THE
HIGH PRIESTS
OF
WASTE

THE

HIGH PRIESTS

OF

WASTE

BY A. ERNEST FITZGERALD

W · W · NORTON & COMPANY · INC · New York

TO
Nell

CONTENTS

FOREWORD

The staggering military budgets which burden American society so cruelly contain enormous waste. Those who pay for this waste through taxes, inflation, and deprivation of benefits the wasted money could buy are asked to believe the waste is an inevitable part of buying complicated equipment supposedly needed for our military protection. In fact, some defenders of the process would have us believe that the waste is good for us.

I was a part of the arms-buying process for most of twenty years. As an industrial engineer, I had opportunities to see the stupendous waste at first hand and sometimes to document it. While this concerned me greatly, I also saw it as an opportunity. The folklore about the inevitability of waste notwithstanding, I knew how to eliminate much of it, and so did many other people I worked with over the years. Now and then we would get a chance to trim a little fat from one of the obese weapons programs. This happened just often enough to keep us convinced we were on the right track and to encourage us to keep trying to learn why costs were not cut dramatically on all the big, expensive weapons projects.

Why not go ahead and save the money? I heard very few sensible answers to this question as I progressed through several jobs in industry, into the management consulting business, and then became head of a good little industrial consulting firm. When I was appointed Deputy for Management Systems in Air Force Headquarters in the Pentagon, I was determined to solve the mystery of "Why not?" in my new post. Gradually the answer unfolded: Waste was the Pentagon's policy.

I didn't want to believe it. As a matter of fact, I *refused* to believe my own hard evidence for a long time. Indirectly, my stubborn refusal to believe that the policy of waste was genuine and to accept it as a fact of life led to my departure from the Pentagon.

Given my own reluctance to accept the unpleasant truth even after it was proclaimed and demonstrated to me on an almost daily basis, I can appreciate that the American taxpayer (the most docile in the world) might have difficulty believing that the squandering of his money is deliberate.

Most Americans of my generation and older were brought up on a steady diet of complete trust and faith in our military establishment. At our grandfathers' knees and from our schoolbooks we learned of our country's proud military traditions and of the accomplishments of our military hero leaders. The statuary in almost every park and courthouse square in the country reminded us of our martial heritage. We were made ashamed of the parsimony of the public in past support of the military and were indoctrinated to provide without question whatever money our bluff but honest military chiefs said was needed to keep our guard up. Those who fretted about the huge sums involved were assured that the check-and-balance system our founding fathers had thoughtfully built into our government's structure would make sure that the money really was needed and would be spent wisely. Some of us wondered about the wisdom of conducting this biggest of public businesses behind the veil of military secrecy. Don't worry about secrecy, we were told, it's for your own protection. Besides, military matters, especially the modern weapons systems, are so complicated that you wouldn't understand them anyway.

In the years after 1939, we were urged not to worry about waste and inefficiency which might creep into military activities. In vague, fuzzy ways, we were assured that a little waste, a growing amount actually, was good for us. We were taught that our modern industrial society was so incredibly productive that some of the excess output had to be wasted in order to keep things humming. As long as the waste effort was needed anyway, the military was the place to apply it. We could make jobs and fend off foreign aggressors at the same time. And, since the military spending made us rich, why not go ahead and build up an ever-increasing military capability? You could never have too much. Better to overequip ourselves and "err on the side of safety" than to get caught short.

Now, a man from Mars—or an American from the nineteenth century, for that matter—would recognize instantly that the conditions I have just described created a climate where scoundrels could flourish. Only through several generations of mass brainwashing could citizens fail to perceive that they were perfectly set up to be fleeced whenever unscrupulous or weak men came to occupy the unique positions of unaccountable trust in our monstrous military establishment. The central theme of my story is simply that the inevitable happened to us, given the conditions and the climate which were created. We are being fleeced.

I have described my own experience with the military spending complex in some detail. It is my hope that readers, especially those having backgrounds similar to my own, can share vicariously my difficult educational experience and thereby become wiser less painfully than I did.

Those readers who begin my story already believing the Pentagon's management to be rotten may also gain new insights. Many of the Pentagon's severest critics, especially among the young, seemingly view the Pentagon as monolithically bad and more or less uniformly populated by scheming, greedy, blood-thirsty villains, and it is true that easy pickings in the military spending coalition have attracted disproportionately large number of unprincipled rascals. However, I also encountered a large number of exemplary citizens—civilian and military—in the Department of Defense and its suppliers. Unhappily, public attitudes and political conditions have favored the bad actors, and they dominate the exemplary citizens in the spending coalition. I hope that my accounts of the sincere and brave efforts of some of the more conscientious public servants will encourage critics to try to create conditions in which the good guys may thrive rather than damning the whole Pentagonal crew.

Another area in which I hope to adjust the aim of some vitriolic military critics is that of overall Pentagon objectives. It is an article of faith among some of these critics that the U. S. military is primarily an adjunct of a new form of colonialism aimed at promoting and protecting American business interests abroad and exploiting subject populations. Now, I think it probable that business opportunities in far-off places have stimulated a good number of military adventures. There is little doubt that armed might could be employed as a form of insurance for overseas interests. Also, it is obvious that U. S. business interests follow closely on the heels of friendly troops to establish their branch operations. However, I believe most such actions are primarily the results of aggressive businessmen doing what comes naturally—reacting to existing situations to make a profit. If such considerations were prime factors in the long-range plans whose enormous costs we bear year after year, the secret was well kept in middle management levels at the Pentagon. Many examples of horrendous waste had nothing to with military capability of any kind, whether intended to subdue the savage or not.

However, it is undoubtedly true that subject population exploitation is a major objective of the military spending coalition. The people marked for exploitation, though, are not masses of troublesome, illiterate, disease-ridden peasants in underdeveloped countries who can barely sustain their own miserable lives. The exploited masses are United States taxpayers, the most productive and easily managed subject population in the history of the world. If my stories can convince the neocolonial school of Pentagon critics of this fairly obvious fact, perhaps they will shift some of their concern from the exploited foreign masses, who don't vote here, to the exploited domestic masses, who do.

The final group I would like to reach are those who defend the Pentagon, right or wrong, out of sincerely patriotic motives. If you are among those who really believe that uncritical, unquestioning support of our military establishment is the way to protect our traditional freedoms, pay particular attention to the ways in which an immensely powerful, unaccountable military establishment has affected the lives and freedoms of some of the patriotic, conscientious United States citizens I have written about. Compare the actuality of these real human situations with our ancient ideals. Then consider whether exempting the

Pentagon from criticism contributes to achieving our ideals and protecting our freedoms.

Think especially hard about governmental power. The founders of our country taught us to distrust concentration of power in individual hands. As for privileged, unaccountable power, these same founders resorted to violent revolution to be free of it. Now, we are again confronted with great concentrated, unaccountable, privileged power. True, it is native power and appears benign or even benevolent to most citizens. This protective coloring makes it all the more dangerous, and citizens must learn to control the military spending juggernaut before they are robbed of their resources and their freedoms.

Cost estimating for major weapons systems was inspired
by a passage from *Alice's Adventures in Wonderland*:

"You ought to have finished," said the King.
"When did you begin?"
The Hatter looked at the March Hare, who had followed
him into the court, arm-in-arm with the Dormouse.
"Fourteenth of March, I think it was," he said.
"Fifteenth," said the March Hare.
"Sixteenth," said the Dormouse.
"Write that down," the King said to the jury;
and the jury eagerly wrote down
all three dates on their slates,
and then added them up,
and reduced the answer to shillings and pence.

THE
HIGH PRIESTS
OF
WASTE

COUNTRY BOY IN THE AEROSPACE BUSINESS

I reacted to an offer to go to work in the Pentagon in September of 1965 with a feeling approaching elation. True, the appointment as Deputy for Management Systems in the Air Force would cost me money, and my wife complained about that. Also, it was a bad time to leave the small but solid industrial engineering consulting firm which I had helped form and where I had been serving as president. However, these drawbacks appeared insignificant when weighed against the professional opportunities of the new appointment.

It was an exciting and promising time in the business life of the Pentagon. Robert McNamara was riding high as Secretary of Defense, probably at the peak of his power, prestige, and influence. From all outward appearances, he and his associates seemed completely dedicated to bringing the hitherto unmanageable military machine under tight, businesslike control. I was particularly impressed by Mr. McNamara's seeming determination to end the pork-barrel distribution of military procurement funds. I had found Mr. McNamara's posture statement introducing the fiscal year 1966 military budget especially impressive. Among other things, he said:

The Defense Department, however, cannot and should not assume responsibility for creating a level of demand adequate to keep the economy healthy and growing. Nor should it, in developing its programs, depart from the strictest standards of military need and operating efficiency in order to aid an economically distressed company or community.

3

Mr. McNamara underscored this policy by pointing out that this was also the policy of the Congress, and that the annual appropriation act forbade "the payment of a price differential on contracts . . . for the purpose of relieving economic dislocations." Further on in his statement, he nailed down his policy regarding assistance to ailing firms:

In a free enterprise, competitive economy, it would be inappropriate for the Government to subsidize individual firms, even those engaged primarily in supporting the Defense program. To do so would be to discriminate against non-defense firms.

Mr. McNamara commented further on the flexibility and adaptability of the free market economy:

The ability of our free enterprise economy to adjust to change is one of its greatest strengths. It is through the free market mechanism that resources are shifted from areas of expanding demand, and from less profitable to more profitable use, to the benefit of the entire nation.

This was music to my ears. My work as a cost-cutting consultant to private industry and to the government on weapons programs had been reasonably successful and satisfying, and I had even made a fair amount of money, for a country boy. But nearly always there had been some philosophical obstacle to full realization of attainable cost savings on the big weapons programs. Usually the excuses had to do with keeping surplus personnel for whom no necessary work was in sight. In military contractor plants this was called "maintaining capability" and was rationalized in general, nonspecific terms of "military needs," "attainment of social goals," and "keeping the economy healthy."

A department manager for one of my private clients, a military contractor, explained the general philosophy in an unusual way. This gentleman had been the beneficiary (or victim, depending on one's viewpoint) of an analysis of his department's work load and work force by one of my associates. His department had 105 employees, but our analysis showed that forty-six people could easily perform his projected work load. We had previously done similar analyses dozens of times for this and other companies, and our usual procedure was to negotiate with the manager to arrive at a personnel budget which would achieve and maintain a balance of people with available work within a few months.

We did not expect the manager to be overjoyed at the prospect of losing 56 percent of his people. Most managers in similar situations fought like tigers to keep or even expand their work forces until experience proved they could get along without the supernumeraries. This particular manager, though, had a unique defense. He did not challenge our findings. He agreed with them and praised the thoroughness and professional caliber of my associate's analysis. Nonetheless, reasoned our manager, he should keep all his employees, supernumeraries and all, and even hire more people if they could be found (the area had a severe labor shortage at the time, 1961). His rationale was that he and his company, our client, were doing a fine thing by keeping the excess people not only employed but also nonproductive. Obviously, he said, it wouldn't do to let the excess folks go, because that sort of thing was old-fashioned and just wasn't done anymore. He mentioned that they might even vote for radical political candidates if they were unemployed.

Given the then severe labor shortage and his own company's rapidly expanding business, we pointed out that any surplus employees he might release would most likely be snapped up by another department within the company, and that even if they should find themselves on the street, they should have no trouble getting relocated. Ah, said our manager, but what if someone were to hire them and put them to work *producing* things, items which would compete in the commercial marketplace? That would never do, our manager said, because competition might set in, driving prices down, and some of the less efficient companies might go broke. This sort of thing could develop into a chain reaction and ruin the whole business climate.

This was a weird and wonderful rationalization. We were to hear it many times, often clothed in erudite economic jargon.

In dealing with our military clients, my little firm had encountered a variety of reactions to cost-cutting and cost control. At one extreme were a few managers of relatively small and poverty-stricken weapons programs who welcomed any help they could get and afford on their limited budgets. The trouble was that they couldn't afford much expensive help, so we and our clients often endured relative poverty together. We found ourselves doing lots of free work. Nevertheless, our assignments on the smaller weapons projects helped to save lots of money. In one case, a cost reduction program we designed and helped install resulted in a 65 percent reduction of the principal contractor's cost for each unit of his product. At the same time, a general improvement in management disciplines cured the contractor's problems of late delivery and improved the quality of his products. From a strictly professional standpoint, our work with small weapons programs was productive and satisfying.

Our work with large, generously funded weapons programs was another matter. There was never a problem finding places to cut costs. All of them were as fat as lard hogs. The difficulty lay in getting action. Always there was some excuse, some compelling reason for avoiding actions needed to actually save money. Many of our military clients, particularly the managers of the huge intercontinental ballistic missile programs, just didn't care what things cost and said so. For example, an Air Force officer responsible for a portion of the Minuteman missile told us that his financial responsibilities consisted of making sure "his" contractor had all the money he needed to "get the job done." It did not matter what things cost.

This was a common attitude during the early 1960s. The whole country was then mesmerized by the "missile gap" myth, later shown to be a complete deception. The essence of this myth was that the Russians were far ahead of the United States in deploying intercontinental ballistic missiles with nuclear warheads. It was further assumed that the godless Bolsheviks intended to incinerate us all as soon as they got together enough missiles to do the job. The only way to deter the Bolshevik was to close the missile gap as quickly as possible. The approved method of closing the gap was to authorize practically unlimited money for contracting. It was then generally believed that any problem could be cured by pouring money on it.

Among the many disastrous results of applying this philosophy was the evolution of the Ape Theory of Engineering. A psychologist who had belatedly and unfortunately discovered the mathematics of probability speculated that if enough chimpanzees could be put to work at enough typewriters, one of them would eventually reproduce the works of Shakespeare. After the payrolls of the larger military contractors were stuffed to overflowing with surplus engineers as a result of the indiscriminate hiring campaigns of the missile-gap period, the Ape Theory was widely applied to solve engineering problems. One manager of a contractor missile project told me he never worried about engineering problems. "I just assign a thousand or so guys to the problem," said this managerial giant. "One of them is bound to come up with a solution."

Based on his outstanding record running the missile project, this gentleman was later put in charge of one of his company's major nongovernmental undertakings. The results were predictably calamitous.

Ape Theory management was not restricted to engineering, of course. Classical factory management was blighted to an even greater extent. To thinking industrial engineers, this caused greater immediate concern than the degradation of engineering management. Superior industrial management was generally considered to be the cornerstone of American economic strength. Until the early to mid-1960s, the exceptional efficiency of manufacturing in the United States more than offset lower wages and salaries in foreign countries. Because of our superior overall efficiency, we were able to remain competitive in world markets despite the higher wages and enviable standard of living of American factory workers. Whereas the European industrial revolution had its beginnings in automation (the spinning jenny, etc.) and the use of mechanical power, the American industrial revolution was rooted in the subdivision, measurement, and management of human labor. This was the essence of "scientific management" which changed the face and nature of our country between 1860 and 1960. Whether applied somewhat inhumanly by disciples of Frederick Winslow Taylor or compassionately by followers of the Gilbreths, the effect was dramatic.

Wage incentive plans tied to systematically measured productivity became commonplace in most United States industries.

Analyses of human labor requirements became prime factors in equipment selection and other investment decisions. Reduction of labor content of manufactured articles became a major factor in product design. In short, reduction of labor required per unit of product became the major focus of American industrial management. Output per worker soared. For good or ill, we became the world's dominant industrial power.

Use of the Ape Theory turned back the clock in big contractor factories during the missile gap madness. Labor efficiencies, as measured by traditional industrial engineering methods, sank to unbelievably low levels. Typical efficiency levels in the Air Force's ballistic missile contractor factories ranged from 5 to 40 percent of the efficiency normal to competitive, commercial manufacturing. As a specific example, overall factory efficiency on the guidance set for the Minuteman II missile was 12.5 percent of normal. This meant that the big aerospace contractor would spend about eight times as many labor hours as an old-fashioned factory for an equivalent amount of work.

Production control techniques which had been carefully evolved and refined over a period of sixty to seventy years were effectively abandoned. Orders for parts to be made in the factories would be released and immediately lost. Hordes of "expediters" or "parts chasers" would then be unleashed to find the orders and shepherd the parts through the manufacturing process. By dint of much scurrying about, the parts chasers would round up enough parts to assemble a missile from time to time.

The expediter phenomenon gave the big contractor operations their most obvious visual characteristic: droves of people walking about. Usually they looked quite busy, for the first principle of the expediting art is to stride purposefully from hide-out to resting place. In addition, of course, the accomplished aerospace expediter never leaves a place of refuge without carrying something—a part, a clipboard, or a sheaf of papers. The harried and dutiful expediter image is completed by a serious facial expression, seldom smiling and peering intently with a hard eye.

The ambulatory work force characteristic gives rise to curious misconceptions at times. Early in my professional career, I was employed for a time in a large Southeastern aircraft modification and maintenance plant. At that time, our operation was newly established, and we had imported large numbers of experienced expediters, since few were available in our benighted section of the country. Our typical expediter was a Californian or a Texan with a pencil-line mustache and a loud sports coat. Usually he was a prosperous looking citizen who drove a Cadillac and exuded an air of good living long enjoyed.

One day while working on a problem in our warehouse for incoming materials, I met a young black man I had more or less grown up with. My friend was driving a delivery truck for a local mill supply house. For several months he had delivered supplies to all parts of our sprawling complex, and he was much impressed with the operation and the apparent prosperity of our employees. In fact, he asked me if I could help him get a job with us. I told him I would do what I could but that his practically nonexistent education and limited experience (truck driving) would be handicaps. I told him we were then hiring mostly skilled mechanics, machinists, welders, and the like.

"Oh, that's all right," my friend said. "I don't want none of them complicated jobs. I just want to be a walker."

I had to admit that strolling did appear to be a pleasant and rewarding occupation for large numbers of our employees. Unhappily though, I had to explain that the job description "walker" did not exist as such, and a person would therefore not be able to apply for the work straightforwardly. I am not certain I was completely convincing.

At this particular company we had many other jobs whose actual duties differed sharply from the official job descriptions. The most interesting of these was the real assignment of one of our high-level managers. This lucky man was intelligent, handsome, and personable. He was well liked by both men and women. In truth, he was phenomenal in building close and lasting friendships with ladies. He had been married a number of times, and his ex-wives still loved him dearly. His numerous girl friends would do anything for him. Oftentimes his large and lively parties would be completely staffed on the distaff side by his retinue of female admirers. To top it off, he had an absolutely incredible capacity for strong drink.

Recognizing the value of this unique talent, our top management simply let nature take its course. They very wisely avoided burdening their social genius with the grubby details of factory management. Assistants could handle the drab routine of the official job, leaving the genius free to exercise his God-given talents for fun and profit. This was particularly useful when high-ranking military customers visited the plant.

The typical military visit started with briefings enumerating the company's unique capabilities, our contributions to the national defense, and further contributions which could be made if a few minor problems, especially money limitations, could be solved through cooperative efforts of the company and its military customers. Then, after a proletarian luncheon in the company cafeteria, demonstrating an austere and democratic way of life, an extensive walking tour of the large facility would be organized for the visitors. Usually the tour was conducted by the social genius, who really did know a great deal about the operation despite the large proportion of his time spent on outside activities. After the tour, involving a walk of several miles, it was entirely natural for the social genius to suggest that the party adjourn to a nearby watering place for refreshments while talking things over. In the course of discussing the plant tour in a relaxed atmosphere, the social genius could generally determine the diversionary preferences of his guests. In many cases, members of the gifted one's devoted circle of lady friends would be called on to help out.

Jealous associates and outclassed competitors for the affections of his female friends gave unkind names to the semiofficial activities of the social genius. They overlooked his real contributions to the business health of the company. For an investment of a relatively small amount of expense money, the company built an enormous amount of good will and cemented close and warm relations with important military customers.

An illustration of the effectiveness of our talented social specialist was the high incidence of visits to our plant by Air Force generals. This is a relatively rare occurrence even for an aerospace giant. Not so for our new and relatively unglamorous company. General officer visits were commonplace, and we often had visits from four or five at a crack.

I later learned that extra-official diversions were widely used by military contractors for a variety of purposes. Whereas the prime purpose of the social genius' efforts was to improve customer relations, social diversions are often employed to fend off bothersome, overly inquisitive types. One of my little consulting firm's assignments on the Minuteman missile program was to evaluate the contractor's methods of determining where they stood on their contracts, whether they had spent more or less money than planned for work done through a given point in time. We had notable success in similar appraisals ourselves, on one occasion identifying an incipient cost overrun of $100,000,000 on a $150,-000,000 contract six months before the contractor's own sluggish appraisal systems had signaled the problem. Even though we could not convince our client, the Air Force, to head off the upcoming cost increases by insisting on simple corrective measures, it was agreed that "early warning" of such increases would be useful in that more time would be available to get money to pay for the overruns. Therefore, it was reasoned, the contractors should be asked to modify their own internal procedures so that they could give early warning themselves without the necessity for appraisal of contract status by outside groups.

There were obstacles, of course. The big contractors did not *want* to give early warning of cost overruns. If overruns were identified as such when they occurred, it would be much more difficult later on to confuse the issue by citing the extreme difficulties of Extending the Frontiers of Man's Knowledge and Inexorable Economic Processes, such as inflation. This, in turn, might cause embarrassment when changes to the contract (called "contract nourishment" in the trade) were authorized to allow the overrun contractors to offset possible losses. Furthermore, it was feared that early, unvarnished overrun projections might unduly alarm the nervous nellies of Mr. McNamara's budget department. It was widely believed that full revelation of impending financial disasters could lead to cancellation of contracts.

Since the requirement for objective reporting of status of contracts appeared to have customer backing, direct opposition by the contractors was not prudent. They had to appear to go along with the scheme without actually revealing damaging facts. This was an old dodge, of course, having been employed many times before. Basically simple schemes are made ever more complicated, and new hordes of specialists are employed to furnish the trappings and appearance of control. Eventually a complicated jargon, a new language, is created which completely confuses the uninitiated. With the esoteric language it is then possible to establish a management cult whose services can be peddled on subsequent contracts long after the original purpose of the activity has been forgotten. It is fashionable for aerospace contractors to grumble about the paperwork and reports that go along with cultish schemes, but they don't really mind so long as no meaningful information is revealed and the government pays for the stuff. One manager told me he made as much money on the paper as on missiles and that it was a whole lot easier to deliver.

My little group, by insisting on looking at basic control features and examining end results, was slowing down the natural evolution of a profitable and salable management cult and threatening exposure of damning facts at the same time. We had to be diverted, preferably in a way which would not upset the customer.

Sad to say, the diversions were never so pleasant as those provided by my friend the social genius. This was probably due to the scarcity of such talent, because some of the contractors worked hard at the tactic, often substituting quantity for quality in the diversionary art.

One of the best organized practitioners of diversion among the Minuteman contractors was General Electric's Reentry Systems Department in Philadelphia. General Electric employed a tactic which we labeled the Ordeal by Alcohol, which required several shifts of GE drinking buddies. My own first exposure to the process is typical.

When an associate and I arrived at the Philadelphia airport late one afternoon, we were met by two GE representatives, both old acquaintances and very pleasant people to work with. They drove us to our hotel and once there insisted on our joining them for drinks in the bar. After several drinks, my associate and I pleaded pressing work. This apparently was the signal for the next shift to appear. The potted palms parted, and we were hailed from the next table by another pair of GE acquaintances who had been looking all over for us. It was a good thing they recognized our voices, they said. They had made dinner reservations at a fine restaurant in the suburbs, and we just had time, after one more drink, to hurry on out and meet one of their management people who wanted to discuss our visit to the plant. Going along with the gag, we went to the suburbs and had an excellent but long, wet, and convivial dinner in a place with an indoor water-fall. During the after-dinner drinks, we were joined by a new GE man, a stranger this time, who was to drive my associate and me back into town. Everyone else was going the other way.

We went back to town but did not go straight to our hotel. Our new friend, Big John, knew a place we just had to see. This place, the Zu Zu Club, was an after-hours place with a police-man at the door and a number of unescorted ladies seated at intervals along the bar. We were immediately accosted by the ladies, who were really not very attractive and were aggressively entrepreneurial besides. Big John ordered drinks for the three of us and three of the enterprising ladies. At the time, I couldn't help thinking of my old friend the social genius, and reflecting on the sad decline of the aerospace diversionary art.

At this point, my resourceful associate rescued us. He told one of the ladies and the bartender that we were paid companions of Big John, who, my friend said, was a Texas oil magnate. My associate explained that Big John liked to go adventuring in places like the Zu Zu, and that we went along to protect him, since his judgment was poor and he tended to throw away large sums of money when he was in his cups. For some reason, Big John got very drunk after only a couple of drinks. Moreover, all three of the ladies began to show great affection for him. My asso-ciate and I left quietly, unnoticed by Big John, and went to our hotel for some badly needed sleep.

The next morning we were greeted cordially but with some surprise on our early arrival at the GE plant. We were shown into the GE Minuteman program manager's large and comfortable office, which had been set up as a kind of recovery room. The room was mercifully dim, lighted only by some subdued desk lamps and a large illuminated aquarium, in which tropical fish were swimming about soothingly. The table was laid out with cold orange juice, steaming pots of coffee, breakfast rolls, and quantities of ice water. There were also aspirin and stomach remedies available. The friendly manager suggested that we could conduct our business in the quiet and comfort of his office. We wouldn't have to venture out into the harsh glare and noise of the outside world. In fact, he had arranged a series of briefings which he was sure would answer all our questions.

I must confess that it required considerable exercise of will to leave that sanctuary. I am certain I could not have done it if we had stayed any longer with Big John. Incidentally, we never saw him again. I've often wondered what ever happened to him.

One of my private clients, also an aerospace contractor, employed a somewhat more genteel but equally effective delaying approach. My firm had been retained by the old-fashioned top management of this medium-sized company. They really didn't fit in with the aerospace giants since they were genuinely concerned about rising costs in their operations and had hired us to help correct the problems. In spite of, or perhaps because of, the strong backing we received from the client's top management, the middle and lower levels of client management did not count me and my associates among nature's noblemen. Their secret weapon was the company chauffeur and man of all work, whom I shall call Calhoun. Calhoun was a black gentleman of the old school, born and raised in the Deep South and practiced from birth in manipulation of white folks who thought he was being helpful and servile. A real Tom, but shrewd and clever as a Wall Street wolf.

Calhoun took charge of me immediately on my arrival in the client's Midwestern home city, and I didn't escape for nearly a week. He met me at the airport, fetched my baggage, and announced that he was at my service as long as I was in town. By the time he got me to the hotel he had arranged for me, which was as far as possible from the client's plant, he knew my life's history. After settling me in my room, he said he would pick me up "first thing" the next morning to deliver me to the plant.

Eager to start the new job, I was ready to go before seven the next morning. But no Calhoun. Starting about eight o'clock, I made several increasingly anxious telephone calls to inquire into Calhoun's whereabouts. Each time I was told not to worry, that Calhoun was on the way. Calhoun was very reliable. He finally showed up about 10 o'clock, very apologetic and very vague about car trouble which he could get fixed in no time at all. If I would just go into the coffee shop and relax, he would be right back. He got me to the plant just in time for lunch.

About two in the afternoon, after lunch and a few introductions, Calhoun appeared and asked if I would mind being taken back to the hotel a little early so that he could get back to the plant by 3:30. His shift ended then, he explained, and his cost-conscious management wanted to avoid paying overtime.

In the following days, I managed to lengthen my effective time in the plant, but not much. I finally had to dismiss Calhoun and rent a car.

We were not always put off with gentlemanly and indirect methods by Minuteman contractors. We were thrown out of the Autonetics Division of North American Aviation (now North American Rockwell) without ceremony. However, I must admit that the action was not without some provocation. The consultant we first assigned to examine Autonetics was an experienced and skillful industrial engineer. He was very intense and dedicated to his work. He had a bad habit, though, of pacing back and forth as he talked and making sweeping gestures with his hands. On our first visit to Autonetics, we met with the manager of their Minuteman Division, a former Air Force colonel, in his big luxurious office. In fact, their entire headquarters building was downright gorgeous. We called it the Taj Mahal. As my associate was explaining the purpose of our visit, he was pacing back and forth and gesturing broadly as he usually did when caught up in enthusiasm. Just as he paced in front of the former colonel's huge desk, he made an especially wide hand gesture, swept a beautiful silver water jug off the colonel's coffee table, and drop-kicked it across the room with his next long stride. Water and ice flew all over, along with shards of the jug's vacuum lining when it broke after bouncing off the opposite wall. It was apparent we were off to a bad start.

Things went downhill from there. Shortly after he had sullied the cost-plus splendor, our consultant got one of the Autonetics vice presidents out of bed in the middle of the night to answer a question needed for a report due the next day. To add injury to insult, the information completed the data we needed to predict that Autonetics' guidance set would last only one third as long as the contract specified. The Air Force covered up the problem for nearly four years after that, but my associate was never forgiven for digging up the information.

Next we unearthed the huge undisclosed cost overrun cited earlier, which embarrassed both Autonetics and the Air Force. Again, the bad news was unwelcome. The incipient overrun, about $100,000,000 on a contract of about $150,000,000, was difficult to explain. The contract was less than a year old at the time the huge increase was uncovered, which made it hard to rationalize with the standard alibis. Considerable time is needed to becloud original premises, and this contract was too new. The Air Force tried to explain away the overrun by attributing the increase to changed requirements, but they were frustrated by troublesome facts.

First, basic requirements had *not* changed, and the product finally agreed upon after contract changes represented retrogression, not progress, in important characteristics. It was not nearly as reliable as the product it was designed to replace. Second, analyses showed that the lion's share of the increase was due to increased overhead expenses, poor factory efficiency, and bad quality control, none of which had anything to do with the supposedly changed requirements. The issue became critical when a faction within the Air Force accepted our appraisal of the situation and tried to say "No" to the impending but avoidable cost increases. We had to go. The Air Force project officer who sided with us had to go too. Suddenly and without explanation, I, my associates, and the friendly tightfisted project officer could no longer get into the Autonetics plant. Our passes and our permission to enter the building were canceled. We were banished from the Taj Mahal. No longer could we enjoy the sumptuous surroundings. No more lunches in the salubrious California weather on the tastefully designed patios. My associates could no longer ogle the droves of uncommonly attractive girls employed in the Taj Mahal. Most importantly, we could no longer collect hard facts on the bungling and boondoggling at Autonetics.

To keep our exclusion from the delights and challenges of Autonetics in perspective, I should acknowledge that there were further provocations. At about this time, we learned of the tent episode which my former associate, Mert Tyrrell, recounted in his book *Pentagon Partners, The New Nobility*. This was the unsuccessful attempt by Autonetics, a self-proclaimed giant of space-age technology, to invent the tent. With the advice and prodding of the subsequently banished Air Force project officer, we began questioning the observation shelter (tent) project which, strictly speaking, was none of our business. This project, in which a million dollars or so was expended, was a fruitless attempt to protect airmen manning the Minuteman sites from the bitter winter winds of North Dakota and Montana. The Minuteman missiles based in these cold states were supported by huge springs in their underground silos. The springs tended to sag unevenly, which resulted in the missile leaning from the vertical.

For a number of reasons, it is important that Minuteman missiles point more or less straight up. One of the functions of the airmen manning the missile launching sites was to go to the missile silo periodically and check to make sure the missile was standing straight up. The airmen got cold doing this chore, so Autonetics was commissioned to solve the problem. Autonetics' brilliant engineers correctly concluded that a tent would be a good shelter from the bitter northern wind, confirming the decision of countless generations of Indians who inhabited the region in times past. Unhappily, even though the ignorant savage had solved the problem after a fashion, missile gap technology was not equal to the task. All the Autonetics tents blew away, computers and wind tunnels notwithstanding. Perhaps it was a random failure of the Ape Theory of Engineering. In any event,

it was embarrassing, and our probing of the project did not en-
hance our popularity.

An interesting and somewhat ominous aspect of this adventure
was the authority for our banishment. We were not thrown out
of the Taj Mahal by Autonetics, whom we had admittedly dis-
comfited. Our passes were canceled by the government's agent in
residence at Autonetics, the Air Force Plant Representative. This
gentleman later retired and became a division manager at Autonetics. This man's career pattern was not unique, of course. The
pattern of active duty military officers protecting big contractors'
interests, then going to work for a contractor after retirement
was so common that the practice was hardly commented on in the
industry. However, this instance made a particularly strong impression on me because poor stewardship of a government emissary gone native affected me directly. Until that incident, I didn't
really appreciate how much and how badly military officers'
conduct of the government's business was affected by the prospect of post-retirement employment.

Another factor which was beginning to worry me and my associates was the degree to which the poor management practices
and work habits of the aerospace contracting industry were in-
fecting other segments of industry. Most management people
didn't think about this aspect of military contracting waste at all.
Of the few who did think about it, most assumed it was somehow "good for the economy" or, if not, that our country was rich
enough to afford the luxury of a little boondoggling. A handful
of businessmen with a mixture of commercial and military contracts recognized the infection problem, but they thought geo-
graphic separation of the different types of activity would control
the problem. In this way, workers in the commercial operations,
where high efficiency and productivity were important, would not
see what a soft touch their colleagues in military work had. I suppose this quarantine approach was partially effective for a while.
Commercial factory workers were partially protected from the
loafing virus, and government auditors were usually satisfied that
they had at least theoretical protection against contractors using
government contract funds for the benefit of private commercial
projects.

However, even if factory workers had been as stupid as visualized by the corporate managers who thought the quarantine would work in the long run, the approach was doomed to ineffectiveness. Factory workers are not stupid, of course, and they understood full well that the high output levels required in cost-competitive commercial activities were not required in government contract activities. A bigger problem, though, was that management attitudes and practices proved readily transferable, and usually in the wrong direction. The tough, cost-conscious attitudes generally found in competitive commercial operations were not adopted by military contract operations. Rather, the permissive attitudes toward spending and the management fads so prevalent in government contracting were widely adopted by commercial divisions of companies with a mix of government and commercial business. The beneficiaries of the government's free-spending ways began to brag about their good fortune. Employees of the fat California aerospace companies would chide their less fortunate friends, urging them to get on the gravy train. "If you're not working at Ace Aerospace, you're working too hard," was a typical appeal, often proclaimed loudly in the bars of the shiny new boom towns. The secret was out, but who cared? The good life beckoned.

At that time, competition from foreign producers not infected by the live-it-up, make-work philosophy was only a tiny, fluffy cloud.

Finally, many thoughtful people were becoming concerned that we were not really buying many effective weapons, despite all the cost-effectiveness rhetoric out of Washington and the enormous sums allocated to "defense." It should be remembered that at that time, 1965, most Americans felt threatened by the Soviet Union and that we were just embarking on large-scale military operations in Southeast Asia, an undertaking with overtones of high idealism, almost a holy war. Even on the free-spending Minuteman missile program, some of the working-level Air Force officers were becoming concerned. Despite the fact that the then current new model was costing much more than previous models, it was not working well. Contractor cost indicators were spiraling out of control. Analyses of trends of Minuteman con-

tractor overhead expenses were especially alarming. Given a continuation of trends established in the early 1960s, most of the
huge Minuteman spending budget would be used to cover overhead expenses within two years. No missiles, or a few at best.
Just overhead and direct subsidies to "maintain capability."

We had some Air Force planes older than the crews that flew
them. The Air Force had not developed a really successful new
bomber or fighter plane since the 1950s. So, even though my
consulting work in the military contracting business had been
fun most of the time, and occasionally professionally satisfying,
my new job in the Pentagon seemed tailor-made for my experience and capabilities. The time looked right. Pressures for more
military spending were building up, while the national administration's official pronouncements endorsed economy and frugality
in military programs.

In briefings I attended prior to going to work in the Pentagon,
outgoing Secretary of the Air Force Eugene Zuckert talked a
tough line on cost control. Incoming Secretary Harold Brown
talked tougher. Assistant Secretary Leonard Marks, who was to
be my new boss, said they meant business, as did Secretary
McNamara and his assistants. Comptroller of the Air Force Lt.
Gen. Jack Merrell expressed great concern over the rising costs of
weapons systems.

My predecessor as Deputy for Management Systems briefed
me thoroughly and in addition wrote a long report to the Secretary of the Air Force summarizing major weapons systems
management problems. It was a good road map. Privately he told
me that the major problems were that key military people, especially major generals and above, were indifferent to our cost control efforts because they didn't understand what we were trying
to do, and they lacked training in business and industrial management.

I couldn't wait to get started. I was sure we could save billions.

PENTAGON NOVITIATE

Seen from a distance, the Pentagon looks like a huge grim fortress or perhaps a prison squatting on its low rise in the Virginia countryside. It remains grim looking as you approach it from the south side, which looks out on acres of paved parking lots and is marked by several stark pedestrian entrances and an exhaust-blackened opening for motor vehicles. The impression changes, though, as you approach from the other four sides. The landscaping is good, in some spots downright beautiful, with well kept grass, azaleas, taxus hedges, and massed tulips and other flowers in season. The WPA-austere exterior of the building is modified too, especially at the colonnaded River and Mall entrances. I was allowed to park just outside the Mall entrance, and to me the building's outward aspect there seemed well suited to its function. It projected about the right mixture of simplicity, frugality, and attractiveness for a public building. Its imposing size and setting, along with its muted harshness, seemed particularly appropriate to the headquarters of the world's largest and most powerful military establishment.

The overall impression of appropriateness continued as you entered one of the three main doors at the Mall entrance. First, you were reminded of security and vigilance. You had to pass several uniformed guards. Perhaps as a gesture toward civilian control of the military, the guards were not soldiers or marines. They were civilian employees of the General Services Administration, with uniforms similar to those of city policemen. Just inside the entrance was a large, counter-enclosed reception area, where pleasantly brisk ladies would draw a map to direct a visitor to his destination in the 17½ miles of Pentagon corridors.

Proceeding toward the innards of the building from the Mall entrance, the visitor would pass one of the Pentagon contributions to culture. The main hallway leads from the outer ring of the Pentagon, called the E ring, to the inner or A ring. This hall was hung on both sides with GI art, mostly dating from World War II. Some of these paintings were memorable. When I first went to work in the Pentagon, the first picture on the right entering the hall showed an American soldier in the Aleutians shooting a Japanese soldier. The Japanese soldier was leaving a broad, red smear of blood as he slid headfirst down a snow-covered slope. Another painting had a head and shoulders picture of a battle-shocked GI in the foreground. He was gaunt and stubble-bearded, and his jaw hung slack. His eyes were large and round, with a vacant, horrified stare. The background was littered with corpses and smashed equipment. Another painting showed a U.S. Navy aircraft carrier blowing up under attack by a swarm of Japanese aircraft.

This long hallway art gallery symbolized one of the very real worlds the Pentagon operated in. I worked in another one. The civilian secretariat in the Air Force, as in the other services, was primarily concerned with research and development, procurement, training, maintenance, and various administrative matters, including financial management, where I was assigned. My particular responsibilities were to develop improved management controls and methods of analysis throughout the Air Force. This was a dull sounding job, but the Air Force was a huge organization, with more than a million people and a budget of about $25 billion, so it was a big job. Also, I was expected to undertake trouble-shooting assignments from time to time. I had one assistant and two secretaries to help me do all this. However, I had some things going for me in addition to my experience in the business. In the first place, I was allowed to spend most of my time working in the area I knew best—assessment and controls for the big weapons programs being developed by Air Force contractors.

The most important factor, though, was the quality of the people I worked for. My new bosses in the Pentagon were very impressive people. My immediate superior was the Assistant

Secretary of the Air Force for Financial Management, Dr. Leonard Marks, Jr., called "Ted." Prior to accepting the Pentagon appointment a couple of years before, Ted Marks had been a professor in the Graduate School of Business at Stanford University. He had earned his Ph.D. at Harvard, where he had also worked as a consultant to the Air Force on financial management problems. In addition to his good academic background and consulting experience, Ted Marks' personality seemed well suited to the job of squeezing fat out of the Air Force's huge budget. In our early conversations, he exuded an air of cheerful determination while at the same time recognizing the formidable opposition we would face. Among other things, he spoke of the need for perseverance, particularly on the part of civilian appointees. He cited the short service of my two immediate predecessors as contributing to the lack of continuity, and hence perseverance, in the past. Both my predecessors had been on leave from Harvard. One had stayed only about a year, the other about two years. Just about the time they got a program going, it was time to return to Harvard. I agreed that this was bad, and promised to stay on until the job was done or at least until we came to a good stopping place. Ted Marks seemed pleased. He even suggested that I might like the work well enough to make a career of government service.

Dr. Marks' counterpart in the Office of the Secretary of Defense was Dr. Robert Anthony, the Comptroller of the Department of Defense. Dr. Anthony had just come to the Pentagon from Harvard Business School, where he had made a truly outstanding reputation as a teacher of accounting and financial management. He was the author of several successful books on his specialties. He too had extensive experience as a consultant to the Department of Defense. In fact, he, Dr. Marks, and Mr. Neil Harlan, Dr. Marks' predecessor in the Air Force, had worked together on a consulting project for the Air Force in the early 1950s when all three were at Harvard. Dr. Anthony was a longtime friend of Secretary McNamara, and appeared to be operating under a sweeping reform charter from the Secretary, who also had a Harvard background.

Dr. Anthony showed a keen perception of the practical problems of bringing about change. His solution to the problem of bureaucratic inertia was to set up a small, select group under his personal control to help formulate needed reforms and see that they were carried out. He staffed this organization, innocuously titled the Analysis Group, entirely with recent graduates of the Harvard Graduate School of Business. The men Dr. Anthony recruited for the Analysis Group were all top students, with high levels of energy and intelligence. It was hoped that this talented group of young men could either persuade the Pentagon bureaucrats to join in reform efforts or bypass them if necessary.

Of all my new bosses, Dr. Harold Brown, the Secretary of the Air Force, had the most imposing credentials. He had been a youthful prodigy in nuclear physics prior to his appointment as Deputy Secretary of Defense for Research and Engineering in 1961. In that job, which he held for four years before his appointment as Secretary of the Air Force, Dr. Brown was responsible for all the research, engineering, and military systems development sponsored by the Department of Defense. Certainly in terms of money spent and perhaps in terms of responsibility, it was the world's top technical job. Dr. Brown was highly regarded in the technical community, and Secretary McNamara appeared to have complete confidence in him. Many of us who were concerned about the waste and ineffectiveness of the Air Force's weapons development and buying activities believed that Harold Brown had the necessary qualifications, especially brains and high-level backing, to clean up the mess in the Air Force.

Dr. Brown's performances in meetings I attended during my early days in the Pentagon increased my confidence in our bright young Secretary. (I believe he was thirty-eight years old at the time.) While I was in the Air Force, major weapons programs such as the Minuteman intercontinental missile system and the F-111 fighter bomber were reviewed periodically by an assemblage called the Designated Systems Management Group, or DSMG. Membership in the Group included the Secretary, the Under Secretary, and the assistant secretaries on the civilian side and the Chief of Staff, the Vice Chief, and the deputy chiefs of staff on the military side. In addition, certain members of the next lowest organizational layer, of which I was one, were invited to attend DSMG meetings. In short, the group included the entire top management of the Air Force. At most meetings of the DSMG, the Air Force managers of the big programs, who were called System Program Directors, or SPDs, would make presentations to the assemblage. SPDs were always Air Force officers, usually colonels or brigadier generals, occasionally major generals. The SPDs were invariably accompanied by large numbers of their subordinates, or weenies, as they were called in the irreverent vernacular. Occasionally the SPDs would bring along representatives of their principal contractors, sometimes even the presidents of the giant firms when an especially hard sell was scheduled.

In a DSMG meeting shortly after I entered the Pentagon, the Minuteman System Program Director put on an unusually frightening show. According to the SPD, unimpeachable sources in the intellience community had learned that the Soviets were about to invent a gadget which might render our Minutemen ineffective. However, all was not lost, according to our SPD. Our guys, his contractors, could invent something to overcome the Soviet threat for a measly hundred megabucks (a "megabuck" was Pentagonese for one million dollars) plus change.

Young Harold Brown listened politely to the presentation, interspersing a few brief questions. When the pitch was completed, Brown leaned back in his chair, smiled, and said, "Well, if their developers lie like our developers, we've got nothing to worry about."

The proposal was thereby rejected out of hand. Most people in the meeting appeared taken aback. They didn't seem accustomed to such abrupt rejection of their sales proposals. I was delighted. Here at last was a service secretary with enough technical knowledge to see through the phony "threat analyses" that had spawned so many useless weapons spending programs. Here also was a man with enough courage to reject such proposals and with enough top-level backing to make his decisions stick.

My confidence in Harold Brown grew as I saw him in action. I remember, in particular, sessions in which Dr. Brown was being briefed on the Cost Management Improvement Program, a collection of projects ostensibly aimed at correcting some of the management horrors so much in evidence in developing and producing the Air Force's planes, missiles, and other military systems. The Cost Management Improvement Program was being conducted by the Air Force Systems Command, the organization responsible for inventing and buying the Air Force's new weapons. The work involved in the program, which was considerable, was directed and approved by a group called the Control Board, of which I was a member. The titular head of the control board was the commander of the Air Force Systems Command, a four-star general. The board's working head was the Comptroller of the Air Force Systems Command, Brig. Gen. (later Maj. Gen.) Wendell Carter, a graduate of the Harvard Graduate School of Business Administration. The program was generally referred to as the McKinsey Program, because of its domination by McKinsey & Company, a firm of management consultants who had contracted with the Air Force to help out on the Cost Management Improvement Program.

It was easy to see why McKinsey & Company dominated the program. The McKinseys, as their consultants were called, were models of modern management advisors. Invariably bright, calmly intense, dressed like fashion plates and well connected in the business and government establishment, the McKinseys awed most potential opposition. Their connections were especially imposing. They moved easily in the highest social and managerial circles, and discussed matters of import with high governmental officials on a first-name basis. The McKinsey partners claimed they were the world's largest employer of graduates of the Harvard Business School. Many of their consultants were former classmates or students of high government officials.

Dr. Brown's good insight was demonstrated in the first review of the McKinsey program I attended. The lengthy briefing was presented by the senior McKinsey partners assigned to the job, and followed the time-honored consultant's format for such affairs: progress to date, plans for the future, and obstacles to be overcome. The presentation was a dizzying display of forms for collecting data, proposals for computer data banks, new organizations to perform the work, and the like. Nothing was said, though, about actually stopping or rolling back the huge increases in costs on the new weapons programs. Harold Brown picked this up and asked what was being done about contract changes which were granted by the Air Force to help contractors "get well" on overrunning contracts. These changes were the "contract nourishment" changes we had observed on the Minuteman missile program, usually marginally valuable changes with staggering price tags. Contract nourishment made the contracting process a bad joke and helped wreck all attempts at controlling costs. Happily, the new Secretary was on to the dodge. Unhappily, nothing substantive was being done to actually control these costs, although there was a plan afoot to study the problem.

I was uneasy about other aspects of the Cost Management Improvement Program, especially the cost-estimating project. The heart of the system which was being invented was a set of forms for recording costs incurred on the big weapons contracts. The forms weren't really new, despite the large amount of money and high-powered talent expended in their invention. They were adaptations of the cost study forms which had been in use for some years. However, this did not concern me so much as the intended use of the information which was to be collected. I was afraid the vastly inflated costs of weapons then being built would become the bases for estimating the costs of similar items in the future, thereby inflating budgets by building in all the fat and waste we were experiencing. This practice had been bad enough in the pre-missile-gap days, but perpetuation of the wild cost escalation of the early 1960s seemed to me to be sheer lunacy. So I set out to determine what was going on.

At first, the cost-estimating experts responsible for the project professed to have no clear idea of what would be done with the huge store of historical cost information which would be deposited in the computer data banks. They had thought mostly about deposits till then, and hadn't really got around to thinking about who would make withdrawals and what for. Many of the experts, the McKinseys especially, expressed the hope that all functional groups in the Air Force would find the data bank useful and that withdrawals would be made by systems analysis people who would use the data for estimating costs of proposed new weapons systems, by comptroller people for establishing budgets, and by procurement people for setting contract prices. The big job, they said, was to sell the various sets of cost estimators—systems analysts, budgeteers, and buyers—on the use of the giant new collection of cost histories. Meanwhile, it was hoped that if only we could collect enough data and store it in computers, our statisticians could score management breakthroughs by discovering hitherto unsuspected cost-estimating relationships. It was the application of the Ape Theory to cost estimating.

However, as I kept probing, I began to uncover little nuggets of information about the intended use of the new cost-estimating system. The necessity for "selling" the system cropped up repeatedly in briefings and conversations. Then one day I asked a briefer, a senior Air Force colonel, just what it would take to sell his forms to potential users. "That's easy," said the colonel. "Just as soon as the program managers discover they can justify more money for their programs by using our forms, we'll have it made. Everybody will want to use them."

At the time, I thought this was an outrageous answer. However, I later realized that the colonel had simply blurted out one of the secrets of bureaucratic success in gaining approval for ever increasing costs. I named it the "back-up" principle. Let's look at a hypothetical case to show how it works.

The Aardvark Missile Case

General Palmy, the System Program Director of the Aardvark missile program, had a cost overrun. This was not unusual. He always had a cost overrun. It was one of the challenges of the job. He needed a new explanation every year, and this taxed the imagination. Palmy had got through the DSMG meeting with a beautiful set of VuGraphs (full-sized lantern slides) in six colors which described Palmy's own brilliant analyses of the latest series of test failures. Palmy did not mention that these calamities were caused in the first place by sheer stupidity on the part of his own engineers and his favorite contractor. The technical discussion in the DSMG meeting had left little time for the few pesky questions about the annual cost overrun raised by the Assistant Secretary for Financial Management. Palmy had not escaped scot-free, however. The Assistant Secretary for Financial Management (the "FM," in Pentagonese) had requested a private session on the Aardvark financial situation. Among other things, the FM, Dr. Dudley

Doe, had to have a good story when questioned about the matter by the Comptroller of the Department of Defense at budget time. General Palmy understood this and was prepared to help the FM. Included in the string of weenies (assistants) Palmy took with him to the FM's Pentagon office was Major Buck, who had a master's degree in business administration from the Assistant Secretary's alma mater. Palmy and all his entourage were, as usual, decked out in full military regalia, uniforms, wings, campaign ribbons, and battle stars. The Assistant Secretary had been a supply officer in World War II and had earned an American Theater ribbon and the Victory Medal. He was known to be somewhat overawed by sure-enough combat types.

Palmy introduced his associates to the FM and the FM's military aide. Palmy was careful to mention that Major Buck was an MBA graduate of the university the Assistant Secretary had attended. The military aide, Colonel Clapsaddle, never let Dr. Doe out of his sight if he could help it. (The FM had to lock the door for privacy in the restroom.) The aide sat in all the Assistant Secretary's meetings. He had been carefully selected and coached for this delicate duty by his military superiors. Colonel Clapsaddle had many important assignments. He made the complicated arrangements for the FM's many out-of-town trips. He always went along on these trips and was personally responsible for carrying the liquor kit. His most important duty, however, was to prevent surprises, especially surprises embarrassing to high-level military officers. He maintained constant, close communication with military aides in other civilian appointees' offices, with the Air Staff, and with other key people like General Palmy. Colonel Clapsaddle had done his job well in this instance, so Palmy had a good book on the FM and knew generally how to proceed.

The FM's aide had arranged for a VuGraph projector and a screen to be set up, so as soon as Palmy's assistants turned out the lights the General began to show his slides and give his pitch. He had a presentation of interminable length for such occasions, which gave the entire background and history of the Aardvark program, along with detailed organization charts, graphic descriptions of contractor responsibilities, and so on. Sometimes he succeeded in consuming the entire time allotted for a briefing with this boilerplate. Palmy had become a legend in his own time by these performances. He had once put to sleep an under secretary, two assistant secretaries, three generals, and assorted colonels and deputies in a single briefing. But not this time. The FM was tough. He had been around too long to be put off by this old ploy. The oldest trick in the military bureaucracy is to explain how a watch is made when asked the time of day. The FM got right to the point. What about the overrun?

Palmy explained sadly that he could only discuss the financial situation in general terms, since he was just an old worn-out airplane driver who was hard put to keep up with all the engineering and scientific problems that were unavoidable when Pushing the State of the Art. However, he was fortunate to have the bright young MBA, Major Buck, who was a real expert on matters financial. Would the Secretary (as assistant secretaries are flatteringly called to their faces) care to be briefed by the Major? The Secretary would, and the Major was on. It was his big chance.

Now, Major Buck knew all too well the reason for the current staggering overrun on the Aardvark missile program. Until a year before, the principal contractor on Aardvark, Granite Aircraft, had two big military programs, the Aardvark missile and the Dodo fighter-bomber. Dodo has been canceled due to two unfortunate circumstances: First, it would not fly; second, Granite Aircraft's tame senator had died, thereby depriving Granite Aircraft of needed congressional sponsorship. Despite the loss of almost half their total business, Granite Aircraft had made only token layoffs, just enough to arouse public sympathy for Granite employees whose jobs were endangered. (Strangely, no one worried too much about those who had already gotten the ax.) Most of the people formerly supported by Dodo were now supported by Aardvark. Those whose time on the job could not be charged directly to Aardvark charged their time to various overhead accounts, which in turn were allocated to Granite's contracts in proportion to the direct charges on each contract. Since Aardvark was the only project Granite had left, all the charges to overhead accounts were allocated to the Aardvark contract. Granite's top financial people had worked closely for several months with the government auditors, their own certified public accountants, and the Air Force officers in the Aardvark project office to invent new charts of accounts, new accounting pools for accumulating overhead expenses, and new classifications of direct and indirect expenses. All sorts of combinations of accounts and classifications were tested on computers. The results were always the same: Aardvark paid.

Major Buck, being an intelligent young man and an experienced financial manipulator besides, naturally did not need computers, CPAs, nor his MBA training to pinpoint the cause of the current overrun. What tested his mettle was explaining it while *avoiding* the basic cause.

Major Buck had the new estimate for the Aardvark program (with the overrun buried throughout and indistinguishable) broken down in marvelous detail. He had computer printouts which sorted the astronomical costs by contract, by contractor, by appropriation, by fiscal year, and by hardware and task subdivision. He needed it all, because the FM bored in. The FM was in his element now.

"Do you have back-up for this shocking estimate, Major?" the FM asked sternly. "Show me the breakdown by work breakdown structure element. I want to see it for the air vehicle, the support equipment, training tasks, and all the subdivisions." The Major had it, and on VuGraphs, which showed he was well prepared. The shadows on the screen were in the shape of boxes connected by lines in the manner of an organization chart. Inside the top box was the label "Total Program," and under that was the cost estimate for the Aardvark program. The other boxes were arranged in a horizontal row beneath the top box, and each had its own label: Air Vehicle, Aerospace Ground Equipment, and so on. Beneath each label was the associated cost estimate. The FM was a trained accountant, so he did what came naturally. He added up the cost estimates in the subordinate boxes. He prided himself on his prowess at sight-adding. The sum of the numbers in the subordinate boxes equaled the figure for the Total Program box. All right so far, but the FM was just getting started. He selected the Air Vehicle for similar treatment. He knew what that was. It was the missile. He had seen pictures of it on General Palmy's VuGraphs. The FM demanded to see the back-up for the Air Vehicle. Major Buck complied, showing the breakdown and estimates for subdivisions of the Air Vehicle: Air Frame, Propulsion, Guidance, and other categories. The testing process was repeated with the same results: the whole equaled the sum of its parts.

The FM pressed on, requesting back-up for the guidance estimate. By now he was far beyond his depth. He had no idea what the strangely named pieces of guidance hardware were. Moreover, there seemed to be no end to the progressively smaller subdivisions of the program estimate. He felt he was being caught up in an infinite regression. He was reminded of the cow on the Pet Milk can. As a child, Dudley Doe had been fascinated by the picture of the cow on the Pet milk can. The cow on the label was looking out of a Pet milk can which had a cow looking out of a can on *its* label. The progression continued with successively smaller pictures of cans, cows, and labels until the pictures finally receded into infinite, invisible smallness. Little Dudley had often wondered how small the pictures of cows, cans, and labels could become. Now Dr. Doe wondered how infinitely small the successively smaller subdivisions of the Aardvark Program could get. He felt dizzy and a little ill. However, his accounting training finally paid off, to his visible relief. The sum of estimates for the pieces of the guidance system was $50 million more than the total estimate labeled "Guidance." He had them, and about time too. His conference table was stacked high with VuGraphs, back-up VuGraphs, and computer printouts to back up the back-up VuGraphs.

"How do you account for this discrepancy, Major?" the FM asked in his Assistant Secretary tone. "I just don't know, Mr. Secretary," Buck replied. "I'm sure something went wrong with our new computer program." This was not true. Buck had deliberately put in the mistake himself so as to provide a focus of attention for examiners of back-up data. Major Buck was destined to become a general. "This is very embarrassing to me, Mr. Secretary," Buck said humbly as he pawed through a new pile of back-up data. "But if you'll just give me a minute or two, I'm sure I can straighten it out."

"Well, get cracking, Buck," said General Palmy. "Full throttle. Balls to the firewall. We can't keep the Secretary all day."

"Yes, I do have an appointment with the Under Secretary," said the FM. (They had a date to play squash.)

"Here it is," Buck said brightly after rapidly copying several figures from the back-up stack onto a pad and striking a total. "It's the PIGA."

"The piga?" mumbled the FM.

"Yes, sir. The PIGA. The pendular integrating gyroscopic accelerometer."

"I see," said the FM. "Well, there is one more thing I want to make sure of. Can all these estimates be supported statistically? Were they derived from audited, actual costs?"

"We can support them. I guarantee it," said Buck. He could, too, although he had practiced a subtle form of military mendacity by giving a future-tense response to a past-tense question. The reason for this undetected waffling was that the financial experts at Granite Aircraft and their subcontractors were still working on the detailed estimates. Major Buck's confidence was based on three factors: first, Granite's estimators were the world's foremost experts in the black arts of creative accounting; second, the program estimate had started with the grand total of what would be necessary to support the employee populations at Granite and the subcontractors, with the detailed estimates derived from subdivisions of the overall; and finally, Granite's creative accountants always did as they were told by their customer, and they had their orders from General Palmy.

This didn't mean that Granite's estimators had an easy job. In truth, it was a fantastically complex task. The detailed estimates, part actual cost experience and part extrapolation of the established unit cost trends, had to be carefully constructed to equal the directed amounts. The trend lines weren't simple straight lines, either. They were exponential hyperbolae. Numerous "accounting adjustments" had to be made to recorded past costs to establish trend lines so that the estimates would come out as directed. This was where most of the creativity came in. On top of everything else, they had to make sure that most of the cost overrun was attributed to contract changes worked up by Granite engineers and given to General Palmy, who then directed Granite to carry them out.

Blissfully ignorant of all this (and hoping to stay that way), the FM wound up the meeting. "That was an excellent briefing, gentlemen," he said. "A very professional job. And please don't take my nitpicking your figures to heart, Major. Just reflex action for an old accountant. As a matter of fact, General Palmy, I'd appreciate it if you and Major Buck could accompany me next week in my meeting with Secretary Quill-pen, the Department of Defense Comptroller. I want him to see this briefing. I think we can kill two birds with one stone. We're going to get some flack from old Crumley Quillpen about the new Aardvark budget, but I believe the briefing will convince him we have the financial situation under control. In addition, I believe we can sell him on adopting our new back-up system in place of the scheme his whiz kids are working up. Of course, the presentation will have to be cleaned up a bit. Be sure that extra fifty megabucks for the pendulum—for the piga—gets cranked into the total estimate because this will be the basis for our budget request. Aardvark is our top-priority program, and we can't afford to get caught short on funding. Also, that computer program problem should be solved. General Palmy, why don't you talk to Proctor Pinstripe of Ivy Consultants about that? His fellows are really good at that sort of thing."

Pinstripe was a close personal friend and classmate of Crumley Quillpen. The FM was very pleased with himself for thinking of this angle. Pinstripe could be depended upon to endorse whatever was being done (his fees were very high), and his endorsement would carry a lot of weight with Crumley Quillpen.

"Finally," said the FM, "I'll want to say a few words of introduction when we brief the Comptroller. You gentlemen work up a short statement on Aardvark for me. Clear it with Colonel Clapsaddle."

With that the FM excused himself, said his smiling goodbyes, and left for his squash game with the Under Secretary. General Palmy bolted out right behind him. He was late. The president of Granite Aircraft was waiting for him at the airport in the Granite corporate jet. They were going to Granite's executive training center in Jamaica for a working weekend.

Major Buck and the other weenies gathered up the VuGraphs and back-up data and departed. Buck stopped in the outer office and used the FM's telephone to call his wife in California. He told her to go ahead and buy the fur coat.

Colonel Clapsaddle stayed on. He had lots more work to do. He was responsible for security in the FM's office. He had to make sure none of the VuGraphs or computer tabulations had been left behind. They were all classified documents. He also had to make sure that none of the Assistant Secretary's personal letterhead notepaper had been lifted by General Palmy's entourage. Sometimes the weenies would take a few sheets and use them for floating forged notes around in the field. This created all kinds of confusion. He also had to start laying the groundwork for selling the new back-up system to the Department of Defense Comptroller. Among other things, he would need an acronym.

Back-up System. BUS. Department of Defense Back-up System. DODBUS. It had possibilities.

He left to have coffee with Crumley Quillpen's military assistant.

I had seen the situations and strategies illustrated by the Aardvark Case in real life. Since it was apparent that the Back-up Principle had wide acceptance and was about to gain official endorsement through the Cost Management Improvement Program, I had no time to lose if I was to have any chance of heading off an official stamp of approval for the Back-up Principle. So I went to work on the problem.

I remembered that my predecessor as Deputy for Management Systems, Ronald Fox of Harvard, had told me that the high-level military managers were indifferent to management improvement efforts because they didn't understand the problems and needed training. What was needed, then, was a good clear explanation of the dangers in the way we were proceeding and simple suggestions for improvement. The explanation had to be brief, too, because it was hard to get the generals' attention for very long at a time. It was also very important to try to determine the interests and concerns of the generals in this area.

One area of interest was quite clear. Everyone talked about the desirability of constructing "credible" cost estimates. Credibility derived from two factors: the approval by recognized cost-estimating experts of the methods used in making the estimate, and whether or not the estimate came true. It seemed obvious that an extremely high cost estimate, full of fat and extra allowances for unforeseen difficulties, would be easier to meet than a lower, lean one which would tax the management abilities of government and contractor managers. Accordingly, I expected to find that the recognized cost-estimating experts would have established criteria for "credible" estimating techniques which would produce difficult but attainable cost goals for weapons systems contracts. If cost history from old programs had to be used on occasion, I would have expected a requirement to identify separately the cost of inefficiencies, waste, and redundant expenditures so that future contract costs and program budgets would not be inflated automatically by our contractors' runaway cost increases.

I was disappointed. All the recognized experts—the Rand Corporation, McNamara's Systems Analysis people, the Air Force estimators—were pushing for the use of historical cost figures with the fat built in to the exclusion of all other approaches to estimating costs. All these highly regarded experts were pushing the same old snake oil. The only thing new was the huge size and expense of the data collection and processing effort. When the reasons for my concern and my inquiries became apparent, advocates of the scheme shifted their justification for the program. They tried to argue that estimates derived from the high-cost historical data were not intended for evaluating proposed contract prices, and that the procurement people had their own separate system. I found that the procurement cost estimators did indeed have their own system, but the only difference was that essentially the same information was arranged differently on the forms. The only significant reason I could find for the differing paperwork was intense but petty bureaucratic jealousy. The procurement estimators made it very clear that they had no intention of changing their ways. Furthermore, the policy guidance which had been issued from my office prior to my arrival in the Pentagon was quite explicit:

A weapons system cost estimate derived separately from a contractor should be used for:
   a. Planning, including cost effectiveness studies;
   b. Budgeting;
   c. *Evaluating the reasonableness of contractor proposals* [emphasis mine];
   d. Managing on-going programs.
Whenever possible, historical data on prior systems should be used as the basis for developing a cost estimate.

As if this were not bad enough, the official cost-estimating manual prepared by the McKinseys for the Cost Management Improvement Program specifically prohibited the use of industrial engineering techniques which could have given indications of the amount of fat in cost estimates. The manual was entitled *Cost Estimating Procedures* and was published on October 1, 1965, by the Air Force Systems Command. In the section labeled *Estimating Methodology*, the manual gave this direction: "The estimating methods are based on projections from historical data. Historical data are used to project future costs."

The expert writers then went on to explain that there were two basic approaches to estimating the cost of new equipment or services. One they called the industrial engineering, which they described as a summing up of material and labor estimated as necessary to do the job. This approach was forbidden. Instead, the second approach, which they called the statistical approach, was to be used. The approved approach involved correlation of historical costs with systems characteristics such as aircraft weight, speed, complexity, and the like. Not only had the experts arranged to build in all the inefficiencies of past and current procurements, they had also forbidden use of an approach demonstrably effective in pinpointing opportunities to save money. I could see the Aardvark Case becoming universal and, worse, gaining complete respectability through high-level acceptance.

My fears were heightened when I learned that McKinsey and Company had been hired to improve the procedures for collecting cost and economic information for the Office of the Secretary of Defense. The Systems Analysis people, McNamara's so-called "whiz kids," had been struggling for several years to develop and install such a system without much success. Their proposed system was essentially just another battery of forms for contractors to fill out. Many of the forms were rehashed versions of old forms, some of them dating back to World War II. However, the contractors and the individual services—the Army, Navy, and Air Force—weren't sure what the whiz kids intended to do with the information. They didn't trust the whiz kids. On the other hand, the Air Force approach and its implementers were known quantities. In keeping with their free-enterprise theme song, the contractors felt that they should complain about *any* government-imposed reports, but in their hearts they knew the Air Force approach was harmless, perhaps even good for the business of selling overruns. Therefore, nearly everyone was happy when the McKinseys reinvented the old Air Force cost collection forms.

In fact, the Air Force cost estimators and the Cost Management Improvement Program advocates were jubilant. At last their estimates would be "credible," at least in the eyes of McNamara's whiz kids. They would be backed up in a manner mutually agreed upon by the Air Force and the powerful Office of the Secretary of Defense. The Air Force Systems Command management experts gloated over their coup. They had helped convince the Defense Department Comptroller and the Systems Analysis people that the McKinseys should be hired to invent the new system. "Five of our forms," they crowed, "have been adopted for universal use by OSD." (OSD was the abbreviation for Office of the Secretary of Defense.) "Just think what this will do for our management image. We're the leaders in management." They then set up a subproject in the Cost Management Improvement Program which was named straightforwardly the Management Image Project. Air Force officers were assigned to tell the world about how the Air Force Systems Command was leading the Pentagon out of the woods in managing big new weapons systems. Nothing was ever said about such unmentionables as high costs, waste, overruns, and hardware that didn't work very well. The emphasis was on paperwork systems.

Pentagon contractors were pleased too. After the word got out, *Business Week* reported the good news. In their January 1, 1966, issue, they wrote:

Defense contractors applaud the Pentagon's new comptroller, former Harvard Business School Professor Robert N. Anthony, for modifying a proposed new cost and economic information reporting system.

The purpose of the new system is to give the Defense Department better data on past weapons costs as a basis for judging bids.

Business Week printed the last-quoted sentence in boldface type to make sure everyone got the glad tidings.

It was clear by now, of course, that my educational project was going to be too late to head off official ratification of the Back-up Principle. On the other hand, I still had hopes that somehow the monster reporting scheme could be made to work to our advantage in cutting costs. With this in mind I consulted the cost-estimating oracles at Rand Corporation to make sure I hadn't overlooked any hidden advantages of the historical estimating approach, then asked my boss to arrange a meeting with Mr. McNamara's cost-estimating experts. The Secretary of Defense's leading expert on cost estimating was Dr. Harold Asher, who had learned his trade working with the Rand Corporation and the Air Force. Dr. Asher's principal assistant was Mr. Saul Hoch. They were part of the Systems Analysis group ("whiz kids") headed by Dr. Alain Einthoven.

Dr. Marks, very helpful as usual, set up the meeting with the two experts. It went pleasantly, and Dr. Asher and Mr. Hoch listened politely but somewhat uninterestedly to my concerns about the Back-up Principle and my proposals for saving money. I had prepared for the meeting by digging up some cost indicators from the Minuteman program, which represented my most recent experience at the time. I showed the two experts some figures from the Minuteman guidance system contracts, which were then the worst of a bad lot of Minuteman contracts. For example, factory labor efficiency on one recent contract had been planned at an average of 8 percent of the level normally expected in competitive commercial manufacturing. The planned efficiency ranged from a low of 7.2 percent up to a peak of frenzy at 11.5 percent of normal. Actually, even those dismal plans were not achieved. Actual overall efficiency was 4.2 percent of normal, with a range from 3.2 to 7 percent. I showed them examples of comparable work then being performed in the aerospace industry at efficiency levels of 60 to 80 percent of commercial standards. The responses from the two experts were slightly glazed stares and faint, condescending smiles. I had the sinking feeling that neither of them had the foggiest notion of what I was talking about.

Nonetheless the issue was important, so I pressed on, moving to an area which I hoped would be somewhat less esoteric. This had to do with rates of pay and indirect or overhead expenses. Again, I drew on my experience with the Minuteman missile program. In my early days in the Pentagon, I found it necessary to use cost figures from my earlier consulting experience for the simple reason that analytically useful cost information was not available in Air Force headquarters. Gross cost figures were reported routinely, as were increases in actual and estimated costs of weapons. The elaborate explanations for the increases always avoided routine accounting analyses starting with the traditional breakdowns into labor costs, material costs, overhead costs, and so on. Since I did not feel free to use data from my private, non-military consulting, and Air Force functionaries viewed experience on Army and Navy programs as inapplicable, I was usually forced to use data from my Air Force consulting experience, which was mostly on the Minuteman program.

I showed Drs. Marks and Asher some of the increases in rates of pay and overhead which had occurred in a typical Minuteman contractor's operation. With little change in composition of the work force, factory direct labor pay had increased from an average of $2.81 per hour in 1962 to $3.23 in 1964, an increase of $.42 per hour. This increase of 15 percent over two years, or 7½ percent per year, compared to an average annual increase of around 3 percent per year for similar work in more competitive businesses during the same period. Union demands were generally accepted as the cause of this abnormal rate of increase, although skeptics, myself among them, had pointed out that there was no discernible resistance on the part of the contractors' management. Why bother? They could pass on the increases to their tolerant government customers.

The skeptics' viewpoint was strengthened by the history of rates of pay in this same contractor's engineering operations which were not unionized and therefore not directly affected by the union. Whereas factory labor rates had gone up 7½ percent per year, average hourly pay in engineering had gone up 12 percent per year over the same period. No union excuses here, but the contractor claimed he was competing for badly needed engineering talent. Again, their excuses didn't seem to hold water. In addition to an extremely low level of activity on the part of this contractor's engineers, obvious even to the most casual observer, the contractor's own records refuted his presumed pressing need for engineers. As illustrated by the Aardvark Case, the engineers who were needed for work on specific contracts charged their time directly to those contracts. If they were not assigned directly to contract work, the engineers charged their time to overhead, or indirect accounts. The incidence of engineers without direct assignments had increased at an average of 100 percent per year over the 1960 base period, with the rate of increase accelerating over the period 1962–1964. Along with other abnormal factors, this increase in engineers on the payroll without direct assignment had caused the contractor's overhead rates to increase sharply. For every hour of direct work on contracts, the company had an engineering overhead charge of $4.01 in 1962. By 1964 this figure had increased to $5.99, a total increase of 49 percent or 24.5 percent per year. Increases in factory overhead rates, also largely due to avoidable causes, were also shown. Factory overhead rates had gone from $2.72 per hour of direct labor to $3.75, a total increase of 38 percent or 19 percent per year.

I had a large stack of well documented examples of avoidable cost increases to show McNamara's cost-estimating experts, many pinpointing specific opportunities for saving money. Taken together, just the specific examples in my samples represented potential annual savings of about $500,000,000. In addition to the horror stories, I showed Dr. Asher and Mr. Hoch some success stories, instances in which straightforward analyses, problem identification, and good management had produced dramatic reductions in weapons costs. My purpose in reciting all these details to the cost-estimating experts was to illustrate to them that we were not necessarily prisoners of historical cost trends, and that relatively simple corrections could produce results radically different from statistical indications.

All my work was in vain. Dr. Asher explained that he and his colleagues knew all about what he called "engineering estimates," and that my proposals were not practical. I suggested that perhaps the Pentagon was big enough to accommodate both approaches to estimating costs—the Systems Analysis statistical approach for making gross estimates for comparing alternative weapons proposals and my approach for negotiating prices and assessing ongoing projects. Couldn't we, I asked, make some simple modifications to the back-up forms to give us some rudimentary information about what the weapons should be costing in addition to what they actually were costing?

Sorry, said Asher, our policy is to depend on historical costs.

My sales attempt was a complete flop. Hoping to salvage some kind of cost-saving commitment, I suggested that we use the Systems Analysis estimating approach in an attempt to hold down some of the weapons costs which were then escalating rapidly. If we were tied to historical precedent, couldn't we find a situation where a change in the product had resulted in proposed cost increases far in excess of anything which could be justified empirically, then try to hold down or even roll back the cost increases? Somewhat cautiously, Dr. Asher asked what I had in mind. I suggested the Minuteman guidance system. Introduction of a new model had resulted in a unit price increase from $177,700 for the last batch of old models to $1,081,000 for the first batch of the new models. I pointed out to the experts that the new model had been justified in the first place partly on the grounds of its relative simplicity, which should have made it less expensive to manufacture. It didn't appear to me that the increase was justified on any basis, statistical or otherwise, but I was willing to see my premise tested using the Systems Analysis approach.

Dr. Asher replied that he would consider my suggestion, adding that historical projections might be abandoned on occasion but that the timing of abandonment of historical cost standards was important. He then suggested that we need not take up any more of Secretary Marks' time discussing esoteric details. He, Mr. Hoch, and I could talk about it separately.

We did. After the discussion, I wrote Ted Marks the following memo:

MEMORANDUM FOR MR. MARKS
Following our discussion with Dr. Asher and Mr. Hoch in your office on December 6, I had a conversation with Dr. Asher and Mr. Hoch which clarified my impression of their thinking. In some respects their clarified position seems more dangerous than the unclarified position. It seems that their discussion regarding the timing of the "abandonment" of historical projections from past programs as a performance standard depends on the availability of new actual costs. Once actual costs are available for a weapons system program, these become the new standard for that program regardless of the relationship to the past historical or parametric estimate.
We need further discussion on this subject.

In other words, the standard for evaluating costs of weapons was whatever the contractors spent. In the permissive environment of Pentagon procurement, the statistical estimating procedures functioned as the ratchet in the mechanism for jacking up prices.

It dawned on me that Mr. McNamara's cost-estimating experts were cost Calvinists. They believed that ultimate costs of big weapons systems were preordained. They gave little weight, perhaps not even recognition, to the interdependence of reliability of cost estimates, quality of management, and skill and energy of the people doing the work. My own viewpoint was different, no doubt due mainly to different work experiences. Whereas much of my adult life had been spent helping to make ridiculously low cost estimates look good, McNamara's experts had seen even their most generous estimates exceeded consistently. Even on those rare occasions when good cost performance had occurred on portions of the big weapons programs, the statistical estimators probably had not detected it. In my own experience in military hardware production, savings in isolated portions of programs were generally dissipated elsewhere and consequently lost from overall view. In any event there was no discussing cost reduction with McNamara's estimators. Even if they had been disposed toward dialogue with the lower orders, which they were not, the concepts were foreign to them.

In our discussions of this situation, Ted Marks appeared to share my concern and my views, but he shied away from direct action. In his position, he could have directed a change in the policies and practices within the Air Force. However, this was not his way. "Just keep selling," he advised. He suggested that I put together a pitch for the Air Force managers in charge of buying weapons systems and managing on-going programs. Following Ted Marks' suggestions, I put together a presentation (with VuGraphs, of course), illustrating the futility of various manifestations of the Back-up Principle being peddled as "cost control systems." I drew up diagrams showing the essential elements of any control system—identification of variables or attributes of the process to be controlled, standards or benchmarks for these characteristics, sensors of actual characteristics, mechanisms for comparing actual characteristics to the desired benchmark, and feedback provisions for adjusting the process when actual characteristics varied from those desired. The presentation emphasized that all these parts had to be present, either in the form of mechanisms or human participation, for any control system to work. I emphasized that this was true whether we were concerned with a thermostatic temperature control system for a house, controlling the speed of an automobile, guiding a ballistic missile, or controlling the cost of the F-111 airplane program. I pointed out that the principal emphasis in the Air Force-OSD-McKinsey project was a collection of historical statistics, both in the back-up system and the separate project to determine status of on-going weapons programs. There were no provisions for systematic correction of unfavorable conditions such as cost overruns. The highly touted "cost control systems" weren't really control systems at all. They lacked essential parts. In reality, they were analogous to recording thermometers or speedometers. At best, they might carry the bad news.

I gave this pitch to all the Air Force program managers and procurement people who would hold still for it. Practically all of them agreed with my analysis but disagreed with my conclusions. They were contemptuous of the massive data collection projects, which they considered boondoggles dreamed up by consultants aimed at expanding the functions and span of control of the bean-counters, as they called comptroller people. The procurement people viewed *any* comptroller attempts to collect information on procurement programs as unwarranted intrusions by bean-counters into procurement affairs. The procurement people agreed with me that the back-up data was of marginal value but disagreed with my contention that we needed something better. According to the procurement experts, they had the key to controlling costs of the big weapons systems. What we had to do, they said, was to get competitive bids on fixed-price incentive contracts, award the business to the lowest bidder, then leave the contractor alone until he delivered his product. Speaking of companies who had contracted to develop and produce new airplanes, Lt. Gen. Tom Gerrity, the energetic head of Systems and Logistics (S & L) in the Air Staff, said, "We'll write tight contracts and won't see the contractors again till we meet them at Edwards." Edwards Air Force Base in California was where the Air Force tested most of its newly developed airplanes. "If the new aircraft don't meet our specifications," the General continued, "we'll call the sheriff."

In theory, this approach had great appeal to me. I was convinced that the spurs of real competition, coupled with rewards for success and ruin for failure, would encourage lower costs and better products. However, as I tried to point out, there were problems. In the first place, competition for contracts for major weapons contracts were rare. Most contracts on the big programs were negotiated with a single "selected source," with the criteria for "selection" having more to do with entrenched position, political clout, and the contractor's need for the business than with true capability.

Even when there was more than one bidder for a contract, the competitive process left a lot to be desired. Practically speaking, only large, established aerospace companies were adjudged to be "responsible bidders." Given the low efficiency levels and high-cost operations common to these giants, "competition" for the big contracts among the favored few could not be depended on to produce the lowest prices attainable or high-quality products. I likened this situation to a track meet with participation limited to middle-aged ladies, each weighing in excess of 300 pounds. My irreverent view of the capabilities of our large industrial partners was topped by one of the few maverick generals I briefed. He said the so-called competitions reminded him of contention among bullmoose for the privilege of servicing the government cow. There was a good deal of bellowing, snorting, panting, and pawing of the dirt, with an occasional clashing of antlers, but none of this activity signified any great concern for the welfare of the taxpayers' cow.

Furthermore, I argued, even if we did have effective initial competition, it would be meaningless unless we enforced provisions of the contracts we let. The Air Force had never been known to enforce the original requirements of any major weapons contract if a large contractor had difficulty meeting the requirements. Smaller contractors frequently had their feet held to the fire, but the giant firms were given relief by changing their contracts to match their actual performance.

Finally, I contended, we need good information on what equipment and services ought to cost in order to protect ourselves from overpricing of follow-on contracts and spare parts. Follow-on contracts, or contracts for additional equipment following the initial order, were almost invariably negotiated with the original supplier without competition. The Back-up Principle was used to rationalize whatever prices were paid. We were usually skinned. Spare parts were also usually bought sole-source from the original supplier. The manufacturers viewed this business much as shaving goods companies look at razors and blades. Razor manufacturers can sell razors at cost if this can get the customer to buy their high-profit blades.

Some of the Systems and Logistics people acknowledged that my arguments might have had some validity in the past but that things had changed for the better. They had largely shifted away from cost-plus contracts, which everyone agreed had been ruinous. They now had fixed-price incentive contracts for major weapons programs which placed a strict ceiling on the amount of money the contractor could receive from the government. In addition, the procurement experts said, they were writing contracts which emphasized performance specifications rather than design details. The contractors would be saddled with complete responsibility for meeting the performance requirements, and any changes they made in design details in order to meet the performance requirements would be their own responsibility. The government would not pay extra for these changes. All these improvements would facilitate strict enforcement of contract terms.

As for the problem of excessive prices for follow-on orders and spare parts, the procurement experts had devised an ingenious solution. Under the leadership of Robert H. Charles, the Assistant Secretary of the Air Force for Installations and Logistics, they had developed a scheme called Total Package Procurement or, more popularly, the Charles Package Plan. The Charles Package Plan required the competing contractors to commit themselves during the initial competition to prices for contractual options to buy more equipment and spare parts. By getting firm commitments on prices and specifications for future needs during the heat of initial competition, we could harness the mating drive of the bullmoose to get lower prices and better products. What I should do, the procurement people suggested, was to let them brief me on the

Charles Package Plan as it had been applied to the Air Force's program for a huge new transport plane, the C-5A.

The C-5A briefing was a slick job based on twenty VuGraphs. It covered Item A (RDT&E, standing for Research Development, Test, and Engineering) and Item B (Production) of the contract with Lockheed. The Total Package contract included $618,600,-000,000 for RDT&E and $787,800,000,000 for production in the single contract target price of $1,406,000,000. It was a fixed-price incentive contract, which meant that the government would pay a share of overruns, but only up to a point. The ceiling price of the total package contract was $1,662,000,000. Any costs above the ceiling price would be borne entirely by Lockheed.

It was the largest single contract ever let by the Air Force up to that time. And what did we get in return? We got the "total package, a lock-and-key job on an aircraft system ready to use."

VuGraphs numbers 3 and 4 summarized that aspect. VuGraph number three read:

WHAT WE BOUGHT

Item A—RDT&E

- System integration and assembly
- Aircraft/Mission kits
- Training/training equipment
- AGE
- System test
- System management
- Data and reports

The line item labeled "AGE" stood for Aerospace Ground Equipment, which would typically include equipment need in checking out electrical, electronic, hydraulic, and other functional systems of the aircraft, work stands and other maintenance aids, materials handling equipment to help load and unload the plane, and numerous other items needed to make the aircraft a useful and ready-to-go part of an overall system for airlifting equipment and men. In past programs, contractors had typically charged enormous sums for Aerospace Ground Equipment after they had gained a dominant position by winning the business for the basic equipment, usually airplanes or missiles. This time, according to the briefer, there would be no running up of casual initial cost estimates for developing AGE. We had them all locked up in the total package commitment.

VuGraph number 4 illustrated how the procurement specialists had headed off the usual runaway increases in the cost of production of airplanes. Again, the contractor's enthusiastic estimates made in the heat of competition were tied down as firm contractual commitments. The VuGraph read:

WHAT WE BOUGHT

Item B—Production
- Aircraft/Mission kits
- Training and training equipment
- AGE
- Contract technical services
- Provisions for
- Initial spare and repair parts
- Replenishment spare and repair parts
- Updating/modification changes

In summary, said the briefer, we had bought a complete package of development and production of fifty-eight C-5A airplanes, which would be required to meet our original specifications. In addition we had binding commitments for the ancillary equipment, services, and spare parts necessary to a complete and workable airlift system.

What about the rest of the airplanes for the 120-plane program? The total package deal described by the briefer included only fifty-eight aircraft. Glad you asked that, the briefer said. He had some VuGraphs—numbers 17, 18 and 19 in the presentation— which described the contractual options for the additional airplanes we planned to buy. The price for the planned second batch of fifty-seven airplanes, called Run B, was already firm as long as the contractor's actual cost for the first batch of fifty-eight airplanes was between 90 percent and 130 percent of the planned cost, called the contract target cost. If actual costs of the first batch, Run A, were less than 90 percent of the target cost, the price of Run B would be adjusted downward. If the actual costs of the first batch were more than 130 percent of the planned cost, there would be "an upward revision of planned costs."

I jumped on this latter point immediately, but the briefer was quite vague about the exact mechanism for the "upward revision of planned costs." However, he pointed out that 130 percent of the target cost of the first batch was the contract ceiling price, which was the limit of the government's liability for the total package contract. Above that amount, every dollar the contractor spent would be a dollar lost to him. In any event, said the briefer, the contractor had no assurance that he would get the second order, Run B. His over-ceiling costs on the first order would be lost forever to him, and if the repricing mechanism for the second order indicated substantially higher prices, then the second order would probably not be placed, or at best would be reduced. McNamara's cost effectiveness people would be watching the C-5A project like hawks, and any sizable increase in the cost of the program would be a signal to look for less expensive alternatives to the C-5A airlift system. Anticipating the possibility of ordering fewer than the planned fifty-seven C-5A's in Run B, the Air Force procurement experts had agreed in advance with the contractor on the price increases due to smaller quantities. For example, as illustrated on VuGraph number 18, if we should decide to buy only the first lot of twenty-one airplanes in Run B, we already had agreement that contract target costs for each of the twenty-one airplanes would increase only 1.9 percent over the unit costs based on the full second order of fifty-seven airplanes.

The briefer moved rapidly to VuGraph number 19, which described the pricing for the third batch of C-5A's, called Run C. Prices of Run C airplanes—the 116th through the 200th C-5A's—were to be based on "straight line unit curve projection" of actual costs of Run B airplanes. This was bad news. It showed that the philosophy manifested by Cost Calvinism and the Back-up Principle was not dead. Indeed it was alive and well, and a cornerstone of the new order of things represented by the Charles Package Plan. On the other hand, I had been assured that there was little possibility of the current 120-airplane program being expanded. Since the first two orders totaled 115 planes, Run C probably would be only five airplanes. Besides, the decision was years in the future.

At that moment, I made the first of a series of horrible mistakes I was to make in the Pentagon. I dropped my questioning of details of C-5A option pricing. Instead, I asked that a copy of the C-5A contract be sent to my office. I thought I could get more specific information by studying the actual document than by listening to the slick-talking colonel who was briefing me.

I continued to be troubled by the C-5A briefing without quite knowing why. The colonel who had briefed me had been entirely too glib and too superficial, but on the other hand, Mr. McNamara was neither, and the Secretary had reportedly pronounced the C-5A scheme "a damn good contract." It really did sound as though the Air Force had the C-5A contractors, Lockheed and General Electric, pretty well tied down to binding contracts. Having seen Air Force procurement and program management repeatedly let big contractors off the contractual hook, I found it difficult to believe that they would suddenly turn around and enforce the C-5A contract if it was as tough as pictured and if the big contractors got in genuine trouble performing their commitments. I was skeptical of the intentions of the procurement and program management experts, but I had no firm foundation for presuming bad faith in this instance. It was, after all, a special case. It was the Air Force's showpiece, and the wave of the future in military contracting. By adoption, it was McNamara's scheme too. One enthusiastic reviewer called it "a Miracle of Procurement." There was a lot of high-level pride involved, and many firm public stands taken. I suspected my past bad experiences might be prejudicing my judgement. Maybe I was just too untrusting.

Little things kept cropping up to feed my suspicions. While working on the Minuteman program, I had been disgusted by the end-of-the-fiscal year spending sprees. Nearly every June there was a big rush to get left-over funds "obligated," or earmarked for contracts, before the start of the new fiscal year on the first of July. Once the money was obligated, there was then pressure to get it spent. I had thought this practice was an example of lower level bureaucratic irresponsibility. I never imagined it could be a formally expressed policy. I was dead wrong. In my reviews of management information available in Air Force headquarters, I came across a series of graphs in the Management Summary booklet furnished to us by the Air Force Systems Command. These graphs were labeled "Unexpended Funds for Current and Prior Fiscal Years." These graphs had millions of unspent dollars on the vertical scale and months of the fiscal year on the horizontal scale. A broken line was drawn from the number of unspent dollars available at the beginning of the year to zero dollars at the end of the year. This depicted the goal. Spending all the money was the financial objective. The actual amount of unexpended money was shown by a solid line. Anytime the actual spending lagged behind the planned spending, the graphs were enhanced by stern little minilectures. One of these read:

Goal: (AFSC) * to attain a zero unexpended balance by 30 June 1966. All unexpended balances are susceptible to withdrawal by Headquarters USAF unless justified as a valid requirement.

On the next monthly graph, actual spending had picked up briskly but was still behind the plan overall. Again, there was a little lecture:

Goal: (AFSC) to attain a zero unexpended balance by 30 June 1966. Unexpended balances in the old programs are extremely susceptible to criticism.

Total funds available in weapons programs always exceeded the amounts under contract. Because of the pressure to obligate and spend all the available money, total funding plans were more reliable guides to total expected costs than contract amounts in anticipating ultimate total costs. In the usual program, contracted for in many pieces, some of the additional funding was for legitimate purposes. Even though many of the added items were vastly overpriced, such things as ground equipment and spare parts were not provided for in the basic contracts as they supposedly were in the Charles Package Plan. Furthermore, large numbers of engineering change orders (ECOs) were usually anti-

* Air Force Systems Command.

cipated in planning funds for the typical airplane program, whereas the total package approach on the C-5A was supposed to minimize government-generated engineering changes.

As a basis for comparing the amount of funding over and above contract target prices on the C-5A, I obtained funding figures for the C-141, a routinely overrun jet transport plane then being produced by Lockheed. Total funding was about 37 percent more than the total of target prices for the several basic contracts for airplanes and engines. Then, on December 21, 1965, I asked the Air Staff for comparable figures for the C-5A. Here is what I got:

A. Funding for total program		$3,431.9 million
B. Contracts for:		
1. Research and Development plus production of 58 airframes (Lockheed)	$1,406.4 million	
2. Production of 57 airframes (Lockheed)	538.9 million	
Subtotal (Lockheed)	$1,945.3 million	
3. All engine contracts (General Electric)	574.0 million	
Total contracts		$2,519.3 million
C. Funding in excess of target prices (A—B)		$912.6 million *

I read the figures with a sinking feeling of having been there before. My slide rule showed me that the $912,600,000 of funding in excess of the contract prices was 36.2 percent of the sum of the basic contract prices totaling $2,519,300,000 million. Extra funding for the C-141 was 37 percent. It was close enough for government work. The Air Staff, at least, was anticipating routine additions plus the usual dreary overrun on the C-5A, the Miracle of Procurement. If there was a bright spot, it was the appearance of this comparatively low slush fund factor of 36–37 percent for cargo transport airplanes. In the missile programs, the Minuteman

* "Hearings on Military Posture," before the Committee on Armed Services, U.S. House of Representatives, Ninety-first Congress, First Session, pp. 3018–3019.

especially, slush fund factors were often several hundred percent of basic contract values. And, in accordance with the zero-balance policy requiring expenditure of programmed funds, the extra money *would* be spent. Spending all the money was a military order. Good soldiers always followed orders. A C-5A overrun, at least a modest one, was inevitable unless we could change long-standing policies and practices.

I attempted to get clarification of the C-5A funding plan from the officer who had briefed me, but my questions were shot down by a barrage of doubletalk. So I telephoned an Air Staff officer known for giving straightforward answers. He had sat in the C-5A briefing I had received.

"Why all this extra money, nearly a billion dollars, for the C-5A?" I asked. "Doesn't total package contracting lock up all the odds and ends on which contractors have gotten fat in the past?"

"Not really," my friend replied. "The contract does commit the contractors to a price on the first production run, but not on all AGE and spares. We got an agreement on how these items would be defined and priced later on, but it's the same old cost-plus-percentage-of-cost contracting for AGE and spares when the rhetoric is stripped away."

"But what about the briefing?" I protested. "Wasn't I told that 'What We Bought' included AGE and spares? What about the 'Miracle of Procurement' that fast-talking colonel with all the VuGraphs told me about?"

"Don't feel too bad about that," my friend said. "We don't call that guy Horseshit Harry for nothing. You were taken in by an expert. Your problem was that you were listening to what he said. Go back and read the actual wording on the VuGraphs Harry used in his presentation."

Sure enough, when I looked up the presentation VuGraphs, the actual wording under "What We Bought" was *"provisions for"* (emphasis mine) aerospace ground equipment spares and so on. In other words, we hadn't really bought the stuff after all, just the "provisions" for buying it in a sole-source environment later on. Total package was nowhere near total except in the public relations outpourings of the likes of Horseshit Harry. Once again,

I asked the Air Staff to send me a copy of the contract for the C-5A. I wanted to study the actual, written agreements between the Air Force and the contractors. I also asked for the composition of the C5A slush fund of $912,600,000. For once, I got a quick answer from the Air Staff to my question, "What accounts for the difference between the value of the Total Package contracts of $2,519,300,000 and the program funding plan of $3,431,900,000?" The summarized answer was:

Item	Amount in millions
1. ECOs (Engineering Change Orders)	$100.0
2. GFE (Government Furnished Equipment)	15.0
3. Depot AGE	10.0
4. Common AGE	20.0
5. Base AGE	35.0
6. First Destination Transportation (Cost of delivering equipment)	15.0
7. Price Point Estimate (estimated cost overrun)	54.0
8. Initial Spares	250.0
9. 5 Additional Aircraft	65.0
10. Incentive Payments	20.0 *

Aside from the fact that the list contained many items we had been led to believe were contained in the prices of the Total Package contracts, the figures were suspect. For one thing, they were all nice, round numbers, giving rise to the suspicion that they had been plucked from thin air to provide a *pro forma* response to a nosy new civilian in the Secretary's office. Furthermore, the list of figures added up to $584,000,000. When this total was subtracted from the slush fund of $912,600,000, there was still $328,600,000 unaccounted for. "What was it for?" I asked the Air Staff.

This time I didn't get a written answer. Instead, the Air Staff sent an emissary to explain the figures to me. They did not send an artful declaimer like Horseshit Harry. They sent a mumbler. After poring over the list for a long time as though he had never seen it before, the Mumbler ventured an opinion that something had been left out. I agreed with this possibility. But what was it?

* *Ibid.*

The Mumbler said something about these figures being the result of "negotiations" and "management decisions," which told me nothing. Furthermore, even if the bureaucrats had picked a figure arbitrarily, they would back into a breakdown of figures which would rationalize the overall amount. What was the rationalization?

"It must be replenishment spares," said the Mumbler. These were spare parts for the system after the airplane was in service. The Mumbler said he would check on it. I never heard from him again.

Despite the flimflam from the Air Staff, one thing was clear. The military expected the cost of the C-5A airlift system to increase, they had anticipated the increase in the funding plan, and the money would be spent. So much for the Miracle of Procurement.

I took this assessment to my boss, Ted Marks. I suggested that he set up a procedure to withhold slush fund money and control these contingency funds in the office of the Secretary of the Air Force.

Ted said he would assign another of his deputies, an expert in these matters, to study the suggestion. Meanwhile, he urged me to continue my educational activities, and to keep trying to sell my ideas.

So it was back to the VuGraph drawing board for me. This time I decided to try to deal with the combined effect of historical pricing, Cost Calvinism, the Back-up Principle, slush fund financing, arbitrary spending goals and the like, rather than to discuss each of these bad concepts and practices in isolation. In order to minimize the defensive reactions to criticism of other functions, I decided to focus the new pitch on the syndrome of the so-called "credible estimate," a concept of my own functional area, financial management.

When the new pitch was ready, Ted Marks gathered an all-star audience. He had generals from procurement and program management, research and development, the Comptroller's office, and the Air Force Systems Command. In addition, he had the Under Secretary and the assistant secretaries for Research and Development and for Installations and Logistics (I&L), which included procurement. The Assistant Secretary for I&L, Bob

Charles, was the key man in the audience. As inventor of record of the Charles Package Plan, or Total Package Procurement, Bob Charles was the darling of the military procurement community. Secretary of Defense McNamara's endorsement of the Total Package Procurement had sent Bob Charles' stock sky-high in the Pentagon management circles. The trade press hung on his every word and viewed him as the final authority on buying weapons. Bob Charles was unquestionably the most influential Pentagon official with the big contractors. Prior to entering government service, he had held a number of high positions in industry. Most of his business career was with McDonald Aircraft Corporation, where he had risen to Executive Vice President. The big firms considered him to be one of the few high Pentagon officials who truly understood contractor problems. Ted Marks thought that if we could convince Secretary Charles and the Air Staff generals who worked with him that our ideas were sound, our cost-control program would have smooth sailing. Until then, as Ron Fox had observed, Bob Charles and his generals had been indifferent to the financial management efforts.

My presentation on the credible estimate syndrome covered eight major points:

1. Contractor operations generated actual cost trends, which were then projected to price subsequent similar work.
2. *De facto* Air Force policy restricted visibility of contractor cost factors. For example, industrial engineering measurement of labor efficiency was not even recognized in most cases, much less recorded. I showed a number of examples of blind acceptance of dismal labor efficiency in Air Force programs, including instances where the incriminating data had been readily available but not examined because of the belief that it was improper to look behind the actual cost projections.
3. Formal Air Force policy required the use of "projections from historical data" in estimating contractor costs. I pointed out that efficiency indicators and other industrial engineering data could not be used, even if it had been collected, because of the flat policy prohibition.

4. Aggressive fact finding was generally discouraged. I cited instances, including our adventures at Autonetics, where Air Force officers and civilians had got in trouble for getting too nosy.

5. Contract negotiations were conducted under conditions unfavorable to the government, resulting in higher-than-necessary prices. In addition to being partially blinded by the Air Force's policy on fact gathering and cost estimating, government contract negotiators were confronted by overpowering contractor negotiation teams. Whereas the usual government team was small, composed of relatively low-ranking people, the contractor teams were large and could call on the full resources of their giant corporations. The big contractors always knew how much money the government team had to spend, and they generally held out for most of it. On some programs, they were told, in considerable detail, just how much money the Air Force had in both basic contract funds and in the slush fund (Ted Marks had been shocked to witness the open distribution of this supposedly closely guarded information during Minuteman SPO meetings with contractors). The giant contractors knew the government's deadline for letting the contract. A delay in contracting could delay availability of military hardware. Delaying a program because of a fuss over mere money was a responsibility no one wanted, so a favorite contractor tactic was to stall until the government negotiator had to settle. If all else failed, the contractor president could usually overcome a stubborn low-level negotiator by the simple expedient of taking his case to a high-ranking general or civilian appointee who was a fellow member of the old-boy network.

6. Additional money, over and above identified contract requirements, was programmed and budgeted in advance. This was the slush fund for cost overruns, contract changes, ground equipment, spare parts, and so on.

7. Air Force policy required obligation and expenditure of all program funds, slush funds and all.

8. Money for the original contract plus money for contingen-

cies, changes, additional items and overruns was pumped back into contractor operations (Point One), thereby generating new actual cost trends and starting the cycle all over again.

In summing up, I pointed out that the combined effect of Air Force policies and practices affecting buying and financing of major weapons systems guaranteed cost overruns. Far from being unhappy accidents or inevitable byproducts of Extending the Frontiers of Man's Knowledge, overruns were planned in advance, directed with the force of military orders, and carried out by the obedient soldiery. The "credible" estimate, then, was a self-fulfilling prophecy *if it were fat enough!*

These last words were printed on my VuGraph but concealed by an opaque overlay until I spoke them. When I peeled off the overlay and flashed the conclusion on the screen in huge, bold letters, Ted Marks burst into uproarious laughter. Nobody else uttered a sound. General Gerrity turned beet-red and clenched his jaw with a visible working of facial muscles. Bob Charles blanched a bit, especially around the mouth, but kept his cool in the best traditions of Yale and St. Louis Country Day School. Norm Paul, the Under Secretary, just sat and looked inscrutable.

I went on to recommend modification of our policies to give us factual visibility of what was going on in the big weapons programs, negotiations of prices based on what equipment and services should cost with achievable efficiency, strong backing for negotiatiors in the field, withholding of contingency funds, and so on. I urged the group to consider these suggestions especially for the C-5A, which was our showpiece, and also for the F-111 fighter, which was more or less a personal project of Mr. McNamara. The F-111 fighter had already gone through several cycles of the process I had described, and its cost had begun to head for the stratosphere, even though the plane had not flown as of then.

Unfortunately, nobody was listening. Ted Marks was still chuckling, and the other dignitaries were obviously furious except for the Under Secretary, who remained silently inscrutable.

I had made a monumental blunder. The key people whose indifference my predecessor had lamented had been educated. Those who had previously been indifferent to cost-control efforts had become violently opposed once they understood what we were doing.

THREE

PLAYING THE GAME

In the weeks that followed my dreadful mistake of revealing my overall objective, most of the people I worked with were very kind to me. After all, anyone can make a mistake, and I was a greenhorn in the Pentagon, despite my years of experience in the military contracting business. The first thing that was done was to educate me in the basics of the Air Force-contractor partnership. I was instructed in the mysteries of the lodge in much the same way one is indoctrinated before being taken into a secret society. Within six weeks after my big blunder, eighteen old hands, by actual count, brought up the subject of our partnership with big contractors in conversations with me. These old hands—senior colonels and civilians of GS-15 and GS-16 rank—represented the middle management of the Air Force's Pentagon and Systems Command headquarters. (GS-15 civilians are equivalent in rank to colonels, GS-16s to brigadier generals.) At that time, I was not instructed by any of the generals, or by any of the assistant secretaries or their deputies.

The old hands introduced me to the oral traditions of the Air Force. According to this folklore, General "Hap" Arnold, the commander of the victorious Army Air Forces during World War II and a patron saint of the modern independent United States Air Force, originated the concept of a permanent, interlocking arrangement of military and contractor organizations. General Arnold and his associates had been much impressed during World War II by the innovative and productive capacity of the American aircraft industry. All during the war, the Air Force and its industrial partners had worked, according to the tradition, almost as one organization in carrying out the mission of developing and supplying aircraft to our fighting forces. Given the highly successful outcome of this venture, it was only natural, with the victorious completion of the war effort, that both the Air Force and its industrial suppliers should want to continue a good thing. According to the folklore, there was practically unanimous consent at the end of World War II that the military's partnership with industry should be perpetuated and made even closer than it had been during the war. Other government and business leaders endorsed the concept and advocated its continuation, but General Arnold was credited with parenthood of the concept.*

In 1947 the Congress set up the Air Force as a separate agency within the national military establishment. Whereas the Army and the Navy were old, mature organizations dating back nearly to the founding of our republic, with well established traditions and ways of operating, the Air Force was starting fresh, with most of its tradition and experience dating from 1941. Prior to World War II, the old services had depended very heavily on in-house or organic support activities such as arsenals, shipyards, and technical laboratories to assist them in the development and production of new weapons and other equipment. Suddenly divorced from their parent organization and thrust out on their own, the chiefs of the fledgling independent Air Force bound themselves even more closely to their industrial partners with whom they had worked so successfully during World War II. It quickly became apparent that there were political as well as technical and

* *Pentagon Capitalism*, by Seymour Melman, published by McGraw-Hill Book Company, 1970, contains a text of a memorandum by General Eisenhower written in 1946 while he was Chief of Staff of the United States Army, which lends credence to the Air Force oral tradition. One paragraph of General Eisenhower's memo is particularly pertinent: "The possibility of utilizing some of our industrial and technological resources as organic parts of our military structure in time of emergency should be carefully examined. The degree of cooperation with science and industry achieved during the recent war should by no means be considered the ultimate, there appears little reason for duplicating within the Army, an outside organization, which by its experience is better qualified than we are to carry out some of our tasks. The advantages to our nation in economy and to the Army in efficiency are compelling reasons for this procedure."

logistical advantages to the new and closer partnership with industry. The Air Force had gained powerful new allies in the business and banking communities, in local and state governments whose districts benefited from Air Force contracts, in labor unions and, to a great extent, in the university research community. These powerful interests provided the political support necessary to sell the Air Force's expensive programs to Congress and the American taxpayer. In return the Air Force did its best to keep its partners generously supplied with contracts and research grants.

All the old hands who indoctrinated me made it clear that they heartily approved of the partnership approach employed by the Air Force. Whatever one might think about the ethics of the approach, there was no denying that it had been brilliantly successful in obtaining money from Congress. It was not uncommon for the Air Force to receive as much research and development money from Congress as the other two services combined. Given our relationship with our industrial partners, said the old hands, why should we not obtain all the money we could for them and see that it was distributed judiciously. After all, their financial prosperity was in our interest. We were totally dependent on them. Moreover, the easy contractual relationships and generous procurement policies had become a way of life and probably could not be changed even if we wished to do so.

For one thing, according to the old hands, our national economy was dependent on this spending. Surely, my instructors told me, I was aware that only the massive military spending of World War II had ended the Great Depression of the 1930s. The 15 percent unemployment rate of the Great Depression was cured only by the enormous increase in military spending from about $1,500,000,000 in 1940 to more than $81,000,000,000 in 1945. After the early post-World War II boom, unemployment began climbing again. In 1949 it reached a postwar high of nearly 6 percent. Once again, though, the massive upsurge of Korean War military spending cured the problem and reduced unemployment to less than 3 percent of the work force. Even then (early 1966), the relatively high unemployment which had persisted since 1958 was being reduced by a combination of high spending for strategic weapons and the spending for the steady build-up of conventional counterinsurgency forces then thought to be necessary to oppose the so-called "wars of liberation."

I tried to counter economic arguments in favor of a deliberate overspending policy by citing Secretary McNamara's ringing disavowals. The old hands' rebuttal was that this was nothing more than propaganda for public consumption. The operative policy, they said, was just the opposite. As proof, three colonels and one GS-15 civilian quoted a statement which they said had just been made by Dr. Eugene Fubini, deputy to Dr. John Foster, Harold Brown's successor as Director of Defense Research and Engineering. Dr. Fubini's pronouncement, they said, was that "we have an arsenal economy, and we can't change it without violent dislocation."

I listened to all this instruction as patiently as my nature would allow. It seemed clear to me that many of the old hands had come to me on their own and were really trying to help me, to keep me from going wrong in my new job. However, I did counter with the argument that the operational forces were constantly clamoring for newer, better, and more equipment. I argued that if all these requests for equipment and weapons were legitimate, we could divert any savings we might capture to the procurement of the things the operating forces said they needed. I heard no logical counter to this proposition, but I did receive a new series of indoctrination lectures, this time from somewhat higher ranking old hands. David Novick, the head of the Cost Analysis Department of the Rand Corporation, tried especially hard to set me straight. Because of his long experience and his position in the Rand think-tank as reigning sage of military cost estimating, I listened closely to what David Novick had to say.

In addition to sharing his personal experiences with me, he recommended that I read a number of Rand documents dealing with Air Force procurement and cost estimating. One of the Rand documents made a particularly strong impression on me. This was Rand Memorandum 4500-PR, dated May 1965, and entitled "A Review of Air Force Procurement," 1962–1964. Among other things, this document pointed out that the new "tough look" in Air Force procurement was more theoretical than real. Of the

$30,000,000,000 worth of procurement examined in this study, less than 3.2 percent involved formal advertising for bids, which is the strongest form of price competition. Only 14 percent of the dollar volume of procurements involved so-called "negotiated price rivalry." Typically the "negotiated price rivalry" would involve only those contractors selected by the Air Force as qualified to bid, a practice which usually resulted in elimination of all but the inner circle of firms favored by the Air Force. The Rand memorandum also pointed out that the shift from cost-plus contracts to fixed-price incentive contracts, supposedly representing a hardening of the Air Force attitude toward its contractors, had been accompanied by a contradictory decline in firm fixed-price contracts, which traditionally had been regarded as the toughest form of contracting. The Rand paper rationalized these anomalies by philosophizing that the contractual relationship was only one part of the process of obtaining equipment necessary to "the social service of defense." It stated that "the relationship between buyer and seller transcends the individual transaction" and that "negotiation is used because the results are believed to be socially superior to less personal arrangements."

In short, the Rand report cast grave doubt on the validity of the new "get tough" line on contracting. At the same time, they excused the cozy and incestuous relationship between buyer and seller as a good thing, certainly superior from a social or political point of view.

Mr. Novick took pains to explain that he understood very well my desire and intent to do what I could to squeeze the fat out of Air Force procurement. He said that he had felt very much the same way himself when, as a young man just starting out in the business, he had pushed very hard in the same direction. However, he said, he had been the beneficiary of some excellent advice from a seasoned veteran of the military procurement business who had advised him to avoid if possible the specific and the controversial and to concentrate instead on improved procedures and theoretical knowledge. Mr. Novick then suggested that we place greater emphasis on the program for cost research—that is, research into ways to evolve more credible cost estimates.

He had not heard my briefing. I did not have the heart to subject this nice man to my entire contentious diatribe. Instead I told him I was not opposed to more research into cost-estimating methodology, but that additional knowledge in that area at that particular time reminded me of the circumstances of a rather shiftless farmer in my home county in Alabama. This gentleman owned a large and fertile farm which had once been a very productive piece of property. However, in his shiftlessness he had allowed the place to run down so that he barely scratched out a living in his half-hearted attempts at cultivating the place. The county farm agent was constantly badgering the shiftless gentleman to improve his ways of farming and to attend demonstrations and classes to learn up-to-date farming methods. The shiftless one always responded: "Hell, there ain't any point in my learning all them newfangled methods. I ain't farming as well as I know how now."

The next senior citizen of the Pentagon to give me good sound, straight-from-the-shoulder advice was Maj. Gen. Harry Goldsworthy. I met with General Goldsworthy to discuss our plans for reviewing contractor's compliance with our requirements for systems which would routinely report to us the status of contract work while it was underway. This was a continuation of the approach we had employed on Minuteman and which had subsequently been adopted with modifications for use throughout the Air Force. The reviews of contractor systems for compliance with our requirement had evolved into rather formalized analyses involving plant visits during which the contractors were required to demonstrate to the visiting Air Force teams the workability of their systems for reporting overruns or underruns on work done through a given point in time. None of the contractor systems reviewed or demonstrated at the time of my conversation with General Goldsworthy had met our requirements. Certainly none were as effective as the simple poor-boy analyses we had done for ourselves on the Minuteman and other programs.

With the support of my boss, Dr. Marks, I had been applying all the pressure and persuasion I could muster in an attempt to get compliance with our rather simple requirements. However, because of their natural reluctance to disclose overruns as they

occurred and before the issue could be confused, the big contractors, their trade associations, and their sympathizers within
the Air Force had stoutly opposed the approach. Our opponents
were particularly vociferous in opposing the tough-minded and
factual reviews by the demonstration teams. Publicly the top management, including the generals in the headquarters of the Air
Force systems command, supported the bothersome demonstration visits. However, General Goldsworthy told me that they were
doing so only because of the high-level support this approach
was receiving in the Pentagon, and that the Systems Command
management's true feelings were different. He told me bluntly
that the Systems Command opposed the demonstration process
and that he did too. Furthermore, he told me, there was no visible support at any level for my proposals for systematic cost control and cost reduction. In particular, he said, there had been "no
expression of support from the top guy," meaning Secretary Mc-
Namara. He said that if I was to have any chance of success,
I would have to obtain an explicit expression of support in writing from the office of the Secretary of the Air Force as a minimum. Secretary Brown's approval would be required, but most
of all, according to General Goldsworthy, I would have to obtain
the backing of Assistant Secretary Robert H. Charles. Then the
General laid it on the line: "We will proceed at our own pace
and in our own way. If you don't agree with us, then we can
take it up with higher authorities."

I had no reason to doubt that the many people who had advised me were anything but sincere, and the advice was no doubt
sound for any aspiring bureaucrat. I understood perfectly what
they were trying to tell me, and I was not ungrateful for their
efforts. I rejected the advice because I was simply not in agreement with their objectives. At the same time, I felt more than a
little sorry for these people. It seemed tragic to me that such obviously talented people should waste their lives perpetuating,
excusing, and otherwise propping up the traditional wasteful and
dishonest approaches to military procurement. There was work
to be done and money to be saved, and I felt very strongly that
we should get on with the job. However, I had to admit that
General Goldsworthy had a point. While it was true that Secre-

tary McNamara's public statements were ringing declarations of dedication to economy and to rooting out boondoggling, it was also true, so far as I could tell, that no one in a position of responsibility in the Pentagon had directed the kind of specific, hard-nosed cost-reduction actions I was proposing. The military bureaucracy responded to orders, and no one had ordered or otherwise instructed them to reduce the unit cost of Minuteman missiles, of F-111 fighter bombers, or any other major weapon so far as could be determined.

When I told my boss, Ted Marks, about the results of my informal indoctrination by the old hands, he suggested that I ignore all of the folklore and myths about deliberately fat contracts and other loose procurement practices and throw myself wholeheartedly into the Cost Management Improvement Project (CMIP) efforts then underway at the Air Force Systems Command. In particular, he urged that I keep selling and that I keep up my educational efforts. "Just keep hammering away" he said. "They'll come around." I objected that this was not the point, and that the more the civilians and military bureaucrats understood, the more they opposed cost reduction and control efforts. They simply did not believe that the Department of Defense and Air Force top management sincerely desired actual reductions in cost, especially if such reductions in cost were likely to result in lower employment within the military contracting industry. I contended that we needed both specific, unequivocal direction to cut costs and examples on our part that we meant business. We desperately needed to get tough on some specific project. Otherwise the people in the Air Force Systems Command and the field officers would never believe that we were really serious about wanting cost reduction. I suggested that some of the conscientious objectors to contractor cost reduction might even be relieved to have strong direction from headquarters. They could continue to maintain the good relations with contractors which they prize so highly by blaming the unwelcome direction on "those guys across the river," as they referred to the Secretary of the Air Force and his staff.

When I recounted to Ted Marks the essence of my conversation with General Harry Goldsworthy, he relented somewhat and said that perhaps we could work up a policy memorandum on cost reduction for Dr. Brown to sign. He said that he would set up a committee to draft the memorandum. He would head the committee himself, and I would assist him. In addition we would bring in the two senior McKinsey and Company partners working on the CMIP and Gen. Wendell ("Red") Carter, AFSC comptroller, to assist in the project. It did not seem reasonable to me that we should need so many high-powered people to draft a simple cost reduction memorandum. On the other hand, it was possible that participation by McKinsey and the AFSC headquarters might serve to soften criticism of the directive when it finally came out. In any event, I was so pleased that Ted Marks had finally agreed that we needed specific direction to the field that I did not object.

Subsequently, the committee met every few weeks over a period of a year or more. Between meetings we would draft memoranda which we would send out if we were in Dr. Brown's shoes. The meetings were always congenial and stimulating, and were marked by lively discussions of the various proposed memoranda, exchanges of management philosophy, and unanimous agreement on the rottenness of military procurement. But we never did get out a letter directing unit cost reductions on the Minuteman, the F-111 fighter-bomber, or anything else.

I was making a mighty effort to work within the system and to play the game according to the bureaucratic rules. One of these rules was not to push too hard and to make as few waves as possible. So I let the cost-reduction policy project take its natural course while I busied myself with other jobs. There was plenty to do, and several segments of the Cost Management Project appeared to be worth sizable investments of time. Despite having been shot down repeatedly in my efforts to reorient the cost-estimating project, I still had hopes of converting it to a useful cost-reduction aid.

I was also interested in the project to study contractor overhead expenses. Overhead rates had run out of control for years, often with the active connivance of the Air Force procurement hierarchy. This layer of contract cost had been pictured as very mysterious, perhaps beyond the ken of mere man. "Overhead is like the dark side of the moon," one of the procurement sages told me in that pre-Apollo era. The Pentagon's military and civilian bureaucrats and Harvard-educated financial appointees professed inability to understand the arcane art. Every one-window shopkeeper in the world understands overhead expenses, but the Pentagon's giants of management did not, if one swallowed the excuses. Feigning ignorance was a phony excuse, of course. Anyone with walking-around sense could understand why contractor overhead had gone out the roof. Engineers without direct assignments charged their time to overhead and administrative accounts. Taj Mahal office buildings and gorgeously appointed offices were paid for through overhead. The hordes of superfluous office workers were supported by overhead charges. The money for corporate executive jets, limousines, and chauffeurs came out of overhead. Likewise the ubiquitous "Washington representatives" and "technical representatives." Plush jobs for retired officers and, alas, consulting fees for renowned academicians were also financed by these unfathomable expenses.

The real reasons Pentagon management people played dumb on this subject were legion. Some involved convoluted reasoning, but some of the considerations were perfectly understandable. One night, while traveling with one of our most brilliant management generals, I was in an ornery mood and decided to pin down my companion on military motivations for inaction on runaway contractor overhead expenses. This gentleman could not very gracefully plead ignorance with me, because we had both seen gross examples of deliberate inflation of overhead expenses by contractors we were visiting. Furthermore, he was well aware of the rather consistent success of my former consulting associates in cutting overhead. Surely, if a group of sharecropper industrial engineers could understand the problem, the bright, beautifully educated Harvards could. My companion's standard excuses of the necessity for keeping up contractor capability and maintaining the war mobilization base didn't make sense, either, because all the generals were clamoring for more and newer hardware. Savings from overhead reductions could be used to buy weapons. The overhead accounts were also the safest places to make cuts, even if arbitrary reductions were made. Even an overly harsh reduction of personnel in a contractor's sales department would have little or no immediate effect on the principal operations of engineering, manufacturing, and testing. Certainly there would be no danger of delaying delivery of weapons then in production.

I persisted in this discussion all through dinner and long afterward. Finally the general lost his patience and ended the argument. "Look, Fitzgerald," he said angrily, "I'm going to retire in a year or two and I'll become part of some contractor's overhead. If I cut overhead allowances, I'll be cutting my own throat." *In choler veritas.*

The CMIP contractor overhead project then underway was only the latest of a series of studies of the subject. When overhead rates began their dramatic upsurge during the Missile Gap fraud of the early 1960s, Pentagon procurement experts reacted by setting up a group to study the problem. And they did, for several years. During that period my associates and I were working on a relatively poverty-stricken Navy program where rising contractor overhead rates had contributed to the program managers' financial difficulties. With some help from my group, the program's prime contractor had done a good job of rolling back his overhead rates. The contractor had reduced overhead rates by about 20 percent in the face of a declining volume of business. This contrasted so sharply with the otherwise almost universal increases elsewhere that I was called before the study group to explain what was going on. To my surprise, the group was generally hostile. They were really searching for confirmation of their beginning premise that overhead rate increases were altogether the result of Inexorable Economic Processes, that they were something that just happened to us, like the weather, and that nothing could be done except to try to anticipate the increases so that plenty of money would be available. The study group was offended by my suggestion that they stop dealing in generalities and get down to specific contractor situations. They were outraged when I urged them to shift from a subjective, qualitative approach to objective, quantitative analyses aimed at identifying waste and cutting it out. When I told them that no sophisticated new management tools were needed, and that skilled, old-fashioned cost cutting would do the job, they all but threw me out. So far as I could tell, the only result of this universal study was to fend off proposed corrective measures for two or three years.

I was hopeful that the CMIP overhead project would not follow the earlier pattern. I dug up my old horror stories illustrating the costly effects of uncontrolled overhead and added a few new ones. I presented these, along with some success stories, to show that improvement was possible, to other members of the CMIP Control Board. Again, I urged objective, quantitive analyses for the express purpose of cutting costs.

There was very little overt reaction to my proposals from most of the Control Board members, but General Red Carter was very complimentary in private. My suggestions were just what we needed to make the project go, he said, and he would personally go to the field with the Air Force Systems Command overhead team to explain the program to the contractors. This reaction encouraged me greatly, and my appraisal of the program's chances for success shifted from hopeful to optimistic. I was eager to hear how the contractors would respond.

The official reports of the team's visits to contractor plants didn't tell me much, but unofficial and detailed reports from friends working for the contractors were most enlightening. A good example was a contractor report of the team visit to the Boeing Company in Seattle.

According to my secret sympathizer at Boeing, Brig. Gen. Wendell Carter led the AFSC overhead cost management improvement team which visited Boeing on March 7, 1966. In addition to General Carter, the team included a number of Air Force officers and a consultant from McKinsey & Company. After General Carter introduced the team, the McKinsey & Company consultant kicked off the presentation to Boeing's management. The McKinsey consultant stated that the AFSC-McKinsey team was building a framework to present an overview and guidelines for cost management. After the consultant had finished describing the framework, an Air Force major was introduced for the next segment of the presentation. The major stated that the overhead project, which had the personal support of Lt. Gen. Austin Davis, Vice-Commander of the Air Force Systems Command, had four major objectives: (1) to identify effective methods, (2) to examine possibilities of developing new systems, (3) to provide common concern and adherence to principles, (4) to provide a basis for joint government-industrial programs.

The major then lauded Boeing (a "great litany of praise," according to my reporter) for their cooperative and constructive reply in working with the Air Force. The major concluded his presentation by saying that General Davis believed in effective evaluation while avoiding the risk of "overcontrol," the cardinal sin of procurement.

He then introduced General Carter to summarize the presentation. My reporter said that General Carter's summary covered eight points:

1. Overhead is the most complex and variable element of contract cost.
2. The "graph drawers" in the Pentagon were implying that the Air Force was doing a miserable job in overhead management.
3. The Air Force was depending on its contractors to help with this problem.
4. He castigated "those guys across the river" who were putting on pressure and pot-shotting.
5. The current project was a slow approach to the problem in the face of criticism.
6. There was grave danger that critics of overhead increases might mount a "witch hunt."
7. Statements claiming that contractor overhead expenses could be cut significantly were out of line.
8. The government was seeking to develop a qualitative approach to document the conviction that certain contractors appeared to be controlling overhead.

I had made a point of keeping contact with friends and acquaintances working for our contractors. Most were secret sympathizers with my cost-saving objectives. Many were convinced that their companies would buckle down and start rolling back costs if their military customers were really serious about the cost reduction ballyhoo. They kept alert for signals of serious intent. Sadly, they were not to hear the signals on the overhead project. All they could do was report the bad news to me.

Reports of Red Carter's conduct in the field were in sharp contrast to his attitude in private meetings with me and in the strategy sessions with Mr. Marks, where he had sold himself as a true believer in our supposedly common cause of cost reduction. Emasculation of the overhead project was an accomplished fact, so I decided to accept it gracefully. I did not make an issue of the unhappy reports I was receiving from the field, although I did let Carter know about the feedback I was getting. He didn't seem concerned. His promotion to major general had just been announced, so from his viewpoint he must have been doing something right. I was learning to play the game. One just did not press too hard on an issue. If there was resistance, one backed off and moved on to something else.

The something else I moved on to was deeper involvement in obtaining information on status of contracts. The approach developed on the Minuteman program for detecting cost overruns as they happened had been accepted as a good idea, at least in theory. The process had been named "performance measurement," and requirements for it had been written into a number of contracts for big weapons systems. However, beneath the surface enthusiasm for the scheme, all was not well. There were enormous pressures to convert the potentially useful performance measurement procedures into another "management image" façade. To this end, it was important to the management image faction to avoid the surfacing of embarrassing facts on the validity of information the big contractors were giving us. The demonstration teams checking out the accuracy of this information were accumulating a vast store of proof that status information which contractors were giving us was misleading and that their management systems which produced the data were faulty.

Opposition to inspection by the demonstration teams grew stronger as the evidence of deceit accumulated. With encouragement from their big contractor friends, many of the generals, especially those in procurement, had been dragging their feet. Some, like straightforward Gen. Harry Goldsworthy, opposed the inspections openly. Another fundamentally sound scheme was in danger of being dropped or subverted. Without tough factual inspections, the big contractors could not be expected to modify their management control systems to produce facts on overruns on work as it was being done. It was clearly in the contractors' best financial interests to confuse the situation as much as possible. The management image faction in the Air Force didn't care about substance, though, and were pushing hard to approve whatever status information systems the contractors offered so long as the contractors' descriptions of the system conformed to the requirements. The procurement experts contended that the scheme was superfluous because we didn't need to know what was going on. With our new fixed-price incentive contracts we could practice "disengagement," leaving the contractor alone until he finished the job. General Gerrity's assurance was sung out in answer to all contrary argument: "We'll meet the contractor at Edwards and call the sheriff if his plane doesn't meet the specifications." Indeed, the procurement experts said, if we knew too much about what was going on in the contractor operations, we might be tempted to dabble in things which were none of our business. This would lead to "overcontrol."

These dream-world arguments overlooked the fact that we were responsible for fielding military weapons systems which presumably were badly needed. Air Force flight tests at Edwards Air Force Base were scheduled near the end of years-long development programs. Symptoms of trouble always occurred much earlier in failing programs, and we would waste both the time and the effort invested in unusable junk if we closed our eyes to developing trouble. Besides, we had the practical problem of going to Congress for fresh money. With a lead-time of about eighteen months for congressional appropriations, early warning of trouble was important.

Even though I was committed for the moment to the gentlemanly Ivy League code of behavior for civilian appointees, I had no intention of allowing the general officer corps to undercut the performance measurement project. I had fair warning of their intentions and could only blame myself if I failed to control the project. Many of the lower-ranking officers were trying hard to make the performance measurement project meaningful. By accompanying them on their visits to contractor plants, I could support them by giving first-hand testimony to the determination of the Air Force Secretary's office to get the facts. My personal involvement in these inspections was deeply resented by the generals, but Mr. Marks and Secretary Brown seemed to appreciate the information I brought back to the Pentagon from these forays into the field. Very often our field inspections would smoke out hitherto concealed cost overruns and other problems as a by-product of checking out the contractor's information systems.

Knowledge of systemic problems was useful too. For example, we found that most of the contractors were holding up their end of the self-fulfilling prophecy syndrome by releasing internal budgets far in excess of the money covered by their contracts. They were gambling (at minimal risk) on subsequent contract nourishment change orders to cover their built-in cost overruns. None of the big firms could give sound accounting for final usage of material bought for use on their contracts. Unsupported "accounting adjustments" shifted incurred costs around to hide overruns. Plans too were juggled to conceal indications that completed work had cost more than planned. In fact, the adjustment of plans to match whatever had been spent was prevalent enough to have acquired the common name of "rubber base line" planning. The variations of the rubber base line seemed infinite. After our teams began to document capricious changes to overall planned costs for contracts, contractors became increasingly inventive in devising new ways to conceal overruns. One common dodge was to leave total planned costs for a contract unchanged but to "borrow" budget or planned costs from future work and add it to the planned costs for current work for which actual costs were exceeding plans. In the creative accounting trade this process was called "sucking upstream," an inelegant but descriptive title.

In earlier attempts to provide for systematic status reporting for big contracts, the rubber base line adjustments had evolved to such a high state of refinement that equating planned costs to actual cost was done automatically on computers. In the early 1960s a planning and scheduling scheme known as PERT (Program Evaluation and Review Technique) was developed by the Department of Defense. The technique became widely used for schedule planning, and it was decided to take advantage of the wide industry acceptance of PERT to develop a uniform method of planning the cost of contracts and detecting cost overruns or underruns as the work progressed. The objectives were the same as for the scheme later developed on the Minuteman program, but the two schemes differed in approach.

Both schemes depended on breaking the total planned contract work down into smaller segments of work to be performed over relatively short spans of time. Each of these segments of work, called "work packages," had its own estimated or planned cost. Then, as the work packages were completed, the planned cost of the completed work could be compared to money actually spent to get an objective picture of overruns or underruns as the work went along without having to depend on guesses or live in ignorance until money for the contract ran out with the work undone. On the Minuteman program we had found that schedule and cost planning were done separately but in such enormous detail that we could construct our own plan made up of short-span work packages, each with its own planned cost, without contractor involvement if necessary. In fact, these more or less naturally occurring subdivisions of work were so small that for our purposes we could ignore the effect of work started but not completed for rough assessments of status. This simplified matters greatly, because we would simply add up the planned costs of all the completed work packages, then compare the total planned cost to total actual costs. That way we were able to use existing contractor breakdowns of actual costs accumulated, and thereby avoided arguments about changing contractors' accounting systems, which were considered sacred and unchangeable. PERT-Cost, on the other hand, required that the contractors compare actual cost incurred to planned cost for each individual package of work. This meant that the contractors' accounting systems had to provide separate cost accounts for each work package.

The accounting nightmare created by this requirement gave the contractors a valid excuse to negotiate longer and longer time spans for their work packages in order to reduce the number of separate accounts. Finally, when PERT-Cost matured as an "acceptable system" for the contractors, individual work packages commonly embraced work to be done over a two- or three-year time span. This, of course, invalidated the whole original concept of the scheme. There were no longer enough short segments of planned work to permit meaningful periodic evaluation of completed work. (Unhappily, the specialists who worked at PERT-Cost, called Pertniks, had long since evolved into a cult, most of whose members had forgotten what they set out to do in the first place and were mostly concerned with advancing the interests of their sect.)

To remedy this fatal shortcoming, the Pertniks invented a formula to estimate planned cost of work done in work packages started but not completed. Originally, it was intended that the formula would be used rarely and that most of the planned cost information would result from the completion of segments of work. With "maturation" of the system and growth of length of work packages, the formula became the whole show.

The basic formula was

$$V = \left[\frac{A}{A + E} \right]\left[B \right],$$

where

V = value (planned cost) of work accomplished,
A = actual cost to date,
B = budget (planned cost) for the total work package, and
E = estimate to complete the remaining work.

It was a simple enough formula for the space age, and it appeared to contain a measure of rough logic. For example, if actual cost to date (A) was $500,000, the total budget (B) was $900,000, and the estimate to complete remaining work (E) was $500,000, the planned cost (V) of work done would be

$$V = \left[\frac{A}{A + E} \right]\left[B \right]$$
$$= \left[\frac{\$500,000}{\$500,000 + \$500,000} \right]\left[\$800,000 \right]$$

$$= \left[\frac{\$500,000}{\$1,000,000} \right]\left[\$800,000 \right]$$

$$= \$400,000$$

Therefore, the Pertniks could report that the planned cost of work done was \$400,000, the actual cost was \$500,000, and there was an overrun of \$100,000. Among other shortcomings, the assessment was still basically dependent on the subjective estimate to complete the work. The folks doing the estimating could still draw any picture they wished for the government. Actual practice produced even more amazing results.

On most programs, monthly status reports were required, and making up new estimates to complete was bothersome. So the process was automated. Since the contractors only told the government about overruns when they chose to anyway, actuals to date plus the estimate to complete equaled the total budget until the contractors decided to break the bad news. Therefore, instead of fooling around with new estimates each month, the same results could be obtained by subtracting the actual cost to date (A) from the total budget (B) to derive the estimate to complete (E). Moreover, the computation $E = B - A$ could be performed on computers untouched by the human brain. Here's what resulted when $B - A$ was substituted for E in the formula:

$$V = \left[\frac{A}{A + E} \right]\left[B \right]$$

$$= \left[\frac{A}{A + (B - A)} \right]\left[B \right]$$

$$= \left[\frac{A}{B} \right]\left[B \right]$$

$$= A, \text{ or}$$

planned cost of work done to date equals actual cost of work done to date.

Here at last was the perfect cost status reporting system from the contractors' viewpoint. Any number of Pertniks, accountants, and other cultists could play. Huge amounts of computer time could be used preparing the reports. All this made the scheme delightfully expensive, with the government allowing its costs and a fair profit in contract prices. With a little forethought in setting up the scheme and employing the lunatic formula, the reports to the government could be made utterly meaningless. It was just complicated enough to discourage nosey troublemakers, especially high-ranking people whose group ethic forbade getting into detail on any subject.

It was easy to see how the big decisionmakers committed to the avoidance of "details" (and, as a consequence, of facts) could get snowed by the Pertniks. In one of my early indoctrination visits to a big contractor's plant, I asked about performance measurement on their principal project. Luckily, the monthly report was then in preparation and I could see it if I wished. I wished and was conducted to the computer department. This was a huge, cool aerospace-looking room full of intimidating machines. The magnetic tape reels on the computers rapidly wound and unwound, making a scientific, softly whirring noise. A bewildering array of colored lights blinked off and on faster than the eye could follow. A printer was spewing out the PERT-Cost monthly status report onto a wheeled cart. (Each complete copy of the report weighed more than 100 pounds.)

Now, the proper reaction of a visiting management expert to such a dazzling display was to mutter something about the marvels of modern computerized management, maybe ask a few questions about the type of computer employed, and move on to something less esoteric. However, I wondered out loud who ever had time to read all those reports and what action they led to. I was told that the reports were "analyzed" by a group of specialists in the plant, then sent to the customer, the Air Force, at Wright-Patterson Air Force Base in Dayton, Ohio. This was the headquarters of the Aeronautical Systems Division (ASD) of the Air Force Systems Command.

On one of my trips to ASD, I looked up the people who received the PERT-Cost reports to see what they did with the monthly mountain of paper. They said they picked off some of the PERT-Cost figures for other reports and occasionally prepared summarized data in response to special requests. Mostly, though, the reports were just filed away. The oldest citizen could not recall an instance of the reports being used as a basis for corrective action. I asked one of the PERT-Cost experts what he thought the purpose of the exercise was. He stared blankly at me for a moment, then said, "Why, to justify overruns, of course." The Back-up Principle was being applied to performance measurement.

Some of the Pertniks acknowledged that the scheme still had shortcomings and needed work. They were making a mighty effort to improve their computer programs. The trouble was, they said, that they needed expert help with this job and didn't have it. They had previously had a consulting contractor who was skilled in the art of PERT-Cost computer programming. They had suffered a grievous loss when an unreasonable colonel in Systems Command headquarters cut off the money for their ace consultant. They asked if I could help gets funds restored so that the PERT-Cost computer program could be properly maintained.

I said I would look into it, and I asked the name of the colonel. I wanted to meet him. He sounded like my kind of ogre. The Pertniks said the villain was Col. Joe Warren, the head of Management Analysis in the Systems Command headquarters at Andrews Air Force Base.

As soon as I returned to Washington, I requested an indoctrination briefing of the management analysis functions at Air Force Systems Command headquarters at Andrews Air Force Base. Colonel Warren spent the better part of an afternoon giving me this briefing. It was unique. Colonel Warren did not use Vu-Graphs. Instead he showed me first-hand the facilities—the chart rooms, the closed circuit television set up, and the like—that were employed to keep the Commander of the Air Force Systems Command and his staff informed of what was going on throughout the command. Instead of showing me VuGraphs which told me about the types of reports prepared for the Commander, Colonel Warren showed me the actual reports and answered all my questions about them in a simple and a straightforward manner. In a refreshing departure from standard military briefing techniques, Colonel Warren made no attempt to cover up or evade in discussions of shortcomings, errors, and omissions in the Systems Command's management information systems. All in all, I was so impressed with Colonel Warren and his performance that I began to inquire about his background and experience with an eye to getting him involved in our weapons systems cost control projects.

Unfortunately, Joe Warren had not attended Harvard. However, he had absorbed the higher education offered by East Texas Baptist College prior to entering the Army air forces early in World War II. After outstanding service as a pilot during the war and several operational assignments immediately thereafter, Joe Warren had picked controllership as a specialty and had become involved in the weapons acquisition business. Meanwhile, he had continued his education by attending a variety of night schools and taking correspondence courses. He had spent a number of years in the ballistic missile procurement business, where he had learned about the great missile boondoggle from the inside before moving to his job at Systems Command headquarters. He had a quick and incisive mind and exceptional energy. His blunt and direct manner did not particularly endear him to some of the more squeamish generals and high-ranking civilians, many of whom preferred a diet of management information consisting solely of good news, optimistic projection, and other happy talk.

As I learned more about Colonel Warren's abilities, experience, and character, I became convinced that he could lead the Cost Management Improvement Program out of the woods. At the time, it was bogged down in briefings, meetings, drafting of new proposals, presentations of breakthroughs accomplished, problems to be overcome, and plans for the future. Numerous manuals were being drafted to solidify and officially endorse the several manifestations of the Back-up Principle and, in the process, add mountains of paperwork. All the while, weapons systems costs were continuing to run out of control, and opportunities to save vast sums were going aglimmering. I began working on Joe Warren to convince him he could help. He was skeptical. He had seen the great procurement boondoggle relentlessly grow larger in spite of all efforts to control it. He had seen officers and civilians who aided its expansion prosper, and those who had opposed it fail. He had taken a few lumps himself. He was then thinking of moving on to another line of business and had started discussions with the Air Force personnel people about other assignments. He was thinking about foreign service as a military attaché. A tour of duty in London, Paris, or some other major world capital would be interesting, broadening for his children, and would get him out of the weapons system acquisition mess. On the other hand, he agreed that some pieces of the panoply of management image schemes contained germs of usefulness and could become vehicles for saving money if properly applied. Also, he could see that there were islands of solid management effort in the procurement morass. Individuals and small groups were trying hard to control costs on a number of programs. What these people needed most was encouragement, sensible direction, and evident support from on high. They especially needed supporters in the Air Force Systems Command Headquarters who would fend off subversion of their work and help them overcome resistance by recalcitrant contractors and their Air Force allies. Joe finally agreed that he probably could help out if he had the proper backing.

Fortunately, many of the officers then assigned to the Cost Management Improvement Project at Systems Command Headquarters were scheduled for reassignment on July 1, 1966. Colonel Warren could be assigned as the working head of the project in the normal course of personnel shuffling. I suggested to Ted Marks that, in view of our need for an action-oriented leader, he should try to get Joe Warren assigned to the job. Mr. Marks recognized our need for action and shared my enthusiasm for Joe Warren's abilities, but he was reluctant to inject himself into personnel assignments within the Air Force Systems Command. However, he agreed to discuss the matter with General Carter, with General Merrell, the Comptroller of the Air Force, and with McKinsey and Company, who had in the past exerted considerable influence in the assignment of personnel to the Cost Management Improvement Project. He did, and thereby caused considerable consternation in the Air Force Systems Command Headquarters. There were several candidates for the working head or secretary of the control board, each backed by a different faction. Until then no one had nominated Colonel Warren. Moreover, the dominant management image faction was not about to risk losing control of the entire project by putting a maverick colonel in charge. On the other hand, they were reluctant to invite unnecessary trouble by ignoring Assistant Secretary Marks' suggestion entirely. They worked out a compromise.

Both Secretary Marks and I had been urging rather persistently that a small but select trouble-shooting group staffed by real "tigers" be established in the Systems Command Headquarters to help perform the most difficult of the field tasks, such as the inspection of the big contractors' performance measurement systems. So, as a means of mollifying Secretary Marks' office, a "tiger team" was established as a separate organization. However, Joe Warren was not nominated to head up the new "tiger team." Instead the Systems Command Headquarters nominated as chief tiger a more conventional colonel, a predictably safe bureaucrat who could be depended upon to keep the "tiger team" inert and toothless. Red Carter was selected as the emissary to carry this proposal to Secretary Marks. Secretary Marks referred the proposal to me and I rejected it. This was the first in a series of proposals for staffing the "tiger team."

For some time poor General Carter was kept shuttling back and forth across the Potomac between Andrews Air Force Base and the Pentagon with lists of proposed "tigers." Each successive list proposed tigers more toothless and timid than the last. We kept rejecting them. Later on, Red Carter prepared a "talking paper" for limited circulation among his fellow generals and other close associates which described this episode. He lamented, "It seemed initially that all the individuals I nominated to Mr. Marks, as either the head of or members of the implementation team, were considered by Mr. Fitzgerald to be incompetent on the grounds of inadequate motivation." In point of fact, they were all conscientious objectors to active warfare on high costs.

Finally, the Systems Command generals relented and nominated Joe Warren as "Chief Tiger." Once the test of wills was ended, Joe Warren's nomination was accepted with outwardly good grace and even a little enthusiasm by his former opponents. For example, on June 1, 1966, McKinsey & Company wrote a "Dear Red" letter to General Carter in which they said:

Although we firmly believe that Joe Warren is an excellent candidate for this new job, I think there is one reservation that we must face— his reluctance to work with consultants. I am sure Joe has his reasons for feeling this way and we, of course, would not attempt to force him to change his mind. However, I am sure you will agree that the Change Cost Project will require some further nurturing by our people before it can be completely turned over to the Command. Therefore, we would suggest that if you do consider Joe Warren as a candidate for the new position that you temporarily detach the Change Cost Project from the new directory and have it report directly to you until our participation has been terminated.

The "Change Cost Project" referred to in the McKinsey letter had been initiated in response to criticisms by Dr. Brown and others of the practice of allowing overrun contractors to "get well" by giving them overpriced change orders of questionable necessity. Colonel Warren was known to favor a much tougher approach than was then being taken in this project.

Naturally, I was very pleased with the assignment of Colonel Warren to head the new tiger team. In addition, Mr. Marks had arranged for the assignment of a very capable colonel from the Air Staff Comptroller's organization to work with us. This assignment solved a major protocol problem for us. Most of the people in the Air Force's top management recognized that the Air Force's organization structure contained entirely too many levels, that the intermediate layers often added little or nothing to the management process, and that direct communication by the Secretary's office with the field organizations was often a practical necessity. Despite general recognition of the unwieldiness of the overly deep organization, nothing was ever done about it except to occasionally bypass a layer or two. Each time this was necessary, the generals would go around for some time grumbling about the sanctity of the chain of command. Representation on our team from each of the layers in the organizational structure prevented technical violations of the chain of command dicta but did not unduly impede our team effort.

We immediately scheduled a whirlwind tour of Systems Program offices and major contractor plants to spread the word that the Air Force was dead serious about cost control. In spite of the fact that I had been unsuccessful in my attempts to persuade the Secretary's office to issue specific cost-reduction directions and management goals, we did have numerous strongly worded commitments to economy and efficiency by Mr. McNamara and his subordinates. I decided to take these statements at face value and place the burden of contradicting me and the general statements on the conscientious objectors. Many of the people we visited in the field were skeptical, some downright incredulous. But, at the same time, we got an enthusiastic reception from those few brave souls who had been laboring in loneliness and without support in their attempts to control the ever-rising weapons systems cost.

Joe Warren and I were greatly encouraged by the response we received to our early trips to the field. Over and above the warm welcome we got from our hitherto secret sympathizers, we observed another heartening phenomenon. We noticed that even among those program managers and procurement officers who opposed us privately, none was willing to oppose cost reduction and control in the semi-public gatherings of lower ranking officers, their peers, the contractors, and representatives from the top headquarters organizations. In those circumstances, even the worst actors appears inclined to at least give lip service to economy and efficiency in procuring weapons. Joe and I concluded that this was probably a psychological phenomenon of the same sort that compels abject sinners at religious camp meetings to confess their past misdeeds, to testify to the salubrious effects of clean living, and to take the pledge to go forth and sin no more.

We decided to test this theory on a grand scale. We immediately began planning a big revival meeting at Systems Command Headquarters. We proposed inviting the Air Force and contractor managers of the big weapons programs, key Air Force procurement and comptroller people, and as many high-level government official as we could round up to attend the revival. We planned to let those managers who had promising improvement programs underway brag about their accomplishments. By elevating these good guys to administrative hero status, we hoped to motivate the recalcitrants to step up their own management improvement efforts.

Both Mr. Marks and Secretary Anthony thought this was a great idea and agreed not only to endorse the revival but also to serve as visiting preachers. General Red Carter went along with the proposal but got cold feet as the revival date approached. A few days before the scheduled meeting, the General suggested to Colonel Warren that we consider calling off the revival. He thought there was a strong possibility that the session would degenerate into a confrontation between hard-liners on cost control (especially Fitzgerald) and the known opponents who would constitute a majority of the attendees. "Don't worry about a thing, General," Joe assured him. "They won't lay a glove on us."

The revival was produced and managed expertly by Joe Warren. The meeting took place in a large auditorium at Air Force Systems Command Headquarters, across the Potomac from the Pentagon in suburban Maryland. The big room was full of generals, colonels, high-ranking government officials, contractor executives, and assistants to these notables. The visiting preachers, Secretaries Marks and Anthony, gave good speeches, praising and encouraging those who appeared to be on the right track and exhorting the troops to greater effort. Then came the administrative heroes, military and contractor, to testify to the beneficial effects of sharper management. The testimony of these people was the most impressive part of the show. For the most part, they had worked in relative obscurity and without obvious high-level support to accomplish their small improvements. All had made headway against the tide of inertia and often outright opposition from the powers of the procurement community. Recognition of the good work of the conscientious and persistent people had the desired effect on the fence straddlers and opponents of tougher management. Several of the more reluctant managers professed to be converted on the spot. Joe Warren was delighted. "They're signing off our sheet of music," he said.

The stage was set for the "Come to God" sermon winding up

the revival. I gave this message myself. I had worked hard to prepare my presentation. I had a number of new VuGraphs, without which no Pentagon preachment was complete. My pitch focused on methods of using performance measurement systems to identify avoidable costs and inefficiencies so that we could avoid perpetuating this waste by building it into subsequent contract cost estimates. My key VuGraph depicted a success story. Stimulated by a temporary shortage of money, one of our contractors had carried off a remarkable reduction of labor cost of missile system hardware. My VuGraph summarized this happy story in the plotting of the aerospace estimators' principal analytical tool, the unit cost improvement curve. One of the beauties of this curve is that it is complex enough (an exponential hyperbola of the general form $y = kx^{-m}$) to intimidate the uninitiated, yet is ideal for graphic presentation. It is a straight line when plotted on logarithmic graph paper.

The first part of my example was a typical example of application of the improvement curve. A plan for man-hours per unit of hardware had been negotiated at the beginning of the contract which anticipated spending about eighteen thousand man-hours on the first unit made, with a planned improvement to about five thousand man-hours per unit for the 150th unit. The contract plan had been overrun, with actual man-hours per unit exceeding the plan by five to eight thousand man-hours per unit in the early going. The plan was shown as a straight line on the logarithmic graph paper, and the actual man-hours were plotted by x's marked on the chart. Between 100 and 150 units, the x's fell neatly on the solid line representing the plan, which supposedly proved that the cost estimates underlying the plan were "good." The estimates were coming true, and that was the final test.

However, a troublemaker came on the scene. One of the government contract negotiators began asking questions. What was this exotic spage-age hardware? What *should* it cost? Never mind that the actual cost was tracking the plan. If the plan was fat enough, all that was necessary to accomplish this was to round up enough extra people to charge their time to the hardware as it passed through the shop.

The unit of hardware turned out to be a collection of a couple of hundred pounds of altogether mundane structural parts and insulation for each missile. Such miscellaneous parts were called "pots and pans" in the trade. The collection of parts for each missile was called a "missile set." Based partly on his own generalized experience, but mostly on intuition, the negotiator realized that five thousand hours per missile set was outrageous and that the earlier actual costs had been preposterous. His judgment was that two or three hundred man-hours per missile set of hardware would have been generous, but, lacking facts to back up his judgment, he was unable to negotiate significantly lower man-hours per unit for the subsequent orders. He had to settle for an average of about four thousand hours per unit for the next 550 missile sets. However, he did negotiate a clause in the contract which provided for resetting the contract target costs if actual experience supported his judgment that man-hour costs should be much lower.

Then the negotiator arranged to have the government representatives assigned to the contractor's plant watch the factory operations closely for a while. Under close inspection, the man-hours per missile set of hardware just melted away. From the previously rather steady level of five thousand hours per unit, the costs dropped precipitously to less than two thousand hours per unit. Subsequently, several progressively lower contract targets were set, finally reaching a level of less than eight hundred hours per unit. This notable saving was achieved without significant changes to work methods or tooling. All that happened was that the supernumeraries stopped charging their time to the job.

I decided to use this small success story as a vehicle to expound on the philosophical underpinnings of our problems with the recognized cost-estimating experts. Pointing to my VuGraph image on the screen, I described the situation for the benefit of the audience. The speech was captured by the omnipresent tape recorder:

"I have a chart here of an actual situation. The contractor projected a plan depicted here in man-hours per unit of hardware, then contracted for it. He plotted his actual man-hour cost, which showed that he was overrunning his plan up until this point. Then his performance became increasingly better, and he followed the projection shown in the latter portion of the contract. That's a fairly typical thing and familiar to most of you, I believe. Given this picture, what do we do to calculate man-hours for the follow-on contract? Well, you go to the books and read them. Read the Rand documents and similar writings, and it is very obvious from reading the books that you should draw a line through these *x*'s and extend it out here. Right? That is exactly the way you do it.

"In this case the contractor got religion and drove his cost down as shown on the second part of the. VuGraph. The point here is that we didn't really know how much fat was in the first contract. Our negotiators thought they knew, but they didn't have facts to support them. So, in the final analysis, these good results were something of an isolated happy accident. The process, with its undeniably good results, was not systematic or scientific enough to inspire confidence that it could be repeated. This problem could be remedied with better criteria for cost information to be provided through our contractors' cost-control systems.

"I think the reason we have a problem of establishing sound criteria for our control systems is that we are not really very scientific in establishing our criteria. I think it is symptomatic of a problem with the High Priests of our cost estimating community. The estimators for the contracts depicted on the VuGraph should not be criticized because they were following faithfully the traditional practices employed by our High Priests of estimating. We are victims of tradition. We are also victims of the fact that, at least in my opinion, the High Priests are in the Dark Ages of the science of cost estimating.

"Now the Dark Ages weren't nearly as dark as you might believe. In actuality they were marked by a goodly amount of system and order. The scholars knew a great deal. They studied all the time, probably much more than our scholars do now. The difficulty was that (1) they knew a lot of things which weren't so, and (2) they didn't learn anything new. If they wanted to solve a problem they would go to the Holy Writ or perhaps to the works of the ancient Greeks and try to search out the answer by reading books. They depended on elaborate logic and massaging a very slim body of facts, a lot of which, as I said before, weren't so, to arrive at their solution.

"When I was in college I had an excellent philosophy professor, and he told a story to illustrate a point I just made. A novice in a monastery in Europe during the Dark Ages sat around for days and days listening to an argument among his senior monks about how many teeth a donkey had. They searched all the sacred works of Aristotle and all the rest, but still they couldn't agree. So, during a break of some sort, the novice stole down to the stables, went up to a donkey, and counted his teeth. He went back to the discussion and announced he had the answer. The senior monks were astounded and outraged. The novice had cheated. He had broken all the rules of the game. As punishment he was kicked out of the monastery.

"We are not quite that bad, but we are close to it. This mental block wasn't actually removed in our general intellectual life until about four or five hundred years ago. I have taken some quotes from Francis Bacon, the father of the scientific method, which illustrate what we have to do in order to overcome our current difficulties. Bacon, in about the late fifteen hundreds, became a critic of the Greek philosophers and their dogmatic followers. He said they spent too much time in theory and too little in observation. He said, 'thought should be the aid of observation, not its substitute,' and that in order to learn new things, we must have an 'expurgation of the intellect.' That is what I would call 'unlearning.' Unlearn those things that are not so, so that you can learn something new. We must destroy what Bacon called the Idols of the Mind, of which he enumerated four.

"The first of these he called Idols of the Tribe. These are fallacies natural to humanity in general. As we illustrated, just a moment ago, 'everybody knows' that you draw a line through those x's on the man-hour chart to properly estimate the follow-on contract.

"Next are the Idols of the Cave. Everyone has a 'cave or den of his own which refracts and discolors the light of nature.' This is our personal prejudice. We all know our personal prejudices or our limited experiences tell us that there is nothing we can do other than to draw a line through the x's on the man-hour chart to arrive at cost of subsequent units.

"The third set of idols is the grabber, Idols of the Market Place, which Bacon says are 'a wonderful obstruction to the mind.' These are the stories which men tell one another in their dealings with one another in commerce and the like. In simplest terms, they lie to one another. Bacon went on to say that Idols of the Market Place are 'a collection of fig leaf phrases used to cover naked ignorance.'

"And then, the final category of fallacies, which he called Idols of the Theater. 'Stories invented for the stage are much more compact and elegant and more as we would wish them to be than that of the true story of history,' he said. And that is very true here. How simple it is to draw the line through the x's and to extend it on out. The real world results on the VuGraph upset all of the high priest's theories. How do you account for what really happened? None of the theories fit."

I then showed the gathering some examples of situations in which performance measurement systems had been used to gather systematically information which identified soft spots and inefficiencies in contractor performance as the work progressed. In the examples, the pinpointed areas of avoidable cost had been attacked as they occurred with good effect on actual cost performance. Follow-on planned contract costs and internal budgets had been constructed from the bottom up using proven industrial engineering techniques. After making attainable allowances for each element for planned cost, then adding generous allowances for expected inefficiencies, redoing work and the like, these "should cost" budgets were invariably far less than the extrapolation of past trends of actual costs. In my examples, the contractors had come close to achieving the "should cost" goal in each instance, with significant savings to the government.

I summarized the "come to God message" by reminding the assembled generals and contractor executives that we already knew how to save enormous sums of money. "New tools" might prove useful in the future, but we could go ahead and save money while they were being invented. A major reason for our costs being too high was that they were planned that way. We lacked objective factual information needed to determine what our complicated weapons ought to cost. Again, we lacked these needed facts because the system was planned that way. If we really wanted money to replace the creaky old airplanes our boys were flying in the widening Asian war, we could find it within existing budgets by squeezing the fat out of our procurement programs.

Overall, the response to the revival was all that Joe Warren and I had hoped for. Not only had we avoided the fistfights General Carter had feared, but also we appeared to have made a number of new converts. Many of the previously recalcitrant managers had testified and taken the pledge. Most of the attendees asked for copies of my talk, which pleased me no end, since this represented my first venture into the field of philosophy.

Since I had spoken from notes, the tape recording had to be transcribed and cleaned up a bit for printing. But a strange thing happened on the way to the printers. Several days after I had sent the laundered copy of the speech to Mr. Marks' office for his review prior to going to press, Mr. Marks' military assistant informed me that the speech would have to be cleared by an organization called "Security Review" before it could be printed and distributed. Now I had never heard of "Security Review," but I was not concerned since I had assumed that their sole purpose in reviewing the speech was to make sure that I had not inadvertently leaked any military secrets.

Time passed. The speech had been submitted to Air Force Security Review about the third week of August, and along toward the middle of September I began asking the head of Security Review, a nice gentleman named Flint DuPre, what had happened to my speech. After several inquiries, Mr. DuPre told me that the Air Force Office of Security Review had reviewed the document and forwarded it to Security Review in the Office of the Secretary of Defense for their consideration.

Finally, on September 29, after much prodding, we got our answer from the Office of the Secretary of Defense. My speech was suppressed. It could not be printed or distributed even within the Department of Defense or the Department of the Air Force. The rejection of my speech was accompanied by a scathing letter from Mr. Charles Hinkle, Mr. NcNamara's director of Security Review, commenting on my speech. Mr. Hinkle wrote: "It is a caustic, inappropriate depreciation of the costing techniques which have been sponsored and encouraged by OSD for the past few years." I complained loudly that this had nothing whatever to do with military security, and furthermore that my job was to improve on past practices, not to condone them if they were bad. The Security Review experts explained to me that it was, too, a security problem. Unfavorable comment on established practices might cause the public to lose confidence in the management in the Department of Defense, and this, in turn, would undermine security.

Brushing aside this silly argument, I demanded that the Security Review people identify for me a real live human being who could give me a sensible reason for suppressing my speech. Relieved at getting rid of me so easily, the Security Review experts identified Mr. McNamara's cost-estimating specialists in Systems Analysis as the villains. I attempted to get through to Dr. Harold Asher, the head of the Cost Estimating section in Systems Analysis, but, as usual, he was not available. However, his assistant, Mr. Saul Hoch, would talk to me.

Mr. Hoch gave me the word. If information was available which indicated that dramatic changes in production techniques, production practices, or manufacturing tooling were in the offing, such information could be used to modify estimates for follow-on contracts. However, efficiency measurements, particularly those based on industrial engineering standards, were forbidden. I argued that industrial engineering measurements were the best indication of the existence of superfluous employees, but to no avail. Systems Analysis did not believe in industrial engineering measurement. It complicated their mathematical techniques. Mr. Hoch told me that, in the absence of information regarding dramatic changes in manufacturing methods or tooling, "extensions of previously experienced recurring cost provide the most reliable basis for estimating follow-on cost." I tried to point out that I was not challenging the way in which Systems Analysis made their cost estimates. Sitting as they did at the right hand of Secretary McNamara, they could prepare estimates any way they pleased, of course. I was simply suggesting that we be allowed to get objective evidence of the existence of fat in contracts and seek to eliminate it in negotiating with contractors for follow-on work. No dice, Hoch said. Stick to the policy.

From my standpoint, there was one beneficial side effect of my conversation with Mr. Hoch, despite the fact that I had gone nowhere in my arguments. He agreed to give me his personal comments on my speech and also to tell the Security Review people that he had no objection to my reviewing the Department of Defense comments which had led to their suppression of the speech. I got copies of these comments and read them carefully. Many of the written comments provided enlightening insights to the bureaucratic mind, but one made a particularly strong impression on me: *McNamara's weenies had totally censored Francis Bacon!*

Needless to say, I regarded the phony "Security Review" suppression of my cost-control speech an outrage, and I said so to everyone who would listen to me, including my boss, Secretary Marks. Mr. Marks, of course, could have cleared the speech for distribution himself, but at considerable risks to his own position. Since I had been suppressed by the Systems Analysis function in the Department of Defense, I asked Mr. Marks where Secretary Anthony, the Comptroller of the Department of Defense, and our functional supervisor, stood in the matter. Mr. Marks said he didn't know but that he would submit the speech to Secretary Anthony and find out. By that time, of course, the speech was a hot potato in the Office of the Secretary of Defense. Secretary Anthony delegated review of the speech to one of his deputies, Mr. George Bergquist. Mr. Bergquist, in turn, delegated review of the speech to one of his assistants, Col. Herbert Waldman. Weeks later, on November 14, 1966, Colonel Waldman wrote me a nice note of seven and one half lines suggesting that poor communication was perhaps the culprit. At the bottom of the formal note, Colonel Waldman, on loan from the Air Force, penned in, "Your talk would help by getting out the word."

By then, it had become painfully obvious that my stand on cost control was not supported by the powers in the Pentagon. Months before, I had decided to proceed as though genuine, hard-nosed

cost reduction and control was really the clearly stated and understood policy of the Department of Defense, and to hold to the
course until someone contradicted me. The Security Review caper
had contradicted me, and very effectively. I was unmasked as
something of a one-man band playing the cost-reduction tune.
It was perfectly clear that the Back-up Principle, the systematic
justification of ever-rising prices, was still the dominant theme of
the top management of the Pentagon. Naturally, this revelation
undid all the good effects of the revival meeting which had come
off so successfully the previous August.

I soon learned that suppression of a speech or research document by the authorities in the Pentagon was the surest way to
draw attention to an issue. Within days after the rejection of my
speech by OSD, the word was passed throughout the military
procurement community that my ideas had no backing, particularly at the level of the Office of the Secretary of Defense. An
interesting phenomenon, a byproduct of the suppression of my
ideas and, incidentally, those of Francis Bacon, was that bootleg
copies of my talk were in great demand. The reaction was similar
to having a book banned in Boston in the days before pornography
became commonplace.

Another example of the banned-in-Boston phenomenon came
to my attention during this same period. One of my friends
slipped me a copy of a Rand Corporation document entitled
"Cost Incentives and Contract Outcomes: An Empirical Analysis,"
written by Irving N. Fisher of the Rand staff. This document,
dated September 1966, had also been placed on the Index Ex-
purgatorius by the Security Review censors. The copy slipped
surreptitiously to me was covered with notations such as "This
document has been suppressed!" and "Do not use this information," and so on. On reading the suppressed document it was easy
to see why Security Review was having a difficult time putting
down heresy. Embarrassing facts kept cropping up which refuted the official dogma. Most of Irving Fisher's document was
devoted to complicated statistical analyses which were difficult for
the layman to follow. However, the narrative summaries were perfectly clear. Anyone could understand them. Some of the passages

marked and questioned by the security review censor, our Protector of the Faith, were particularly revealing. For example:

The statistical analysis presented here suggest that many of the advantages attributed to incentive contracts may be unimportant. It is commonly believed that such contracts provide substantial motivation for increased contractor efficiency and tighter cost control and lead to significant cost reductions.

Farther on, commenting on the results of his analysis, Mr. Fisher wrote:

. . . it has been impossible to discover a statistically significant relationship between the sharing rate and any of the various measures of cost outcome. These results imply that the incentive effect on cost and efficiency may not be as important as customarily believed. They also suggest that cost underruns commonly observed for incentive contracts are due to biased target costs and inflated costs of supplemental changes.

The heretical comments went on and on: "It is difficult to see how such contracts provide any real incentives for cost control as long as the contractor can overstate both the target costs and the cost of supplemental changes." Mr. Fisher also took a shot at the cozy partnership arrangement between the government customer and military supplier: "So long as costs are determined under the present government-contractor relationship, there exists a substantial probability that contractors will bias these costs upward, thereby defeating the intended effects of incentive contracts."

Apparently nothing was sacred to the irreverent Mr. Fisher. He also attacked the totem of competition:

It might be expected that the bias in contract costs would be negligible because of price rivalry. However, contracts awarded on the basis of price alone account for only a small proportion of the total number of contract awards. Design and technical rivalry and sole source solicitation are the primary methods of contractor selections. Consequently, the competitive forces that normally constrain contract cost bias are absent in most weapon systems contracts. Moreover, there seem to be no effective constraints limiting the tendency to bias the cost of supplemental changes.

"In summary," Mr. Fisher wrote, "the main point is that incentive contracts are probably not saving the government much money."

From the standpoint of the dogmatic defenders of the status quo, Irving Fisher's heresy had to be suppressed. It was. On October 21, 1966, after a long and presumably thorough review, Mr. Roger Delaney, the Deputy Director of Security Review in the Office of the Secretary of Defense, formally forbade publication of the document. Suppression of my speech for phony "security" considerations was outrageous enough, but I thought the suppression of Irving Fisher's paper was even worse. In addition to the fact that military "security" was in no way involved in the Fisher suppression, he was not even an employee of the Department of Defense. The Rand Corporation was a contractor to the Air Force. Mr. Fisher's study had been performed, and the ensuing report prepared, under this contract. It had been distributed by Rand with the notation "Distribution of this document is unlimited." The Security Review censors, in violation of their own rules regarding true military security requirements, had taken upon themselves to stamp the document "Confidential," a classification usually reserved for important military secrets. As an official of the Air Force, I decided to test the system to determine whether I could obtain a copy of our contractor's product through official channels. I requested that David Novick, the head of Rand's Cost Analysis Department, send me a copy of Mr. Fisher's report. Old friend Dave turned me down, writing that "the manuscript is involved in administrative processes, which means that it is not now available for distribution." I telephoned Mr. Novick to reiterate my request, but he turned me down again, this time confirming that the Office of the Secretary of Defense had indeed suppressed Mr. Fisher's findings. I attempted also to talk to Mr. Fisher at Rand but was told that he was not available and that he would soon be leaving Rand's employ.

Now, it happened that Irving Fisher's analysis of the effectiveness of the new "magic" contracts confirmed the experience of many people involved in Pentagon procurement who were concerned about the effect of blind adherence to dogma in the face of contrary facts. It seemed grossly unfair to me that Mr. Fisher should be fired for adding to our inventory of facts. So I set out to see what I could do to head off Mr. Fisher's firing. In the process, I also hoped to find a way to control the worst effects of the absurd censorship by the Security Review people. Fortunately, I was assisted in this chancy undertaking by Bill George, one of the bright young Harvard graduates hired by Secretary Anthony for his analysis group. Bill George had been assigned by Mr. Anthony to work closely with me and others in the Air Force to provide better and more timely information on the status of several of our major weapons programs, especially the F-111 fighter bomber in which Mr. McNamara had a personal interest. In addition to being exceptionally bright, well educated, and energetic, young Bill George was perceptive enough to see that Secretary McNamara's worst enemies were those of his assistants and underlings who sought to suppress embarrassing facts. He seemed as outraged as I at the treatment given Irving Fisher.

As a start, Bill George and I met with Mr. Flint DuPre, our Air Force Security Review chief. I am afraid I was not very kind to poor Mr. DuPre in this session. After some fairly rough questioning, Mr. DuPre finally had to admit that suppression of the Fisher document had absolutely nothing to do with military security. He tried to take refuge in the old public confidence smokescreen but finally admitted that key individuals in Air Force procurement objected to Mr. Fisher's document because it made them look bad.

I then showed Mr. DuPre my bootleg copy of the Fisher document, one of many then being circulated in the Pentagon. It was stamped "Confidential." I asked Mr. DuPre what would happen to me if I reproduced and distributed this document myself. "Would I be violating security?" I asked him. He conceded that I would not be violating security and that, in all probability, nothing would happen to me unless the act offended my boss, Mr. Marks. I then told Mr. DuPre that continued suppression of the document could do nothing but make the Security Review function and the defenders of the dogma look more foolish than they already did, and I suggested that he get together with the Rand Corporation and work out arrangements to clear the paper for open publication.

I then called Rand Corporation headquarters in California and asked them to arrange for Mr. Fisher to visit me in my office in the Pentagon. I wanted to meet him and discuss with him in detail the analyses and findings set forth in his report. In addition, I hoped that an expression of interest in Mr. Fisher and his work from Air Force Headquarters, the Rand Corporation's principle customer, might give them second thoughts about firing him.

Several weeks later, Irving Fisher came by to see me, and we had an interesting talk. He had gone through a rather shaky period, but Rand had not fired him. Apparently, news of his impending sacking had aroused a number of rather outraged comments from the Pentagon in addition to mine. Finally, Security Review had relented somewhat and had agreed to "negotiate" revisions in Irving's report which would render it fit for public consumption.

Many months later a considerably laundered version of Irving Fisher's paper was released by the Rand Corporation. However, even the laundered document was not approved for unlimited distribution, as was the original version. It bore the classification "For Official Use Only." The laundered version also included a disclaimer that views and conclusions contained in the report "should not be interpreted as representing the official opinion or policy of the United States Air Force." Despite extensive revisions, the revised report bore the same date—September 19, 1966—and serial number as the original suppressed document.

My exposure to dogmatic thinking in the suppression of my speech and Irving Fisher's report convinced me that Francis Bacon's Idols of the Mind were very real and were worshipped in the Pentagon. There was no question that they were indeed "wonderful obstructions to the mind." On the favorable side, the Fisher case illustrated that defensive obstructionism on the part of the Pentagon's mindless bureaucracy could be overcome, or at least brought to a standstill, if high-ranking officials required the obstructionists to justify their actions.

Despite all this diversionary nonsense with the censors, I remained very active in working in the field with Joe Waren and his tiger team. In fact, we had redoubled our efforts following the revival at Air Force Systems Command Headquarters in August.

Our major effort at the time was an in-depth review and inspection of the performance measurement system for the C-5A at Lockheed Aircraft Corporation's Marietta, Georgia, plant.

I had been interested in the C-5A transport plane program since my first days in the Pentagon. Moreover, my early skepticism about the authenticity of the miraculous nature of its procurement had grown. Despite a continuing din of publicity about the "Miracle of Procurement," the project had, in fact, gone badly from the very start. I found definite indications of incipient cost overruns during a plant visit to Lockheed's Marietta facility in January 1966. As the year had progressed, indications of financial trouble had become increasingly clear. Even the relatively uninformative performance measurement reports sent to the Air Force by Lockheed indicated trouble.

Lockheed's C-5A contract contained a specification for cost planning and control which we believed would give us the measurement of their progress needed to avoid major surprises and hopefully to permit us to stimulate corrective action if the need was indicated. Our visits to the Lockheed plant and cursory examinations of their existing internal control systems had convinced us that Lockheed could keep us well informed of progress with only minor modifications to their existing systems. Unfortunately, Lockheed had not chosen to give us this information. Instead they had installed a PERT-Cost system, mad formula and all, which restricted our visibility considerably. However, at that early stage of the program the Lockheed employees operating the cumbersome system had not yet come to depend completely on the crazy formula for status reports. We were receiving periodic re-estimates of the cost of pieces of the program which, although admittedly subjective, gave us positive indications that the working-level people at Lockheed expected to have big overruns.

The reaction to my early attempts to call attention to the C-5A cost problems, especially the reactions of Secretary Charles and the procurement generals, convinced me that I would need much more evidence if there was to be any hope of heading off or containing the growing problem. Therefore, I decided to "lay in the weeds," as the expression goes in Alabama, and bide my time until our tiger team could get into the C-5A situation more thoroughly. Joe Warren, other members of the team, and I made a number of visits to the Lockheed plant during the late summer and early fall of 1966. It became increasingly clear that not only was the project in financial difficulty, but serious technical problems were brewing as well.

The generals at Systems Command headquarters and in the Air Staff grew increasingly uneasy, in some cases even agitated, as the tiger team concentrated on the C-5A program. Why were we wasting the efforts of our hotshot team on the C-5A, we were asked. Didn't we know that the project was in great shape and that in the unlikely event of difficulties, Lockheed would be fully responsible for making good on their contractual commitments? No, we replied, we did not know that, and we were concentrating on the project because it was the Air Force's model of weapons systems management, the wave of the future. We wanted to make certain that our showpiece was a good one.

The tiger team had really touched a nerve. Our more faint-hearted supporters began putting as much distance as possible between themselves and the team. General Jack Merrell, the Comptroller of the Air Force, attempted to bail out and abandon the cost-control project entirely, apparently, without prior approval of Secretary Marks, who was supposedly General Merrell's functional supervisor. General Merrell gave away practically all his responsibilities in the Cost Management Improvement Project to General Tom Gerrity, the Deputy Chief of Staff for Systems and Logistics (including procurement), a known opponent of our approach to cost control. General Red Carter also wanted out. He was particularly eager to give away the systems demonstration function, the on-the-scene inspection of contractor performance measurement systems. Earlier, General Carter had suggested to me that the big contractors be allowed to hire their own private acounting firms to inspect their systems, thereby relieving us of that onerous chore. General Carter described my reaction to his proposal as follows in a "talking paper" circulated among his fellow generals:

"This suggestion was objected to on the grounds (rather astonishing to me) that accounting firms were not sufficiently ethical to be depended upon to give an unbiased evaluation of the client-contractor system. In fact, the reaction against this idea was so strong that I had to withdraw and destroy the paper that suggested it."

I had pointed out to the general that in many cases the big contractors' own accounting firms had themselves designed and installed the defective systems they would be reviewing. In effect, we would be asking them to tell us whether they had done their own work properly in the past. As his fellow generals became increasingly jittery with the tiger team's probing of the C-5A "miracle," General Carter suggested that the comptroller's management systems review responsibilities be given to the Contract Management Division of Air Force Systems Command, which fell under the procurement chiefs. Here too, we had a large concentration of conscientious objectors with a vested interest in the status quo. In any event, the Contract Management Division was under orders to "disengage" and look the other way and wanted no part of the tough approach at that time.

The Lockheed C-5A situation came to a head during a visit by the team to Lockheed-Georgia on November 14 and 15, 1966. Lockheed officials stuck stubbornly to their position that there were no problems on the project, even in the face of overwhelming evidence to the contrary. Lockheed readily admitted that they were not meeting the official Air Force requirements for objective performance measurement information, but they stated that their system was good enough for the Air Force Systems Program Office and provided all the information they desired. Lockheed was supported in this position by the Systems program Office representative. In fact, the representative of the Air Force SPO repeated the tired old argument that visibility into status of the contract such as we were insisting on was undesirable and "could lead to unwarranted meddling by the Air Force in the contractor management." One Lockheed official, an old friend, told me privately that he believed Lockheed would be in serious trouble with the military side of the Air Force if they complied completely with our requirements.

Just before we left the plant, I was told by a very nervous Air Force officer assigned to the Air Force Plant Representatives

Office that the SPO had already agreed with Lockheed to relax certain of the C-5A specifications so that Lockheed could meet them. The officer told us that no formal contractual agreement had been made as of then, but that Lockheed and the Air Force Systems Program Office had reached a "meeting of the minds" on a revised set of requirements which Lockheed could meet with an airplane less sturdy than the one originally contracted for.

We had a long, gloomy airplane ride back to Washington. On the way, after an extended period of silence, I said to Colonel Warren, "Well, Joe, they've flimsied up the airplane." "Yes," said Colonel Warren, "I can see it now, the big tin balloon burbling along and shedding parts." It was a prophetic insight.

Our immediate problem, though, was what to do about our performance measurement requirements. The contractor and the Air Force SPO representatives had just told us to go to hell, that they were not going to comply with the requirements. With all eyes on the Miracle of Procurement, our new model of contract management, we had to put up or shut up. If Lockheed got away with repudiating their contractual commitment, we could forget about enforcing the requirement elsewhere. We discussed at length the problems we would encounter in attempting to get the big contractors to reveal overruns as they occurred. The principal contractor trade association, the Council of Defense and Space Industry Associations (CODSIA), was already objecting strongly to our specifications for performance measurement and especially to the tough demonstrations required of contractors. We all agreed that, in all probability, the Pentagon military and civilian chiefs would, in the end, cave in and go along with whatever CODSIA wanted.

Back in Washington, I decided that I could no longer "lay in the weeds" and that I had to give my bosses the bad news that the Miracle of Procurement was not a miracle after all and that it had all the earmarks of another of the unbroken series of big procurement disasters. My information was received very gravely by Secretary Marks, so much so that, uncharacteristically, he and I both walked directly to Assistant Secretary Robert A. Charles' office to fill him in on the situation. Bob Charles, too, seemed greatly concerned and, for a change, did not brush us off with "disengagement" slogans.

I had scarcely returned to my office before my telephone started ringing. It was Colonel Guy Townsend, the C-5A Systems Program Director. Colonel Townsend, I thought, was one of our best program directors. He was exceptionally hard-working and well qualified for his job. At the same time, he was pleasant and easygoing in his personal relationships, just a good old country boy from somewhere near Columbus, Mississippi. I thought very highly of Colonel Townsend, but he didn't think much of me, at least not then. Over the telephone he screamed at me. He wanted to know what I was doing discussing "engineering matters with the contractors." I explained to him that there appeared to be serious engineering problems on the C-5A, that correcting these problems was likely to cost money, in all probability an enormous amount of money, and that some sort of corrective action was badly needed. Colonel Townsend then suggested, rather sarcastically, that we allow him to precipitate the corrective action. I replied that this would be entirely appropriate and that I would meet him at Lockheed in the near future for the kick-off of the corrective action program.*

The next visit to Lockheed loomed as a crucial meeting. Joe Warren and I decided that we would need all the backing we could get to have any chance of getting the C-5A problem · recognized and corrective action started. Accordingly, we decided to utilize the camp meeting testifying phenomenon and take as many generals as we could round up to Lockheed with us. By that time we had employed this device so often that it had become widely recognized among the big contractors. Secret sympathizers in the contractor plants told me that they had observed that whenever their managements got stubborn, Fitzgerald, Warren, and a whole raft of generals would appear as if by magic. The generals, however reluctantly, would testify in behalf of our cost-control program. Wags in the industry named the process "instant generals."

---

* See "Hearings on Military Posture before the Committee on Armed Services, House of Representatives, Ninety-first Congress, First Session, pages 2981 and 2982, for my memo of this conversion.

We thought the "instant generals" treatment might prove a cure for the Lockheed ailment. Ted Marks thought so too, and on November 25, 1966, he wrote to the Deputy Chief of Staff for Systems and Logistics and to the Comptroller of the Air Force, Generals Gerrity and Merrell, respectively:

We have indications of significant incipient cost problems from the Lockheed C-54 contract. At the same time, we are experiencing difficulty in obtaining adequate visibility into causes of these indicated problems. Based on reports I have received it appears that Lockheed is holding back full disclosure of the information generated by their own systems because of a belief that our cost planning and control specification is not supported by all elements of Air Force management. In order that this misconception may be squelched, I solicit your assistance in conveying the message to Lockheed management that we intend to enforce the contractual requirements for cost planning and control specification and the cost status information which should derive from implementation of this specification. To this end we are planning a meeting with Lockheed management on December 5, 1966 at eleven hundred hours to which you or your representative are invited. Ideally, your representative would be of general officer rank.

Key generals from the Air Force Systems Command were also invited to the meeting at Lockheed. Of course, all the generals fingered for this duty realized that they were to be figuratively dragged, kicking and screaming, to Lockheed to testify in favor of a tough approach to cost control of which they wanted no part. The "volunteer" generals immediately set their assistants to calling around, particularly to members of the tiger team, to inquire if it would not really be better if the generals sent subordinates better versed in the "details" of cost control. One of the tough guys on the tiger team devised a standard response to the reluctant general officer warriors, one which he called the first commandment of the Lockheed revival: "Send not thy weenie, come thyself."

And they did. On December 5, the big briefing room at the Lockheed Georgia plant looked like a West Point reunion. From the standpoint of numbers of stars present, it was our most successful "instant generals" visit. The generals were well prepared too. As a result of our previous visits to the Lockheed plant, the generals had received a number of reports on contractor overhead expenses and rates of pay far in excess of those envisioned when the C-5A contract was priced. They had also received reports in some detail of crucial engineering work packages with cost overruns of more than 100 percent of the original estimate, with the work still undone. Overall, even the sluggish Lockheed performance measurement reporting system, which tended to understate overruns, was showing a 50 percent cost overrun in the all-important airframe development category. Through October of 1966, Lockheed had completed work on the airframe development for which they had budgeted $36,586,000. For that work, they had actually spent $55,486,000, an overrun of $18,900,000. To make doubly sure the generals were well prepared for the meeting and also to give them an opportunity to express reservations about our approach, Ted Marks had convened a dry run of the Lockheed visit in his office in the Pentagon on November 29. The meeting had ended with the attendees in full agreement on the necessity for full disclosure by Lockheed of status of the C-5A program.

Lockheed had pulled all the stops in preparing their presentation. They had great piles of VuGraphs, in color of course, for their management team's briefing of the Air Force visitors. The Lockheed briefing was masterful. They started out by conceding what we had already established—namely, that on work done through that point in time they had vastly exceeded their planned cost. However, they said, this was due solely to minor perturbations inherent in starting up any new, large-scale development program. In any even, they said, the overrun problem had been fixed. How? By increasing the budget, of course. With this single masterstroke of management, the overrun in airframe development had practically disappeared. With the new budget, the upwardly revised planned cost for airframe work done through November was $61,740,000. The work had been accomplished at an actual cost of $62,310,000, an overrun of only $570,000.

Overall, Lockheed had increased their planned cost by $211,-000,000. Whereas they had previously planned an overall contract underrun of $173,000,000, they were now projecting a total contract overrun of $38,000,000. Still, Lockheed said, this sort of adjustment was "within the normal range," and our problems were now behind us. As a matter of fact, they said, they expected privately to vastly underrun future budgets, especially in production. They acknowledged some slippage in "minor milestones" but contended, overall, they were on or ahead of schedule. The Lockheed presentation on the technical status of the C-5A was especially skillful. They flatly and forcefully denied that there were any significant problems whatever in the technical area. They denounced "rumors" to the contrary as nothing but spiteful gossip.

Since Lockheed was obviously lying, the moment seemed ripe for the Systems Program Director, Guy Townsend, to "precipitate corrective action." I looked at him intently. Colonel Townsend returned the look for a moment and seemed about to say something. Apparently, however, he thought better of it, readjusted his cigar, and looked back at the mesmerizing shadows on the VuGraph screen.

The overall effect of the Lockheed presentation was devastating. The generals had been told exactly what they wanted to hear, and they accepted the Lockheed position gratefully and without question. The joint Lockheed-Air Force party line on the status and glowing outlook for the C-5A had been reestablished. No one was fooled, of course, but the generals had a ringing and authoritative statement from Lockheed that all was well with the Miracle of Procurement. They could cling to that for years to come. For the first time in all of our "instant generals" visits, we got absolutely no favorable testimony from the visiting military dignitaries.

With faith in the miracle duly restored, the generals and civilian procurement chiefs see no point in pressuring Lockheed to live up to their contractual requirements on performance measurement. Joe Warren and I and other members of the tiger team were naturally extremely disappointed that we had been blocked in our attempts to gain visibility into what was actually going on in the C-5A program. We were even more disappointed that the C-5A, our model of weapons/systems management, was clearly doomed to be just another routine disaster. Joe summed up our feelings beautifully in a report which he prepared for Secretary Marks on December 13, 1966, describing his reaction to Lockheed's December 5 briefing as compared to the earlier briefing we had received on November 14 and 15:

The second briefing was very much like seeing the rerun of an old movie; the plot still has drama and suspense, the script was excellent, the acting superb, but the outcome will be the same as it was the first, second or tenth time it was shown. The contract costs will be exceeded.

Regarding the effect of the C-5A's "magic" contract, he wrote:

The provisions of the contract will not act as a brake on cost increases, in fact the contract almost guarantees increases. The coming cost increases will be more than justified, supported, rationalized and explained by the contractor. His position will be supported by the Air Force, the costs, whatever they are, will be duly entered into data banks, to prove beyond any doubt that they are the true costs. Who can argue that they should have or could have been different." *

The embarrassing activities of the tiger team had been effectively contained, for the moment, at least. However, General Red Carter was in serious trouble with his fellow generals. He had lost control of the tiger team, and as long as it existed in its present form and with the present personnel, new embarrassing disclosures were likely. Red Carter circulated a detailed talking paper among his fellow generals to explain how they had got into the mess in the first place and to suggest a way out, saying, in part: "After considerable pressure from Mr. Marks last spring to nominate a tiger I gave the job to Joe Warren, who had been identified as being the appropriate kind of tiger, and he has been saddled with the job of satisfying Mr. Marks' office since July of 1966."

That was true, of course, and Joe Warren had satisfied Mr. Marks' office very well indeed. The talking paper continued: "We have been proceeding for nearly six months under the 'Joe Warren tiger team approach.' The major effort has been concentrated on Lockheed Marietta, with almost no effort being placed by this tiger team on other contracts."

This was only partly true. We had spent a good deal of

* The complete text of Colonel Warren's remarkable report is contained in Appendix A.

effort on other programs but began concentrating on the C-5A at Lockheed Marietta after it became apparent that the project was in serious trouble. Red Carter then went on to give his fellow generals the good news that Joe Warren would soon be leaving: "The departure of Colonel Warren offers an excellent chance to review this entire program to make some decisions about the future and stand up for them as a command." He then suggested that "once we have made our decision I think we should get with DCS/S&L headquarters USAF, explain what we intend to do, get their support, then explain to Mr. Marks what we are doing and why and get on with it."

General Carter's suggestions were apparently accepted by his fellow generals, for they finally got up nerve enough to take some action. On December 14, 1966, General Carter wrote directly to me to inform me that I had been fired from the Management Systems Control Board, which directed the activities of the Cost Management Improvement Program (CMIP). He put it this way: "—attendance at control board meetings will not be requested unless topics of significance to everyone concerned are scheduled." My attendance was never requested again.

That still left unsolved the problem of what to do about Joe Warren. As long as the chief tiger was anywhere near by, he remained dangerous and could become a big problem at any moment. The problem was solved wtih dramatic suddenness when it was found that Joe Warren possessed absolutely unique qualifications to be air attaché in Addis Ababa. His immediate presence in Ethiopia was essential to the national defense.

Secretary Robert Anthony saved Joe Warren from African exile by finding him a higher priority job in the office of the Secretary of Defense. However, it was clear that Colonel Warren would never again fill a responsible management job in the Air Force and that his chances for further promotion were zero. The object lesson was widely noted and taken to heart by other Air Force officers.

FOUR

SHOOTING TROUBLE

The administrative atrocities perpetrated by the generals club in gentling the tiger team and firing Colonel Warren presented an excellent opportunity for a small demonstration of civilian control of the military. A few quiet but firm words from the Air Force Secretary's office could have kept our chief tiger on the job and given us a fighting chance of saving some rather enormous sums of money. At worst, we might have had a minor flap over loss of face on the part of the generals. Instead, the civilians in charge were simply too gentlemanly, or something, to raise hell. True, Joe Warren and his family were spared the worst consequences of his doing his job too well, but the damage to our systematic approach to cost control was fatal. The program lingered for years, but it was increasingly devoted to construction of the "management image" façade of ritualistic paperwork systems. The sickness of our model of good management, the C-5A, was "cured" by allowing its symptoms to be hidden by a curtain of secrecy and lies.

As things developed, I had little time to brood over all this. For one thing, I was doing very well personally. Despite my obvious unpopularity among the generals, my superiors gave me outstanding performance ratings and nominated me for an award in embarrassingly laudatory language. Getting fired from the CMIP Control Board didn't hurt me either. In addition to saving the time I had previously wasted in the Board meetings, I actually received more hard facts on field activities than before. Knowing that my access to official communication had been limited, my secret sympathizers stepped up their assistance.

Friends in the contractors' plants kept me well informed, in several cases giving me advance warning of Air Force program managers' plans to undercut our requirements for factual status information. Secret sympathizers among the working-level military did even better. Roused to silent indignation by the generals' treacherous treatment of one of their own, Joe Warren, they provided me with a steady supply of closely guarded "talking papers" and other memoranda intended for very limited distribution within the lodge. Most of the stuff dealt with minor plots of the sort one would expect from ten-year-old members of a tree-house club, but some of it was of great value. Finally, I continued my frequent visits to Air Force field installations and contractor plants. In the kind of work I was doing, there was no substitute for being present at the scene of action.

The most interesting development, however, was the increasing interest by the Office of the Secretary of Defense in factual status information on the big programs and also in my proposals for pricing contracts without building in historical waste. Most of this OSD interest had been stimulated by Bill George of Secretary Anthony's Analysis Group. Bill saw these approaches as offering hope for controlling runaway costs of the big systems, especially the F-111 fighter-bomber, which was then in deep trouble and reflecting unfavorably on Secretary McNamara due to his strong support of the program in face of congressional and other criticism. Bill George's interest and assistance were most heartening, but at that time the most important diversion from the tiger team fiasco was the surfacing of the old, long-concealed Minuteman missile reliability problems. My associates on the Minuteman consulting project had pinpointed these problems in the summer of 1963, almost three and a half years before they surfaced at Air Force headquarters. The 1963 evaluation had revealed serious, inherent reliability problems in the advanced guidance system for what later became the Minuteman II missile.

The Minuteman II missile system had started life in 1963 without fanfare simply as the sixth wing of Minuteman missiles. The first five wings, consisting of three squadrons of fifty missiles each, were well on the road to full deployment. The cost overruns on the first five Minuteman wings had been monumental, but the program was adjudged a great technical success. Tests had indicated that the missile system would be highly reliable. For its time, the missile was exceedingly accurate and apparently capable of delivering its nuclear warhead on Soviet population centers if ever the unthinkable should come to pass.

The sixth wing of the Minuteman missile system was justified primarily by frightening intelligence assessments of the Soviet Union's capabilities and intentions. The intelligence spooks reported that the Russians were deploying a large number of truly monstrous ballistic missiles, each capable of carrying a nuclear warhead with destructive force equivalent to 100,000,000 tons of TNT. Thus, each of the Soviet warheads would be five thousand times as powerful as the atomic bomb which destroyed Hiroshima (by way of comparison the Soviet SS-9 missile which frightened opponents of increasing military appropriations into submission in the late 1960s and early 1970s was said to have a warhead equivalent in destructive force to 25,-000,000 tons of TNT.). No one thought to ask at the time why the Soviet would need such huge warheads on their missiles. In any event, the threat posed by these horrible weapons was viewed as serious enough to require that the United States prepare to destroy them before they could be launched. This would be an exceedingly difficult mission, requiring considerably more missile accuracy than could be provided at that time by the Minuteman missiles of the first five wings. A more accurate guidance system was required, and this was the first justification for the wing-six Minuteman missile.

A second major justification was to develop a guidance system which would have a longer service life. The mean time between failure (MTBF) of guidance systems for the first five wings of Minuteman missiles had been low to begin with but increased rapidly as refinements were made over the years. Eventually, though, a point of diminishing returns was reached in spending money to improve the MTBF of the guidance systems for the first five wings. The Minuteman program's technical experts reasoned that a Wing VI or Minuteman II guidance set, designed to make maximum use of the high reliability parts developed for the first five wings of missiles and substituting new parts of inherently greater reliability, would produce a Minuteman II guidance set with an initial service life, or MTBF, equal to the ultimate life achieved on the earlier system. Then, starting from an already high service life plateau, the technical experts projected that evolutionary refinements to the Minuteman II guidance set would produce a rejuvenated growth in MTBF similar to that experienced on the "young" Minuteman I guidance systems. In addition to building on already proven parts and adding only parts thought to have inherently greater reliability, fewer parts overall were to be used. Based on the inferential metehods of calculating projected reliability then in general use in the military contracting business, a reduction in the number of parts was expected in itself to improve reliability.

Guidance systems with long and reliable service lives were very important to the Minuteman system. First, the longer the time between overhauls of the guidance systems, the fewer the missiles out of service at any given point in time for replacement of guidance systems. Military strategic thinkers then believed that any nuclear exchange between the United States and the Soviet Union would be completed in an hour or so. This, in turn, meant that the only missiles that counted were those in place and ready to shoot. A second reason for wanting a longer-lasting guidance set was that it would save money. Because of the importance of keeping a maximum percentage of the deployed Minuteman missiles ready to fire at any moment, it was necessary to provide spare guidance systems for quick replacement of those that failed on the missiles in the underground silos. A longer average time between failure meant that fewer spare guidance sets would be required. Given the high cost of these guidance sets, the projected longer MTBF for the Minuteman II guidance set was expected to save enormous amounts of money.

When my associates and I first reviewed the Minuteman II program in the summer of 1963, we predicted that huge cost overruns would occur and that service life of the guidance set would be short unless the Air Force took corrective actions.

Unhappily, little or nothing was done to head off the cost overruns, and they took place on schedule. Whereas our estimates of the Minuteman cost overrun were acknowledged (they were so large that they were difficult to hide for very long), the Air Force and its technical advisory consultant on the Minuteman program, the Space Technology Laboratory Division of Thompson Ramo Wooldridge (later TRW Corporation), tried to ignore our warnings of quality and technical problems. While my associates were preparing reports which showed quantitatively that the Minuteman II guidance system would last only about one third as long as anticipated, the Air Force's technical experts were proclaiming in their reports that the outlook for the guidance systems reliability was "favorable." No figures, no quantitative data at all, just "favorable."

Incidentally, this matter illustrates a problem which persisted throughout my years of experience in the weapons business. I noticed that weapons systems managers and engineers showed a distinct preference for narrative, qualitative reports focusing on estimated accomplishments at the end of the program. This enabled them to avoid exposing many embarrassing facts on current conditions without actually lying. If later events proved them wrong, they could always take refuge in the fact that their earlier estimates stemmed from "engineering judgments" which could not be expected to be precise when working on the Fringes of Man's Knowledge. Of course, good weapons systems soldiers would lie if absolutely necessary to avoid embarrassing disclosures, but they usually tried to avoid it.

In any event, the Air Force, with the cooperation of their development contractors and technical consultants, managed to keep the Minuteman guidance problems under wraps for more than three years. I first learned that our 1963 assessments had been confirmed during a trip to audit the Autonetics plant in Anaheim, California, on October 25 and 26, 1966. Again, as in the case of learning about the C-5A technical problems, I learned about the Autonetics guidance systems failures in informal conversations with contractor engineers and worried working-level Air Force officers. The Air Force officers were particularly concerned that the exceedingly high failure rate of the Autonetics guidance sets had put a high percentage of our deployed Minuteman II missiles out of commission. The quantities of spare guidance systems provided to our operating forces in the field were based on the assumption that the guidance systems would have the long life indicated by the System Program Office and the contractor. Therefore, the operating forces were caught short of spares when the guidance systems began breaking down much faster than anticipated.

When I returned to the Pentagon with the alarming news of the guidance systems failures and resulting high out-of-commission rate for the deployed Minuteman missiles, Ted Marks asked his military assistant to request that the Inspector General of the Air Force look into this situation and report to us as quickly as possible. The Inspector General's organization was generally considered to be an objective gatherer of facts that spared no one's feelings and let the chips fall where they would. Unfortunately, the Inspector General of the Air Force reported to the Chief of Staff of the Air Force, the senior military official, and not to the Secretary of the Air Force, the civilian chief. Consequently, they often protected the military side of the Air Force against civilian criticism. The Inspector General chose to be protective in this case, even though the out-of-commission situation was exceedingly grave if one accepted the premise that Minuteman missiles ready to fire were essential to the national defense.

The Inspector General waffled. He tried to stall. He gave the excuse that the Minuteman II program was still undergoing development and that he tried to avoid getting involved in weapons systems programs while they were still in the development process. We pointed out that the Minuteman II was supposedly in operational status concurrently with its development and that Minuteman II missiles were being supplied to several operational wings, not just to Wing VI, under the Force Modernization Program. The Inspector General people continued to evade the issue, but they did say that the military authorities with a "need to know" would be aware of any problems with Minuteman readiness and on top of the situation. We countered by reminding them that if the proper authorities with the "need to know" were indeed on top of the problem, they should have provided sufficient spare guidance sets to keep the Minuteman fleet in commission. Furthermore, we argued, those of us in the financial management organization also had a "need to know." If additional spare guidance systems and expensive fix-it programs were to be required, we would be expected to come up with money to pay for them.

Finally, even the long-suffering Ted Marks lost patience with the military evasions on the Minuteman situation and directed that the Minuteman System Program Director (SPD) appear in person in the Pentagon in early January 1967. He also invited the other assistant secretaries and a large assortment of deputies and generals to attend the meeting so that everyone could get to the bottom of the Minuteman situation at once. The program director, Brigadier General Arthur Cruikshank, came to the meeting in the Secretary of the Air Force's large and impressive conference room armed with the usual collection of VuGraphs and charts. In the finest traditions of military briefings, General Cruikshank started out telling the gathering a great deal that they already knew and presenting a lot of new boilerplate information irrelevant to the question at hand. He didn't get far, though. Ted Marks rather gently brought Cruikshank back to the main theme of the meeting, and I began questioning him on the Autonetics guidance systems situation. After a very half-hearted attempt to follow the standard evasion procedures, Art Cruikshank broke down and told all.

"Look," he said, "I've only been in charge of this program since last summer. When I came aboard I was told that the Minuteman was the best program in the Air Force. There are no problems, it was in great shape, I was told. The briefings I got sounded too good to be true. And guess what? They weren't true."

At this, several of the generals began to squirm and attempted to inject questions on other subjects. However, it was clear that General Cruikshank was ready to talk, and Ted Marks and I were both determined to see that he got a chance.

"What about the guidance system?" I asked.

"It stinks," Cruikshank replied. "It's sick now, and it's been sick for a long time. The problems have been glossed over. After I had made a number of trips to the field to see first-hand how bad the guidance system was really performing, I confronted the Autonetics president, Norm Parker, with the situation. Parker acknowledged that there were some problems but claimed that they were minor and would soon go away of their own accord. 'Don't worry about it, Art,' he said to me. 'This system is like old wine—the older it gets, the better it is.' I said to him, 'Bullshit. It's like old cheese. The older it gets the worse it smells.'"

Consternation reigned. Several generals tried to talk at once, but for once we were in charge of the meeting.

"Are you going to hold Autonetics to their contract?" I asked. "Can't you require them to make good on the faulty guidance sets?"

"No," Cruikshank answered. "The contract's no damn good. It was written so that the MTBF requirement was just a 'goal,' not a firm contractual specification."

I then asked, "But what are you going to do? Isn't a big portion of the Minuteman fleet out of commission?"

"Yes, about 40 percent of the new missiles are down," he answered. "I've already beefed up our testing procedures to weed out the guidance sets that don't work at all when we first get them. We've had lots of zero time failures. We're going into more extensive testing of components and selective assembly. I made a personal review of the quality control situation at Autonetics, and we hope to have some corrective action there. We are also taking another look at what went wrong in the design phase. Even with all of this, though, we're just not going to get the MTBF we need. We've got to buy more spare systems."

From Autonetics?" I asked.

"Where else?" Cruikshank responded.

"Will you pay them a profit on the additional systems?" I asked.

"Yes," said Cruikshank.

"Then Autonetics is in the position of the light bulb manufacturers," I offered. "We've got to have their guidance sets, and the faster they wear out the more money they make."

"That's about it," conceded Cruikshank.

At that point Gen. Tom Gerrity broke in. "Not necessarily. We'll see about that," he said with determination.

The meeting then settled down to speculation about how much additional money would be required for the Minuteman. Shortly afterward, we adjourned and went our separate ways.

A few days later, General Gerrity called a meeting of concerned fellow generals from the Air Staff and the Systems Command to discuss the Minuteman problem and what to do about it. The meeting took place in a conference room in the Air Staff section of the Pentagon. Adjoining the conference room was a sort of control room containing audio and visual aid equipment. One of my most audacious secret sympathizers stationed himself in the control room to take a few unofficial notes. He later told me that he had a very bad moment shortly after the meeting started. He could not hear clearly at first, and in adjusting the unfamiliar sound system to get more volume, he caused the speakers to squeal. Providentially, according to my secret sympathizer, the assembled generals were so intent on their subject that they did not appear to notice. At least no one investigated, and the secret sympathizer remained undetected.

The secret sympathizer told me that the consensus of the conference was that the principal problem was A. E. Fitzgerald, the Deputy for Management Systems. He said there was much bitter talk about how intolerable it was for Fitzgerald to go directly to the scene of action and bring back "premature" reports of trouble. Information of that sort should come through channels and be "staffed" at each level. "Staffing" was the bureaucratic process whereby reports, letters, position papers, and the like were circulated among department heads at each level of command. Once all the department heads had their shots at changing a document and had finally approved it, a "fully coordinated staff position" could be presented to the Commander for his approval and transmittal to the next level of command, where the process would be repeated. "Staffing" and "coordination" were marvelous information filters. In effect, communications were voted on in a kind of bureaucratic popularity contest at each level of the ponderous, multilayered organization. Much bad news died along the way, and a lot more was overtaken by events. All in all, military staffing and coordination strained out a lot of unpleasant stuff which would have spoiled the tranquil ignorance of civilian presidential appointees. If unpleasant facts had been allowed to go through unfiltered, unrefined, and in time for reaction, some of the appointees might have been jolted into attempts to manage the affairs of the Air Force, and that would never do.

My secret sympathizer said that the generals' lamentations about Fitzgerald were loud and mournful. One kept referring to "that bastard Fitzgerald" until another reminded him that he was being redundant. The second general said that the name Fitzgerald was Norman-Irish for "bastard son of Gerald." Scholarship flickered on in the Air Staff. The generals were particularly bitter, my sympathizer said, about the dialogue where Cruikshank played straight man for my questioning about Autonetics' failures. General Cruikshank, who was not present at the meeting, of course, had made them all look bad, and would have to be dealt with. However, General Cruikshank was controllable and his fate could be decided later. The immediate problem was Fitzgerald. I was not controllable by the generals and, most alarmingly, seemed to have the confidence of Secretaries Marks and Brown. The assembled generals then decided that they had to make sure I was competently escorted when I want to the field, and that I should get no information which had not been "coordinated." Procedures for staffing documents up through the Air Staff would have to be followed more strictly. For the moment, anger and frustration had befuddled the general's collective reasoning, and they forgot that I seldom got any useful information from official Air Force sources anyway. Further filtering of information from the field would confuse no one but themselves and would make them more vulnerable than ever to embarrassing revelations at high levels.

Alerted by my secret sympathizers in the Air Staff and the field, I knew better than to depend on the creaking and malfunctioning military bureaucracy for corrective actions or even accurate information on the Minuteman program. So I scheduled a series of trips to the Minuteman systems program office at Norton Air Force Base in San Bernardino, California, and to the plants of the Minuteman associate contractors. I took along the people assigned by the Air Staff and the Systems Command Headquarters to keep an eye on me. I found them very capable people. I worked hard at convincing my traveling companions that we, the Air Force, could benefit greatly by gaining control of the floundering procurement program. I believe that I was at least partially successful in this attempt, because my new associates became deeply involved in the work and, outwardly at least, shared my concern.

On one of my many troubleshooting trips to the Minuteman systems program office in early 1967, I received the first threat of my Pentagon career. My former associates in the little consulting firm I had left to join the Pentagon were at that time working on performance measurement and other cost-control systems on the Minuteman program and elsewhere in the Air Force Systems Command. The little firm, Performance Technology Corporation, or PTC, had by then gained a considerable reputation for tough, incisive analysis of weapons systems management problems and, where they were allowed to perform, for effective cost reduction. One of the senior civilian employees in the Minuteman program office took me aside and told me bluntly that my former associates were going to "suffer" if I did not "ease up" on my probing of the Minuteman situation. I thanked him for the warning but told him that he had just removed any doubt that I would continue and even intensify my efforts to clean up the disastrous Minuteman mess. I felt bad that my probing promised to cause trouble for my former associates. However, the threat convinced me that the Minuteman situation was even more unwholesome than I had previously suspected.

I also felt bad, somewhat guilty and quite angry, about Brigadier General Cruikshank's treatment at the hands of his superiors. Officially, General Cruikshank was still the Minuteman's System Program Director, but in actuality most of the program responsibility had been assumed by General Cruikshank's immediate superior, Major General John McCoy, the commander of the Ballistic Systems Division, of which the Minuteman program was part. General Cruikshank's superiors had made it very clear that Cruikshank was in disgrace because of his candor in revealing the Minuteman problems to the Secretary's office. Cruikshank's subordinates were regularly summoned to meetings on the Minuteman problem at which General Cruikshank was pointedly excluded. Cruikshank's subordinates told me that they had been instructed not to give certain sensitive information to him for fear that he would "leak" it to the Secretary's office.

The Air Force procurement gang's behavior in rubbing out Joe Warren's career had been vicious, stupid, and brutal, but at least it was done quickly. Not so with poor Art Cruikshank, perhaps because Cruikshank was a general and an initiate of the inner circle. His punishment for truth-telling and embarrassing contractors and fellow generals was more cruel. Whereas Joe Warren had been removed swiftly from his post, Art Cruikshank was kept in place for systematic humiliation for about six months. He was allowed to occupy the chair of the Minuteman System Program Director but without any real authority. In addition to being bypassed and excluded from meetings and decisions concerning the Minuteman program, his attempts to control the program were thwarted or ignored. For example, Cruikshank and one of his few remaining loyal assistants attempted to get help from the Air Force Contract Management Division to examine contractor personnel levels that the Minuteman program was required to support financially. Ordinarily, an Air Force systems program director could have simply directed his own staff to carry out this work, but Cruikshank had been effectively stripped of authority to supervise his employees.

Insiders on the Minuteman program had long realized that their contracts were worthless as limitations on spending and that the operative statistics in controlling Minuteman costs were numbers of people in the Minuteman operations of their contractors and those being supported by the overhead accounts. Before I left the Minuteman program in 1965, we had helped to deflate contractors' spending plans somewhat by a quick-and-dirty manpower and overhead analysis. With the program careening out of control in the spring of 1967, Cruikshank attempted to get help to perform a similar review. On March 24, 1967, General Cruikshank wrote to the Commander of the Contract Management Division, Brig. Gen. Dan Reilly, soliciting his help in this effort. He wrote:

Excess contractor manpower in the R & D (Research and Development) area is felt to be a major contributor to the FY 67/68 Minuteman R&D deficit. Minuteman contractor manpower loading has not been seriously worked since 1965, and needs a critical review to assure that R&D manpower is phased down commensurate with Minuteman R&D effort. This problem needs critical attention at Boeing, Autonetics and Avco.

Cruikshank's assessment of his program's financial condition was, if anything, understated. When the Minuteman II program had started life as the Wing VI Minuteman in 1963, the R&D estimate for the program was $490,400,000. The entire research and development effort had been scheduled for completion in fiscal year 1966. After the program was renamed Minuteman II, the estimates for research and development passed one billion dollars, reflecting the program's vast overruns, mostly covered by spurious contract changes. After the decision to proceed with the MIRV (Multiple Independently Targeted Re-entry Vehicle) in 1966, a portion of the Minuteman II program was split off and, with the addition of certain new items such as the Post-boost Control System and an improved third-stage rocket motor, became the Minuteman III.

With the Minuteman program thus redescribed, the original 1963 estimate of $490,400,000 dollars in development funds was lost from view, and the slate was wiped clean. The redefined Minuteman II development program, really less ambitious in scope than the earlier Wing VI program, was given an initial base line price of $953,900,000. By early 1967, with panic reigning because of the Minuteman's technical disasters, the lid was off on plans for higher spending. The top military people were clearly prepared to "pour on money" in their blind attempts to make good things happen. The associate contractors scrambled frantically to increase their estimates so that they would get their share of the loot to be scattered about. Contractor estimates for the Minuteman II R&D program skyrocketed to more than $2,700,000,000. In this climate, it was not surprising that General Cruikshank's sincere but feeble efforts to slow down the runaway cost increases would be ignored. And they were. When General Reilly finally got around to responding to Art Cruikshank's urgent request for assistance about three weeks later, he brushed off Cruikshank's plea. Instead of helping, Reilly suggested that Cruikshank refer any information he might have to the appropriate contracting officers.

Contracting discipline was never good on the Minuteman program, but it appeared to collapse completely in the confusion of early 1967. The panicky disorder was not restricted to the critically sick Minuteman II either. The greedy contractors and ambitious Air Force project managers took advantage of the disorder to charge ahead into the Minuteman III program, especially the MIRV project, without defining exactly what they were buying and without effective limits on the contractor spending. Typically, new work would be authorized by either a change to an old contract or a new so-called "letter contract." Practically speaking, these contractual documents did not commit the contractors to do anything but did commit the government to pay them money up to a stated limit, called the limitation of cost. As the contractors' spending approached the cost limit, the compliant Air Force contracting officers would simply raise the limit to permit the contractor to continue his unfettered spending. Frequently, the work to be done would not be officially described in the contract and a price set for the work (called "definitization") until the work had been underway for many months. In some cases "definitization" was not accomplished until after completion of the contracted work. Specifications would then be set to match whatever the contractor had been able to produce, and the contract price would be based on the contractor's actual costs. A specific example of this process as it applied to a portion of the MIRV project was described in a trip report by Mr. Charles Donahue, Jr., of the Office of the General Counsel of the Air Force, regarding his visit to the Autonetics division of North American Aviation on March 3, 1967. Mr. Donahue wrote:

Then too, the major contract at Autonetics, contract number 786, for Post-boost Control Systems research and development is, so far as Minuteman III is concerned, still in a letter contract stage. It is not expected that this contract will be completely definitized until well into 1968. Thus, there is no total price. The contractor is not working against any incentive. Rather, he is incurring costs and getting increases in the limitation-of-cost clause as he goes along.

An interesting sidelight of this situation was that the Air Force had given Autonetics the contract to develop the guidance system for the Minuteman III without competition and, indeed, without even effective negotiations before work started in spite of Autonetics' miserable performance on the Minuteman II guidance set.

With the Minuteman program leaderless, with the frantic money-grabbing by the contractors proceeding unchecked, and with a sizable percentage of the Minuteman missile fleet still out of commission, the confused state of the program degenerated to absolute chaos. With no constructive corrective actions in sight, and with the cover-up and deception growing, I decided that a real jolt was in order.

My determination to jolt my leaders into constructive action was strengthened when I found that reports on the Minuteman II accuracy had been misleading. To me, this was the last straw in irresponsible behavior. As in the past, reports and briefings on the missile's accuracy emphasized that outlook was for "outstanding" Minuteman II accuracy. The primary indicator of accuracy was CEP or Circular Error Probability. CEP was demonstrated graphically by plotting test warhead impact points on a target of concentric circles about the central aim point. The graphic displays looked just like rifle targets used in shooting matches, and a tight grouping of shots near the bullseye was the objective. In one of the briefings I received in the Minuteman control room at Norton Air Force Base, I noticed that the Minuteman II test shots showed a tight grouping all right, but that all missed the bullseye by a startling margin. The test results depicted precision but not accuracy, just like a rifle which shot consistently high and to the right. Furthermore, the number of impacts plotted was far less than the total number of test shots. The Minuteman management people were counting only the relatively good shots, omitting entirely the worst misses.

The jolt for my bosses took the form of a trip dated June 21, 1967, covering a visit to the Minuteman systems program office on June 5, 1967. I was accompanied on this visit by a representative from the Air Staff, Colonel Larry Killpack, who worked in the Systems and Logistics section, and by Mr. E. L. Kirschbaum and Mr. Gordon Arthur, both of the Air Force Systems Command headquarters. Mr. Kirschbaum was the technical advisor and the assistant to General Wendell Carter, the Comptroller of the Air Force Systems Command, and Mr. Arthur was the assistant chief of the pricing section in Procurement at Systems Command Headquarters. We found that even routine administration of the program had collapsed. For example, there had been no overall compilation of the contractor's financial requirements since the previous December. Routine reports submitted by the contractors in March 1967 were still lying around unprocessed on the fifth of June. The performance measurement applications in which the Minuteman program had previously shown good progress had been allowed to die. Contracting continued to be a bad joke, with after-the-fact negotiations serving only to confirm whatever the contractor had done by way of performance and paying him his cost plus a profit, regardless of how poorly the work had been done. Commenting on one of the large Minuteman contracts at Boeing, one of my associates wrote: ". . . it appears that this contract is being used merely as an instrument to transfer funds to Boeing, rather than as an instrument to exercise control." Despite the generally acknowledged ineffectiveness of contracts as controls or restraints on contractor performance, we reported that "BSD procurement people told us that Air Force policy prohibits any other form of contractor cost control or restraints." We reported that the "subsidy accounts," which previously had been separately identified and tracked on the Minuteman program, had been lost from view, buried in the overall financial requirement, and presented to the Air Force top management as part of the absolutely necessary financial requirements for the program. We also reported that there had been no effective, large-scale competition for contracts on the Minuteman program for nine years, and that efforts to stimulate competition were resisted.

These were serious charges and they were true. Nevertheless, taken alone, these discrepancies, even backed up by our extensive documentation, probably would not have generated any action on the part of the Air Force top management. To some degree the same charges could have been leveled against any of the major Air Force programs. However, our charges regarding the degradation of discipline and the deplorable ethical situation on the Minuteman program succeeded in catching the attention of our bosses. We roused a number of high-ranking people by writing that the "general decline in discipline and attention to duty" was leading to indefinite delays in complying with directions from higher headquarters "up to and including the Office of the Chief of Staff." Military people could flaunt orders from the Secretary but not from their military leader, the Chief of Staff.

Commenting on the ethical situation, we wrote, in part:

Although it is impossible to quantify its effects, the ethical situation in the management of the Minuteman program has a derogatory impact in program management. There are many examples of failure by BSD and Minuteman management personnel to exert maximum effort in the government's interest, compounded by strenuous efforts to cover up problems and stifle criticism. A glaring example is the manner in which attempts to pinpoint responsibility for failure have been dealt with in recent months. It is generally believed that the Systems Program Director is being relieved of his responsibilities because he told the truth regarding failure of one of the Minuteman contractors to deliver as promised. Citing the failure of this contractor is viewed in some quarters as a reflection on the Systems Program Director's superiors. It is very difficult to envision anyone conveying an unpleasant truth to the headquarters in these circumstances. The outlook for full visibility by higher levels of management is dim indeed. Worse, the ethical and moral climate makes it nearly impossible to motivate people properly.

That did it. I delivered a single copy of the report to Mr. Marks on June 21 as he was leaving for an out-of-town trip, and gave a copy to Colonel Killpack. By the next day, it appeared that everyone in the Air Force Headquarters had a copy. No one was indifferent to the report, and there was no middle ground. My secret sympathizers were delighted. Others, particularly procurement generals, were furious, especially so at what they took as a slur on the honor and integrity of high-ranking Air Force officers. There were dark mutterings to the effect that Fitzgerald had finally gone too far and that something would have to be done about him.

We had a DSMG review of the Minuteman program on June 22. The meeting was quite tense, with many of the attendees obviously wondering who would first mention the damning report. As it turned out, no one did. The presentation to Secretary Brown consisted of the usual drivel. His choices were limited. He could (1) provide more money, or (2) cancel or defer part of the program. None of the military people present suggested financing even part of the necessary "fix-it" project out of either savings, which could be obtained by squeezing fat out of existing programs, or enforcing contractual requirements so that contractors who failed to meet specifications would pay for at least part of the corrections with their own funds. In discussing how to present the problem to the office of the Secretary of Defense, one of the generals brazenly suggested that we merely "change the numbers." Others made the same proposal somewhat more obliquely.

I was encouraged by the fact that Harold Brown rejected out of hand the proposals that we "solve" the Minuteman program simply by lying about it. He also solicited ideas for "small cost reductions" to help solve the financial problems. Without elaborating on this last request, and without any specific instructions to the assembled generals, Brown then adjourned the meeting by asking the Chief of Staff and the Assistant Secretaries to join him in a private session in his office to discuss "some very serious management problems" on the Minuteman program.

I later learned that the "very serious management problems" included those outlined in my report to Secretary Marks. The upshot of the meeting was to authorize a huge group of Air Force officers and civilians under the direction of Maj. Gen. Jack O'Neill to study the Minuteman program for ninety days.

During this period no "outsiders" would be allowed to visit, question, or otherwise attempt to obtain information on the Minuteman program. I was not included in the study team, of course, so the prohibition against "outsiders" had the effect of getting me out of the Minuteman program for the time being at least.

I was never allowed to see General O'Neill's final report. A "summary report" was issued for general distribution within the Air Force, but all my requests, including official communications through Secretary Marks' office, for a copy of the complete report were refused. We were told that the complete report was a "military matter" and could not be released without permission of the Chief of Staff. We civilians could not get that permission.

Meanwhile, plans moved ahead to begin "solving" the Minuteman problem by pouring more money on it. On June 21, the day before the DSMG, Harold Brown wrote to Secretary McNamara requesting additonal emergency funding for Minuteman to see the program through the remaining nine days of fiscal year 1967. One June 23, Mr. McNamara approved the addition of $18,600,000 to the Minuteman program for fiscal 1967. The budget department of the Office of the Secretary of Defense was also alerted that vast increases would be needed for fiscal year 1968 and subsequent years.

Then, on August 1, I learned belatedly that news of the Minuteman problems had been reported in *The New York Times*. *Missile/Space Daily* for August 1, 1967, carried the story headline "Guidance System Causing Problems in Minuteman II Readiness." They reported in part:

> The Air Force, responding to a story in last Friday's *New York Times*, admits that it is having some maintenance problems with the Minuteman II guidance and control systems, but insists that it "is indeed a reliable weapon systems."

The futility of this deception was revealed in the next paragraph of the quote:

> According to the *Times* story, as recently as this Spring reliable sources say nearly one hundred missiles—about forty percent of all of

the advanced Minuteman II missiles and ten percent of the entire one thousand missile Minuteman force—"were out of action because of trouble with the weapons guidance and control system." The Autonetics division of North American Aviation is the producer of the Minuteman II guidance and control system.

As this passage indicated, the outside world's knowledge of the Minuteman system was reasonably accurate. And it was clear that Air Force denials were fooling no one—the *Times*, *Missile/Space Daily*, or the Russians.

This publicity, along with internal Air Force reports on the Minuteman troubles, reached McKinsey & Company, our consultants on the Cost Management Improvement Program, at about this time. Even though I no longer attended CMIP control board meetings, the McKinsey partners and consultants called on me frequently to give me reports of progress on the program I was responsible for. Shortly after news of the Minuteman disaster got out, the McKinsey partner in charge of their Air Force work called on me to ask what I had done to stir up the generals over the Minuteman program. The generals were absolutely enraged, he said, about a report that I had written. He asked if he could read the report. Of course he could, I told him. The document was not classified (we had transmitted the failure information separately). The McKinsey partner read the strongly worded, fifteen-page report quickly but intently. He turned a bit white as he read it. When he had finished, he dropped the report on my desk as though the paper was hot. He looked at me for a moment, said, "Holy mackerel," got up, and walked out of my office. Although McKinsey & Company continued to work in the Pentagon throughout my tenure, I never saw this gentleman again.

Near the end of General O'Neill's ninety-day study, the Inspector General of the Air Force finally came to life. About a year too late, the Inspector General got into the Minuteman act with his own investigation. I suppose the Inspector General organization felt compelled to maintain their image as the impartial watchdog of Air Force readiness and stewardship.

General O'Neill's summary report and the Inspector General's report on Minuteman were circulated at about the same time.

Neither was a complete whitewash. On the other hand, neither report dealt with the most basic problems of the whole affair: systematic deception, concealment of critical failings for nearly four years, and the upside-down rewards and punishment system which castigated people trying to protect the public interest and coddled those who helped cover up blunders.

As usual in serious bureaucratic flaps, a reorganization was recommended. Reorganization is a favorite device because it gives the appearance of action with a minimum of genuine change. Under General O'Neill's plan, the Air Force Systems Command's two West Coast buying divisions—the Ballistic Systems Division, of which the Minuteman program was part, and the Space Systems Division—were to report to a new organization called Space and Missiles Support organization, or SAMSO. Whereas the older buying divisions had been headed by major generals, SAMSO was to be headed by a lieutenant general. As commander of a buying division, the Electronic Systems Division, General O'Neill was a major general. He was tapped for the new job he had recommended, and as commander of SAMSO, he became a lieutenant general.

General McCoy, the Commander of BSD, was also transferred, but without a promotion. He was transferred to the Air Force's Logistics Command, known among Air Force officers as the Old Elephants' Graveyard. Usually generals assigned to the Logistics Command never returned. However, the duty was considered good, and John McCoy could look forward to serving until retirement under his friend and patron, General Thomas Gerrity, who had recently been given his fourth star and assigned to command the Logistics Command.

Initially, the procurement generals had planned to consign Art Cruikshank to the Old Elephants' Graveyard also. However, as contrasted to General McCoy's situation, Cruikshank could not have looked forward to a pleasant tour of duty. Had he been assigned to the Logistics Command, Cruikshank would have been subordinate to his old bosses, who made no secret of the fact that they hated his guts. I and others who believed that Cruikshank was being mistreated protested his proposed reassignment strongly. Ted Marks also supported Cruikshank's cause. As a result of intervention from high levels in the Air Force, Cruikshank's proposed assignment was canceled, and he was transferred instead to an operating command in the Military Airlift Command. His punishment for candor was lightened, but in the final analysis his reward had been humiliation and removal from his post as Minuteman systems program director.

The investigators of the Minuteman program capped the scandal by attributing the Minuteman II problems to, of all things, a lack of money. The Inspector General was especially strong in promoting this outrageous misconception. Actually, the major cause of the disaster, in addition to simple incompetence and dishonesty, had been a superabundance of money which permitted the program managers to indulge in Ape Theory management without thinking. Autonetics claimed they had been denied money to conduct testing. In fact, they had been denied additional money for one of their testing programs because they were already being paid for it. The vastly inflated prices paid them for Minuteman II hardware, especially as compared to similar hardware for Minuteman I, would have covered several times as much testing as they performed on the successful Minuteman I program. The choice to waste money was theirs. The incentive contracts on Minuteman II placed minimal restrictions on the way they spent the vast amounts of money they received. Rather than being told what to do, as was the case with Minuteman I, they were to be rewarded for producing a quality product on Minuteman II. However, the opportunity to grab off additional hundreds of millions of dollars by raising Ape Theory management as a revived idol was irresistible to the Minuteman spending complex. All of my attempts to reason with the new boss, General O'Neill, were rebuffed. He was polite, to be sure, and willing to exchange pleasantries at length, but he successfully evaded substantive discussions. Finally, after I had made several trips to the West Coast to attempt to dissuade O'Neill from swallowing the Ape Theory and other fairy stories, he cut me off with finality, saying, "Write me a letter."

My letter, written on December 16, 1967, in response to General O'Neill's request, was to come back and bite me years later.* In the letter, I explained to General O'Neill the

* The text of this letter is included as appendix B.

background of the problems he was inheriting on all his programs, especially on the Minuteman. In addition I offered suggestions to General O'Neill for improving the management of the several billion dollars a year for which he would be responsible.

There was little or no hope of reviving meaningful cost controls on the Minuteman program after the great flap of 1967 was laid to rest. With the help of Mr. Anthony's Analysis Group, my civilian bosses and I made several subsequent attempts to stimulate interest in cost reduction and control on the program, but nothing came of them. Also, I attempted to keep track of progress in improving the Minuteman guidance system's mean time between failure. Some improvement was reflected in the figures reported to us, but I learned that much of the apparent improvement was due to changes in methods of calculating the averages. Guidance systems which didn't work at all, called "zero time failures," had previously dragged down the average life, the MTBF. These were omitted from the new calculations. Also, field failures which could be repaired without removing guidance systems from the missiles were omitted under the revised method of computation.

Gradually, as high-level interest in the Minuteman subsided, detailed information on the program dried up. As was the case with the C-5A, much of the Minuteman program went underground (literally and figuratively), to be heard from only when there were spectacular test failures or when new transfusions of money were needed. Unlike the C-5A, the Minuteman program was destined to stay out of sight. Minuteman was protected by a veil of military secrecy, whereas practically all of the information on the C-5A carried no national restrictions whatever.

While the Minuteman debacle was proceeding to a state of perpetual boondoggle, I was also heavily involved in another procurement disaster, the F-111 fighter bomber. The F-111, earlier known as the TFX, has been the subject of bitter controversy and political debate since its inception. The Air Force contract source selection board had chosen Boeing Airplane Company to build the plane but had been overruled by Mr. McNamara's associates, and the contract was awarded to the

General Dynamics Corporation in Fort Worth, Texas. Charges of political influence in the contract award, coupled with serious questions about the wisdom of building the plane in the first place, had led Senator McClellan, Chairman of the Senate Permanent Investigating Subcommittee, to hold extensive hearings into the project in 1963 and 1964. The project had been started in 1962 as one of the first great applications of McNamara's cost-effectiveness doctrine. By using one airplane to satisfy the requirements of the Navy for a fleet air defense airplane and the Air Force for a tactical fighter-bomber, McNamara had hoped to save vast sums by making one development program do for both services and by taking advantage of the lower unit costs which were supposed to result from larger production orders for similar aircraft.

The project was doomed to failure from the start. Neither the Air Force nor the Navy wanted any part of the program at first, and high-ranking representatives of both services worked assiduously behind the scenes to undercut McNamara's project. Each service wanted to build its own airplane and selectively leaked information which would support their respective cases, both to the press and to McNamara's congressional critics.

To make matters worse, key people in the Pentagon apparently were misled by the "optimistic" (read "wholly false") assessment of the potential of the variable wing sweep concept which was central to the whole idea of the F-111. The plane's wings were hinged to the fuselage by means of large pins in a central yoke attached to the fuselage. The purpose of this arrangement was to permit the wings to be swung nearly straight out from the fuselage for slow-speed flight for landing and taking off from shorter than average fields and for safe operation from aircraft carrier flight decks. Unhappily, the promoters of the concept, first the National Aeronautics and Space Administration (NASA) and later the contractors and military people with vested interests in the program's continuation, glossed over major problems.

The beautiful theoretical concept had practical problems. First, the airplane carried excess weight because of the massive yoke, the hinge pins, and actuating mechanisms for varying the wings' sweep. More weight was added because of the loss of structural continuity between the hinged wings and the fuselage. Modern aircraft are generally constructed so that the skin of the craft bears most of the stresses. This results in great structural efficiency. They are strong structures for their weight. Some of this structural efficiency advantage was lost on the F-111 due to the fact that the stress-bearing skin of the swiveling outer wing panels could not be connected to the skin of the wing roots. The pylons for carrying bombs, missiles, or fuel tanks under the wings had to be swiveled so they would continue to point straight ahead as the wings were moved, and this added weight and complications avoided by similar aircraft. With the wings fully swept back for supersonic flight, the F-111 had a sizable portion of its wings tucked away inside the fuselage and the thick "glove" or wing root so that the hidden surface contributed nothing but weight to the aircraft in the supersonic configuration. All in all, especially when rigged for supersonic flight, the F-111 carried tons of dead weight not needed on other supersonic aircraft.

In addition, the F-111 concept had inherent aerodynamic drag problems. The thick glove and provision of fuselage space to accommodate the folded wing increased the cross-sectional area of the aircraft, which in turn increased drag, as did the break where the wing met the glove.

The inherent problems were widely known, but except for one engineer at Grumman Aircraft, where the Navy's F-111B version was assembled, no one was willing to criticize the concept openly. The Grumman engineer was dead right in his criticism, but he was declared crazy and eventually outlawed from the industry. Despite the fairly obvious practical problems, the F-111 was officially proclaimed a grand idea. Adherence to this party line was required as an article of faith. Although doubts persisted regarding the practicality of the concept, there were sufficient money and power behind the project to make adherence to the party line attractive for those who valued their careers and businesses.

I became involved in the F-111 program during my first few days in the Pentagon. On October 11, 1965, Secretary Anthony assigned my boss, Ted Marks, the responsibility for improving the reporting on the cost status of the program for Mr. McNamara's personal use. Reports were to be submitted to Mr. McNamara on a quarterly basis, but in actuality as the program got deeper into trouble, reports were submitted much more frequently, finally settling down to an everyother-week affair to coincide with Mr. McNamara's renowned "Saturday meetings" of key government and contractor personnel in his office. Mr. Anthony assigned two of his brightest and most aggressive young Harvard Business School graduates to work with me on this project. At first, I worked with Lt. Commander Steve Lazarus, Mr. Anthony's military assistant, and later with Bill George of Anthony's analysis group. Both of these men were incredulous at the sloppy record keeping and, in some cases, total absence of vital financial information on the program. For example, they could not believe that no one knew the actual cost of each airplane as it was completed. They also seemed surprised to learn that each of the many new estimates of the program's total cost was made from scratch and bore no necessary relationship to previous estimates. It was as though the program was born again with each new and always higher cost estimate. Differences between the cost estimates were usually attributed to Air Force-directed "changes" and previous "estimating errors." Each time a new Air Force estimate was generated which was higher than the amount on contract, the contractors and their Air Force partners would go to work generating new changes which would take up the slack and then some. The net effect of the multitudinous contract changes on the F-111 was to diminish the specified performance of the airplane, but the cost went up nevertheless.

I had long become accustomed, of course, to the "rubber baseline." The cozy relationship between government buyer and contractor customer did not surprise me either. However, the closeness of the Air Force and its principle contractor, General Dynamics, was a little unusual in the cost-estimating function. The Air Force and General Dynamics were united not only in purpose but also functionally. For example, I was working very late one night to prepare one of our periodic submissions of

F-111 cost data. This was a particularly urgent submission, and I was preparing part of the material myself while the rest was being put together by a group of officers and civilians in the Air Staff with help from Systems Command Headquarters cost specialists. As frequently happened, we were getting new instructions from staff specialists in Mr. McNamara's office and Secretary Anthony's analysis group. It soon became obvious that this particular project would be a night-long affair, and about 1:30 in the morning I decided to walk to the Air Staff offices, where our specialists were working to deliver the latest instructions and discuss the work remaining to be done. To my surprise, all our cost experts were sitting around relaxed and drinking coffee in the outer office of their suite. They were all friends of mine and seemed glad to see me. I asked how the work was coming and they said "Fine, no problem." "Let's go over the work sheets," I suggested. "Where are they?" They replied that the work sheets were in the back room and became somewhat agitated as I walked back. When I entered the back office I saw why. There, seated at a big table, surrounded by working papers and estimating manuals and beavering away, was good old Chester May, ace cost estimator from General Dynamics. Chester May in the back room was the Air Force's "computer" for F-111 cost estimates.

I was astounded when Mr. Anthony's assistants told me that McNamara really believed that the new magic incentive contracts would penalize contractors who failed to meet their commitments, and that General Dynamics, in particular, would be highly motivated to keep their costs down and their performances up to avoid losing their shirt on the F-111. According to Anthony's assistants, Secretary McNamara was surprised to learn that General Dynamics stood to make more money on their overrun development contract than they had anticipated in their original bid. General Dynamics had won the F-111 development contract in 1962 with a proposed price of $543,500,000, including a planned profit of $42,900,000. By early 1966, the development contract estimate had increased to almost $1,300,000,000, and it was estimated that General Dynamics would earn a profit of more than $80,000,000. By producing an airplane inferior to the one they had promised to build originally, General Dynamics had nearly doubled its profits.

Secretary McNamara might have been less surprised if he had become better acquainted with some of the government people administering the F-111 contract for him. In some quarters, lack of interest in cost control was total. I came across a prime example of this attitude during a trip to the General Dynamics plant in Fort Worth, Texas, in early January of 1966. General Dynamics had been given a letter contract for $1,779,906,000 to start building production models of the F-111. Negotiations were then underway to "definitize" the contract, to set an official price and agree on specifications, schedule, and quantities of airplanes to be delivered. In preparation for the negotiations, one of the DCAA (Defense Contract Audit Agency) auditors had analyzed the overhead rates proposed by General Dynamics in pricing the contract. In common with other giant aerospace contractors, General Dynamics' overhead rates had increased rapidly, and further increases were projected in spite of their rapidly growing business base. Even the usually myopic Inspector General of the Air Force had remarked on the increase in General Dynamics' overhead. The IG viewed with alarm the fact that overhead rates for the F-111 were 97 percent higher than overhead rates on General Dynamics' previous project, the B-58, even after allowing for inflation and changes in overhead content. Based on his analysis of General Dynamics' overhead, the DCAA auditor recommended a reduction of approximately $82,500,000 from the contractor's proposed production price. The Air Force price analyst resident in the General Dynamics plant was outraged at the auditor's recommendation:

The contractor is entitled to his cost of operating the facility, and if we think his costs are too high we should seek a cheaper facility, but since we have engaged him then he is entitled to his costs.

This analyst apparently thought he was dealing with a cost-plus contract. He was not. He was supposedly negotiating a fixed-price incentive contract. Furthermore, the facility that our cost analyst was suggesting we might abandon belonged to the

United States government, lock, stock, and barrel. General Dynamics was a tenant.

Despite vast cost increases and evidence of almost equally vast opportunities to save money, I was unable to generate any interest in substantive actions to drive down F-111 costs at that time. For one thing, the combined forces of the historical costing cult and the incentive contract sect were too strong. For another, I was told there wasn't time. The production contract had to be definitized as quickly as possible. Why? So it could be changed. Big doings were in the offing. The contract schedule, the mix of airplanes for different customers, and quantities of airplanes were to be changed immediately after definition. "What about the performance specification?" I asked, thinking I was prepared for anything in the prevailing madhouse atmosphere. I was not. The F-111 program managers were proposing to base specifications for the F-111 production model on whatever the Air Force accepted in the nineteenth development prototype, which had not been built at that time. Since, on form, the Air Force could be depended upon to accept practically anything one of their pet giants produced, we weren't really guaranteed anything at all.

The only bright spot in the dismal F-111 picture was the performance of Mr. Anthony's young assistant, Bill George. Bill did an outstanding job, especially in selling Dr. Anthony, Mr. McNamara, and McNamara's deputy, Paul Nitze, on the desirability of departing, at least on occasion, from the rigid policy of using historical costs of price contracts. It was becoming increasingly clear that this relic of Dark Age thinking was not only bleeding the taxpayers white but was also destroying Secretary McNamara's reputation. Bill kept hammering away at the advantages of determining what goods and services should cost if produced efficiently as opposed to what they were likely to cost if nature were allowed to take its course. The tightwad approach I favored came to be called "should cost" estimating, and the traditional approach was called "will cost".

In the spring of 1967, Bill George's selling efforts finally bore fruit. Mostly because of his tenacity, the cost-estimating issue had become sharpened and brought to the attention of the top civilians in the Department of Defense. The top procurement officials, military and civilian alike, continued their strong opposition to "should cost," despite the fact that their own written procedures instructed cost analysts to estimate ". . . the degree to which contractors proposed cost represent what performance of the contract should cost assuming reasonable economy and efficiency." This instruction, contained in Defense Procurement Circular #12, dated October 16, 1964, was also incorporated in the Armed Services Pricing Manual. Although this appeared to be clear instruction to price analysts to perform "should cost" analyses, the pricing chiefs disagreed. They claimed the instruction was poorly worded and didn't really mean what the words conveyed.

The first opportunity for using "should cost" analysis on the F-111 came when estimated cost of the plane's engines began increasing dramatically. The contractor for the F-111 engines was Pratt & Whitney Aircraft Division of United Aircraft Corporation. Pratt & Whitney's original estimate for the F-111 engine, designated the TF-30, had been $273,910 each. Somewhat later, Pratt & Whitney had committed themselves to a firm unit price of $460,000 for the engine in the version of the F-111 which was to be supplied to the British. In early 1967, Pratt & Whitney's informal estimates for the TF-30 engines they were building under an unpriced letter contract rose to around $700,000 per engine. This was bad news indeed for Secretary McNamara, who was having a difficult enough time as it was defending the F-111 program to a hostile Congress. As usual, Mr. McNamara got little help in solving this problem from his own cost estimators and their consultants who depended mostly on statistical analysis of historical costs. The statisticians' own procedures could have been employed as an arguing point to help Mr. McNamara hold down the skyrocketing Pratt & Whitney prices. For example, when the characteristics of the Pratt & Whitney TF-30 engines were substituted in the Rand Corporation's statistical formulas, the following results were obtained: Cumulative average through unit 150—$442,000; cumulative average through unit 500—$381,000; cumulative average through unit 1000—$348,000.

Unfortunately for Mr. McNamara, statistical analyses of the actual cost then being experienced by Pratt & Whitney in manufacturing the TF-30 engines indicated that the unit cost would soar much higher, perhaps to $900,000 per engine. Following their usual practice, the statistical cost estimators abandoned their old formulas which produced lower estimates and eagerly embraced the new data, thereby allowing the ratchet mechanism to function in jacking up prices. Apparently this was too much for Mr. McNamara, and he directed the Navy, which was buying the engines for the bi-service project, to conduct a "should cost" study of TF-30 engines at Pratt & Whitney. The Navy was also urged to employ outside industrial engineering consultants to assist in the study.

The Navy's Air Systems Command and their procurement specialists wanted no part of the "should cost" study. They decided to have the outside consultant do the whole job. The Navy asked for competitive bids on the study from a number of outside consulting firms. My old company, Performance Technology Corporation, or PTC, was the only firm to respond with a proposal to actually perform a "should cost" study. Other firms either flatly refused to bid on the controversial project or proposed doing something more bland, such as a review of management procedures and manufacturing techniques.

PTC won the competition, and moved several consultants into the Pratt & Whitney plant to begin the study. They immediately encountered a united front of opposition from Pratt & Whitney management, the Naval Air Systems Command, and the Navy's plant representatives at Pratt & Whitney. (Incidentally, the Navy captain in charge of the plant representative detachment at Pratt & Whitney, who was particularly vigorous in opposing the "should cost" study, later retired and was rewarded with a job at Pratt & Whitney.)

Despite being denied access to the usual sources of "should cost" data, PTC managed to glean enough information to submit an interim report on May 1, 1967, about a month after they had begun the study. The interim report contained a number of intriguing bits of information:

1. Controllable unfavorable labor variances at Pratt & Whitney had been increasing steadily, growing from 23 percent in 1962 to 35 percent in 1966.
2. A study of machine utilization in Pratt & Whitney's factory showed that, on the average, 62 percent of the machines were neither running nor attended. This was particularly important at the time because Pratt & Whitney was asking the government to furnish them large numbers of additional expensive machines. PTC suggested that Pratt & Whitney first make full use of machines already in their plant.
3. Observations of the activity of Pratt & Whitney assembly workers showed an average of 40 percent idle workers.
4. One-time, nonrecurring costs included in recurring categories inflated projected future prices by as much as $134,000 per engine.
5. The numbers of people charging their time to Pratt & Whitney's General and Administrative accounts had increased 34 percent between August 1966 and April 1967. This increase was considered to be purely discretionary on Pratt & Whitney's part and could have been avoided or mitigated by simple management decisions.

PTC's interim report stirred up a storm of controversy and increased opposition from Pratt & Whitney and their allies in the Navy. However, the interim report apparently impressed the top officials in the Office of the Secretary of Defense, and the Navy was directed to stop their opposition and assist PTC to gain access to the data they needed to complete the "should cost" studies.

After many more difficulties, and working under a tight contractual deadline, PTC prepared and submitted a detailed report of about 200 pages on June 12, 1967. Their findings were shocking. They estimated that the TF-30 engines at Pratt & Whitney probably would cost between $620,000 and $685,000 each with then-projected efficiency levels at Pratt & Whitney. This was very close to the figure of approximately $700,000 per engine contained in Pratt & Whitney's informal proposals, none of which PTC had been allowed to see. PTC then estimated that various models of the TF-30 engine should cost from $344,000 to $450,000 each with the fat squeezed out. Using the probable cost or "will cost" estimates, PTC calculated that the entire order of TF-30 engines would cost $1,438,700,000. Using "should cost" unit cost figures, and allowing time for attainment of better levels of efficiency, PTC recommended that the Navy should attempt to negotiate a target cost of $771,000,000 for the huge orders of engines. Their proposed cost reduction goal of $667,000,000 was unheard of both in absolute magnitude and as a percentage of a major contract proposal.

The Naval Air Systems Command and, for that matter, the entire Pentagon procurement hierarchy, were outraged at the PTC "should cost" recommendations. The furious bureaucrats in the Naval Air Systems Command, feeling that they had been made to look bad by the PTC upstarts, and also eager to protect a pet giant contractor, initiated their own "evaluation" of the PTC report. On July 17, 1967, Mr. Graeme C. Bannerman, the Assistant Secretary of the Navy for Installations and Logistics, prepared an "Official Use Only" memorandum for Mr. Paul Nitze, the Deputy Secretary of Defense, summarizing the Navy's evaluation of the PTC "should cost" findings. He wrote: "The Naval Air Systems Command evaluation, concurred in by Admiral Gallantin and me, has stated that the obvious errors in the PTC report are such as to render all of its conclusions suspect."

Previously, in the Secretary of Defense's June meeting on the F-111 program, it had been agreed that Mr. Bannerman would use the PTC recommendations as a starting point for negotiating lower TF-30 engine prices with Pratt and Whitney. Mr. Bannerman rejected this course of action, writing: "This conclusion is based primarily on the fact that the report contains so many mistakes and gaps that it would raise many unanswerable questions and would be a source of embarrassment rather than help."

Mr. Bannerman concluded his blast at PTC, saying, "I have discussed the substance of this memo with Bob Frosch, who agrees completely." Dr. Frosch was the Assistant Secretary of the Navy for Research and Development. Thus, in one memorandum

Secretary Bannerman had arrayed all of the admirals of the Naval Air Systems Command, Admiral Gallantin, the head of the Navy Matériel Command, himself, and another assistant secretary solidly against the PTC "should cost" recommendation. However, it appeared that Mr. Bannerman neglected to clear this stand with his boss, Under Secretary of the Navy Charles Baird. Although Mr. Bannerman had written in his July 17 memorandum on the PTC study, "I have personally studied this report . . .", Secretary Baird was apparently unimpressed with the level of scholarship among the Navy procurement types. Commenting on the affair in an interview with a reporter afterward, Secretary Baird was quoted as saying, "I think I was the first official above the Captain level to see the report." * Mr. Baird had read the Naval Air Systems Command's scathing and somewhat emotional response to the PTC suggestion but then had taken the step, unusual among high Pentagon officials, of personally reviewing the PTC report itself, not just a second-hand interpretation of it. After reviewing the Naval Air Systems Command report, Mr. Baird told a reporter:

I asked to see the original PTC report and the two seemed so much at odds I got the PTC people in here and talked to them myself. I felt they had done good service . . . an important service. Time will show it was a service to Pratt & Whitney too.†

A detailed review of the Naval Systems Command's "evaluation" of the "should cost" recommendations showed that they consisted for the most part of restatements of negotiating positions taken by Pratt & Whitney. Moreover, the Navy was apparently fed some bad numbers by Pratt & Whitney. Recalling the period in which his firm's findings were being challenged by the Navy, David Howard, then President of PTC, told a reporter: "They found some of the figures in the company records were entirely different than those cited in our report. That was a bad moment. Fortunately, we had copies of the original records." ‡

It quickly became apparent that the Naval Air Systems Com-

* Washington *Evening Star,* February 10, 1969.
† *Ibid.*
‡ *Ibid.*

mand was functioning as Pratt & Whitney's sales force and negotiating team on the Pentagon payroll. They were summarily relieved of responsibility for negotiating the Pratt & Whitney production contract. Full responsibility for fact-finding and contract negotiation was assigned instead to Gordon Rule, one of the Navy's toughest and most experienced contract specialists. For the record, Gordon Rule reported directly to Admiral Gallantin, the head of the Naval Matériel Command. In reality, Mr. Rule drew his authority directly from Deputy Secretary of Defense Paul Nitze.

Gordon Rule made good use of his new charter. He assembled a large team of cost estimators, auditors, and industrial engineers from all over the Department of Defense to perform another "should cost" study at Pratt & Whitney. This team, which utilized at one time or another more than fifty people was chartered on July 28, 1967, and was finally disbanded on July 15, 1968. The "should cost" study itself lasted approximately six months. By contrast, PTC had been allowed about eight people and about nine weeks to complete their study and submit their report. Whereas PTC spent about half their time attempting to get access to cost information, Gordon made sure that this problem was solved before he started work. Allowing for savings opportunities lost through the passage of time and a reduction in planned quantities of engines, Mr. Rule's "should cost" recommendations were fairly close to those of the earlier PTC study. He opened negotiations with Pratt & Whitney with a Navy position about $500,000,000 less than Pratt & Whitney had expected to get.

Mr. Rule conducted a tough, tenacious negotiation. He flatly rejected Pratt & Whitney's first definitive price proposal. On August 30, 1967, he wrote to the President of Pratt & Whitney, Mr. A. E. Smith, that his proposal was rejected and was being "returned as unacceptable for the reason that the proposed costs contained therein are considered to be excessive and unreasonable." He responded to Pratt & Whitney screams of anguish with little minilectures on the stewardship responsibilities of government procurement officers. For example, on November 9, 1967, having been accused of trying to tell Pratt & Whitney how to run their business, Mr. Rule wrote again to President Smith of Pratt & Whitney:

The "should cost" method of pricing must not be construed as an attempt on the part of the government to tell a contractor how to conduct his operation. If, for example, a contractor wishes to conduct a patently inefficient operation with excess indirect employees, poor estimating, labor that consistently fails to meet standards, lack of proper competitive subcontracting, abnormal spoilage and rework, etc., that is his business. It is the government's responsibility however, not to pay taxpayer's money for demonstrable inefficiencies in the manufacturing process of a sole-source supplier, regardless of the quality of the ultimate product.

Presidents of giant aerospace firms did not expect talk like this from their partners in the Pentagon. Pratt & Whitney got stubborn. Gordon Rule responded by putting Pratt & Whitney in the newspapers. Readers of Washington newspapers were treated to blow-by-blow accounts of Mr. Rule's negotiations with Pratt & Whitney. It was much more interesting than similar stories of holdout baseball stars dickering with their team managements. Moreover, the money at stake belonged to the taxpayers and the sums were huge. Gordon continued this refreshing and useful tactic throughout the long, complicated negotiations.

The F-111 program was beginning to come apart at the seams, and this, of course, complicated Gordon Rule's negotiations. The Navy's sabotage of the F-111B portion of the program was far advanced, and the British pulled out of the project before the engine negotiations could be completed. In addition, Secretary McNamara was replaced by Clark Clifford in early 1968, and this too removed some of the urgency, Nevertheless, Gordon Rule finally salvaged a negotiated reduction in engine prices totaling almost $200,000,000. In addition, he obtained commitments from Pratt & Whitney to improvements in their management practices, which it was hoped would result in further savings.

After negotiations with Pratt & Whitney were completed in June of 1968, administration of the F-111 engine contract was returned to the Naval Air Systems Command. Even though subsequent changes to Pratt & Whitney's contracts and further reductions in quantities of engines bought dissipated most, if not all, the negotiated savings, the work of Gordon Rule and his team was rightly regarded by cost control advocates as an outstanding achievement. As a minimum, they had fought Pratt & Whitney to a draw.

PTC, too, came in for a share of the praise and credit. On July 25, 1968, Deputy Secretary of Defense Paul Nitze wrote to David Howard, President of Performance Technology Corporation:

Dear Mr. Howard:

At his weekly staff meeting on June 17, 1968, the Secretary of Defense commended the Navy on the outcome of its negotiations with Pratt & Whitney Division of the United Aircraft Corporation. Performance Technology Corporation undertook the initial studies at Pratt & Whitney and many of the recommendations made in your report will be adopted by the company.

I want you to know of my personal satisfaction with the results of the Navy's efforts and my appreciation of the initial assistance provided by Performance Technology Corporation.

This was a note to gladden the heart of almost any long-frustrated cost control consultant in the military contracting business. It was small comfort to PTC, however. As a result of their "success" they had been made outlaws and for all practical purposes put out of business by the military procurement hierarchy. When, in the summer of 1967, the Naval Air Systems Command had failed in their attempts to discredit PTC professionally, and it had become apparent that the position they had taken in their Pratt & Whitney "should cost" study would be vindicated, they had been encouraged by one of Mr. Anthony's assistants to draft a proposal for applying their "should cost" skills to other large, overrun weapons contracts. PTC complied and drafted a paper outlining suggested applications of "should cost" throughout the Department of Defense. Subsequently, dozens of copies of the draft PTC proposal were distributed throughout the procurement hierarchy and to politically powerful giant contractors. The procurement community panicked. They lashed out at the nearest vulnerable group, which was PTC. In his post-mortem interview with the Washington *Star,* PTC President Dave Howard, commenting on his disastrous proposal, said: "Somebody got hold of it, made copies and circulated it throughout the Pentagon. One guy came to me and said, "Dave, you just committed suicide!" *

The Air Force procurement gang got the contract to rub out PTC. The Air Force set them up by the simple expedient of "forgetting" to pay them on contracts they were performing.

According to Dave Howard's newspaper interview, the Air Force began withholding payment in the summer of 1967. By October the Air Force owed PTC about 150 percent of the company's net worth. However, they were assured by their Air Force project officers that payment would be forthcoming and were urged to stay on the job. By December, the Air Force owed the company about 170 percent of its net worth, and PTC could no longer borrow money to stay in business. At that time, the Air Force issued a contract change notice to PTC's principal contract unilaterally moving the contract's projected completion date from several months in the future to two days in the past and adjusting the total price of the contract downward drastically. In effect, they were told that their contractual period of performance was terminated retroactively but that they would have to continue work until the assignment was finished without additional pay. PTC was given the chance of accepting the illegal termination with a huge loss or fighting the case through the Armed Services Board of Contract Appeals and the courts. The latter course might have taken years with no money coming in meanwhile. PTC would have been bankrupt immediately. Since they were in no position to conduct a long legal fight, PTC had to give in to the Air Force's blackmail and accept a completely arbitrary change of contract terms which, in the end, cost them about half their net worth.

The combination of the financial catastrophe which the government had contrived for PTC and their blacklisting which prevented their getting new business caused the company to cut its staff from twenty-four to two people. In the spring of 1968, PTC went out of business entirely for a time and thereafter was revived only periodically when various of its former consultants used the firm as a vehicle for doing consulting business they had obtained.

* Washington *Evening Star,* February 10, 1969.

At the time of the great "should cost" scare in the summer of 1967, the entire military spending coalition was eager to kill PTC as an object lesson to other consulting firms. If PTC had prospered or, for that matter, even survived their recommendations to take $600,000,000 from one of the most respected of the procurement lodge brothers, every hungry consulting firm in the country would have been tempted to emulate them, and the flood gates would have been open. It could have ruined the entire racket.

The Air Force procurement and systems management people had independent reasons for wanting to kill PTC. For one thing, they were very angry with me over the Minuteman disclosures, and as demonstrated by their threats, they seemed to think they could somehow deter me in the future by hurting my former associates. Most importantly, however, they wanted to guard against repetition of the office of the Secretary of Defense's TF-30 strategy in which PTC's consultants were employed as shock troops. The Air Force was especially worried about the new Mark II avionics program for the F-111. "Avionics" was the term applied to collections of radar and communications sets, navigation aids, and other flight and fire control equipment in aircraft. The F-111's original set of avionics, called the Mark I, was considered good by the Air Force but not good enough. Consequently, beginning in 1965, the Air Force mounted a concerted sales effort to promote an improved system called the Mark II. At the time, the system they envisoned was pictured in Air Force and contractor presentations and in trade journals as a natural evolutionary improvement in the Mark I system. While it was acknowledged that some additional development and start-up cost might be anticipated, these were pictured as minimal because of the already advanced state of development of components of the system. As early as June 6, 1966, the competitors for the new Mark II system, especially Autonetics, were releasing pictures of their new equipment already designed and manufactured and ready to be plugged into the F-111. Based on their glowing picture of technical excellence, coupled with a low price, Autonetics won the Mark II competition over its competitors, Sperry-Rand and Hughes Aircraft. After winning the competition,

Autonetics ran paid advertisements announcing their success in the competition and offering their equipment, already developed and ready to install in other aircraft.*

Sad to say, none of this was true. Before the contract was even awarded, the Air Force had detected 1,062 deficiencies in Autonetics' technical proposal. The Air Force contract people contended that Autonetics had agreed to correct all these deficiencies without cost. However, this proved too difficult for Autonetics. Their technical proposal was, quite simply, a fairy tale. So the technical requirements for Autonetics' Mark II avionics system were downgraded, and a new set of specifications, called the A-1 specifications, were drawn up in September of 1966. Again, according to the Air Force records, Autonetics agreed to meet these degraded specifications and very generously did not increase their original bid of $39,000,000 for research and development and $106,000,000 for the first production order of just over 200 sets. Autonetics' contract, a modification of the Charles Package Plan or Total Package Procurement, was put in force as a subcontract on General Dynamics' overall F-111 program. After the Air Force had added estimates for General Dynamics' portion of the Mark II, money for additional production, provisions for change orders support, and other slush fund items, they arrived at a total cost for the entire program of $610,000,0000. The Air Force program management people had once again overestimated the efficiency of total-package contracting and underestimated the brazenness of their contractors and their ability to jack up prices. By March 30, 1967, Autonetics' asking price for a further degraded 200-set system had risen to $356,700,000. Still, Autonetics was proposing 350 deviations from the A-1 specification. Some of these deviations represented such serious degradation in the systems performance that the prime contractor, General Dynamics, would not accept them without approval from the Air Force. At the same time, General Dynamics announced that their price for modifying the airplane to accept the Mark II system, installing it, and testing through the first pro-

* See the Military Budget and National Economic Priorities hearings before the Subcommittee on Economy in Government of the Joint Economic Committee, Part II, June 17, 1969, page 820.

duction batch would be $494,800,000. This resulted in a total for the two contracts of $851,500,000, without Air Force slush fund additions.

Meanwhile, the entire F-111 program was out of control, with cost increases pouring in so rapidly that even keeping track of them became a major chore. The Pentagon's multilayered organizational structure and cumbersome communications simply could not keep up with the rapidly escalating cost increases. In addition to the F-111 systems program office in the Aeronautical Systems Division at Wright Field, there were F-111 systems offices at the headquarters of Air Force Systems Command at Andrews Air Force Base, in the Air Staff in the Pentagon, and finally, Mr. McNamara, with the assistance of Secretary Anthony and Bill George, were attempting to keep up as well. For a time, each of the several offices had different sets of figures, none of which matched the figures being used by the contractor. In an attempt to bring some order out of this chaos, a single central office for collecting and disseminating F-111 program cost estimates was established in the headquarters of Air Force Systems Command. One of the Systems Command's best cost analysts, with additional assistance from time to time, manned this office and served as the single source of F-111 cost estimates for Air Force headquarters and the Office of the Secretary of Defense. Bill George, I, and the Air Staff analysts responsible for keeping our respective bosses informed all obtained our F-111 program estimates directly from the office at AFSC headquarters.

By April of 1967, the Air Force could no longer pretend that the Autonetics situation was just another General Dynamics subcontractor problem. General Dynamics had pitched it back to the Air Force. Even though Autonetics' $145,000,000 contract had been highly advertised as another in the series of miraculous total-package procurements, the alternative of simply enforcing the contract was apparently not considered by any of the parties involved. Autonetics had supposedly made firm commitments to performance specifications, but these requirements had been degraded again and again. Apparently ignoring the fact that the contract included an absolute ceiling of $187,000,000 in payments to Autonetics for the specified guidance sets, not degraded ones, negotiations between the Air Force and Autonetics started with the contractor's latest revised proposal of $357,000,000. A tentative agreement was reached with Autonetics on a price of $297,-000,000 for development and production of the degraded avionics sets. The Air Force also stipulated that the not-to-exceed price would be reduced if Autonetics could not demonstrate that any increases above their original price were due to changes directed by the government.

At that point the Air Force's latest procurement miracle was less than ten months old, but already it was in deep trouble. Estimates of the cost overrun had skyrocketed and were increasing almost daily. For all practical purposes Autonetics' technical guarantees had dissolved. Instead of attempting to correct the program's multitudinous problems or, failing that, to terminate the contract for default, the Air Force rushed forward to commit the Department of Defense as deeply as possible to continuation of the program. Sensing that the Mark II program might be canceled if the full magnitude of the financial disaster became known at the Office of the Secretary of Defense, the generals in the Air Staff and the Systems Command decided to do what came naturally and lie about it.

A new estimate for the Mark II Avionics program was prepared to be included in a memorandum to be sent by Secretary of the Air Force Harold Brown to the Secretary of Defense, asking for approval for a full-speed go-ahead on the Mark II program. In this estimate, the generals deliberately omitted the costs of several items and arbitrarily reduced others. On May 4, 1967, Harold Brown's memorandum for the Secretary of Defense went forward. It said:

I recommend that you approve proceeding with the Mark II program as defined by the April 17 proposal which provides a firm baseline in terms of specifications and a "not to exceed" target price on the current schedule.

I do not know whether Harold Brown was a party to this deception or an innocent dupe of his generals. What is clear, however, is that despite the definite wording of the memorandum, the "firm baseline in terms of specifications" was being ignored by the contracting parties. Worse, the cost estimates were plucked from thin air, or from someplace else, by the generals. Harold Brown included in his memorandum to the Secretary of Defense an estimate of $704,000,000 for the Mark II program, including the F-111K (the British model), or $580,000,000 without the K model, which was expiring at the time.

All the while, our ace analyst in charge of keeping control of the "official" cost estimates on the F-111 was trying to keep up with the fluid situation. He received a call from an officer in the Air Staff who directed him to delete the support items from the official estimate and to make certain other "adjustments." Unluckily for him our analyst had already furnished "unadjusted" figures to his other customers. I had been given an estimate a week or so before which was $229,000,000 higher than the "adjusted" figure provided the Secretary of Defense. With the estimated cost leaping forward almost daily, our analyst at the Systems Command headquarters had, just the day before the "adjustments," given Bill George an estimate $385,000,000 higher than the figure included in Secretary Brown's memorandum.

In a departure from his usual practice, Secretary Brown had not asked either Mr. Marks or me to comment on the "revised" figures. The reaction to Harold Brown's memorandum by the Office of the Secretary of Defense was also unusual. On the bottom of this memorandum sent forward was the notation "Approved by:" with a blank for the approving officer's signature. Harold Brown's memorandum had been promptly returned with the initials "CRV" penned in the approval space. These were the initial of Cyrus R. Vance, then Deputy Secretary of Defense. Neither Bill George nor, so far as I know, Robert Anthony were consulted by Mr. Vance prior to his approval of the very questionable Mark II program.

Bill George, in possession of "unadjusted" Mark II cost estimates, quickly spread the word in the Office of the Secretary of Defense that they had been snookered by the Air Force. It was worse than they thought. Once I learned of the deception, I went to our fountainhead of F-111 cost information at Systems Command headquarters to find out what was really going on. I learned that in addition to the arbitrary reductions in the cost estimates made by the generals, they had included only the cost of research and development and the first order of 207 production units in the figures sent forward to the Office of Secretary of Defense. The total program was about 800 production units (the exact number was classified). At the time Deputy Secretary Vance had given his go-ahead to the Mark II program, the official "unadjusted" Air Force estimate for the complete program was $1,232,100,000, excluding the dying F-111K British model. This was $752,000,000 more than the comparable figure in Harold Brown's memorandum to the Secretary of Defense.

Uncovering this bit of high-priced, high-level hankypanky caused a strong reaction, but not the sort a hard-pressed taxpayer might expect. No general officers were asked to resign. The only person reprimanded was our ace analyst at Air Force Systems Command manning the office responsible for disseminating consistent if not altogether accurate F-111 cost information, and he was not reprimanded for furnishing false information. He had nothing to do with that. He got in trouble for supplying Bill George and me with "unadjusted" cost figures. Even though he had supplied us with the figures before receiving instructions to phony them up, our conscientious cost analyst was in serious difficulty for telling us the truth. Presumably he should have anticipated the need to lie and done his duty. The civilian cost analyst, having betrayed his masters, however inadvertently, was removed from his job and replaced with a more pliable and perceptive military officer. For several months thereafter, the cost analyst was given nothing to do. He became a social outcast. He was moved to a remote corner of a large bullpen with no one near him. Except for his bravest friends, no one would talk to him. He usually had to eat lunch alone. Periodically, the colonel in charge of his section would summon him to be belabored verbally for consorting with Fitzgerald and Bill George. After a long period of penance, our ace cost analyst was finally allowed to run an adding machine again.

Bill George made so much noise about the Air Force's deliberate deception on the matter of the Mark II cost estimates that it could not be completely ignored, although most of the high-level civilians and generals seemed to hope the incident would just be overlooked. Dr. Al Flax, the Air Force Assistant Secretary for Research and Development, was elected to explain the matter to Mr. McNamara. It was decided to acknowledge what Mr. McNamara presumably already had learned from Bill George and to account for the $385,000,000 discrepancy rather than the true larger discrepancy of $752,000,000. A simple, straightforward story was concocted. Using the simplest possible application of the Back-up Principle, the $385 million discrepancy was accounted for as follows:

"Error"	$170 million
"Omission"	$215 milion
Total	$385 million

The sum of the two figures equaled the total discrepancy, and that made everything all right.

At the luncheon table in Air Force Mess #1 (incidentally, the best restaurant in Washington) Al Flax told us of his visit to Mr. McNamara's office to explain the Mark II cost estimate discrepancy. Dr. Flax said that Secretary McNamara looked very grim at the outset of the session and that he expected an explosion when he broke the news. Dr. Flax said that he did the best that he could with his material and then was surprised that the Secretary of Defense simply stared at him for a long while. Dr. Flax said this was the worst part of the whole session. Finally, Dr. Flax told us, Mr. McNamara said quietly, "Well, all right, Al, thank you," and dismissed him.

In terms of strategy for controlling the Mark II cost growth, I favored an attempt to hold the procurement generals to their commitment on the Mark II. The fact that the cost estimates for the program which Mr. Nitze had approved was revealed to be a deliberate lie had embarrassed the generals greatly. It was my hope that fear of further embarrassment might motivate our procurement and program management people to attempt to control the runaway cost for once. At the time, I was convinced that if our procurement people were to spend half as much time and energy attempting to control cost as they spent in deception and concealment, our cost problems would be minimal.

I hoped, as did many of my coworkers, that our bosses would simply enforce the Mark II contract. After all the noise about "calling the sheriff" if big contractors failed to live up to their commitments, and the use of this shibboleth to fend off cost controls, we had a chance to employ the principle. For once, we had a definitized contract to work with. True, the Air Force had already started to cave in by agreeing tentatively to technical changes, but all the changes had been for the convenience of the contractors. The net effect of the tentative changes, as usual, was to degrade the product. Significantly, no one, least of all Autonetics, really expected the Air Force to enforce the Mark II contract. Autonetics immediately began spending money with their usual carefree abandon. The supposedly firm contractual price ceiling had absolutely no effect on Autonetics' management behavior.

We hoped for contract enforcement but did not expect it. By then, there was a tacit understanding that contracts with big firms were nothing more than shifting reflections of the financial needs and performance prospects of the giants. This understanding was evident in the behavior, not the talk, of the "call the sheriff" crowd. The principal public declaimers of the "call the sheriff" approach were also the most energetic private opponents of strict enforcement of contracts. The slogan was in fact nothing more than a device to fend off the gathering of facts which could be used to protect the taxpayers' interests when the contractual façade crumbled.

Recognizing that we needed facts to protect against runaway Mark II price increases, a group favoring factual identification of the real effect of Mark II specification changes coalesced within the Air Force. I strongly supported this faction. The exercise favored by our faction came to be called a "technical trace." Clearly, if we were to change the price based on value to the government, the price would be reduced, not increased by hundreds of millions of dollars as Autonetics and their government allies were suggesting.

In addition, realizing that we would sooner or later end up

negotiating a new price based on Autonetics' cost and technical experience, I proposed a quick but thorough overall technical audit and a comprehensive should-cost study for the Mark II. There was a widespread feeling at the time that the Mark II should be promptly canceled and a new start made on improved F-111 avionics. Decisions on the program up to that time had been based largely on the technical assertions in the various sales pitches. A competent technical audit could have quickly provided a factual basis for deciding whether to go forward with program or to cancel it. The price of whatever program was finally decided upon could then have been based on results of the should-cost study. My bosses endorsed the proposed technical trace, but I got absolutely nowhere with my suggestions for the overall technical audit and should-cost study.

Bill George was more successful. He had been following the Mark II program closely for some time, and in a March 29, 1967, letter to Mr. Anthony, he had recommended a number of improvement measures for the Mark II, including a should-cost study. In this letter, he told Secretary Anthony that "from all the information I have it is clear that Mark II avionics represents the largest area of current growth on the F-111 program." His March 29th proposal had not been accepted at the time, but, on the other hand, it had not been rejected either. So, when it became obvious in May that the program was completely out of control, Mr. Anthony accepted Bill George's suggestion and directed my boss, Ted Marks, to conduct an independent cost study which would include estimates of the program's probable cost, or "will cost," and what the system should cost under an improved mode of management.

Unfortunately, Ted Marks did not immediately move to carry out this instruction straightforwardly. Instead, he "negotiated" the instruction with Bob Charles, the Assistant Secretary of the Air Force for Installations and Logistics, before passing them on. The "negotiated" instructions emasculated Mr. Anthony's direction to conduct a should-cost study. On June 30, 1967, using the "negotiated" direction as a basis, the Air Staff directed the Systems Command to follow "the normal contractor proposal fact-finding process" on the Mark II cost study. On July 12, 1967,

Mr. Anthony reinstructed Ted Marks to do a should-cost study and this time volunteered Bill George to assist by working directly with the cost-study team.

This time, Ted Marks made good use of the strong, unequivocal instructions from Bob Anthony on the should-cost study. On July 31, he took Mr. Anthony's instructions to Secretary Brown to get his backing for the project before directing the Air Staff and the Systems Command to carry them out. Harold Brown's reaction was quick and positive. That same day he endorsed the instructions from Bob Anthony, and returned the documents to Ted Marks with a handwritten notation at the bottom:

Ted, I am greatly concerned with the Mark II avionics costs. They are too high to begin with, they may include pyramided profits, and as the program gets into technical and schedule trouble the price for fixing it will also go up. We need a good cost scrub to establish a baseline and to keep the contractors honest. Please get on with it urgently. H. Brown.

Ted Marks immediately instructed the Air Staff and Systems Command by telephone to get moving. He also told them that both Bill George and I would be members of the cost-study team, which caused consternation in the Air Staff and the Systems Command. General Red Carter called Mr. Marks' office to say that neither Bill George nor Fitzgerald could be included in the cost-study team without written instructions from the Secretary's office. They got them. With unprecedented speed, Ted Marks sent the necessary written direction to the Air Staff the next day, August 1. Within hours, the Air Staff relayed the instructions to the field, informing the Systems Command and the F-111 SPO that Fitzgerald, George, and company would arrive at the F-111 program office in Dayton, Ohio, the next morning to kick off "industrial efficiency survey aspects" of the study.

The high-water mark of attempts to gain businesslike control of runaway weapons systems cost was probably reached on the morning of August 2, 1967. The Navy's treachery in attempting to subvert the Pratt & Whitney should-cost study had just been exposed, and Gordon Rule's project was getting underway. The Air Force opponents of tough cost reduction and control measures had been thoroughly discredited, and I was on my way to do what I had wanted to do since entering the Pentagon. I was no longer a one-man band. Seemingly, at least, I had all the authority and high-level direction I needed to get on with the job. Not only that, but everything had been done through channels.

Before Bill George and I met with the cost-study team to lay out the work to be done on the Mark II should-cost study, we met with Maj. Gen. "Zeke" Zoeckler, the F-111 Systems Program Director, and his deputy, Brig. Gen. John Chandler. The meeting lasted more than half the day. The two generals did not want to do a should-cost study, and they tried to talk us out of the idea. Worse yet, they wanted to bury the General Dynamics portion of the Mark II costs in the overall F-111 program, where it would be lost to separate view. This was a more or less standard practice on big programs like F-111 with practically unlimited funds. It was common practice on the Minuteman program and had been on the F-111 until then.

Submerging all or a part of the costs of ill-considered changes in the originally defined program had contributed greatly to basic F-111 program cost growth. This had become a bone of contention between McNamara and the military. McNamara and his close associates wanted to keep separate the cost of "improvements" such as the Mark II, both for better visibility of what was happening on the program and to minimize the appearance of cost overruns on the unfortunate basic program. On the other hand, the Air Force, secure in the knowledge that increases in the basic program would be blamed on McNamara's poor judgment in the early decisions, didn't care what the program cost. Add-ons, though, especially Air Force promotions such as the Mark II, made the military look bad when the cost shot up out of sight. They preferred to show only the tip of the cost iceberg in such cases.

General Chandler gave us his long "type-model series" lecture, killing time to tell us something we already knew. Most Mark II systems were to be installed on the F-111 airplanes. "F" was the type designation for "fighter," Chandler told us, as though instructing the local high school ROTC class. "111" was the model number of the type, and the "D" suffix indicated it was the fourth in the series of the model. General Chandler said he was telling us all this so we would understand why we should be content with another "born yesterday" estimate of the F-111D type-model-series and not attempt to separate incremental costs of the Mark II. It was tradition, he said, to start afresh, with all that had gone before forgiven, with each new series. According to our instructor, we would be violating tradition if we insisted on keeping track of Mark II costs separately.

Bill George and I rejected this argument, pointing out that "born again" cost estimates (called "de novo" estimates by the Harvards) were one reason we lost control of programs. We had separate contractual agreements for the Mark II with both General Dynamics and Autonetics, and for once we were not going to be flimflammed. Besides, we had already been through this argument with the Air Staff and the Systems Command headquarters, and had negotiated an agreement that the Mark II program would be defined by the contractors' April 1967 proposals. The already compromised April 1967 baseline would be our reference point. Finally, we said, we had orders to keep the Mark II program separate from both the Office of the Secretary of Defense and the Secretary of the Air Force.

General Chandler seemed quite upset at our rejection of the proposal to bury part of the Mark II cost. With amens from General Zoeckler, he summed up his underlying fear of full disclosure. Regarding General Chandler's fear, Bill George wrote in his trip report: "Both he and General Zoeckler expressed the fear that the Mark II program will be cut off if we use the April 14 definition because costs are too high. It is clear that they do not want the total cost of the systems stated."

We told the generals that we would just have to take our chances on the Mark II program being canceled, and insisted that we move on to talk to the cost-study team who had been waiting for us nearly all day. Bill George asked General Zoeckler if the General intended to sit in on our meeting with the cost-study team. "Of course I am going to attend your meeting," General Zoeckler replied. "You don't think I would leave you alone to influence my people?"

After General Zoeckler had made a final and futile attempt to talk us out of the should-cost study, we met with the team. Discussion of the upcoming Mark II study quickly focused on various approaches to identification of inefficiencies in the operations of General Dynamics and Autonetics. As the discussion progressed, General Zoeckler became increasingly uneasy. Finally, he played his trump. He simply countermanded my instructions regarding identification and attempts to minimize inefficiency. "Inefficiency is national policy," the General proclaimed. He then went on to explain that inefficiency in the operations of military contractors was necessary to the attainment of "social goals." He said that contractor inefficiency provided for such things as (1) equal employment opportunity programs, (2) seniority clauses in union agreements, (3) programs for employment of the handicapped, (4) apprentice programs, (5) aid to small business, (6) aid to distressed labor areas, and (7) encouragement of improvements to plant layouts and facilities.

Summing up, the General explained that pressing for efficient cost management was undesirable because it diverted management's attention from more important matters. This was the same refrain that had been sung for me by the old hands during my initiation into the mysteries of the Pentagon lodge. However, this was the first time I had heard the philosophy employed by a general officer in specific instructions to the troops. It was plain that if General Zoeckler's instructions were allowed to stand, nothing would come of the should-cost study. I tried to explain to the general and the group that we, as a nation and a society, could afford the nice things the General was afraid we would lose only because our productive activities had been highly efficient. I also cited our very specific instructions in this instance, but the General could not be moved. Finally I said, "O.K. Zeke, let's just identify the cost of all these things you are worried about jeopardizing and let our leaders decide how much money they are willing to allocate to them."

When I returned to Washington, I told Ted Marks that General Zoeckler's policy statement would have to be dealt with quickly and positively if we were to have any hopes of saving money on the Mark II program. Mr. Marks seemed concerned, but he gave no indication of what sort of action would be taken to put the Mark II should-cost study back on track.

Bill George and I continued to work with the cost-study team in the field, but the whole operation was conducted under the cloud of Zoeckler's policy statement. Some of the working-level cost analysts and industrial engineers attempted to identify inefficiencies but without much enthusiasm. At the Autonetics plant, senior Air Force officers actively undercut the should-cost effort.

After several weeks had passed, I again reported to Mr. Marks that the policy conflict was unresolved and was killing the should-cost effort. Again I received no definite indication of action from Mr. Marks. However, a few days later, on September 11, 1967, I received a copy of the talk advocating the should-cost approach which had been suppressed the previous year. The paper bore the notation "Approved for publication, L. Marks, Jr."

I leafed through the document, the transcript of my "Come to God" speech at the Systems Command revival thirteen months before. Not a word had been changed. Even the heresy of Francis Bacon was to be tolerated. I was gratified at being tossed this bone, however belatedly, but I could not help reflecting at the time how different things might have been if any one of my civilian bosses had found the courage a year earlier to write "Cleared for Publication."

As more weeks passed with no action on the part of the top civilians in the Air Force, the procurement generals and their civilians grew bolder in their suppressions of the should-cost concept and of the people who advocated it. General Zoeckler's successful repudiation of both official policy and specific direction had given them renewed courage. However, the Mark II should-cost study was not yet dead. Bill George, with help from Gordon Rule, was still pressing his sales effort.

On October 20, Gordon and Bill met with Dr. Anthony to review progress on the Pratt & Whitney should-cost study, and to discuss prospects for applying the approach elsewhere. The subject of Air Force resistance to the should-cost approach came up, and the discussion was recorded in Bill George's memorandum of the meeting:

Gordon then interjected his understanding that the Air Force was opposed to the should-cost approach. In particular, he noted that Mr. Charles (Assistant Secretary of the Air Force I&L) was opposed to this approach on the grounds that it reflects poorly on past and current Air Force procurement practices, and that the Air Force always does a form of should-cost.

Mr. Anthony was surprised by Mr. Charles' statement. I confirmed that he had made these remarks at a meeting I attended, and added that Mr. Charles' concept of should-cost was very different than that being used at Pratt & Whitney. I also explained that, although some Air Force people (especially those in staff jobs and at higher levels) were opposed to this effort, there were many people in the field who understood and supported it.

With the F-111 program then rapidly degenerating (and with it the management reputations of Secretaries Anthony and Mc-Namara), the report of Air Force sabotage of the cost-reduction and control effort on the F-111 struck home. Eight days later, October 28, the Secretary of the Air Force received an "Official Use Only" memorandum from the Deputy Secretary of Defense, Mr. Nitze. Mr. Nitze wrote in part:

. . . I am concerned about the reports on Mark II costs and Autonetics' attempt to reprice the program without regard to their original contractual commitment. It is my understanding that the Air Force is conducting a "should cost" study of the proposed Mark II program. I am desirous that this approach be used to identify the areas for reduction in Mark II costs and that the results of this study be used as the basis for contract negotiations.

Also included in the two page memorandum were some specific instructions, among them:

1. Identify separately all General Dynamics costs clearly attributable to Mark II and insure that these costs are segregated from the cost of the work already on contract.

2. Identify contractor inefficiencies which can be eliminated through improved management control.

3. Insure that the negotiation proceeds from the "should cost" analysis and not from projections from historical costs.

The leaders of the procurement crowd, the generals and Bob Charles, brazenly ignored these crystal-clear instructions. Finally, on December 22, 1967, the Mark II cost-study team presented its pitifully inadequate findings to a large group of dignitaries in

the Pentagon. With the exception of some fragmentary, discon-
nected information on factory labor efficiency and the results of
a carefully staged but completely phony work sampling study at
Autonetics, the study was nothing more than the usual collection
of back-up data confirming that actual costs had exceeded plans
and would probably go up even higher. There were thirty-one
people in the large meeting, including two assistant secretaries
(Marks and Charles) one lieutenant general, four major generals,
two brigadier generals, assorted deputies, colonels, and senior
civilians. I was the sole objector to the charade.

At the close of the meeting, the Air Staff sent a wire to Air
Force Systems Command instructing them to proceed with
negotiations "with complete flexibility" on the Mark II. The
great should-cost scare was over. Just to make sure there was no
misunderstanding about this, Mr. Gordon Arthur, the Assistant
Chief of the Pricing Division at Systems Command, clarified the
instructions on December 26. Mr. Arthur pounded the last nail
in the should-cost coffin by telling the troops that "the 'efficiency'
studies will not be pursued further for this negotiation."

The Mark II program surfaced only occasionally after that.
However, despite their bravado, the Air Force procurement gang
never quite got up the nerve to definitize the Autontics contract
at a level which would let the contractor make money while I
was in the Pentagon. They did the next best thing, though, from
the viewpoint of picking the taxpayers' pocket, by allowing
Autonetics to continue working as though they had an open-
ended, undefinitized letter contract. Bill George and I and a
number of working level Air Force people in the field had documents which left no doubt that Autonetics was firmly committed
to delivering the originally specified Mark II system for a target
price of $145,000,000 and the ceiling price of $188,000,000 for the
complete development program plus production of 207 units.
This situation made a number of people quite nervous. On
March 13, 1968, an Autonetics representative visited Bill George
to talk over the situation. The Autonetics representative was
fearful that the Air Force might enforce the contract, which could
cause his company to lose $200,000,000 or more. According to Bill

George's memorandum for the record of his meeting with the Autonetics representative, Mr. Eyestone, the president of Autonetics (replacement for Norm Parker) and Mr. Moore, a vice-president for the parent corporation, North American Rockwell, met with a gaggle of generals and colonels to discuss the Mark II cost situation. According to the Autonetics representative, the Air Force delegation included Lieutenant General Terhune, Major General Keeling, Major General Higgins, Major General Zoeckler, Colonel Pugh, and Colonel Hanson.

Although Major General Keeling had originally asked for the meeting because he was concerned about Autonetics costs, the top management of Autonetics got the impression as the meeting progressed that the Air Force was willing to live with the higher costs. According to Bill George's visitor, "Lt. General Terhune did not seem displeased with the company's projections [they were going out the roof]. He said now that the program had been approved, his primary concern was getting the system to perform." What the generals really wanted was a list of "good news" items on the Mark II for their meeting the next day with Mr. Nitze and Mr. Anthony.

The Autonetics official said that his top management's impression of the Air Force's lack of concern about the runaway costs on the Mark II was confirmed three days later on March 8, when they were visited by Lieutenant General Milton and Brigadier General Teubner, General Milton had replaced Gen. Jack Merrell as Comptroller of the Air Force, and General Teubner had succeeded General Red Carter as Comptroller of the Air Force Systems Command. The Autonetics official said that generals Milton and Teubner gave no indication that they were concerned about Mark II costs.

The visitor from Autonetics had heard that certain people in the Pentagon were gravely concerned about the costs of the Mark II system, and said that a small minority within Autonetics management groups were also. However, they kept receiving signals from the Air Force that everything was all right, which made it very difficult to stimulate meaningful cost reductions and control within the company. The Autonetics official was concerned that the Department of Defense might insist on enforcement of the contract. In the absence of meaningful cost controls, this would have meant financial disaster to Autonetics. The visitor said he hoped someone would tell his top management to "shape up" for the good of the company.

Despite giving Autonetics the benefit of every doubt, the Air Force could not identify more than $20,000,000 of Mark II cost increase as possibly attributable to government-directed changes. This set off another bitter internal debate within the Air Force during the spring and summer of 1968. Secretary Robert H. Charles, the great advocate of contractor responsibility, fixed-price contracts, "disengagement," and proclaimed inventor of total-package procurement, rejected the suggestion that the Mark II contract be firmed up and definitized at a target price based on the original bid of $145,000,000 plus the most generous estimate of govenment responsible changes of $20,000,000 for a total of $165,000,000. Secretary Charles' decision was that big contractors should not lose money working for the government. He rejected all suggestions to enforce the Autonetics contract on the basis of the contractor's legal commitments. Still, no one could screw up enough courage to renegotiate the contract at a higher price.

The Mark II went on to become one of the great disasters of military procurement. Unfortunately, most of my subsequent knowledge came from newspaper accounts. On May 11, 1969, the Washington *Post,* in an article on the Mark II, summarized the growth of cost estimates for the program of "about 800 units":

June, 1966	$610 million
December, 1966	$850 million
June, 1967	$1,110 million
January, 1968	$1,510 million
November, 1968	$2,510 million

On September 22, 1969, the *Post* reported that the Air Force planned to abandon the Mark II program after only 172 sets of the equipment had been built. Rising costs were given as the major factor in the decision.

On October 28, 1969, the *Weekly Digest* for the Secretary of the Air Force (a new Secretary by then) reported:

Efforts to definitize the Mark II purchase order #181 between General Dynamics and Autonetics have been in work for almost three years. Cost increases on the Mark II and difficulty in establishing a baseline for the increases have been responsible for the delay in definitizing based on mutually acceptable adjustments to the target cost, price, and ceiling.

This assessment ignored the fact that Autonetics' Mark II contract *had* been definitized immediately after Autonetics had won the so-called competition in 1966. The authors of the assessment, the Air Force's procurement specialists, were announcing that the old contract, too tough for their bumbling contractor, was to be redefined based on Autonetics' actual performance.

The Mark II next made the news in the November 18, 1971 edition of the Washington *Star*. The occasion was the delivery of the first F-111D, the Mark II "type-model-series" so dear to the hearts of generals Zoeckler and Chandler. The *Star* quoted the Air Force press release as saying "the basic aircraft has now been produced and are now being equipped with the recently perfected Mark II avionics package." The *Star* went on to report that the Mark II avionics package was far from "perfected" and that it was known in the Air Force "as the 'D-minus avionics' because it had been degraded so badly from the original specifications." The *Star* reported that the Air Force had originally asked for a guarantee of 270 hours mean time between failure for the Mark II system but was actually getting only twenty-five hours, less than one tenth of the original specifications. The *Star* reported that standards had also been relaxed in such critical areas as accuracy of the navigation system.

The *Star* said that the original $145,000,000 total package contract for Autonetics had grown to $855,000,000 and that the average cost of the F-111D avionics was $4,100,000 per unit. The original cost estimate for the Mark II was around $750,000 per unit.

When the Mark II cost control efforts collapsed in late 1967, I was tempted to conclude that my troubleshooting efforts were wasted. However, when I reflected on the outcome of sick programs I had backed away from, I decided that troubleshooting efforts were probably worthwhile. Sick programs left alone to run their natural course often turned out to be worse catastrophes than those we tried to control even when the control attempts were unsuccessful.

A prime example of a sick program I backed away from was SRAM, the Short Range Attack Missile. SRAM was a nuclear warhead missile designed to be fired at ground targets from the FB-111, the bomber version of the F-111, and the B-52, the Air Force's standard heavy bomber. Development of the program was authorized in 1965. In early 1966, the Boeing Company and Martin-Marietta Corporation were selected as finalists in the competition for the total package contract. Both competitors were given large contracts to finance the definition phase of the program. I was assigned as a member of a team called the Special Air Staff Group, or SASG, with responsibility to assure the Chief of Staff and the Secretary of the Air Force that the source selection followed the established rules and that the final decision would "withstand any subsequent critical appraisal." The procedure was designed to head off a repetition of the intense criticism, much of it well founded, which followed the selection of General Dynamics as contractor on the F-111 program.

It was clear from the start that the senior military officers at Aeronautical Systems Division, where program management responsibility was assigned, favored giving the contract to Boeing. However, both contractors were given considerable help. For example, both were told the Air Force's planned funding limitations. This helped them considerably in preparing their price proposals and, in addition, assured that neither proposal would exceed the amount considered salable to the office of the Secretary of Defense. In reality, the price competition was reduced to a game in which the contractor tried to guess how the Air Force would prefer to see the overall cost estimate allocated. In the technical areas of the proposal, both contractors were benefited by a process known in the trade as "technical transfusion." When weakness in the contractors technical plans were detected, Air Force engineers would give the contractor design teams hints as to how they should improve their proposal to make it more acceptable.

One early example of a seemingly fatal engineering flaw supposedly solved by transfusion was the case of the flight-control system on the Martin missile. The Air Force engineers assigned to the SRAM program had conducted an analysis of the probable flight path of the Martin missile after release from a low-flying aircraft. The engineers showed our team, the SASG, a computerized plotting, or trace, of the flight profile of the Martin missile. Because of the presumed flaws in the flight-control system, the computer trace depicted the missile striking the ground, burrowing deep into the earth, then, a little later on, climbing from the hole to continue on its way to destroy its intended target. Several members of the SASG suggested that perhaps this performance characteristic, assuming the Air Force analysis to be correct, might disqualify Martin's proposal. The Aeronautical Systems Division engineers, however, viewed the problem with calm scientific detachment and, while assuring us that their analysis was correct, stated that the problem would be cured by "transfusion."

Unfortunately, despite numerous technical transfusions (or maybe because of them), the Boeing missile could not meet all of the Air Force's specifications according to the engineering analyses. Although the theoretical studies indicated that the Boeing missile would have a number of outsanding features, they also indicated that it could not fly the basic mission specified by the Air Force. This situation led to considerable tension between the SASG and the staff engineers at Wright Field. The ASD engineers were torn between their desire to please their military bosses by showing the Boeing missile as superior and a natural reluctance to leave themselves open for blame later on when the project went sour. Their solution was to try to avoid discussion of Boeing's technical problems with members of the SASG. Finally, as the deadline for choosing a winner in the Boeing—Martin competition approached, the engineers on our team became more persistent. A few days before the source selection recommendations were scheduled to be given to Secretary Brown and the Chief of Staff, the ASD engineers broke down and told all. The Boeing missile as proposed just would not perform the required mission. We immediately took this issue to General Terhune, then the commander of ASD, who was in charge of evaluating the competing proposals. General Terhune tried to minimize the importance of the engineering analysis and stoutly defended the Boeing proposal. After the engineering members of the SASG had belabored the General for nearly an hour on the Boeing missile's shortcomings, the General blurted out, "If you guys are suggesting that I'm prejudiced, you're right. I have confidence in the Boeing company."

Our exchange with General Terhune took place late on a Sunday evening at Wright-Patterson Air Force Base in Dayton, Ohio. The next morning, after our team had returned to the Pentagon, we received a message from ASD stating that they had received a communication from Boeing guaranteeing that their proposed SRAM system would meet the Air Force specifications regardless of what engineering analyses then showed. They would lay their proud company's reputation on the line in the upcoming total package contract. After lengthy arguments between the SASG engineers and the Aeronautical Systems Division, it was agreed that we would proceed with the presentation of findings to the Secretary and the Chief of Staff without settling the controversy. The ASD team would make their presentation which pointed to Boeing as the winner without making a definite recommendation, and the SASG would separately present the results of the engineering analyses showing the Boeing proposal to be deficient.

The SASG spent most of the night preceding the report to the Secretary and the Chief preparing a detailed presentation, complete with VuGraphs, to be given by our team chief, Brig. Gen. Andy Evans. The next morning, the adversaries and the judges, including Secretary Harold Brown and Air Force Chief of Staff John P. McConnell, gathered in the Command Post deep in the bowels of the Pentagon. Mr. Brown appeared nervous and preoccupied. Even though he supposedly had not received either the source selection report or our dissenting views, he praised the outstanding features of the Boeing proposal. He then told the gathering that he and the Chief had already discussed the matter and excused himself to attend to more pressing business.

The ASD briefing went off as planned, with no mention of the damning analysis of the proposed Boeing design. When General

Evans rose to give the SASG presentation, he appeared jittery and disorganized. This was very unlike Andy Evans, who, in addition to being one of the most capable of the generals I worked with in the Pentagon, was ordinarily one of the calmest. The reason for his discomfort soon became apparent. A higher authority had gotten to honest Andy Evans. He omitted the portion of his presentation showing the worst features of the Boeing proposal. When General Evans completed his presentation without making our case, I started to speak up, but one of my fellow deputies sitting next to me laid his hand on my arm and said, "Keep quiet. There is nothing you can do about it."

Ordinarily, presentations such as the one we had just completed on SRAM were followed in a few days—typically, about a week—by a formal announcement of the winner of the competition. That time, though, Boeing was proclaimed the winner within a few minutes. Before I even had time to complain to Ted Marks about how we had been railroaded, I was directed to meet with the other members of the SASG to draft a public announcement of the award of the SRAM total-package contract to Boeing. That last meeting of the Boeing SASG was as gloomy a gathering as I ever attended in the Pentagon. The work had been extra duty for most of us on the team, and we had invested many evenings and weekends of work in our effort to assure a sound and honest source selection It was most dispiriting to see our hard work go for nothing due to an apparently arbitrary decision at the last minute. Andy Evans was so embarrassed and disconsolate that no one had the heart to press him on what had happened at that time. We later learned that General Evans had been brought back into line at a meeting of senior generals from the Air Staff and the Air Force Systems Command shortly before the briefing of the Secretary and the Chief of Staff.

Andy Evans took a secret ballot poll of the SASG on which contractor should have been declared the winner on the basis of their final formal proposals. The vote came out eight for Martin, one for Boeing.

Needless to say, I was not at all proud of my role in the SRAM source selection. I was even less pleased with my decision to remain silent when the results began to come in. Boeing's total package SRAM contract awarded in November of 1966 specified a target price of $143,000,000 for research and development. By December of 1969, just before I left the Pentagon, the R&D contract cost estimate had grown to $409,000,000 for a missile system inferior to the one originally specified. Estimates of Boeing's manufacturing direct labor had increased by almost 1100 percent, their overhead by 350 percent, and their general and administrative cost by almost 500 percent. These increases laid the foundation for justifying the runaway increases in the cost of subsequent production units after the collapse of the total-package scheme.

Other trouble-plagued programs I had backed away from had not prospered either. Some time before I joined the Air Force I had been involved in the early stages of the development of the Mark 48 torpedo. The development contract for the Mark 48 had been awarded by the Navy to Westinghouse Electric Corporation in July of 1964. At that time, the Mark 48 had been touted as the Navy's model of weapons procurement, a parallel to the Air Force's later and much larger C-5A program. With my associates in PTC, I was working on management information systems under a contract to the program's technical advisory contractor, the Ordnance Research Laboratory of Pennsylvania State University. At that time PTC was a subsidiary, a division, of a larger consulting group called Management Systems Corporation, or MSC. In common with so many other models of procurement, the Mark 48 torpedo was in serious technical trouble almost from its inception. In August of 1964, less than two months after the program started, we saw definite indications of technical difficulties. By December of that same year the symptoms were unmistakable. The program was deathly ill.

It happened that my consulting associate who was primarily responsible for detecting the Mark 48 technical troubles had led our consulting team which had found the technical problem in the Minuteman guidance set the year before. We had been more or less quietly shunted off to other work after our embarrassing discovery on the Minuteman program, but not so on the Mark 48. The reaction in the Navy project office, among our compatriots at MSC, and especially at the Ordnance Research

Laboratory was emotional and nearly violent. This team was working assiduously to conceal the program's problems, and my associate's findings and continued probing literally reduced them to screaming tantrums. Some of the prima donnas at the Ordnance Research Laboratory attempted to entrap my probing associate in a contrived "security violation." Even after the clumsily attempted frame-up backfired and got Ordnance Research Laboratory in trouble instead of my associate, our counterparts in MSC charged him with security violations anyway. Even though the charges were untrue, the individuals leveling the charges, the president and vice-president of our parent company, could have made great difficulty for us. It was only after I promised that we would go away quietly that the charges were retracted.

Although there were mitigating circumstances to my backing away from the Mark 48 torpedo catastrophe, I was not especially proud of that performance either. The Mark 48, too, went on to gain notoriety as a champion in cost overruns, technical deficiencies, and late deliveries. To complete the dreary picture, the early attempts to control the Mark 48 program also hurt a conscientious government servant. The Navy contracting officer assigned to the Mark 48 program strongly supported and encouraged our efforts to get the facts when symptoms of trouble developed. Our conscientious contracting officer was eased out of procurement and eventually out of the Navy. When I last heard from him, he was a buyer for the Agency for International Development (AID) in Ghana.

In balance, as I summed up my experience after a year of intensive troubleshooting work at the end of 1967, it was plain that we could not, in good conscience, simply turn away from the sick weapons programs. They would not be made well by either "disengagement" or contractual gimmicks. The new "magic" contracts weren't working.

On the other hand, we could not afford any more frontal assaults either. We had lost most of our best troops. In addition to the personal disasters visited upon Joe Warren, Art Cruikshank, and the people at PTC, we had been deprived of the services of numerous cost analysts, auditors, and industrial engineers through sudden unscheduled transfers and through severe intimidation.

We even had difficulty keeping people on the relatively bland educational projects. As Red Carter put it, "The cannibals eat my missionaries as fast as I send them out."

There had to be a better way.

FIVE

THE BIG ISSUE

After the experience of 1967, I decided to proceed cautiously in attempting major cost-saving actions until the Department of Defense's policy on genuine cost reduction and control was clarified. Public utterances on the subject by Secretary McNamara and other high-ranking Pentagon officials were unequivocal, but actual practice was poles removed. The clincher was the operative system of rewards and punishment. No one was ever fired for overruns. In fact, program managers with the highest costs and biggest overruns seemed to be promoted fastest. Defenders of wasteful procurement practices and sloppy, deceitful financial management were richly rewarded, while economy advocates were ignored, shunted aside, or put out of the business and destroyed professionally if they became too bothersome or persistent. Motivation for contractors was similarly inverted. The giant boondoggling firms were paid to correct their own bonehead blunders and made money in doing so. This premise was supported by a growing body of statistics. Autonetics' experience on the Minuteman and the Mark II and General Dynamics on the F-111 were unusual only in that their bailouts were challenged. Richard Stubbings of the Bureau of the Budget later published a paper showing that big military contractors with the worst records of meeting their original contractual commitments had consistently showed above-average profits on the military business.[*]

Conversely, firms who did their work quickly, economically, and well did not always prosper. For one thing, the so-called

[*] Washington *Post,* January 26, 1969.

"cost-based pricing" penalized cost reduction in some circumstances. Profits were negotiated as a percentage of expected costs, so the higher the cost estimate, the higher the planned profit. Contractors who underran fixed price or incentive contracts could make more than planned profits on the contract in hand, but projections of their lower costs meant lower prices and profits for follow-on work. In some cases, good performers actually put themselves out of business. In a consulting engagement before entering the Pentagon, I encountered a classic example of this reverse motivation. The assignment involved a sick weapons system development program with a prime contractor and several subcontractors who were far behind schedule, failing their technical tests, and overrunning their planned costs. However, there was one subcontractor whose equipment worked as advertised, was delivered ahead of schedule, and was produced for slightly less than the contracted amount. Shortly after I started work on the project, the on-schedule, on-specification subcontractor finished his work. The successful subcontractor, a paragon of contractual virtue, received glowing endorsements and high praise from both the prime contractor and the Navy, the military customer. Then he shut down his little plant. He was out of work.

Meanwhile, the behind-schedule, failing, overrun subcontractors were investigated, chastised, and belabored almost daily by the prime contractor, the Navy and my associates. They seemed to bear up, though, because they stayed in business. Years later, all the ne'er-do-well subcontractors were still happily blundering around, slipping schedules and receiving more money to try to fix their junk while the paragon was struggling to get back into business.

Overall, I was forced to concede that General Zoeckler was right: Inefficiency *was* national policy. It was not officially proclaimed, *de jure* policy, but inefficiency was in fact the natural, expected result of the procedures and guidelines for personal and corporate behavior, all of which were approved or at least tolerated by our top policymakers. Inefficiency was at least *de facto* national policy.

My own experience was something of a contradiction to this

conclusion. At the end of 1967 I was still doing well personally. I was nominated for another high award, again with laudatory language. However, when I studied the language closely, I could see I was being praised for work in two areas: the performance measurement project and the various F-111 cost studies. There had been potential for cost savings in the performance measurement project in the early days, but the approach was being dehorned rapidly. When our approach was adopted by the Office of the Secretary of Defense, Bob Anthony had inexplicably turned the project over to well known, self-proclaimed opponents of the approach who were also conscientious objectors to smiting high-cost contractors. Once they had got control of the performance measurement project, Bob Anthony's conscientious objectors began working with the most obstructive of the contractor trade associations, CODSIA (Council of Defense and Space Industry Associations), to emasculate the scheme. Ted Marks had backed me strongly in opposing the OSD-CODSIA neutering of performance measurement, but now Ted Marks was gone. He had resigned, effective the end of 1967, and had recommended one of his former students from the Stanford School of Business as his replacement. The new FM, Tom Nielsen, seemed intelligent and sincere but was green as a gourd. He had no experience with big weapons programs. All things considered, there was no hope for cost savings through the performance measurement project.

As for my troubleshooting work on big weapons systems, the message had been clear: Concentrate on the F-111. Both the TF-30 engine and the Mark II avionics project were parts of the F-111 program, then viewed as Secretary McNamara's personal project. Nowhere else had we received backing to even try the should-cost approach to cost savings. Of these, only Gordon Rule's TF-30 should-cost project showed any promise. The free-spending generals and civilian procurement experts in the Air Force had told the Secretary of Defense to go to hell and had made it stick, defying both the stated policy and specific directions.

I had to back off to something less threatening and less frightening to the spending complex. I decided to try again on contractor overhead, which continued to increase out of apparent control. Fortunately, I had a new vehicle.

The Systems Command-McKinsey overhead project had expired more or less on schedule and with the expected results. The Project had served as an excuse to avoid corrective action and to fend off critics for several years, but nothing had been done to reverse the steady upward trends of contractors' overhead costs.

Following the demise of the AFSC/McKinsey overhead project, with the problem still uncorrected, the Pentagon's procurement experts had to do something else to excuse their avoidance of duty and to put off would-be overhead cutters a while longer. Either through lack of imagination or perhaps secure in the knowledge that the dodge always worked, the Pentagon procurement chiefs launched *another* big overhead study. This one was truly a world-wide study, and, as it was described, could last forever. This project was headed by Brig. Gen. Bill Snavely, an Air Force procurement officer on loan to the OSD. Members of the study team included representatives from NASA as well as OSD, each of the military services, and other Defense agencies. Meanwhile, the procurement chiefs said with straight faces that we should hold off on any other actions in the area.

When the latest of the seemingly endless series of studies of contractor overhead was kicked off in early 1967, I was not on the team. However, in view of my long experience in the area, Ted Marks insisted that I be added to the team, and I was. The first meeting I attended was a reunion of sorts. A good number of the members of General Snavely's study group were veterans of the overhead study group I had appeared before four years earlier. They were still talking the same way about the same subjects too. Essentially, nothing had changed except that the overhead problem was worse and the conferees were four years older.

General Snavely's plan was to have the team—the whole gaggle—tour the country visiting contractor plants to catalogue overhead schemes which looked good for eventual inclusion in a grand compendium of Good Things to Do. As in past world-wide overhead studies, specific figures were to be avoided.

The team's first visit was to General Electric's jet engine plant in Evendale, Ohio, just outside Cincinnati. GE was one of the contractors chosen to display their outstanding schemes for controlling overhead. The visit started with a welcoming speech to the drove of government visitors by the GE plant manager. This was followed by another general speech about working together. Then the big group broke into smaller subgroups to pursue specific areas of overhead costs.

I was the leader of the subgroup assigned to look at GE's manpower controls. Fortunately, I was teamed with two other people who also thought the "no numbers" rule was nonsense. We listened with diminishing patience for half an hour or so of a long-winded dissertation on "dynamic interactions within the group situation," the mysteries of managing contracts with "high technical content," and the imponderables of "pushing the state of the art." Then my campanions and I began pressing our hosts for specific techniques of manpower controls and, more specifically, for impact on their overhead rates. What were their overhead rates, we asked, and were they headed up or down?

We got more runaround from the GE presentation artists, so we excused ourselves and went to visit our local steward of the public purse, the AFPR, or Air Force Plant Representative. The AFPR was a bluff, friendly officer who said he was there to help us. What could he do for us? he asked. We asked for GE's overhead rates for the past four years and their projection for whatever new negotiated procurement was in the offing. The AFPR immediately dispatched an associate to collect the data for us while he told us how great GE's cost controls were. Their J-79 jet engine was used in the B-58 bomber, the F-104 fighter, and the highly successful F-4 Phantom fighter. The J-79, the AFPR said, was a great bargain at about $120,000 per engine. The AFPR became absolutely rhapsodic in describing "our" (GE's) new TF-39 turbofan engine being developed for the C-5A. The TF-39 project was then developing an enormous cost overrun, but nobody seemed to mind. It was another total-package contract. No need to worry about that. The major consideration was the prospect of commercial applications of the TF-39. According to the AFPR, the engine was so efficient that it would not only revolutionize *air* transportation, it would revolutionize *transportation*. According to the AFPR the TF-39 would enable freight to be moved by air less expensively than by surface transportation.

After a while the AFPR's assistants brought back the overhead rates for past years for GE's fabrication operations:

Fabrication Overhead Rates

Overhead Dollars per Direct Labor Hour

Year	1963	1964	1965	1966
Amount	$4.36	$5.13	$6.99	$8.15

Our three-man subgroup suggested that these results, taken at face value, did not suggest superior cost controls. Granting that there may have been extenuating circumstances such as fluctuations in volume of business, change in accounts, and inflation, none of these would appear to justify such an increase. No, the AFPR conceded, he didn't think so either. There must be some mistake. He sent his assistants back to recalculate the figures. In half an hour or so they came back with a new set of figures for the same years:

Revised Fabrication Overhead Rates

Overhead Dollars per Direct Labor Hour

Year	1963	1964	1965	1966
Amount	$6.08	$7.55	$7.87	$6.90

Neither the AFPR nor his assistants could account for the great differences in the two sets of figures. The picture, especially the trend, was radically changed.

What program would be principally affected by fabrication overhead rates in the near future? we asked. The J-79, we were told. We asked what rate was proposed for J-79 production for the following year, 1968. After another trip out of the room, the AFPR's assistant came back with the figure. It was $9.82 per hour. With this bad news, the AFPR became thoroughly rattled and reverted to ramblings about Inexorable Economic Processes.

A Minuteman III missile, designed to deliver MIRV nuclear warheads to cities marked for destruction, shown in a test launching. Failures in Minuteman II were covered up for four years. If the "button" had ever been pushed, an estimated 40 percent of them would have been duds. *U.S. Air Force Photo*

The foam-doused wreckage of an F-111B on the Grumman Aircraft field. It crashed a few seconds after takeoff, killing its two test pilots. *UPI Photo*

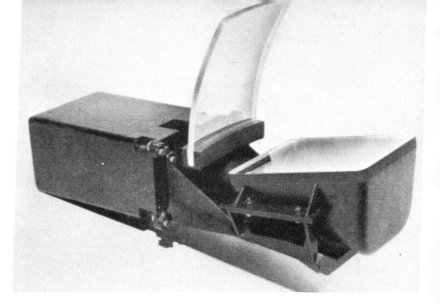

Two units of the infamous Mark II Avionics system for the F-111. *Above:* The head-up display (HUD) projected graphic and numerical presentations of aircraft attitudes and locations onto a glass in the pilot's line of sight as he looked through the windshield. *Below:* The inertial platform which was the heart of the autonavigation of the Mark II system.

The much-heralded Mark II program, contracted for with the Autonetics Division of North American Aviation, became one of the great disasters of military procurement. The cost estimates for delivering 800 units skyrocketed from $610,000,000 to $2,510,000,000 (for a degraded product) in two and a half years.

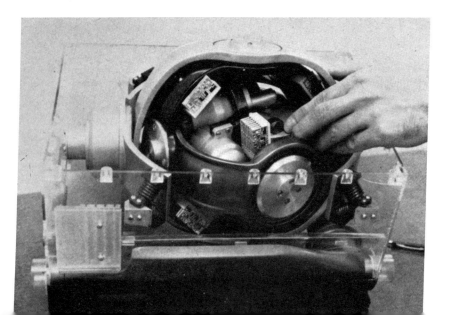

A wheel broken from a C-5A landing gear rolls down the runway as the giant cargo plane lands before a crowd of dignitaries in Charleston, South Carolina. Another tire blew out in the landing, but there were no injuries other than the wounded pride of the assembled supporters of the costly, trouble-ridden C-5A project.

The tangled wreckage of the first C-5A. It was greeted by President Johnson as it came off the assembly line, looking complete but actually missing more than 3000 parts. Later, it blew up on the airport apron in Marietta, Georgia, killing one and injuring one.

Henry Durham, facing the camera, stands outside his Marietta, Georgia, home with one of the U.S. marshals assigned to protect the Durham family. Lockheed supporters threatened to kill Durham, burn his home, and disfigure his teenage daughter after Durham revealed irregularities in the C-5A program. Signs found in the Lockheed plant urged the murder of both Durham and Senator Proxmire.

It was nearing the end of the day, so my trio suggested that the AFPR have his assistants prepare a summary of current and proposed J-79 engine costs for us to look at the next day. Meanwhile, we would tour GE's factory to take a first-hand look at what was going on in the shops.

The next morning our suspicions were confirmed. J-79 prices were going up from a target of $121,420 each in 1966 to $157,651 each in 1968. Direct labor hours were jumping about 15 percent per engine, reversing a gradual but persistent downward trend over the past four years. The AFPR's industrial specialists thought that inherent work content for the various versions of J-79 engines had not changed significantly. As indicated the day before, the overhead rates were taking a sharp jump, even with GE's increasing volume of business. We reminded the AFPR that no matter how impressive GE's cost control procedures looked, the final proof was the level of costs. He responded that he was sure GE was trying its best. I countered that it didn't look that way, especially in the shops. I had counted heads during the plant tour and also observed how many people were working and how many were idle. Only 26 percent of the people I had observed appeared to be working. The AFPR then defended his contractor, reminding us that the J-79 had been a tremendous bargain at $120,000 per copy. We agreed but suggested that GE's management might have decided that it was too much of a bargain, that it was worth more, relatively speaking at least, and that they had simply decided to raise the price. Under the government's rules, the increased prices would have to be supported by increased contractor costs, actual and projected. GE might be just allowing nature to take its course for a spell in order to build a base of higher actual costs to support their higher prices.

At this, the AFPR exploded. He said he had no responsibility for challenging contractor overhead. "That's someone else's job," he said. (He was partly right. No one was responsible.) As for the projected J-79 cost increase, he said that he just did not care: "$120,000, $150,000; these are just numbers." He said he was only interested in "getting engines out the door and in good quality." Warmed to his subject, our steward then stated that he would oppose economy moves aimed at reducing GE's overruns if the cost-reduction efforts involved laying off people. His voice rising to an old-fashioned oratorical pitch, the AFPR then proclaimed GE's Evendale plant "a national resource, a resource of *America*," which should be protected at all costs. "America," he said, his voice quivering, "*is* transportation, and our new product [i.e., the TF-39 for the C-5A] is the new diesel engine of transportation."

With one emotional outburst, the AFPR had rationalized whatever happened at GE as not only unavoidable but for the best and, in his own mind at least, had categorized my trio of questioners as enemies of the state, maybe even of civilization, for suggesting that some small economies might be in order. All three of us had been in the business long enough to recognize the AFPR's affliction. He had gone native. Government representatives resident in contractors' plants, like diplomats posted to foreign countries, often adopted the habits and attitudes of their hosts. Military plant representatives thus afflicted represent "their" contractor to the government rather than representing the government's interest to the contractor. The ailment was widespread, with no known cure, but the progress of the disease was often arrested and the patient made comfortable by an easy, highly paid retirement job with a big contractor.

In any event, there was nothing to be accomplished by argument with the General Electric AFPR, so my partners and I thanked the Plant Representative, left, and proceeded to prepare our report. Although we never got the additional cost facts which both the GE management and our AFPR promised to send us, we had enough information to prepare a meaty report for General Snavely. In addition to reporting our findings, we recommended that the overhead study project be reoriented toward actually saving money. As a start, we suggested that business-type goals be set for the study. We believed that the study group should be charged with pinpointing avoidable costs, devising ways to stimulate actual cost reductions, then following through to see that potential savings were realized. To make the objectives meaningful to the group, we suggested that we set ourselves a goal of saving enough money to buy a new weapons system which our military associates said they wanted but could not afford. Potential savings of several hundred million dollars, perhaps as much as a billion dollars, appeared to be attainable, and we reasoned that the prospects of reinvesting the money in a new weapons system might induce erstwhile opponents of cost reduction to support our efforts. Finally, we suggested to General Snavely that the experience of actually saving money, which each of our subgroup had previously enjoyed, would be excellent on-the-job training for other members who might not have had similar experiences of their own. We thought our suggestions would reverse the nonproductive course the overall group was then following. Summing up this reasoning, we wrote: "As we are now proceeding, the members of our group who don't already understand overhead and how to control it will remain unskilled in the art, and those who do will waste their time."

The majority of General Snavely's Overhead Study Group were shocked, angered, and maybe a bit frightened by our activities at General Electric and by our proposal to put the Study Group on the spot. Our insistence on dealing with facts and figures was analogous to the novice in the medieval monastic gathering counting the jackass's teeth. From the standpoint of the majority of the group, we had violated their rules and proposed a heretical philosophy as well.

Suggesting that we commit ourselves to results roused more than philosophical objections, however. Our subgroup's suggestions posed practical problems for many majority members in addition to their conscientious objection to upsetting big contractors. In the first place, some of them were afraid their bosses might fire them if they endorsed such a radical proposal, and some of them, I suspected, were fearful of having their competence tested by evaluation of results achieved. It was much easier and safer to spend a couple of years touring the country compiling the catalog of Nice Things to Do and writing a report which would be hailed as offering great promise for better overhead cost control sometime during the coming decade.

General Snavely was annoyed with me, of course, but he was an unusually intelligent officer of wide experience and, I believed, basically good instincts. In private conversations, he seemed sympathetic with my objectives. He was unwilling or maybe unable to accept my suggestions, but he told me that he had no objection to my stirring up something on my own. In fact, he told me privately that he thought the time was ripe for some hard cost savings. Like Ted Marks, Bill Snavely was a great believer in education, and he suggested that more education was in order. In particular, he said, the nuances of sharing of contractors' overhead expenses by the contractors' government and commercial activities was poorly understood. As an example, he said that one part of our subgroup report on the General Electric J-79 engine situation seemed most obscure. We had reported that GE's anticipated losses on their current overrun J-79 contracts might be offset by the value to GE of the overrun contracts absorbing additional company administrative expenses. It was then estimated that GE stood to lose about $7,500,000 under the overrun-sharing arrangements of their J-79 contract. At the same time, the overrun contract was charged with an additional $7,000,000 of company administrative costs, which included the costs of various company headquarters activities. We had suggested that GE's overall losses might be less than the $7,500,000 loss on the specific contract if the extra $7,000,000 of administrative expense would have been charged to commercial business or fixed-price contracts if the J-79 overrun had not occurred.

I agreed with General Snavely that overhead sharing could get complicated, especially where contractors had different overhead rates for five or six activities—engineering, manufacturing, test operations, and so on—in each of several divisions, and with a thick layer of corporate headquarters and other administrative expenses spread as a percentage of all other costs. These mechanics were further complicated by the interactions of cost overruns, underruns, and fluctuations in overhead costs. The poor understanding of this complicated business was illustrated by the arguments made by the Pentagon's top procurement and financial people in favor of a scheme called

CWAS (pronounced "quass"), an acronym for Contractors Weighted Average Share in Cost Risk. (Only the first four words were employed in the acronym. Both "CWASICR" and "CWASCR" proved unpronounceable.) Stripped to essentials, the basic idea behind CWAS was that a contractor whose total of commercial business and fixed price contracts equaled as much as half of all his business would be so driven by profit considerations that it would be unnecessary to challenge his overhead costs in contract negotiations.

Even aside from the facts that few big contractors took fixed-price commitments seriously and that pricing practices for follow-on business inhibited cost reductions, I thought the CWAS advocates ignored many real-world motivations in pushing their scheme. To illustrate this point and also to follow through on Bill Snavely's suggestion to educate the troops, I put together a number of simplified case examples which eventually evolved into the Ajax Coat Hanger and Aerospace case example.

Notwithstanding the fact that I was still an adherent of the philosophy of Francis Bacon, I found that Idols of the Theater, "stories invented for the stage," were often useful for illustrating concepts. Maybe it was the influence of the Harvards and their case method of teaching. Anyway, here is the Ajax Case.

The Ajax Coat Hanger and Aerospace Corporation

(Author's note: I know absolutely nothing about the coat-hanger business. I selected that trade as an example to spare the readers fretful detail, which I am told is in the best academic tradition.)

Max Ajax should have been a happy man, but he was troubled. He had a good family and a good business. Several years before, Max's father, Irving, had died, and Max had inherited control of the Ajax Coat Hanger Corporation. The business might not have looked like much, but it had been good to the Ajax family. Old Irving had made a fair living out of the business, and had managed to send Max to the State University. Max had studied Business Administration at State, and the training paid off once Max took over the coat-hanger business. It was not that Max had increased sales of coat hangers. He hadn't. Practically all his output was bought, as had been the case when his father was alive, by Max's uncle Mandel, the late Irving's brother. Uncle Mandel had a big chain of dry cleaning establishments which required a steady supply of coat hangers.

The payoff from Max's business administration training had not come in the form of cutting costs either. The manufacturing end of the business consisted mostly of a single machine which pulled wire from a coil, twisted it, cut it off, and spat out coathangers. This process was rather awe-inspiring to Max, so he left this part of the business to his cousin, Sean, who had also held the same job when Irving was alive. So, all in all, the coat-hanger business practially ran itself, and Max was wise enough to let well enough alone.

When Max first took over the business, he had put together a financial operations summary which he had since updated each week. In fact, he spent most of his working time fooling with the financial summary. Here's what it looked like when he took over:

Ajax Coat Hanger Corporation
Weekly Financial Operations Summary

1. Sales	$1,650
2. Direct Costs	1,000
3. Indirect Costs (Overhead)	600
4. Total Costs (Lines 2 + 3)	$1,600
5. Profit (Line 1 less line 4)	$50
6. Profit on Sales (Line 5 divided by line 1)	3.03%
7. Working Capital Required (4 weeks' operating cost—4 times line 4)	$6,400
8. Weekly Return on Working Capital (Line 5 divided by line 7)	.78%

The $50 weekly profit and the 3.03 percent return on sales looked pretty anemic, but Max knew from his business training at State that the return on working capital invested was outstanding. The .78 percent weekly figure amounted to a more that 40 percent annual return on investment of working capital. Better still, the working capital was all the capital needed in the business. The business was housed in an old warehouse which Irving had bought dirt cheap many years before. After the building, the office equipment and the coat-hanger machine had been fully depreciated, Irving had sold the property, equipment and all, to his wife, Mary, for a nominal sum and then arranged for Ajax Coat Hanger Corp. to rent the property from Mary for $50 per week. This had worked out well for tax purposes, and Mary's independent income had pleased her no end.

Max spent a lot of time analyzing the overhead accounts. For one thing, he didn't have much else to do. He also had learned at State that control of overhead expense was vital to business success. Max's overhead percentage, 60 percent of direct costs, was low for two reasons. First, he had classified all the costs he could associate with Sean's manufacturing operations as direct charges. Even though Sean was a supervisor, Max considered him an integral part of the manufacturing operation and classified his salary as a direct cost. Similarly, the fringe benefits—social security, taxes, and the like—for Sean and his men were also classified as direct charges, along with wages for the helpers and material used to make the coat hangers. Sean and his able assistants took care of all maintenance as well, and this cost too was included as a direct cost of making coat hangers.

The second major reason for Max's low overhead was Miss Quimby, the office manager. Miss Quimby was an ancient maiden lady who operated with superb competence and efficiency. She served as secretary, kept the books, sent out the invoices, paid the bills, paid the taxes, bought the raw material and office supplies, and saw to all the myriad chores incidental to running the administrative end of the business. She also saw to it that nothing was wasted. She saved paper clips, string, rubber bands, uncanceled stamps, and envelopes which could be used again. Each evening before she went home, she cleaned up the office and turned off the lights and heat.

Ajax Coat Hanger's overhead expenses were as follows:

Ajax Coat Hanger Corp.

Weekly Overhead Analysis

Salary—Max Ajax	$300
Salary—Miss Quimby	100
Fringe Benefits	100
Rent	50
Miscellaneous (taxes, insurance, licenses, telephone, utilities, office supplies, Max's business entertainment, etc.)	50
Total	$600

Even though Max's business was remarkably stable and he was reasonably rewarded for his efforts, he realized that the company was vulnerable to any decline in volume of business. There was simply no margin for error or loss of business. Any significant decline in orders from Uncle Mandel would force Max to take a cut in salary. Max was also haunted by fear that the faithful coat-hanger machine might break down irreparably, that Sean would resign, or that Miss Quimby would die.

Therefore, when the opportunity to diversify presented itself, Max jumped at it. Diversification would give him a chance to use his business training for profit. Max's cousin Pierre was a government contracting officer. Pierre told Max of a small group of integrated logistics support systems analysts who had been writing training manuals under contract to the Air Force. The analysts had been working for Amalgamated Systems Corporation, a combination consulting and technical assistance firm. Technical assistance contractors were known as "body shops" or "flesh peddlers," because their basic service was renting experts to assist government and contractor weapons procurement managers. Amalgamated Systems Corporation (ASC) had been founded as a front for university professors consulting with the Department of Defense. University professors consulting as individuals were limited to about $100 per day for personal services, but ASC, as a corporate contractor, could get about $300 per day for the same professors.

ASC had been phenomenally successful as a consulting firm. They had invented numerous paperwork schemes which contractors were required to employ. After ASC had invented a new DoD paperwork scheme, usually described as a "cost-control" system, their usual procedure was to use their professors to spread the word to contractors that ASC's new scheme could be defeated and even turned to the contractors' advantage with a little expert advice. ASC, as inventors of the DoD systems, were uniquely qualified to show contractors how to beat the game.

This had proved to be a winning formula for ASC, but they had overdone it with the integrated logistics systems support caper. This system, which ASC had invented for DoD, was endlessly complicated. All participants, DoD agencies and contractors alike, were required to have approved integrated logistics support systems procedures and training programs to keep up with the constantly changing requirements. ASC had become the *only* consultant in the integrated logistics support systems business. This was bad enough, but when they had gone into the flesh-peddling business and became the only *operators* of integrated logistics support systems, their inside men in the Pentagon had called a halt. ASC's inside men, former professors and ASC consultants, had detected mutterings about management schemes of, by, and for ASC. They warned ASC that some other firm would have to be given at least part of the action. The writing of DoD training manuals was the least glamorous and profitable of the many offshoots of the business, so ASC decided to sacrifice that project.

Pierre Ajax's sensitive antennae, ever alert for opportunities, had detected this signal and arranged for cousin Max to meet the right ASC and Pentagon procurement people.

Max could not believe his good fortune. After a few perfunctory discussions with Pierre and then with an Assistant Secretary for Installations and Logistics, he found himself negotiating a sole-source, cost-plus contract for writing integrated logistics support systems training manuals. He knew absolutely nothing about support systems, integrated, logistics or otherwise, and confessed as much to his unbelievably friendly contracting officer. Not to worry, said the contracting officer. DoD was looking for management ability, and Max obviously had it. He was a successful businessmen.

But where would he get people to do the work? Max had wondered. This problem had been solved when Max received a visit from George Grosbeak, ASC's supervisor of training manual writing. George had told Max that ASC was getting out of the manual writing business. George said the ASC president had told him that Max was going in the business, and had suggested that George call on Max and try to make a deal for himself and his three assistants. Max had quickly closed the deal and had acquired the services of George and his three assistants for a total cost of $1000 per week, including fringe benefits, effective the same date as his contract with the Pentagon.

ASC had generously given George and his boys their old beat-up desks, files, and typewriters, so Max was spared the cost of new ones. Max housed George's group in an unused storeroom adjoining his office in the old warehouse.

Max's contracting officer had turned a little stern with him on the matter of overhead on his new cost-plus contract. Previously, he had been running a steady $600 a week in overhead on a direct cost base of $1000, an overhead percentage of 60 percent. The contracting officer had told Max that this percentage, based on experience, should not be exceeded. Max's problem at the time had not been exceeding the rate but maintaining it. With his accounting practices and his excess floor space, he had incurred no discernable increases in his fixed expenses by taking on George Grosbeak and his associates who would perform the new cost-plus contract. Max's real problem had been how to keep the overhead percentage up. In view of his increased responsibilities, Max had increased his own salary from $300 per week to $500 per week. His fringe benefits had gone up proportionately. He had also increased his "miscellaneous" overhead budget. His contracting officer had told him that the "business entertainment" component of the "miscellaneous" account was not an allowable element of cost. The contracting officer suggested that such effort could be better spent in executive training and seminars. Max got the message and wiped out the "entertainment" budget, substituting a big chunk of money for training and seminars. In the end, the contracting officer told him to shoot for an overhead rate of 50 percent, and his new Weekly Overhead Analysis had looked like this:

Ajax Coat Hanger & Aerospace Corp.
Weekly Overhead Analysis

Salary—Max Ajax	$500
Salary—Miss Quimby	100
Fringe Benefits	150
Rent	50
Miscellaneous (taxes, insurance, licenses, telephone, utilities, executive training & seminars)	200
Total	$1,000

Miss Quimby had received a raise from $80 a week to $100 per week only three years before, and Max didn't want to spoil her, so he had left her salary unchanged. Max figured she could easily absorb the additional duties imposed by the new Pentagon contract. He had noticed that Miss Quimby had developed an uncharacteristic tendency to linger over her lunch of tea and crackers which she took at her desk.

With diversification, Max's weekly summary was as follows:

Ajax Coat Hanger & Aerospace Corp.
Weekly Financial Operations
Summary

	Coat-hanger Business	Cost-Plus Fixed Fee	Total
1. Sales	$1,650	$1,650	$3,300
2. Direct Costs	1,000	1,000	2,000
3. Indirect Costs (Overhead)	500	500	1,000
4. Total Costs (Lines 2 + 3)	$1,500	$1,500	$3,000
5. Profit/Fee	150	150	300
6. Profit on Sales (Line 5 divided by line 1)	9.1%	9.1%	9.1%
7. Working Capital Required	$6,000	($1,500)	$4,500
8. Weekly Return on Working Capital (Line 5 divided by line 7)	2.5%	infinite	6.7%

Even with the greatly increased overhead expenses (mostly Max's $200 per week raise and the extra $150 for executive seminars), the coat-hanger business was made much more profitable by diversification. Whereas the coat-hanger trade had previously borne the entire $600 per week overhead expense, half of the overhead was absorbed by the Pentagon contract after diversification. Thus, even though the total overhead had increased from $600 per week to $1000 per week, the coat-hanger business' 50 percent share of overhead was only $500, $100 less than before. This $100 reduction in total coat-hanger costs was pure profit for Max. At one stroke, he had given himself a huge raise and tripled coat-hanger profits.

Better yet, he got many other benefits from the new Pentagon contract. In addition to the nice fixed fee, at $150 per week equal to his increased coat-hanger profits, Max found his working capital requirements greatly reduced. With the advice of cousin Pierre, Max had negotiated billing and payment procedures for his new contract so that his costs were reimbursed before he actually paid out the money. The secret was in the government definition of "costs incurred." Even though Max only paid George Grosbeak and his associates once a month, he billed the government each week for costs incurred. The incurred costs which Max billed, and was promptly reimbursed for, were those costs which Miss Quimby had accrued on the books as owed to the employees and for overhead expenses, not money actually paid out. So, with the prompt reimbursement of his bills for accrued costs, Max found himself with a "float" of cash in the bank averaging about $1500, equal to a week's operating cost for the training manual project. Instead of supplying an average of four weeks' costs as operating capital as he had to do for his coat-hanger line, Max had extra money always in the bank for his cost-plus contract. In effect, it was payment in advance which resulted in a *negative* operating capital requirement for his manual writing operations. In turn, this meant that his calculated weekly return on investment for the cost-plus contract ($150 fee per week divided by −$1,500) was infinity.

The overall effect of diversification on return on investment had been spectacular. Whereas Max had previously made $50 a week on his average investment of $6,400 for a weekly return of .78 percent, diversification had produced a $300 per week profit on a net investment of $4,500, a weekly return of 6.7 percent. His "float" on the cost-plus contract had reduced his overall financing requirements.

With diversification, Max's business worries had disappeared, at least for the moment. His troubled mind was only indirectly related to the business. Max was really worried about his girlfriend, Suzy, who had become increasingly possessive and demanding. Max was deathly afraid of his wife, Rachael, who would undoubtedly divorce him—with financial ruin—and maybe also do him bodily harm if she found out about Suzy. Max had always fooled around, but Rachael had more or less ignored his lapses. Suzy, however, was beginning to cost Max money, and Rachael would never put up with that.

Max had met Suzy as a result of his expanded executive seminar program. Many of these seminars involved long meetings with Max's government customers. Usually they ended up in places devoted to relaxing and refreshing the weary executive. One of these places was the Club Aristocrat, where Suzy had been featured as an exotic dancer. Suzy's professional name was Erotika, but she had been born Sue Zell Ledbetter in Bug Tussle, Alabama, and she had never really outgrown her preference for the simple life. Actually, she had become an exotic dancer only because it paid more than the waitress job she had before. So, when fortune beckoned, however modestly, in the form of Max Ajax, who was both free-spending and vulnerable to her charms, Suzy had latched onto him with a death grip.

Thus Suzy became the Public Relations Specialist for the Ajax Corporation. In truth, she was a receptionist, but Max couldn't call her that and still pay Suzy what she needed to live, which was $160 per week. Miss Quimby, with her $100 per week salary and heavy responsibilities, was quite sullen about the deal anyway, and Max had to put a good face on it.

Suzy had practically nothing to do at first, which suited her fine. However, as word got around about the new receptionist at Ajax, things picked up. More salesmen began calling even though they didn't sell anything. The most noticeable change, however, was the big increase in visits by Air Force officials, presumably coming to check on progress of George Grosbeak's work. Suzy was instinctively at her best in making the customer's representatives feel right at home.

Max had never been happier. He was so relieved by the solution of his personal problems that he forgot to prepare his Overhead Analyses and Financial Summaries for several weeks. He also neglected to keep after George Grosbeak about staying within his weekly plans for man-hour expenditures. This benign neglect, coupled with the sudden surge of visitors from the Air Force to check on his work, resulted in a vast increase in overtime worked by George and his men.

Finally, a worried Miss Quimby suggested that Max take a look at what the combination of higher overhead (Suzy's salary and fringe benefits) and the huge weekly overruns in Mr. Grosbeak's department were doing to the business. Fortunately, Miss Quimby said, the Air Force was still reimbursing Ajax promptly for the higher costs, but the contracting officer had grumbled about it.

Reluctantly, Max got back to work. His overhead analysis looked like this:

Ajax Coat Hanger & Aerospace Corp.

Weekly Overhead Analysis

Salary—Max Ajax	$500
Salary—Miss Quimby	100
Salary—Miss Ledbetter	160

Fringe Benefits	190
Rent	50
Miscellaneous	200
Total	$1,200

Bad news, Max thought. Suzy had ruined his overhead, but it sure beat supporting her out of his own pocket. He reflected on how fortunate he was to have an understanding contracting officer. Well, on to the Financial Operations Summary, cranking in George Grosbeak's big overruns.

Ajax Coat Hanger & Aerospace Corp.
Weekly Financial Operations
Summary

	Coat-hanger Business	Cost-Plus Fixed Fee	Total
1. Sales	$1,650	$2,950	$4,600
2. Direct Costs	1,000	2,000	3,000
3. Indirect Costs (Overhead)	400	800	1,200
4. Total Costs (Lines 2 + 3)	$1,400	$2,800	$4,200
5. Profit/Fee	$250	$150	$400
6. Profit on Sales (Line 5 divided by line 1)	15.2%	5.1%	8.7%
7. Working Capital Required	$5,600	($2,800)	$2,800
8. Weekly Return on Working Capital (Line 5 divided by line 7)	4.5%	Infinite	14.3%

Max was sure he had made a mistake. Even with his higher overhead to pay Suzy's salary and fringe benefits, his overall profit had gone *up*, not down. It had increased by $100 per week, in fact, from $300 to $400. And, even though the percentage of profit on sales had gone down, from 9.1% to 8.7%, his weekly return on investment had shot up from 6.7% to 14.3%. Best of all, besides the $100 per week increase in profit, it appeared that his working capital requirements had gone down from $4,500 to $2,800 because of his overruns, a savings of $1,700. Before he had got the cost-plus contract, he had needed $6,400. He had freed up $3,600 in capital. He could buy Suzy a "company car" or, alternatively, something for the business.

He decided he had better redo the figures to make sure he hadn't punched the wrong button on his calculator. He hadn't. As he recomputed his Financial Summary figures, Max saw that his big overrun on the cost-plus contract had saved him. He split his indirect expenses, or overhead, between the coat-hanger business and his Air Force contract proportional to the direct costs of each part of the business. Before he hired Suzy and began incurring direct cost overruns, he had $1,000 in overhead and $2,000 in direct costs, with the direct costs evenly divided between the coat-hanger operation and the cost-plus contract, each running $1,000 per week. This meant that each part of the business, having equal direct costs, absorbed an equal amount of overhead, $500. With his direct cost overrun on the cost-plus contract, he had a total direct cost of $3,000—$2,000 on the Air Force contract and still $1,000 on the coat hangers. Using his proportional allocation technique for charging overhead to the separate lines of his business, this meant that the cost-plus contract would now absorb twice as much of the total overhead as the coat-hanger production. So, with the total overhead increased from $1,000 per week to $1,200 per week, it was split two-thirds, or $800, to the cost-plus contract and one-third, or $400, to the coat-hanger business. The reduced overhead absorbed by his coat-hanger business—from $500 to $400—accounted for his increased profit margin. Uncle Mandel paid $1650 for his weekly order of coat hangers regardless of what they cost. On the other hand, Uncle Sam paid him a fixed amount of profit regardless of what the contract cost.

An intriguing idea took shape in Max's mind. *Overruns could make him rich!* Moreover, his latest good fortune had come to him without effort—in fact, without even conscious thought on his part. All he had done was lose control of the business for a time, and nature had taken its course.

Caught up in the excitement of discovery, Max made a special financial operations summary tracing his progress since before diversification.

Ajax Coat Hanger & Aerospace Corp.
Weekly Financial Operations Summaries
(Consolidated Commercial and Government Business)

| | BEFORE DIVERSIFICATION (COMMERCIAL BUSINESS ONLY) | AFTER DIVERSIFICATION (WITH COST-PLUS CONTRACT) | |
		Before Cost Overruns	*After Cost Overruns*
1. Sales	$1,650	$3,300	$4,600
2. Direct Costs	1,000	2,000	3,000
3. Indirect Costs (Overhead)	600	1,000	1,200

4. Total Costs (Lines 2 + 3)	$1,600	$3,000	$4,200
5. Profit/Fee	$50	$300	$400
6. Return on Sales (Line 5 divided by line 1)	3.03%	9.1%	8.7%
7. Working Capital Required	$6,400	$4,500	$2,800
8. Weekly Return on Working Capital (Line 5 divided by line 7)	.78%	6.7%	14.3%

As he reviewed his financial progress, new vistas opened to Max's imagination. Acquiring the cost-plus contract had been the first big break, making possible his big raise and increasing his overall profits by 600 percent. The overrun helped too, and he wondered how much his customer would hold still for. He decided to check out possibilities for increased funding of the contract before speaking with George Grosbeak about his overruns. The really exciting prospect, however, was the possibility of more free working capital if he could get more clost-plus business with his lovely reimbursement procedures. What about the avionics business? he wondered. He had heard his Air Force friends discuss this burgeoning industry. He resolved to ask sometime what an "avionic" was. The fact that he knew nothing about avionics wouldn't deter him though. He knew nothing about integrated logistics support systems either, and he had made a great success of that. With enough cost reimbursement business, his cash float would permit him to expand his commercial business. He could become the Coat Hanger King. He might even put together a conglomerate.

When Max Ajax found himself with half commercial business and half cost-plus, he had a wide range of business options open to him. However, when he got his new cost-plus contract, the option he was *least* likely to choose was to cut his overhead. Max could also have chosen to hire an ace coat-hanger salesman instead of his girl friend, and the government would have picked up half the cost (two-thirds, after the overruns) of Max's attempts to increase his coat-hanger business.

Although I got nowhere in my attempts to dissuade the Pentagon's top management on CWAS, my informal educational efforts produced unexpected results, but not in terms

of improved training. I found that many working-level auditors and cost analysts shared my concerns and understood perfectly how the big contractors were financing increased sales
efforts and a wider range of non-military-related activities out
of DoD overhead allowances. The working-level people didn't
need educating. They already understood what was happening. As usual, our top management people and the procurement chiefs pretended not to comprehend what their subordinates understood perfectly. Also as usual, some of the more
persistent subordinates were getting themselves in trouble.

I settled on General Electric's Philadelphia missiles and
space operations as the first application of my new milder,
greatly scaled down approach to saving a little money. This
situation seemed to offer many advantages. First, it was close to
Washington. Second, we had two large programs underway
at GE Philadelphia, the Manned Orbiting Laboratory (MOL)
and the Mark 12 MIRV Reentry System. The MOL was a
supersecret, so-called "black program" with program control
(such as it was) directly out of the Pentagon. The MOL was
one of history's great boondoggles and was eventually canceled. Unfortunately, it was so enshrouded in secrecy that its
horror stories of waste are probably lost forever to public
scrutiny. The Mark 12, only slightly less secret since the
Congress as a whole had not then knowingly authorized the
MIRV, was part of the Minuteman program. Work had started
on the basic Mark 12 research and development contract in
1963, and the contract had grown steadily through contract
changes, some genuine but mostly of the "contract nourishment"
variety. The Air Force "position" was that DoD-directed
changes to the reentry vehicle caused most of the cost growth,
but facts indicated otherwise. The Air Force contract log on the
principal contract showed that 90 percent of the negotiated
increase in the value of the contract was for paper studies.
Changes to the hardware mockups and to the reentry vehicle
were really quite modest compared to other parts of the wild
and woolly Minuteman program.

Because of this large and suspect cost growth, with the
promise of much more to come when the large-scale produc-

tion for the Mark 12 MIRV was authorized, Secretary Anthony's analysis group was already looking into the project. Rick Kroon, one of Bill George's associates and another bright young Harvard Business School graduate, was checking on the program for Bob Anthony. Rick Kroon had made several trips to Philadelphia, and excerpts from his reports indicated that he had a good grasp of the problem. For example, he included these comments in a November 27, 1967, letter to Mr. Anthony:

Bid and Proposal: the auditors now estimate that B&P and related marketing costs will be $20M in 1967, or 9–10% of cost of sales, vs. $9M in 1963, or 5% of cost of sales.

FFP (Firm Fixed Price): the new Air Force plant representative found a specific example of development costs really allocatable to work covered by an FFP contract being charged to overhead. Total costs would have greatly overrun the contract price.

R&D: it is highly probable that ARPO (Advanced Research Projects Organization) duplicates effort made by other GE groups such as (1) Defense Programs Operations, (2) GE headquarters lab, (3) their flight propulsion group, or (4) another group called TEMPO.

Other Allocations: NASA and/or AEC (Atomic Energy Commission) has disallowed overhead items more applicable to their projects than ours which we later pay for in overhead.

Production Contract: the $400M production contract for the Mk 12 will be negotiated next year. Because the R&D costs are so inflated, the base for negotiation will probably be too high, not incorporating "should cost" analysis. Long-lead items will be negotiated shortly, so the major negotiation will be conducted in an essentially sole source environment.

In the same memo, he also noted Air Staff resistance to cost-cutting efforts despite the fact that the Air Force was paying a large and growing bill for things which did not benefit them.

Rick Kroon also noted in a report to Bob Anthony on December 15, 1967, that "in-plant technical personnel are very sympathetic to the contractor's desire for 'get well' change orders." I had accompanied him on the trip to GE Philadelphia when he had been briefed on the "contract nourishment" process by one of the Air Force resident technicians. I had known the technician since my pre-Pentagon Minuteman days. His candor had often embarrassed his superiors, and he was without pretense

in explaining to Rick how big-time contracting was really conducted. "When your contractor starts running out of money, you
give him a CCN (i.e., contract change notice) to raise the price.
You can always find something to change and tack the extra
money onto. That's contract nourishment."

Rick Kroon knew that was true, of course, but he seemed
astounded that the intent of the parties would be so freely
admitted. As had always been the case on Minuteman projects,
the change mill ground constantly. Large changes would be
authorized, sometimes by telephone, money "turned on" and
spending begun immediately, with negotiation of the price of
the change following months later. Usually final pricing of
changes was based on money already spent by the contractor,
effectively converting the affected contracts—fixed price, incentive, or whatever original type—into cost-plus-percentage-of-
cost arrangements. Rick Kroon described the process to Mr.
Anthony as follows:

Change negotiations seem to be taking place *after* 60–70% of the work
has actually been completed by GE. The work is initiated by a technical directive—a telephone call, TWX or letter—from Ballistics
Systems Division, AFSC. Large changes are often negotiated 6–10
months after work has begun. Thus a principal de facto function of
the negotiators is to verify that costs have been incurred. To the
extent that they do price the changes, they are influenced by the desire to keep the contractor healthy, which I have discussed in an earlier
memorandum.

With GE's contracts growing rapidly through promiscuous
changes, we were confronted with a cost-plus environment
which enabled the contractor to keep increasing the absolute
amount of his overhead expenses without undue increases in
the *ratio* of overhead to direct costs.

The GE Mark 12 situation appeared ideal for capturing
some modest savings and heading off further cost increases.
Moreover, we had some excellent people to work with. The
new AFPR at GE Philadelphia was an eager, sincere lieutenant
colonel who seemed determined to demonstrate that not all
Air Force plant representatives went native. The DCAA (Defense Contract Audit Agency) auditors at GE also included

some exceptional individuals. The resident auditor and his principal supervising auditor were experienced and aggressive and had done a good job of building a case for reducing Government contributions to GE overhead activities.

For a change, I advised caution and adoption of modest savings goals. We badly needed a demonstration, no matter how small, that the Pentagon's top management would back some kind of cost reduction. Both the old-line procurement people and DCAA headquarters had already served notice that they intended to oppose our efforts to limit GE's overhead charges to the government. As Rick Kroon wrote to Secretary Anthony:

Both of these groups now consider this concern over one contractor unwarranted because his costs are not unreasonable when compared to others in the industry. That they *all* could be unreasonable is a new, unaccepted idea. We must make them realize that you and Mr. Nitze expect substantial reorientation of our traditional interpretation of reasonableness.

Rick and I made several trips to GE to review the auditors' data and to discuss the overhead negotiation goals with them and the cooperative AFPR. The AFPR and the auditors agreed on a modest goal of reducing the government's contributions to GE's sales-related expenses.

Just when everything seemed set to demonstrate top management backing for the little savings effort, GE's overhead negotiations were postponed. The two DCAA auditors at GE were abruptly transferred. The Air Force Systems Command ordered the AFPR not to communicate with Fitzgerald and Kroon. The DCAA regional supervisor placed severe limits on the type and amount of cost information Rick Kroon could obtain for Secretary Anthony's office.

As soon as we got this news on February 2, 1968, Rick Kroon made anguished appeals for help to Bob Anthony. I asked my boss to intercede. When nothing happened, I called Bill Petty, the head of the DCAA. Mr. Petty told me that the resident auditor at GE and his assistant were being transferred in response to complaints from General Electric. When I asked him if it might not be worth a few hurt feelings at

GE to save several million dollars, he answered frankly, "No."

No one in authority seemed to care what happened to the banished auditors. As had been the case in earlier incidents of removal or neutralization of cost-reduction advocates, high-level Pentagon civilians seemed pleased when the working troops made cost-reducing motions but were unwilling to buck the giveaway faction to help our would-be cost reducers when they got in trouble.

The tough AFPR at GE kept up the fight on his own, and I was later told that he had won some concessions, but I never saw any figures.

The banishment of the DCAA auditors at General Electric convinced me that I had to change my approach completely. There was no point testing Mr. McNamara's stated policy further. The Secretary of Defense may have believed in it himself, but deviations from the stated policy were the rule in actual operations.

On February 15, Secretary McNamara's "resignation" was announced. His successor, Clark Clifford, had the reputation of a "fixer" in Washington. His Washington law practice was heavily oriented toward serving the interests of giant indus-trial firms, including General Electric. At best, the outlook was not auspicious for the likes of me and working-level audi-tors cutting GE's slush money.

There appeared to be little sentiment among the higher-ups for genuine cost-cutting actions. On the other hand, the need was great. Our financial outlook had never been worse. The Asian war costs were mounting weekly and the Congress was beginning to make ugly noises about the Department of Defense's annual supplemental appropriation, which was be-coming a yearly spring ritual.

Against this deteriorating overall financial backdrop, the C-5A bubble finally burst. My civilian assistant brought me the news that Lockheed's actual costs would likely run three to four hundred million dollars over the ceiling price of their total package contract for development and production of the first fifty-eight airplanes. This information was more in the nature of suspicions confirmed than unexpected news. Ever since our debacle at the "instant generals" visit to Lockheed in December of 1966, indications of trouble had cropped up periodically but were glossed over in each case by the Air Force headquarters military staff and civilian procurement people. In fact the cover-up attempts became so blatant that in November of 1967, Dr. Anthony warned Secretary McNamara that the Air Force Chief of Staff, General McConnell, was lying to him about C-5A costs.*

The surprising news to me was that the miraculous total-package contract contained a built-in loophole. The formula for repricing the second batch, or Run B, of airplanes allowed the contractors to make up losses on the first order. If the contractors' actual costs on the first order exceeded the ceiling price by .1 percent to 10 percent, the price of the second order was increased by a percentage equal to 1.5 times the actual overrun percentage on the first order. For example, if the first order should actually cost the contractor 4 percent more than the ceiling, or maximum price to the government, the price of the second order would be increased by 4 percent multiplied by 1.5, or 6 percent. However, if the contractor's actual cost turned out to be more than 10 percent above the ceiling price, the get-well factor was increased from 1.5 to two. If actual costs for the first order exceeded the ceiling by 20 percent, the second order's price went up by two times 20 percent, or 40 percent. A 100 percent over-ceiling cost on the first buy would jack up the price of the second order by 200 percent. There was no limit other than the good credit of the United States Government and the patience (or ignorance) of the taxpayers.

It was another in the seemingly endless series of mad formulas I had encountered in the Pentagon. The scheme was so crazy, so expensive, and so destructive of the motivations necessary to the success of the Miracle of Procurement that I kept hoping my reliable assistant had made a mistake this one time. Unhappily, the information was confirmed when the C-5A SPO completed a detailed analysis of actual and projected costs at Lockheed in early March of 1968. According to the SPO, Lockheed stood to lose at least $316,000,000 on the first C-5A order. Because of the

* Washington *Post,* May 15, 1969.

repricing formula, however, Lockheed stood to make $182,000,000 in extra profit on the second order which would cut their overall losses to an estimated $134,000,000 for the 115-airplane program.* Fantastically, further cost overruns on the first order could cut Lockheed's expected losses. Air Staff cost analysts later calculated that each additional dollar of overrun on Lockheed's first order of fifty-eight airplanes would increase the price of the second order of fifty-eight planes by $1.70.

Far too late, I realized that I had been faked off by Horseshit Harry and the Mumbler. I had been suspicious when I first heard the vague explanations about repricing the options for C-5A follow-on production, but I had failed to bore in and get specifics. I might have anticipated this debacle if I had not been trying to play the game and be a nice guy when I was new in the Pentagon.

I went back and reviewed the copy of the C-5A contract I had received from the Air Staff after months of delay. The repricing section had been omitted.

It seemed that everything was coming apart at once for the Pentagon. Concurrently with the crumbling of the New Look façade in procurement, we were confronted with the 1968 Tet offensive in Vietnam, which shattered public illusions about the Asian War, and with growing problems in international financial and monetary circles. On March 15 I attended a meeting in Secretary Anthony's office where he laid out the international situation in the starkest terms. "Our top leadership, including the White House, has recognized that the world situation is approaching catastrophe," Dr. Anthony told us grimly. He told the assembled financial management people of a temporary panic in Europe over uncertainty about the soundness of the U.S. dollar and asked that he be notified immediately of any hints of reluctance to accept dollar contracts in Europe. He pointed out the seriousness of the steady losses of U.S. gold reserves and emphasized the importance of the Services minimizing expenditures abroad. Finally, Dr. Anthony announced that he had just agreed with the Bureau of the Budget on a $3,000,000,000 reduction in

---

* "Hearings on Military Posture," before the Committee on Armed Services, Ninety-first Congress (Part 2), p. 2963.

DoD expenditures previously planned for the next fiscal year running from July 1, 1968, to June 30, 1969.* The expenditure cuts were to be genuine reductions too, he emphasized. "No cosmetic actions," Dr. Anthony warned.

At long last, I thought, the true seriousness of our monumental waste had been recognized. I decided to revive my cost-reduction efforts, this time sticking to modest savings goals in areas requiring minimal analytical work. We could save several hundred million dollars just by saying "No" to paying for big increases in contractors' discretionary expenses. These expenses would include such things as independent research and development, proposal writing and other selling expenses, and the costs of undefined "product improvement," "maintaining the mobilization base," and retaining "stand-by" personnel. All these activities were considered desirable things to do, and I was proposing only that we limit the growth of our contributions to support them. We wouldn't tell the contractors how much they could spend on these things, but we would tell them we wouldn't pay for increases. In the mythical Ajax Case, we would not have told Max Ajax that he could not hire his girlfriend. We would have just told him we wouldn't reimburse him for any of her pay. The decision on hiring her would have been left to his discretion.

My overtures for modest cost savings were rebuffed immediately by the procurement community in the Pentagon. They were headed in the other direction. My concerns and the larger ones of Secretary Anthony weren't real-world problems for the procurement people. My proposals would have cut employment in the military contracting industry in a presidential election year. The procurement people were trying to pump it up.

Although presidential appointees and high-ranking military officers could not be drawn into discussion of the supposed policy, the procurement underlings talked freely and gave me documents which supported their case. The period reminded me of my early days in the Pentagon when the Air Force's old hands indoctrinated me in the "partnership with industry" traditions to justify loose procurement practices.

* I believe this is the same reduction the new Nixon administration later took credit for.

I was given a copy of an "Official Use Only" memorandum from Tom Morris, Assistant Secretary of Defense for I & L, to Mr. Nitze to begin my re-education. Mr. Morris' memo began:

We have been very active over the past several months in changing certain of our procurement policies and practices in order to be of maximum assistance in the President's program to employ the hard-core disadvantaged workers.

After pointing out that the Department of Defense was precluded by the annual Congressional Appropriations Act rider from using Defense funds for purposes of relieving economic dislocation, Secretary Morris described the conspiracy to evade this law:

The Small Business Administration does not have this restraint and, under the Small Business Act, the Department of Defense can issue a contract directly to SBA. SBA, in turn, can subcontract the work on any basis it sees fit. This approach has been cleared with the General Accounting Office.

Mr. Morris then described how the Fairchild-Hiller Company, a big aerospace company, had formed a subsidiary company to manufacture wooden pallets for materials handling. In addition to the high technology required, Fairchild-Hiller would supply "management talent." Non-DoD government agencies would provide training funds, loans, and so on. However, even with the government grants and Fairchild-Hiller's "management talent," there were problems:

The problem is the degree to which Department of Defense funds should be used to subsidize this effort. In the present instance, DSA estimates that it can procure the 50,000 wooden pallets in question under competitive conditions at a price of not over $3.30 per pallet. The price SBA has obtained from the new company (called Fair-Mico Company) is $4.59 per pallet.

The proposed price premium amounted to 40 percent, and Secretary Morris suggested that the DoD should maintain the illusion of economy by limiting the price premium to 33⅓ percent. Mr. Morris pointed out that the case he had described would "set a precedent for future procurements through SBA" and would permit achievement of "the primary objective of utilizing an inherently inefficient work force." He assured approval of his sales pitch by writing:

The President is personally interested in this whole program and I understand that a formal announcement of this contract will be made as soon as possible by the White House if we give SBA a contract. I have previously discussed our involvement in this program with Mr. McNamara and he approved our participation and use of DoD funds.

Mr. Morris' memo was dated February 12, 1968. Mr. Nitze approved it that same day.

The Air Force, never to be outdone in giving away money, reacted quickly to the new direction. Assistant Secretary Charles put together a team to carry out the program, and by February 25, 1968, he had solid progress to report to Secretary Brown:

In order to explain the new procurement technique of contracting directly with the Small Business Administration, and to provide a greater sense of urgency at the operating level to support the President's Program, Israel Rubin of my office, with reps from the Departments of Labor and Commerce, the Small Business Administration and the Air Staff recently visited our major buying activities.

Mr. Charles also reported that the first contract under the new scheme had already been awarded and that more would be forthcoming.

I had to admit that the "social goals" faction had scored a point, but I tried to argue that willingness to make a few exceptions to supposedly established policy in order to buy off potential rioters should not be interpreted as repudiation of efficiency goals in general. I didn't convince anyone, though, least of all the Air Force procurement people. As they pointed out to me, there was no problem in getting quick endorsement of the giveaway policy and no delay in carrying it out. Conversely, our only direction to try to reduce costs was Mr. Nitze's instruction to perform a should-cost study on the Mark II, and that did not stick. Actions spoke louder than words. Besides, my procurement friends argued, if the Administration was willing to bend the law to buy minority-group votes, was it reasonable to think they wanted to lay off surplus union members and professional people in the big aerospace plants?

I had to acknowledge the point, assuming the desire to keep people voting right was an underlying purpose of our boondoggle. "But what about political opposition?" I asked. "Won't the Republicans squawk?"

My principal instructor in these matters, one of Bob Charles' subordinates, answered that there might be some grumbling, but most of it would be private. As long as the slush money was funneled through the big corporations, we had little to fear from Republicans. In fact, he said Senator Javits, a senior Republican senator, was heartily in favor of the giveaway scheme and would endorse it in a Senate floor speech.

Senator Javits made his speech on April 19, 1968, and offered an amendment to the bill authorizing military procurement for fiscal year 1969. He didn't specifically endorse extra-cost contracting in the amendment he offered, but both the proffered amendment and his accompanying speech left no doubt that he approved the general idea. For example, the Senator said:

For too long, I think, we have tended to think of our social welfare and manpower programs as a small, compartmentalized part of the budget. In fact, it would be entirely possible to assure that large portions of the defense budget could also serve, at least in part, in the war against poverty in our ghettos and rural poverty areas. All we need to do, and it is the effect of this amendment, is to direct our defense expenditures in such a way as to insure that they have a maximum feasible impact on the problem of hard-core unemployment, which is the master problem in the antipoverty area. There is nothing revolutionary about this suggestion. Our defense expenditures now are used to help sustain certain sectors of the economy. For example, a large proportion of the research and developmental work in connection with the civilian economy and nondefense products is carried along by appropriations for defense research and development.[*]

Senator Javits gave a specific example of the willingness of big contractors to participate in the program. A company in his home state, Republic Aviation, had submitted a proposal to build more F-105 fighter planes using thousands of "hard-core people" in the production process. The Senator said that Republic would

* *Congressional Record*, April 19, 1968, p. S4272.

even build an airplane plant in the ghetto area of Brooklyn "if need be to carry out that policy of employment." Republic was pictured as extremely flexible in "social impact" considerations. "All it wants," Senator Javits said candidly, "is the contract." *

After more rhetoric on how military contracting could help solve the nation's social ills, the Senator even managed to find a good side to the Asian War. He concluded his speech with this suggestion: "If we must fight wars abroad, let us seek imaginative ways to make that war effort bring peace at home, through jobs for the poor."

I conceded that the Administration could probably get away with this caper because of the great fear of uprisings in the cities. Maybe extra-cost government-supported employment of the hard-core unemployed was necessary, at least temporarily. But why not do it through some other agency? It was a well known fact that we had to put four or five or even more dollars in the Pentagon hopper to get one dollar out the bottom for the hourly wage earner. Other agencies could certainly do the job more cheaply. My instructors acknowledged that this was true but that my suggested approach ignored reality: The Congress and the taxpayers would not hold still for the expenditures unless they were disguised as "defense."

When I tried to convince the brighter staff people in procurement, financial management, and systems analysis that the deliberately wasteful expenditures were economically unsound, I learned something which really startled me. In general, the Pentagon's economists professed to believe that government spending, wasteful or not, made the nation prosperous. They drew no economic distinction between wasteful, parasitic activities and productive activities. One seemingly bright young Ph.D. economist, a former Air Force academy instructor, even tried to convince me that our bombing program in Southeast Asia contributed to the nation's prosperity. To such economists, mostly Keynesians of the mindless variety, the economic products of the bombing program were jobs and corporate profits. To me, the products were holes in the ground in an Asian jungle or paddy.

* *Ibid.*

Again, I encountered a sort of religious obstacle to logical thinking. I learned that many Pentagon economists had been highly trained in the mechanics of calculating gross aggregate demand, income redistribution, and the theoretical increases in inflationary spending which they held to be necessary to keep employment high. They really believed that waste was a good thing. Like primitive witch doctors, they had their idols and their mysterious, esoteric rituals which required long training to perform, but they neither questioned nor thought much about fundamental causes and effects. They were our high priests of waste.

During the spring and summer of 1968, I kept hammering away at what I had decided was the central question, the big issue, of Pentagon procurement. Was our prime purpose to buy necessary weapons at the lowest sound prices, as Secretary McNamara had so eloquently proclaimed, or was it to run the world's biggest boondoggle? Obviously, we could not do both. Weapons procurement alone appeared to be difficult enough without taking on the additional responsibility of running a giant, sterile, make-work program. I made a few converts among the military people by arguing that weapons procurement was too important to use as a dumping ground for all the country's social problems. There was ample evidence of the effects of already-poor management disciplines among our big contractors. More supernumerary employees could only make matters worse. Others also worried about this problem. For example, the July 1968 issue of *Armed Forces Management* magazine commented on the misuse of military resources and wondered "whether the military are willing to give up voluntarily the butter in their guns budget."

They weren't. There was a little grumbling, but no military people openly opposed the accelerated giveaways. The prospect of a larger and more potent contractor constituency overshadowed concerns about economical production of weapons that worked. The civilian procurement people, fronting for the military in the Pentagon, went all out in support of the "social goals" boondoggle. Air Force Assistant Secretary Bob Charles, erstwhile advocate of unshackled, competitive free enterprise, disengagement, "calling the sheriff" on contractor malefactors, etc., wanted even more leeway. On July 12, 1968, he wrote to Tom Morris suggesting that DoD do more toward "the amelioration of the critical socioeconomic problems facing the nation." He added:

I believe, however, that DoD is capable of dealing with many of these problems much more effectively and to a far greater extent than at present. For example, certain categories of procurement could be reserved entirely for competition from among firms located in and hiring people from hardcore unemployment areas. In order to accomplish this, many of our present basic assumptions, which are now constraints, should be considered in the light of alternative assumptions which have greater relevance in meeting our domestic crises.

Secretary Charles also suggested that Secretary of Defense Clifford set up a "Citizens Task Force" to seek ways for further evasion or emasculation of rules prohibiting diversion of the taxpayers' contributions to the defense effort to extraneous purposes:

The Citizens' Task Force would evaluate the effectiveness of DoD's current programs and past efforts to accomplish national social and economic objectives, within the constraints of existing statutory authority. In addition, recommendations would be made for new statutory authority. In addition, recommendations would be made for new statutory authority that may be needed by DoD in order to undertake expanded and new socio-economic program roles, to the extent such undertakings are considered advisable.

Mr. Charles concluded by volunteering Air Force staff support for his proposed scheme.

The "social goals" vote-buying scheme gained momentum when Robert Moot replaced Dr. Anthony as Comptroller of the Department of Defense. Mr. Moot had been serving as Administrator of the Small Business Administration and had been an enthusiastic participant in the DoD-SBA-contractor shell game aimed at circumventing the feeble antiboondoggle restrictions on military spending.

On August 12, 1968, Vice President Hubert Humphrey, frantically running uphill for President, jumped on the military contract boondoggle bandwagon. He wrote to Secretary Clark Clifford suggesting that the Pentagon twist contractors' arms a bit to induce them (no compulsion, mind you) to construct new plants so as to maximize "creation" of jobs where they were most needed. He suggested that the already flaccid Armed Services Procurement Regulations be amended to facilitate his job-making scheme:

Neal Peterson of my staff had gone through the Armed Services procurement regulations and set forth the language which I believe is necessary to accomplish this. There does not appear to be any legal impediment to this plan, as it deals only with subcontracts already awarded by the Defense Department.

It appeared to me that Vice President Humphrey did not specifically call for opening the flood gates for unlimited contractor boondoggling, but the Pentagon procurement claque chose to interpret it that way. With the change of top leadership, the Comptroller bureaucracy joined in as well. The Vice President's letter, on top of other indications of top-level support for the social goals faction, was used to block even my feeblest efforts at cost control. Whether or not it was intended, the Pentagon had in fact been turned into a giant, military job-making agency. It was dramatically more expensive and much more wasteful than the much maligned WPA of the 1930s. Whereas the WPA had given us paved streets, parks, post offices, and other useful things along with considerable waste, we got very few tangible benefits from our military boondoggling.

I decided to try again to get a definite expression of policy, hopefully one which would limit the applicability of the now dominant "social goals" philosophy so we could identify a few areas where money saving would be allowed. Air Force Col. Henry Fletcher, Jr., had replaced General Snavely as director of Procurement Policy for the Department of Defense. Since I was seeking policy clarification, it seemed reasonable to consult the fountainhead of procurement policy, so I attempted to meet with Colonel Fletcher. The Colonel was "too busy" to see me, but his secretary said I could write him a letter if I wished. After a fruitless exchange of correspondence in which my polite questions about policy were evaded by Colonel Fletcher, I bundled up my earlier correspondence with General Snavely on the subject and sent it to Colonel Fletcher along with a lengthy cover letter which I concluded with a series of specific questions:

I personally believe that we should try to operate the defense establishment as efficiently as possible, that we should state our intention clearly and that we should act in support of our stated intention. My reasons for this belief are summarized in my July 9, 1968 memorandum to General Snavely along with my suggestions for a combined policy statement and plan of action. If I have misinterpreted our principal top management acquisition objectives, I believe you should tell me so and set me straight.

At the same time, our whole organization would benefit from clarification of procurement policy on several specific points:

1. Are we deliberately supporting an industrial base for social or economic purposes?
2. If so, to what extent, where and for how long?
3. Is there a system of priorities ranking military needs and socio-economic programs within the defense appropriations?
4. In those instances in which we are encouraging the disadvantaged to become defense contractors, is there any reason why we should not encourage efficiency in their operations?
5. If employment of a certain number of people is one of our goals, would it not be desirable to encourage greater efficiency for the purpose of obtaining more and better military hardware and services?
6. Has OSD evaluated the impact of low industrial efficiency on our export trade?
7. How can "policy statements" such as the one quoted on pages 1 and 2 of this memorandum be answered? [Note: the passages quoted dealt with Gen. Zoeckler's "inefficiency is national policy" proclamation.]

Straightforward answers to these questions will clarify large areas of uncertainty regarding our procurement policy. If definitive answers have not been formulated, even a meaningful dialogue on the basic questions would help.

I earnestly solicit your assistance in clarifying the questions outlined.°

I sent my letter to Colonel Fletcher on August 27, 1969. He never replied to me directly, but on September 25 one of Fletcher's assistants, a longtime friend of mine, came to my office, dropped an eleven-page document on my desk, and said, "There's your answer." The document was an advance copy of a

---

° "The Dismissal of A. Ernest Fitzgerald," hearings before the Subcommittee on Economy in Government, Ninety-first Congress, Nov. 17 and 18, 1969, pp. 62–63.

speech Secretary Clifford was to make the next day. It announced a vast expansion of the DoD "social goals" programs.
Mr. Clifford disclaimed any intention of turning the Pentagon
into a social welfare agency, but the substance of his proposal
took a giant step in that direction. In reporting the speech, newspapers carried front page headlines such as "Pentagon to Act on
Domestic Ills" and "Clifford Says He'll Mobilize Resources of
Military to Attack Social Problems." * The stories described the
Pentagon's proposed entry into development of low-cost housing,
invention of "new generation" automated hospitals, expansion of
job-generating activities, and improvement of education. Secretary Clifford also recommended "reexamination" of legal restrictions on using military appropriations for extraneous purposes.

All in all, the Clifford plan was a blueprint for institutionalized
boondoggling and a military-dominated society. It took a while
for these aspects of Mr. Clifford's generally applauded new direction to sink in, but eventually the syndicated columnists began
commenting on it. On October 2, liberal columnist Carl Rowan
wrote:

> How much more difficult it will be to attack this great financial
> sinkhole if the military can boast that they are feeding the hungry,
> healing the sick, and teaching the lame and the halt to do hand-
> springs. We have dozens of agencies that know more about housing,
> education, medicine, and employment than does the Pentagon. If
> Mr. Clifford has excess funds for ventures in these fields, the Bureau
> of the Budget ought to reclaim them forthwith and put them into the
> mangled budgets of some of the agencies of human uplift.
> I know. The argument will be that the Pentagon has to do the job
> because only it can get the money. They will say you couldn't get the
> time of day from L. Mendel Rivers, D–S.C., by talking about poverty
> and illness, but that he will put the scissors to the purse-strings if
> you want guns and bases (preferably in his district).†

Mr. Rowan summed up his objections by saying, "The military-
industrial complex already has more than enough influence on
American life."

Secretary Clifford's official endorsement of Pentagon boondoggling, using social welfare as an excuse, also drew a little fire

---

* *The New York Times,* September 27, 1968.
† Washington *Star,* October 2, 1968.

from the opposite end of the political spectrum. Retired Air Force Lt. Gen. Ira C. Eaker, a syndicated columnist of right-wing, hawkish leanings, reported Clifford's welfare spending plan and then wrote:

Many members of Congress have suggested that one reason why defense appropriations have risen sharply during the past eight years (the proposed 1969 defense bill is the largest in our history) is because DoD takes on the tasks of other departments of government, since it can get the money.

General Eaker summed up his argument as follows:

The best weapon at the cheapest price should be the firm criteria in defense procurement.

If it is wise and necessary for the Pentagon to join HEW, HUD, OEO and the other welfare agencies, why did its proponents wait until the end of the Johnson administration to propose it? *

The General was mistaken on his last point. The Pentagon did not wait until the end of the Johnson Administration to propose the welfare excuse for boondoggling. It had been there all along. It was simply surfaced to get votes.

Actually, I was not totally unhappy with the surfacing of the defense welfare philosophy. Clandestine adherents to the religion of waste had been tripping me up for years anyway, and I figured I could only gain by having the rascals come out in the open with their decrepit arguments. To my mind, this was a far better situation than presenting the pious public face best pictured by Mr. McNamara's classic 1965 posture statement, then behaving contrarily to the stated policy in actual practice. Clifford's endorsement brought the "social goals" issue out in the open where it could be dealt with.

However, before I had time to do anything further on this issue, the C-5A program roused itself to demand money again. The C-5A SPO had been sent to the showers after their March 1968 disclosures of galloping overruns. The C-5A SPO had been told to make another cost study, largely because Lockheed disputed their analyses.

After surfacing briefly, the C-5A overruns had disappeared

* Pentagon Clipping Service, October 25, 1968.

from routine internal Air Force reports. I had made several attempts to get the obviously false reports corrected, but without success.

The C-5A SPO's October 1968 cost estimate was a real shocker. The SPO had estimated in March that Lockheed stood to lose $316,000,000 on the development and production of the first fifty-eight planes. By October, Lockheed's projected loss for the same work had grown to $671,500,000.* General Electric, contractor for the TF-39 engine, was also pictured as badly overrun, but the primary concern centered on Lockheed. Their projected losses on the first order were about twice the net worth of the company.

This generated a great flurry of concern over Lockheed's welfare. Now that we were faced with the actual prospect of "calling the sheriff" to a failing contractor, the tough talkers headed for the hills. The procurement types, previously loud in their praise of "disengagement" and contractor risk taking, and contemptuous of those who insisted on grubbing around for facts on developing disasters, became the most frantic pleaders for bailing out Lockheed.

The Pentagon politicians were panicstricken. Lockheed was assembling the C-5A in Marietta, Georgia, the home state of Senator Richard Russell, Chairman of the Senate Armed Services Committee. The Senator was an awesome figure to the high-level bureaucrats, and the prospect of bankrupting the largest employer in his state paralyzed the thought processes of the bureaucrats. I attended the meeting where the C-5A SPO cost analysts briefed middle-level people from OSD and the Bureau of the Budget on the horrifying Lockheed overrun. The closed-faced superclerks listened to the presentation in silence. When it was over, the spokesman for the Bureau of the Budget said, "This one will have to be settled between the President and Senator Russell."

When the total bill was added up, including the Air Force's share of contractors' overruns, increased prices of spare parts, miscellaneous items such as ground equipment and, above all,

---

* "Hearings on Military Posture," before the Committee on Armed Services, House of Representatives, Ninety-first Congress, First Session (Part 2), p. 2953.

the effect of the nightmarish repricing formula, some high-ranking officials lost their enthusiasm for the Miracle of Procurement, at least temporarily. When all the identified increases were included, the estimated bill for the total Miracle increased from $3,371,000,000 (which included unidentified slush money) to $5,338,000,000, an increase of almost two billion dollars.

Worse, the program was technically sick. In fact it was so critically ill that the C-5A contracting officer had issued an almost unheard of "cure notice" to Lockheed on February 1, 1968. The cure notice warned Lockheed that the Air Force might not accept C-5As built by Lockheed if the company did not correct known shortcomings. This was an extraordinary action. As Bob Charles pointed out in his memo lamenting the possible effect of the cure notice on a big bond offering by Lockheed at the same time, cure notices had not been issued even on such acknowledged technical disasters as the F-111, the Skybolt missile, and the misbegotten Dynasoar project.

The cure notice was only the tip of the iceberg of the C-5A's technical troubles, but the SPO's frightening increases in the estimated costs *assumed technical success*. As the technical trouble surfaced, the costs were bound to go higher in the absence of corrective actions, and neither the Air Force with its "look the other way" policies nor the OSD, mostly Cost Calvinists, believed in corrective actions.

Whereas the OSD and Bureau of the Budget functionaries viewed the problem as bigger than all of them and soluble only by the highest and mightiest, some top Air Force officials were boiling mad about being snookered into the Miracle of Procurement. They were downright bitter about the idiotic repricing formula which would be put in force with the second order of C-5As, or Run B. "We just won't buy 'em," vowed salty old Gen. J. P. McConnell, the Chief of Staff. "We'll haul the goddamned troops in Gooney Birds." ("Gooney Bird" was the common name for C-47 transport planes, a World War II version of the Douglas DC-3.)

Secretary of the Air Force Harold Brown seemed almost equally adamant. In an October 17, 1968, letter verifying his instructions to make Lockheed a "take it or leave it" offer to contract without further recourse to the open-ended repricing formula, Dr. Brown started by making the following points:

a. In view of Lockheed's serious financial position at the end of Run A, they are in a very weak negotiating position, i.e., they have to have Run B to avoid serious dollar losses.
b. The Air Force does not *have* to have Run B. Other alternatives could be pursued.
c. In view of the strong budget constraints, the Air Force will have to fight very hard to get *any* FY 70 and subsequent FY funding from OSD for the C-5.
d. The current contractual arrangement for Run B which provides a "reverse incentive" on Run A costs is unsatisfactory and must be changed if we are to proceed with Run B.

This was the high point of Pentagon resistance to bailing out Lockheed. Significantly, even Harold Brown's October 17 letter was softened between draft and final version. The draft had directed pricing the second buy on the basis of a tough analysis of what it ought to cost, disregarding the crazy formula. The final version, however, directed that the crazy formula be used but with a freeze on further growth. The attitude toward Lockheed softened from then on.

The General Accounting Office, the Congress' barkless and rubber-toothed watchdog agency, chose that moment to make their contribution to solution of the C-5A crisis. On November 1, 1968, four other Air Force people and I met with three GAO representatives to discuss a draft report they had prepared on the C-5A. It was the result of more than a year of study and analysis of the C-5A program, including extensive surveys in the Lockheed plant in Marietta, Georgia. Incredibly, the GAO report (Code 81002) did not contain one word or figure indicating trouble of any sort—cost, schedule, or technical—on the C-5A. Seemingly, the congressional bulldogs had been neutered, then struck deaf, dumb, and blind. Far from detecting and viewing with alarm the catastrophe visited upon us by Lockheed's management, the GAO was full of praise and admiration for noble, fearless Lockheed and the brilliant Air Force creators of the Miracle of Procurement. In fact, the burden of their report was to slap our wrists for trying to find out what was going on at Lockheed. We didn't need to know, they suggested, because of the marvelous total-package procurement concept. They said that the concept envisioned two or more contractors committing themselves in competition to develop the product, to produce it, and to provide selected portions of the necessary logistics support. Mesmerized by propaganda about the Miracle and disdainful of facts, the GAO raved on: "It also envisions that the contractor accept total responsibility for the development and ultimate performance of the system and will be motivated to meet or exceed performance and price commitments." *

The GAO's most specific criticisms were aimed at a series of technical reports on the C-5A's most critical and assiduously concealed problems. One of the reports they questioned, "Strength Summary and Operating Restrictions," dealt with the plane's most serious shortcomings. I had been trying to get the data in the report for more than a year. According to the GAO, we should stop bothering Lockheed because "the C-5A contract contains provisions specifically to motivate the contractor to meet and exceed the performance and specification requirements for the aircraft."

My Air Force associates and I were incredulous that the GAO watchdogs, docile as they were, could have reached such absurd conclusions just at the time the total-package con game was being exposed. I was suspicious that the GAO had been enlisted as part of the cover-up effort and that their criticisms were expected to fend off our factual inquiries. Jim Hammond, the leader of the GAO group, couldn't or wouldn't explain how they could be so wrong. Surely, we thought, someone must have misled them. As Colonel D. R. Boyles, one of our Air Force representatives, put it in his notes:

Hammond was questioned as to what or who had prompted GAO interest in the areas covered by the report. Was it true that Lockheed themselves had requested the investigation as a means of deterring AF monitoring? Hammond was most evasive in his reply and stated that "Mr. Charles had indicated problems and solicited GAO assistance."

Clearly the cover-up had high level support, and the GAO was a party to it. They weren't altogether innocent dupes either.

* GAO draft report (Code 81002), September 1968.

They knew about the cost overruns. Jim Hammond asked if we were considering buying Boeing 747 airplanes rather than more C-5As. Mr. Hammond said we could then buy two 747s for the price of a C-5A. The 747s were being offered at $22,000,000 each. At twice that figure, $44,000,000 each, the 120-plane C-5A program would cost $5,280,000,000, very near the closely guarded October 1968 estimate of $5,338,000,000 for the overrun program.

In the midst of all the furor over the C-5A debacle, I received an invitation to testify before the Joint Economic Committee of the Congress. Months before, the Joint Economic Committee (JEC) staff had invited me to lunch to discuss some of the speeches and papers I had written. The JEC staff was preparing for hearings on the economics of military procurement, and they were considering inviting me to testify on Air Force management systems and the impact of those systems on the prices of things we bought. I had replied that I would be pleased to testify if my superiors approved. The meeting was so unremarkable that I didn't even note the date, and I had forgotten the incident until I received the invitation from the Committee Chairman, Senator William Proxmire of Wisconsin.

When I received Senator Proxmire's letter, dated October 18, 1968, my secretary told me that the envelope containing the Senator's letter had been opened before delivery to our office. The envelope was addressed to me personally, and as I was wondering about it, I received a telephone call from Bob Moot, the DoD Comptroller. Mr. Moot asked if I had received an invitation to testify before Senator Proxmire's Subcommittee on Economy in Government. When I answered that I had, wondering at this phenomenally fast communication, Mr. Moot told me that Tom Morris, the Assistant Secretary of Defense for I & L, was very disturbed by the prospect of my testimony and by the fact that I had been personally invited by Senator Proxmire. Mr. Moot asked if I would turn the matter over to him, in effect assigning the invitation. I replied that I had just that moment received the invitation and had not discussed it with my boss, Tom Nielsen. I told Mr. Moot that Mr Nielsen was out of town and that I would take no action without consulting my boss.

On Tom Nielsen's return, we discussed the situation at length.

Tom observed that the procurement people undoubtedly would be unhappy that I was to testify but added that he thought my views deserved to be heard. We agreed that I should try to work with the procurement people to develop a constructive statement.

The next day, I was informed by Tom Johnson, one of Moot's assistants, that I would not be allowed to testify, and that George Bergquist, Moot's deputy in charge of OSD management systems, would appear in my place. Nielsen confirmed this, adding that I would attend the hearing as a "back-up" witness to support Bergquist's testimony. Nielsen told me that I was not to prepare a statement. Senator Proxmire's invitation had requested that I submit 100 copies of my written statement at least one day before my scheduled appearance on November 13.

In reviewing Bergquist's proposed statement, I saw that he had evaded Senator Proxmire's principal question—the impact of our management systems, controls, and policies on actual procurement prices. In other words, the Senator wanted to know whether our elaborate and costly management schemes were really saving money. George Bergquist acknowledged the omission but said he had been directed to stay away from the subject.

I relayed this to Tom Nielsen, telling him that I could not honestly support George Bergquist's statement, and I suggested that someone who agreed with Bergquist's position be sent in my place as back-up witness. Nielsen agreed with my view and set up a meeting with Bob Moot to discuss the matter.

Secretary Moot listened to our proposal but insisted that I accompany Bergquist to "back him up." At the same time, he was adamant in opposing my testimony and my preparation of a written statement. Moot said it was widely believed that I "intended to present testimony which would leave blood on the floor." "Furthermore," Moot stated, "Secretary Clifford would not agree with your statement."

Both Tom Nielsen and I were amazed at the total illogic of Moot's position. If Moot, Morris, and Clifford didn't want me to testify, surely the best way to prevent it was to leave me in the Pentagon when Bergquist went to testify. I told Moot that since no one had asked me what I intended to say, the fear that I would "leave blood on the floor" was pure conjecture. "Why not," I asked, "let me prepare a statement before passing judgment?" I added that Clifford's assumptions were equally groundless. It did not seem reasonable that the Secretary of Defense would take the position that he would disagree with whatever I might say. I had never met or spoken to Mr. Clifford. I told Moot that anything I would say would be directed toward improved efficiency and saving the taxpayers' money. I could not conceive of the Secretary of Defense opposing such objectives.

Moot dissembled but stuck to his ludicrous position. The matter had been thoroughly discussed in OSD, he said, and the decision had been made.

Having made my views known, I then told Nielsen I was content to let Moot, Morris, and Clifford handle my invitation any way they saw fit so long as they left me out of their game playing. Nielsen agreed that was all we could do, but he expressed puzzlement at the weird reasoning of our OSD superiors. The chiefs just weren't behaving rationally.

The reason for this strange behavior soon became clear. The OSD bigwigs and our procurement people had panicked when Proxmire's invitation came. Before I ever saw the letter, it had been intercepted and opened, and copies had been spread throughout the OSD and procurement offices. All the frightened giveaway artists had immediately jumped to the conclusion that I had leaked my correspondence with General Snavely and Colonel Fletcher to Proxmire. Tom Nielsen told me that Tom Morris and Bob Charles were positive that Senator Proxmire had the entire file and that he intended to use it to "conduct a circus" in the hearings. I told Tom that if Senator Proxmire had the file, he did not get it from me but that embarrassment could be avoided easily if Proxmire did have the file: Simply answer straightforwardly the questions I had raised in posing the big issue of intent in procurement. Did we want to save money or not? An affirmative answer would lay to rest all the questions I had raised.

Unhappily, the procurement people had ceased to think clearly. Their blind, unreasoning panic over possible disclosure of the deliberate giveaway policy was intensified by their fear that Senator Proxmire would learn of the C-5A overruns. One of the

Joint Economic Committee staff men, Richard Kaufman, had been nosing around asking questions about it already. I later learned that procurement specialists in OSD and the Air Force had suggested that Kaufman study the program as a model of how big procurement should be done. Apparently, our procurement experts thought they could confine Richard Kaufman's interest to the flashy gimmicks and keep him away from the repricing formula and the disastrous results. Mr. Kaufman had apparently absorbed all the sales pitches but then had confronted the pitchmen by asking for facts and figures.

A day or so before Senator Proxmire's scheduled hearing, Dr. Brown called Tom Nielsen, Bob Charles, and me to his office to discuss my appearance as George Bergquist's back-up man. Tom and I told Dr. Brown that we were sure OSD was making a serious mistake in their senseless handling of the affair. Dr. Brown didn't disagree, but he said he had concluded that the only thing we could do was go along with their direction. He said he was sure Senator Proxmire would call on me to testify anyway, regardless of my "back-up" status. Dr. Brown wanted to discuss my testimony.

Bob Charles did too. Secretary Charles was normally the coolest and smoothest of operators, but he was obviously shaken then. He had the whole thick bundle of my Snavely-Fletcher file with him and was furious with me for having written it. He was positive that Senator Proxmire had the documents and intended to ask me to vouch for their authenticity at the public hearing. Bob Charles had already marked he passages which he believed would be quoted in the headlines. He was especially outraged that I had recorded General Zeke Zoeckler's statements blocking the Mark II should-cost study. "Just look at this," he said heatedly, showing the marked passages to Dr. Brown. "I can see the headline now in the Washington *Post:* 'AF General Says Inefficiency is Policy.' That's ridiculous, and it's not true. Zeke would never say anything like that."

"It sounds exactly like something Zeke would say," countered Harold Brown with uncommon candor.

I tried to calm Bob Charles' fears by assuring him that I had not given any part of my file on the "social goals" issue to Senator

Proxmire or anyone else except Snavely, Fletcher, and Tom Nielsen. I then told him I thought the Senator's real interest would be in the C-5A cost overruns, which had not been disclosed publicly but which were common insider knowledge, as evidenced by comments by the GAO.

"Stay away from the C-5A," Charles said sternly.

Harold Brown looked at Bob Charles for a moment, then looked to me and said, "Just try to avoid policy disputes." With that advice, Dr. Brown ended the meeting.

Immediately afterward, I met with George Bergquist and David Moran, one of Mr. Bergquist's assistants who was to be another back-up witness. The three of us called on Colonel Fletcher's boss, John Malloy, the Deputy Assistant Secretary of Defense (Procurement) to solicit policy guidance. He had none to offer.

The night before the hearings, George Bergquist, Dave Moran, and I made a last attempt to persuade the OSD people to behave sensibly. A representative of the Secretary of Defense's legislative affairs office, a Navy commander named Dauchess, had been assigned as our keeper. Commander Dauchess supposedly knew the ropes on Capitol Hill and was responsible for seeing that things went smoothly. Bergquist, Moran, and I argued with Dauchess at length, trying to persuade him not to try to force George Bergquist on Senator Proxmire as a witness. We could only look foolish, we argued, trying to run the Senator's hearing for him. We told Commander Dauchess that the Pentagon's shenanigans were sure to be interpreted as an attempt to muzzle me and to obstruct congressional testimony. Aside from looking silly, this was against the law. The Commander understood all this, but he had his orders. He would not be moved and would not agree to ask his bosses to reconsider. We concluded by cautioning Dauchess that we would let him explain the affair to Senator Proxmire if the question of obstructing my testimony came up.

The next day, Commander Dauchess ushered Bergquist, Moran, and me to a big hearing room in the New Senate Office Building. I had never before attended a Congressional hearing, and I was somewhat surprised to see so many spectators, reporters, and television camera crews present. The four of us sat among the spectators, and I was just beginning to take in the scene when Senator Proxmire, whom I recognized from newspaper pictures, called the hearing to order. He was the only member of his subcommittee present. The Senator directed me to come forward to the witness table along with the day's two other witnesses, retired Air Force colonel Bill Buesking and Irving Fisher of the Rand Corporation. Colonel Buesking was then teaching and working toward his Ph.D. at the University of Southern California. After a long career as a pilot, Colonel Buesking had served as a financial control officer on the Minuteman missile program and then worked as an assistant to Bob Anthony and Mr. Bergquist for a couple of years before retiring. Irving Fisher, of the Rand Corporation, had survived (though just barely) the episode of his suppressed study of incentive contracting and was then recognized for calling attention to flaws in the DoD's supposedly miraculous contracts.

I was asked to testify first. After explaining that I did not have a prepared statement, I presented a brief, off-the-cuff discussion of the importance of sound management systems.*

Next, Bill Buesking gave an excellent and comprehensive statement. He stated that he had observed strong resistance to cost reduction in the weapons procurement business in spite of excessive costs, which he estimated at 30 to 50 percent of prices paid. He said that he had detected no correlation between contractor performance and profits, that bad performance was not necessarily reflected in lower profits. He countered the then-current propaganda on low military contractor profits by reporting that contractors on the big Minuteman program had made an average of 43 percent profit on their invested capital. He recommended should-cost pricing and other reforms to save money.

Then Irving Fisher presented an updated version of his previously suppressed study of incentive contracts. He emphasized the likelihood that apparent cost reductions were attributable to fat

---

* "Economics of Military Procurement," hearings before the Subcommittee on Economy in Government of the Joint Economic Committee, Ninetieth Congress, Second Session, Part I, pp. 153–156.

prices for initial contracts and change orders more than to superior contractor cost controls.

While the other two witnesses were testifying, I thought about how I would handle the question of the concealed C-5A overruns when Senator Proxmire got around to asking about them. There was no doubt he would ask, because of questions he had put to previous witnesses. Just the day before, Proxmire had questioned Mr. Malloy, the Pentagon procurement chief, on the program. Senator Proxmire had prefaced his questioning by stating: "I would like to ask you a question or two in connection with the C-5A, in which I understand the Government may pay billions of dollars more, one or two billion more than initially expected." *

Mr. Malloy had taken standard evasive action, pleading ignorance on the Pentagon's largest contract despite assuring the Senator only a minute before that "we have very intimate knowledge of what is going on" in the contractor operations. Finally, in response to a direct question about the C-5A overrun, Malloy replied, "I do not know that." But Mr. Malloy had the same information I had.

After we completed our presentations, Bill Buesking, Irving Fisher, and I sat together at the witness table to answer questions from Senator Proxmire. Before starting his questioning, the Senator first dealt with attempts to prevent my appearance. When asked why I didn't have a statement as he had requested, I replied that Secretary Nielsen, by direction, had told me not to prepare a written statement. I then deferred to my keeper, Commander Dauchess. The Commander had been involved intimately in the maneuvering for almost a month, but he disclaimed all specific knowledge of the affair. Finally, Senator Proxmire got to the key question:

Chairman Proxmire: "Did Secretary Clifford provide instructions to muzzle this witness?"
Commander Dauchess: "I am not aware of any."

Poor Dauchess was really in a bind, and he showed it. He had been standing at attention during the questions, and he was be-

* *Ibid.*, p. 123.

ginning to shake a little. If he had answered "Yes" to the Senator's questioning about Clifford muzzling me, he could have prevented my upcoming testimony, but he would have exposed the Pentagon hierarchy's clumsy, stupid, and illegal actions. Having answered "No," he had to give permission for me to answer questions, and he did.

Senator Proxmire then turned his attention to me. He first established that I was not ignorant of the C-5A, that I was helping to direct the then current cost study. Then he sprang the question:

Chairman Proxmire: "Is it true that the costs of that contract will be approximately $2 billion more than was originally estimated and agreed on?"

I waffled a while but finally acknowledged:

If the total amount of estimated cost variance were to come to pass— and I have no way of knowing whether that will in fact come to pass —on both the Lockheed and the General Electric contract—General Electric provides the engine for the C-5A airplane—if we were to buy the follow-on production runs using the repricing formula, and if our Air Force support items, things that have not yet been contracted for, increase proportionately, your figure could be approximately right.

Translated from bureaucratese, my answer was "Maybe," and I thought for a while that I might have kept myself out of trouble. However, when the hearing ended, about a half-hour later, the reporters closed in on me and began asking about the concealed $2,000,000,000 overrun on the Miracle of Procurement. I knew then that I was in the soup.

SIX

DOWNHILL

"If you must sin, sin against God, not against the bureaucracy. God may forgive you, but the bureaucracy never will." This was Admiral Hyman Rickover's wise and unfailing advice to toilers in the government vineyards. I learned how profound this advice was after my testimony on the carefully concealed C-5A cost overruns.

I had committed truth. I had embarrassed the priestly procurement hierarchy by my blasphemous statements about the Miracle of Procurement. Unknown to me at the time, my blasphemy had also threatened to upset what *The Wall Street Journal* later termed "an artful exercise to rescue hard-pressed Lockheed." * The full enormity of this sin was to unfold before me slowly in the future.

When I returned to the Pentagon after my testimony before Senator Proxmire's subcommittee, I was greeted by my secretary, who had already heard the news. "Have you been fired yet?" she asked fearfully. No, I assured her; the incident would probably blow over after a small flap in the news media. Despite the sensational treatment of my testimony, the factual basis of the testimony was indisputable and would have to be faced anyway by the defenders of the C-5A and other Miracles of Procurement. I told my nervous secretary that the incident might even help us to get a handle on the C-5A program by freezing opponents of cost control in their tracks.

In this assessment, I underestimated the brazenness and desperation of the giveaway faction. The issue of poor intentions in

* *The Wall Street Journal*, December 1, 1970.

procurement had not come up in Senator Proxmire's hearings as Secretaries Moot, Morris, and Charles had feared, but the reaction to the revelations of the previously concealed C-5A cost overruns was so strong that fears of disclosure of my dispute with Tom Morris' assistants were forgotten for the moment. The giveaway faction was momentarily in disarray, but they got their feet back under them when Assistant Secretary Robert Charles took personal charge of countering my testimony. He personally manipulated the figures in Air Force statements aimed at minimizing anticipated overruns on the C-5A. Fortunately for me, my secret sympathizers remained sympathetic and I was furnished regularly with summaries of C-5A estimates, breaking down in detail and comparing "Mr. Charles' position," "Air Force internal position," and "Mr. Fitzgerald's position."

Outside my immediate office, I noticed a definite cooling of relationships. Except for my staunchest friends and the corps of secret sympathizers who thought the disarray of the giveaway faction was hilarious, my peers and superiors gave me a wide berth. None of them mentioned the nasty subject of my testimony to me directly except for my boss, Tom Nielsen, who called from California to assure me that he really had wanted me to testify but that he had been overruled (both Tom Nielsen and Dr. Brown "happened" to be out of town during my testimony). When I passed coworkers in the halls, most would smile sickly, mutter an unintelligible response to my greeting, then hurry on with quickened pace.

My activities on major weapons programs came to an abrupt and permanent halt. I had previously been appointed to the Special Air Staff Group (SASG) to oversee the source selection for the Air Force's new F-15 fighter plane. A long-scheduled meeting of the SASG took place a day or two after my testimony. Whereas all the dozens of SASG meetings I had attended in the course of source selections of the SRAM and maverick missiles had been lively, probing affairs, with especially tough questioning by representatives of the Secretary's office, this standard, formal VuGraph presentation of brochure-type boilerplate aroused little comment. I was the only one present who asked a question. The meeting was quickly concluded, and the F-15

SASG never reconvened, or if it did, I was not invited to attend.

I had also been deeply involved in the C-5A cost review prior to my testimony. My only subsequent connection with this study was informal conversation with the Air Force officers actually doing the work. Tom Nielsen personally took over direction of the project.

Prior to testifying before Senator Proxmire's subcommittee, I had been invited to every meeting of the DSMG since I entered the Pentagon and had attended all that had taken place when I was in Washington. I was never invited to a DSMG meeting afterward.

It was obvious that I was in a heap of trouble. Actually, though, I wasn't too worried. I had been in heaps of trouble before and had always come out on top or at least fought to a draw during my Pentagon tenure. Moreover, I had never in any previous controversy been on firmer ground. In some of my previous controversies, I had occupied very exposed positions, supported in some instances only by my own analyses and assessments. This time, however, I had done nothing more than to confirm that under certain conditions, Senator Proxmire's staff's estimate of probable C-5A cost increases were about the same as the official Air Force position. Admittedly my boss, Tom Nielsen, had suddenly become very stiff, formal, and remote in his dealings with me. However, Tom had always been somewhat overawed by generals, and the embarrassed military procurement types wanted my scalp. Nevertheless I still believed that Harold Brown, who had always backed me in previous controversies, would take a more objective view and might even agree with me that public exposure might be beneficial in the long-festering C-5A situation.

Finally, if all else failed, I could comfort myself that I would not be easy to fire. When I went to work in the Pentagon in September of 1965, I was told that I would be on probation for three years, during which period I could be dismissed at any time without cause. For once, it appeared the bureaucratic machinery had functioned properly. In September of 1968, I received an official "Notification of Personnel Action" informing me that effective September 20, 1968, I was converted to career tenure. Given my newly acquired status as a permanent bureaucrat, the other bureaucrats would be forced to follow the rules—bringing charges and the like, then proving them—if they wanted to fire me. Such an attempt, I thought, might prove to be an interesting action. I was reminded at the time of a story one of my previous bosses had told me just after we had been treacherously done in, foully maligned, and thrown out of a contractor plant where we had been attempting to save some money for the government.

My old boss said that a friend of his, a very proper Ivy Leaguer, was walking one day in a very rough section of South Boston. As he passed a particularly mangy looking bar, the door burst open and a man came hurtling past him across the sidewalk to land in a battered heap in the gutter. Startled by this rude display of violence, the proper Ivy Leaguer rushed to assist the poor man in the gutter. The Ivy Leaguer helped the unfortunate one to his feet and back onto the sidewalk, where the victim stood dazed, bruised, bleeding profusely, swaying back and forth, as he spat out teeth, all the while pressing both clenched fists to his chest. "I say, my man," said the Ivy Leaguer, "you appear to have gotten the worst of it." At that the battered hulk drew himself up, extended his hands, opened his fists, and replied, "So it may appear to the casual observer, but I ask you, sir, whose testicles are these?"

At last, more than a week after my testimony, Harold Brown asked me to come to his office. Immediately on receiving the Secretary's summons, I felt greatly relieved. I liked Harold Brown personally and had found him to be a reasonable man in the past dealings. I was confident that a good talk with the Secretary would clear the air. I was hopeful that Dr. Brown's strong backing and approval of my testimony would bring the military and civilian bureaucrats out of the collective childish pout in which they had been indulging since my testimony.

My euphoria was shattered the moment I walked into Dr. Brown's out office. His usually friendly secretary and assistants were as glum and silent as friends of the family at a funeral parlor. In a hushed voice, Dr. Brown's secretary said, "Go right in, Mr. Fitzgerald, the Secretary is waiting for you."

When I walked into Dr. Brown's huge, impressive office, he was standing with his hands clasped behind his back, looking out one of his giant windows with its view of the Pentagon Mall entrance, the lawn and flower gardens on the terrace below, the Potomac River, and the magnificent public buildings, monuments, and the Capitol across the river. For perhaps half a minute Harold Brown continued to gaze out of the window solemnly. I was sunk and I knew it. The Secretary of the Air Force broke the long silence by turning around and saying, "Hello, Ernie." "Hello, Harold," I replied. I did not ordinarily call the Secretary "Harold," but what the hell, I thought, it's probably all over anyway, so why not behave like grown-up equals.

"You're a damned poor congressional witness," Dr. Brown said wryly.

"I suppose so," I responded. "I hope my testimony hasn't caused you too much trouble." I then started to explain to the Secretary how I had been led to commit truth, but he cut off my explanation with a wave of his hand.

"I had a call from Senator Russell," Dr. Brown said. "He was very upset at reports of your testimony which implied that he was applying political pressure in the C-5A situation. This concerns me greatly. Senator Russell's good will is very important to the Air Force, and I value his personal friendship as well."

I knew exactly what Dr. Brown was referring to. During my testimony on November 13, Senator Proxmire had asked me what kind of pressures were being brought to bear to rush into ordering the second batch of C-5As. I responded that first, the Air Force naturally wanted the airplane; second, that there was a desire to keep the Lockheed plant open, and then I had stepped in it.

Fitzgerald: "And beyond that I can only speculate on pressures that might be generated through elected representatives. I am not subject to these personally. I don't know any pressure that would be brought to bear—at least on people at my level—to keep it—"

Chairman Proxmire: "Pressures from elected representatives? Lockheed is located where?"

Fitzgerald: "They have plants in several states, Mr. Chairman."

Chairman Proxmire: "Where is their principal plant?"

Fitzgerald: "Their principal plant and headquarters is in Burbank, California. The C-5A is being built at the Georgia plant, Marietta, Georgia."

Chairman Proxmire: "The C-5A is being built in the State of Georgia?"

Fitzgerald: "Yes, sir." *

Now I had heard at least a dozen supposedly responsible government officials refer to their fear of Senator Russell's reaction as an excuse for inaction on the C-5A mess, and I must confess that this was in the back of my mind at the time of my testimony. However, neither Senator Proxmire nor I mentioned Senator Russell by name. The newspapers did that for us. The morning after Senator Proxmire's hearings, the Washington *Post* carried a front-page story of the affair. The story included my statement about elected representatives, then went on to explain:

The main assembly plant of the Galaxy [i.e., the C-5A] is in Marietta, Georgia, the home ground of Senator Richard B. Russell (D–Ga.), Chairman of the Senate Armed Services Committee. Three of the new subassembly plants established by Lockheed were located in the districts of influential House Committee Chairmen. The sites were selected from a list supplied by the White House, according to one of the Chairmen.†

The following Sunday, the *Post* deplored the C-5A boondoggle in its lead editorial, again quoting my testimony and explaining that Senator Russell's home state was the chief beneficiary of the generous arrangement. This time they added that the District of Representative Harley O. Staggers of West Virginia, the Chairman of the House Interstate and Foreign Commerce Committee, was another beneficiary.‡

I explained all this and how it had come about to Dr. Brown and asked that he try to set up an appointment for me to talk to Senator Russell. I told Dr. Brown that I was very eager to explain the affair to Senator Russell, to ask him not to take out his unhappiness over my testimony on the Air Force, and to apologize to the Senator for any damage I might have done to his good name.

* "Economics of Military Procurement," hearings before the Subcommittee on Economy in Government of the Joint Economic Committee, Proceedings of November 13, 1968, pp. 207–208.
† Washington *Post*, November 14, 1968.
‡ Washington *Post*, November 17, 1968.

"That won't be necessary," Dr. Brown replied quickly. "Senator Russell has so much prestige and such a fine reputation that no one would believe allegations about his applying political pressure anyway."

"Then what's the problem, Harold?" I asked.

Dr. Brown didn't answer. He just sat there looking thoughtful. Then he said, "Okay, Ernie. Thanks for coming in."

I left. I neither saw, spoke with, nor otherwise communicated with Harold Brown after that.

A few days later, on November 25, exactly twelve days after my testimony, the outlines of my fate began to take shape. I received another official "Notification of Personnel Action." This document, which was delivered to me routinely without any explanation, summarily and retroactively revoked the career tenure which I had been granted on September 6, 1968. I knew next to nothing about civilian personnel regulations, so I dug out my previous official "Notification of Personnel Action," which had converted me to career tenure, and looked up the regulations on both the original conversion and the revocation of my career tenure. Hidden under all the bureaucratic gobbledygook, the net effect of the arbitrary revocation of my career tenure was that I was more vulnerable to arbitrary dismissal without cause. I raised the question of how I could legally be relieved summarily of career tenure with Tom Nelson, one of our personnel experts. I was told that the original granting of tenure had been a "computer error," and a rare one at that, the only one of its kind in the history of the Air Force.

"But wait a minute," I objected, "the notice I got on September 6 did not come from a computer. It was signed by Mrs. A. Y. Kent, the Chief of the Civilian Personnel Division at Air Force Headquarters. Mrs. Kent wasn't a computer. Was the signature on the notice I had received genuine?" "Yes," I was assured. Mrs. Kent's signature was genuine and the document was official.

"Well, then," I asked, "what would a valid conversion to career tenure notice look like?"

I was told that it would look like the one I got.

"Then wasn't I justified," I asked, "in relying on the conversion to career tenure which supposedly protected me from arbitrary dismissal whether or not such dismissal arose from my congressional testimony?"

"You don't understand the problem," my expert adviser told me.

"That's right. I don't. Let's go see the Civil Service Commission."

We journeyed across the Potomac and met with Mr. Seymour Berlin, one of the top officials in the Civil Service Commission headquarters in Washington. Mr. Berlin was friendly and gracious. He patiently explained to me that my conversion to career tenure was not valid because the Civil Service Commission had not been notified of the action. I responded that the explanation sounded reasonable and might be a good one, except for one thing. It was not true. The "Notification of Personnel Action," Civil Service Commission Standard Form 50, was, like most bureaucratic paperwork, prepared in multiple copies, one of which always went to the Civil Service Commission. The record showed that the Civil Service Commission had routinely received a copy of my conversion to career tenure.

Mr. Berlin then gave me a long, lame explanation of how the routine notification did not necessarily come to the attention of top officials in the Civil Service Commission, that it probably just went to "some clerk" who filed it away. This brought out the efficiency expert in me, and I asked why they spent the time and money to prepare, process, and file the notices if they didn't mean anything. Mr. Berlin wasn't sure, but he promised to look into the matter.

Meanwhile back at the Pentagon, my professional career was on an accelerating one-way slide downhill. Word of my losing career tenure spread like wildfire, and the only speculation was when, not if, I would be fired. In early December, one of my secret sympathizers in Mr. Moot's office told me that Secretary of Defense Clark Clifford had announced at his staff meeting that he was "very displeased with Mr. Fitzgerald." I relayed this report to Mr. Nielsen and asked that I be granted an audience with the Secretary of Defense to hear first-hand why Mr. Clifford was displeased with me. I never received a response to my request.

Other indications of Mr. Clifford's displeasure with me were abundant. For example, Mr. Clifford's response to Senator Prox-mire's letter protesting the attempt by the Pentagon to muzzle me before his hearings was a masterpiece of deception which pictured me as a participant in the Department of Defense's silly, amateurish attempt to obstruct the work of Senator Proxmire's subcommittee. Secretary Clifford referred to George Bergquist's nonresponsive testimony "which Mr. Fitzgerald helped review and edit," according to Clifford. This was too much even for timid Tom Nielsen. I had made a point of stating in writing that I wanted nothing whatever to do with George's testimony. Mr. Nielsen wrote to Secretary Brown regarding Secretary Clifford's statement: "The words underlined are not an accurate reflection of Ernie's involvement in the preparation of Mr. Bergquist's state-ment. Ernie was quite concerned with the outline of Mr. Berg-quist's statement and did not agree with its substance or content. In addition, I reviewed the statement and suggested certain corrections. I'm not sure which if any of the changes were made."

Notwithstanding his defense of my position in the Secretary of Defense's cover-up, Tom Nielsen took an active part in the concerted action to put me in my place, which was clearly per-ceived by the bureaucracy as somewhere outside the Pentagon. At that time, with the combination of the Christmas holiday season and the change of administrations, there were a number of official and semiofficial social events taking place in the Pentagon. As a deputy in the Secretary's office, I received in-vitations to these events routinely in spite of my social leper status. However, just as routinely, Tom Nielsen would send his military weenies to see me each time the invitations were issued to suggest that my presence at these gatherings might be em-barrassing.

Tom Nielsen was also responsible for "negotiating" with me to change my testimony regarding the probable $2,000,000,000 overrun on the C-5A program. After my confirmation that Sen-ator Proxmire's estimate of the overrun was about right, the Senator had asked me to furnish exact figures for the record. A day or two after the November 13 hearings I had submitted the then current official Air Force estimates to Mr. Nielsen's office for transmittal through channels to Senator Proxmire and the Joint Economic Committee. The figures I submitted, which were those I had in mind at the time of my testimony, were $3,371,000,000 for the baseline estimate, the official Air Force independent cost estimate of April 1965, and the comparable independent Air Force cost estimate of October 1968, which was $5,338,000,000. Each of these estimates had included provisions for Air Force Logistics Command (AFLC) investment items, principally spares. The April 1965 AFLC line item was $293,000,000. By October of 1968, this figure had grown to $968,000,000.

The question of estimates for spare parts was crucial to the Air Force plan to cast doubt on my testimony. Since the estimated costs for this line item had increased by $675,000,000, the Air Force could make the increase in the total program appear smaller in press releases simply by omitting the Logistics Command from both the before and after figures. However, as my negotiations with Tom Nielsen proceeded, and it became clear that I would not be a party to this flimflam, the official spares estimates included in the October 1968 program estimate were changed arbitrarily against the day when they would have to become public. Fortunately, my secret sympathizers kept me supplied with working papers showing just how this was done. An interesting insight of bureaucratic lying was the manner in which the "support" and "replenishment spares" estimates were changed. Between them, these two categories accounted for six separate lines on the worksheets. The cost estimate for each line item was divided arbitrarily by two. The same result could, of course, have been obtained simply by dividing the total by two. But this simpler approach would not have provided proper "documentation" for the new "estimate." The Back-up Principle prevailed even in support of deliberate lies for public consumption.

The other major Air Force maneuver aimed at discrediting my testimony about the C-5A cost increases was to arbitrarily select a new starting or baseline estimate. Until then, the official baseline estimate had been the April 1965 figure of $3,371,000,000 (rounded to $3.4 billion for public consumption). This estimate was made at the end of the C-5A's contract definition phase and was closely aligned with the airplanes being proposed by the three competitors for the C-5A contract. At that time, both the contractors and the Air Force made detailed projections of then anticipated increases due to inflation, for spare parts, modifications, and other items included in the so-called life-cycle cost estimates.

To muddy this reasonably clear starting point, the Air Force threw out the April 1965 estimate for the C-5A and substituted instead an estimate made in October 1964 for the CXHLS (standing for Cargo, Experimental, Heavy Logistics Support) airplane. The CXHLS was the so-called "parametric" airplane envisioned at the start of the contract definition. This was an entirely different airplane from the machine which finally evolved as the C-5A. Use of this phony baseline enabled the Air Force to rationalize part of the monumental cost overruns by attributing huge, arbitrary cost estimates to differences between the CXHLS and the C-5A. Furthermore, the cost estimate for the 1964 CXHLS was a so-called "ROM" (Rough Order of Magnitude) estimate made in constant 1964 dollars, whereas the detailed estimate for the C-5A in April of 1965 included then-anticipated inflation. By using the rough 1964 constant-dollar estimate as their new baseline, the Air Force manipulators rationalized another huge chunk of the overrun by attributing it to inflation in the economy which had occurred between 1964 and 1968.

There were numerous other creative accounting adjustments made in the frantic efforts to confuse the issue of C-5A overruns. Again, I was kept well informed of these by my secret sympathizers. The closely guarded worksheets reflected the frantic juggling of figures which was taking place at the time.

After much manipulation, the worksheets showed a total C-5A program estimate of $4,362,000,000 in place of the figure of $5,338,000,000 which had been the official estimate at the time of my testimony. At the last minute, it was discovered that the official Air Force press release, already written and "staffed" for release, contained a figure of $4.3 billion. (On the assumption that most of the taxpaying public did not perceive the difference between a billion dollars and a million dollars, most Pentagon press releases on big programs under fire stated the figures in billions rounded off to the nearest hundred million. Obviously, the figure

$4.3 billion is less frightening that $4,300 million, not to mention $4,300,000,000.) Rounded off, the new "official" estimate of $4,362,000,000 would have been $4.4 billion, so the estimate for the line item "five additional aircraft [run C and other Air Force adds]" of $440,000,000 was stricken out and replaced with the figure $425,000,000. This reduction of $15,000,000 dropped the new "official" estimate to $4,347,000,000. The worksheet bore the notation "adjusted by Mr. Charles to make the total less than $4,350 million; keeps estimate at the $4.3 billion in the official Air Force press release."

Tom Nielsen appeared to have his orders in "negotiating" changes in my testimony with me. However, it was clear that his support of the official Air Force lie on the C-5A cost estimate was lukewarm. In addition, I was fairly stubborn in the negotiations. For one thing, my knowledge of the frantic and secret monkey business surrounding the Air Force "position" on the C-5A cost figures had roused my competitive spirit. As a result, Tom Nielsen and I concluded our negotiations by agreeing to use a beginning cost estimate based on the April 1965 figures. However, instead of submitting the precise numbers from Air Force records, I agreed to give in to the extent of rounding them off to the nearest tenth of a billion dollars in accordance with Air Force practice. Substituting the rounded figures for the more precise ones left the situation fuzzy enough to permit the trapped dissemblers a little maneuvering room.

Rounded off, the April 1965 figures were $3.1 billion for development and production and $.3 billion for AFLC (Air Force Logistics Command) investment, mostly spare parts, giving a total of $3.4 billion. The October 1968 figures, rounded off, were $4.4 billion for development plus production and $.9 billion for AFLC, a total of $5.3 billion. I conceded another point in agreeing to accept Nielsen's assertions that common AGE, modification, and replenishment spares were not included in the earlier estimates but were included in the October 1968 projection. The evidence I had seen previously indicated otherwise, but I gave in in the interest of getting approximate figures to Senator Proxmire to complete the hearing record.

Giving in was a mistake. My "negotiations" with Tom Nielsen

came to absolutely nothing. Several weeks elapsed between the completion of the negotiations and the delivery to the Joint Economic Committee of a package of paper without a cover letter or explanation of any kind except for a label, "Inserts for the record of testimony of A. E. Fitzgerald." This package was delivered by a person or persons unknown on the afternoon of December 24, 1968, Christmas Eve. Richard Kaufman, the military procurement expert on the Joint Economic Committee staff, found the material on his desk after being absent from his office for a while. The C-5A cost estimates provided to the Committee compared an October 1964 estimate of $3.1 billion to a figure labeled October 1968 of $4.3 billion. A total cost increase of $1.3 billion. Since the overrun figure was so different from my testimony, Mr. Kaufman immediately called me and asked if I recognized the figures. I did, of course. They were the phony numbers dreamed up by Bob Charles and his military advisers. Someone, I didn't know who, had simply thrown out the results of my "negotiations" with Tom Nielsen and transmitted instead the Air Force "position" figures. Furthermore, the phantom delivery boy (later identified as Lt. Col. Clifford LaPlante) had also "neglected" to deliver several other items included in my submission when it entered the Air Force pipeline for transmittal to the Joint Economic Committee.

With the holiday season in full swing, there was nothing I could do on Christmas Eve about the heavy-handed attempt to discredit my testimony. But in the period immediately following the holidays I raised hell about the perfidious maneuverings. Outwardly my protest evoked only infantile pouting and temper tantrums. Eventually, however, the results of my negotiations were forwarded to the Joint Economic Committee.*

My refusal to back down on my congressional testimony further angered the defenders of the C-5A debacle and its principal contractor, Lockheed, who now included the entire Department of Defense establishment, except for me and my secret sympathizers. My conflict with the top management of the Department was

* "Economics of Military Procurement," hearings before the Subcommittee on Economy in Government of the Joint Economic Committee, Ninetieth Congress, Second Session, Part I, p. 209.

open, as evidenced by the letter of transmittal which accompanied my "negotiated" figures transmitted to the Joint Economic Committee. This cover letter, signed by Brig. Gen. John C. Giraudo, Secretary Brown's Deputy Director of Legislative Liaison, stated: "The inserts for the record previously provided represent our position on the points in question and were considered responsive to your requests." Continuing, General Giraudo wrote: "The attachment which *purports to cover* [emphasis mine] the estimated C-5A program costs is one submitted by Mr. Fitzgerald to back up his previous testimony. The Air Force does not support these figures as a substitution for costs previously supplied to your subcommittee."

All doubts about Harold Brown's attitude toward my committing truth were dispelled by a highly sensitive memorandum prepared at Dr. Brown's request on January 6, 1969. According to subsequent testimony by the author of the letter, Thomas W. Nelson, the memorandum was prepared in response to a question from Dr. Brown: "What are his rights?" referring to me. According to Mr. Nelson, a personnel specialist under Dr. Brown's administrative assistant, John Lang, the question "What are his rights?" was bureaucratic language for "How can I fire him?" The January 6 memo, a response to Dr. Brown prepared by Mr. Nelson and signed by his boss, John Lang, left no doubt regarding my eventual fate. The only question unanswered was how I would be fired. Three alternatives were listed.

First, charges could be brought against me under Chapter 752 of the Federal Personnel Manual. The letter, subsequently infamous as the "Lang Memorandum," went on to detail all the maneuvering that would be necessary to fire me under these provisions. Collectively, the provisions were known as "adverse actions."

The second alternative to canning me was called "reduction in force." It was most explicit: "In the event his job is abolished, Mr. Fitzgerald is in tenure Group I in the excepted service and has the right of full application to all reduction-in-force procedures insofar as 'bumping' and 'retreat' rights *within his competitive level grouping.* However, since he is the only employee in his competitive level grouping, and since he did not progress to this position from other lower grade positions, the net result is that he is in competition only with himself. He could neither 'bump' nor displace anyone."

The third alternative for booting me out of the Pentagon was summarized as follows: "There is a third possibility which could result in Mr. Fitzgerald's departure. *This action is not recommended since it is rather underhanded* [emphasis mine], and would probably not be approved by the Civil Service Commission, even though it is legally and procedurely possible. The Air Force could request conversion of this position to the career service utilizing competitive procedures and consider all the eligibles from the executive inventory and an outside search. Using this competitive procedure, Mr. Fitzgerald might or might not be selected. If not, displacement action would follow."

The arbitrary and unilateral revocation of my career tenure following my congressional testimony had left me particularly vulnerable to alternatives two and three.

Needless to say, documents such as the Lang Memorandum are ordinarily communications of the most private sort, even in organizations supported by the public's tax monies. I received not one but two copies of this sensitive document from unknown but obviously friendly sources. They were left on my desk in unmarked envelopes. The senders, my unknown friends, clearly took considerable risks in reproducing and transmitting the documents to me. I wondered at the time and thereafter what feelings of helpless outrage must have motivated this action. In all probability, the Lang Memorandum was diverted, copied, and sent to me by some of the miscalled "little people" in the Air Force: typists, secretaries, clerks, or maybe messengers. The action must have been accompanied by considerable quickening of the pulses and perhaps followed by misgivings and fears of detection and exposure. In any event, I was greatly in the debt of whoever had taken the risks necessary to warn me of the intended actions by my vindictive superiors.

Two days after the Lang Memorandum was written, on January 8, 1969, I was summoned to the office of my boss, Tom Nielsen. Tom was uncommonly agitated. He rambled on at length about the team concept and the importance of "supporting" one's superiors. In the course of his lecture, he worked himself into quite an emotional state and finally blurted out, "You have lost your usefulness. You work for me, and you are not useful to me."

In reply I objected that my physical and mental capabilities remained unimpaired. I told him that any time he, Assistant Secretary Tom Nielsen, wanted to attack our formidable cost problems I was ready and able to go forth and smite them, hip and thigh. My degree of usefulness, I told him, was a function of the manner in which he intended to employ me. I was not available for lying to the Congress, but I was available for other duties.

Meanwhile, on November 23, 1968, Senator Proxmire had written to Secretary of Defense Clark Clifford, urging him to undertake a comprehensive study of the circumstances surrounding the C-5A contract and its enormous estimated overruns.

"Surely," the Senator wrote, "the option agreement by which the Government could obligate itself to pay an additional $2 billion for this program should not be entered into until the special investigations have been completed and transmitted to Congress." * Simultaneously, the formidable Senator Proxmire had requested the Comptroller General of the United States, Elmer Staats, to personally direct a General Accounting Office study of the C-5A and to report the results to his Committee "no later than January 10, 1969."

Senator Proxmire's continued probing of the unsavory C-5A situation was driving the Pentagon's military and civilian hierarchy crazy. Their frantic reactions clearly were not based on cool and logical appraisals of how best to protect the public interest. To the contrary, the Pentagon hierarchy's thrashing about and lashing out at me was the emotional reaction of prideful men, serving in even more prideful institutions, caught *in flagrante delicto*. Their only concerns seemed to be protection of their own reputations and of the financial health of their pampered pet giant partner, Lockheed.

The Lockheed situation was in fact desperate. Even if Lockheed built C-5s which performed to contract specifications and delivered them on time, both of which were rapidly becoming

* *Aerospace Daily*, November 27, 1968.

improbable, the Pentagon's favorite contractor stood to lose $671,500,000 on the development and production of the first fifty-eight airplanes. As both Dr. Brown and the Chief of Staff had indicated, the Air Force did not need the second order. However, it was perfectly clear that *Lockheed* needed the second order, and this became the driving factor in Pentagon decisions. Based on the Air Force's October 1968 cost projection, Lockheed stood to recover $386,100,000 of their monumental losses under the terms of the absurd repricing formula, leaving them with an estimated loss of $285,400,000. Under the Alice in Wonderland illogic of the repricing formula, additional overruns on the first order could further reduce their losses. Therefore, from the standpoint of facilitating the transfer of the taxpayer's money from the U.S. Treasury to Lockheed, committing the Government to the second order was an absolute necessity. The Lockheed rescue effort faced many difficulties, all of which would become more severe if the aggressive Senator from Wisconsin was successful in completely removing the cover of unwarranted secrecy that had thus far shielded the odorous Lockheed mess from public view. Up to that time, the Senator's efforts had loosened the lid sufficiently to allow some of the smell to escape, but the Air Force had managed to keep the factual situation confused by a combination of lies and flat, illegal refusal to allow the General Accounting Office access to official C-5A cost information.*

One obstacle to completing the rescue of Lockheed at that point was the fact that the Congress had not then authorized the second order of C-5As. True, the Pentagon had ignored or overcome this minor problem in the past, but never where it might become such a noisy issue. In addition, the option to buy the second order expired on January 31, 1969. In a normal situation, this would have presented no insurmountable problem. Not withstanding official assertions that the C-5A was on schedule, Lockheed was in fact many months late in successful completion of many key development segments (some would never be successfully completed). Lockheed's behind-schedule situation provided

---

* "Economics of Military Procurement," hearings before the Subcommittee on Economy in Government of the Joint Economic Committee, Ninetieth Congress, Second Session, Part I, pp. 254–255 and pp. 260–271.

the Air Force ample legal justification for delaying the date for exercising the option for Run B.

The rescue team's major problem was that their own tenure was uncertain. Since the national presidential elections the previous November had resulted in a Republican victory, at least some if not all of the Democratic presidential appointees—the Secretary, the Under Secretary, and the Assistant Secretaries—might reasonably be expected to be replaced after the new Administration took office on January 20, 1969. Even though no one of my acquaintances in the Pentagon believed the new Republican Administration would be less friendly to the giant contractors than the outgoing Democratic group, there was always the danger that the incoming Administration might view the scandalous C-5A situation as a political liability. They might just allow Senator Proxmire to clean up the mess they had inherited from the Democrats by exposing the situation to the purifying glare of public scrutiny.

Senator Proxmire forced the issue by scheduling the new hearing on the C-5A mess on January 16, 1969. He announced that he had invited as principal witnesses the Honorable Elmer Staats, the Comptroller General of the United States, Dr. Harold Brown, the Secretary of the Air Force, and A. E. Fitzgerald. I was in distinguished company but not for long. When Senator Proxmire made it known that he intended to inquire into the change in the course of my career resulting from my earlier testimony, Harold Brown elected discretion over valor and volunteered Bob Charles to take his place. As for the Comptroller General, Mr. Staats had not maintained his phenomenally successful and unbroken climb to the very top of the Washington bureaucracy by incurring the wrath of the likes of Senator Russell of Georgia. The Comptroller General wanted no part of Senator Proxmire's inquiry and he, too, delegated his assistant, Mr. Frank Weitzel, the Assistant Comptroller General, to appear in his place. After all, what are assistants for if not to take the lumps in such situations? I had no one to delegate the invitation to and nothing to lose anyway, so I made plans to appear as invited.

How little I had to lose was illustrated by the handling of my invitation. On the afternoon of January 9, Richard Kaufman of the Joint Economic Committee staff, mailed the invitation from Senator Proxmire to appear at the hearing directly to me and included a copy of the invitation to Harold Brown. When I received the letter on January 11, it had been ripped open and both the envelope and the invitation to me had been mutilated. The copy of Dr. Brown's invitation was missing. The back of my letter of invitation bore the impression of a huge rubber stamp with four separate blocks. The upper left-hand block was labeled "Investigating Division" and had the numbers "1030" inked in. The upper right-hand block was labeled "Correspondence Control" and contained the handwritten numbers "156431." The lower left-hand block was labeled "Action Officer" with the name of Lieutenant Colonel LaPlante printed in by hand. The lower right-hand block was labeled "Date" and was stamped with the date "10 Jan 1969." The envelope had been addressed to me personally, and I again protested the diversion and opening of my personal mail, as well as the pilfering of part of the envelope's content.

When my protests were ignored and my requests for explanation brushed off, I gave the invitation to a reporter for the Washington Star, whose request for explanation could not be ignored quite so readily. Later, the Star reported that the Air Force spokesman questioned by their reporter said that it was standard practice for congressional mail to be sent first to their legislative liaison office, rather than to the addressee, unless it was marked "Personal" or "Eyes Only." The Star went on to report that the Air Force explanation was contradicted by higher authorities: "A Defense Department spokesman said, however, that the policy in the Department itself and in the other services was that mail addressed to an individual should be delivered unopened." *

One of my secret sympathizers was a former "flap and seal" specialist in the Air Force. "Flap and seal" men are experts at removing, reproducing, and reinserting the contents of sealed envelopes in ways which defy detection by the recipient. My friend, the flap and seal man, told me that he and his compatriots would occasionally affix stamps and notations such as those on my invitation on correspondence which they inter-

* Washington Star, December 19, 1969.

cepted, then forward to the addressee. The purpose, he said, was to let the addressee know that he was under surveillance and hopefully to frighten the correspondents into abandoning whatever evil purpose they might have had in mind. My flap and seal friend told me that I was either too dumb or too stubborn to take the hint.

As the date for Senator Proxmire's hearings drew near, the civilian and military people who were helping Bob Charles get ready for his testimony began making gleeful but mysterious allusions to the "big surprise" they were secretly preparing. Mr. Charles' prepared statement, the weenies said, would silence once and for all the critics of the C-5A program. I was told nothing, of course. In fact, I was by then in nearly total isolation in the Pentagon. Except for the good folks in my immediate office, no one spoke to me in the three or four days immediately preceding the hearings. My mail, ordinarily heavy each day, was cut off completely. My secretary told me that it was being "diverted."

On the day of the hearing, January 16, I put a few documents in my old beat-up, accordion-style briefcase and walked alone from my fifth-floor attic office in the Pentagon to the colonnaded River Entrance which had seemed so impressive to me when I had received my coveted appointment only a little more than three years previously. As I walked out the River Entrance I saw below me on the sidewalk a sizable knot of Bob Charles' principal associates—perhaps a dozen people—gathered around the small cavalcade of cars waiting to take them and the Assistant Secretary to Senator Proxmire's hearing. Secretary Charles' car, complete with permanently assigned uniformed chauffeur, telephone, and rear seat reading lamp, was first in line, followed by a couple of G.I. staff cars to haul the lesser weenies. I was riding the bus.

The bus ride from the Pentagon to the New Senate Office Building on Capitol Hill was probably the low point of my adventures in the military spending complex. I was strangely and uncharacteristically depressed by the array of power against me. I had to remind myself that, despite the disparity in numbers of bodies and power of my opposition, I had the rascals outgunned in the unsought adversary position in which I found myself. I was right, and I had all the facts I needed in my head, along with a couple of surprises of my own in the briefcase to be used if necessary. On the other hand, the spokesman for the other side, Bob Charles, had the unenviable task of defending a lie and was dependent on a vast array of back-up witnesses for detailed information which should have been filed away neatly inside his skull.

By the time the Pentagon shuttle bus arrived at the New Senate Office Building, after several stops enroute, I had lifted myself above the nadir of my gloomy sense of being overwhelmed. As I got off the bus, my recovery was complete. There, just across the street at the back door of the New Senate Office Building, was Bob Charles' cavalcade of official vehicles discharging their loads of Assistant Secretary and weenies. For some reason, the fact that I had traveled to our mutual destination just as fast and far more economically completely restored my competitive spirit.

My morale suffered a slight relapse when I entered the huge auditorium where the hearings were to be held. The place was packed. At the front of the room on a raised stage a grimly alert Senator Proxmire sat conferring with several of his staff assistants behind a long judicial bench with places for each of the members of his subcommittee. The stage, the judicial bench, and the equally long witness table immediately below were bathed in the harsh glare of light for the television cameras. The alcove for the television cameras and their crews off to the side of the stage was filled. Immediately in back and to one side of the witness table were tables reserved for the press, also filled to capacity. The first row in the audience seating area was reserved for Secretary Charles and his associates.

I took a seat about midway down the right-hand aisle entering the rear of the big auditorium. At that point I decided to spring the hitherto undisclosed Lang Memorandum when my turn came to testify. This decision was precipitated by a press release shown to me by a friendly reporter after I had seated myself in the audience. It was an announcement by Secretary of Defense Clark M. Clifford that he had, just that day, authorized the Air Force to contract for the first increment of run B of the C-5A cargo airplanes. This decision triggered the repricing formula and reduced Senator Proxmire's efforts to protect the taxpayer's interest to a somewhat academic debate, at least for the moment.

Secretary Clifford's only excuse for blowing several billion dollars of the taxpayers' money was the cryptic statement that procurement of additional C-5A cargo planes would be "in the national interest." *

Senator Proxmire was presently joined by Senator Stuart Symington, the distinguished, well tailored Democratic Senator from Missouri, and tough-talking Democratic Congresswoman Martha Griffiths from Michigan. No Republican members appeared. Chairman Proxmire then called for the first witness, Assistant Comptroller General of the United States Frank Weitzel, to present his statement.

As Richard Kaufman reported in his excellent book, *The War Profiteers*, the Honorable Mr. Weitzel's principal news was that he was retiring. He could have saved the Committee and the Republic considerable time and expense by retiring one day earlier.†

Mr. Weitzel was accompanied by other General Accounting Office luminaries, including Charles M. Bailey, the Director of the Defense Division; Robert F. Keller, the General Counsel; James H. Hammond, Associate Director of the Defense Division, and Mr. George Gearino, the Supervisory Accountant in the Atlanta Regional Office, which had immediate responsibility for reviewing government affairs at the Lockheed Georgia plant.

Although Mr. Weitzel had little news to report, he did recount the feeble pro forma efforts, mostly letter writing, by the GAO to obtain information on the C-5A mess. The only cost figures Mr. Weitzel had at that time for the Congress of the United States were the misleading figures released to the general public by the Air Force a month before. According to Mr. Weitzel, the GAO had come into possession of this information only the day before.

For the most part, the frustrated but restrained questions of the members of the Subcommittee on Economy in Government

* *The New York Times,* January 17, 1969.
† *The War Profiteers,* p. 162.

were pitched progressively from Weitzel to Bailey and Keller to Hammond to Gearino. In each case, Mr. Gearino pleaded either ignorance or weakness in the face of Lockheed and the all-powerful Air Force.

Next, Chairman Proxmire called Secretary Charles to the witness table. Mr. Charles was accompanied to the table by Thomas W. Nelson, the personnel specialist who had written the Lang Memorandum outlining the three best ways to fire Fitzgerald. He was also backed up by the dozen or so weenies in the front row, leering in expectation of their hero, Bob Charles, demolishing the hated Proxmire.

Secretary Charles was eager to present his carefully prepared statement, but Senator Proxmire had a number of preliminary questions. First, the Senator got Mr. Charles to admit that he had been concerned about my November appearance because of the fear that I would not place all elements of the C-5A program "in perspective," that the public would get the impression that the C-5A was a bad program, and that the manner of its procurements was equally bad. Mr. Charles said his fears had turned out to be justified.

Senator Proxmire then turned to the matter of my career status. Bob Charles wisely allowed Tom Nelson, the personnel expert, to handle this. Mr. Nelson had with him the transcript of a telephone conversation that same day with the malleable Civil Service Commission in which the Chairman of the Commission, the Honorable Robert Hampton, repeated Mr. Berlin's earlier assertion that my conversion to career tenure was invalid because of the inadequate communication between the Air Force and the Civil Service Commission. After a great deal of Who-Struck-John over the alleged computer error, Tom Nelson finally admitted that the supposed error in my case was the only mistake of its kind on record.*

After questions about falsification of my submissions for the record of C-5A cost figures, on which Bob Charles pleaded ignorance, Senator Proxmire moved abruptly to another matter. He produced a copy of the Lang Memorandum and read from it the three preferred methods for firing Fitzgerald suggested to the

* *Ibid.,* p. 286.

Secretary of the Air Force. As the Senator was reading from the document, his assistants placed huge stacks of copies of the Lang Memorandum on the press tables and then went up each of the two aisles in the big auditorium passing out additional copies to members of the audience.

As most of the reporters left the room to file their stories, Yale man Bob Charles kept his cool and would concede only that the wording of the Lang Memorandum "may have been unfortunate." * On the other hand, the less blasé Tom Nelson was visibly affected. Even from my seat in the audience in back of the witness table, I could see that poor Tom, a ruddy individual in normal circumstances, had turned purple. Richard Kaufman later told me that from his better vantage point in back of Senator Proxmire, it appeared that the unfortunate Tom Nelson might suffer a stroke.

Senator Proxmire had beaten me to the punch in disclosing the scandalous Lang Memorandum, but I had to concede that his handling of the situation was superior to my plan. As most of the reporters were scurrying out of the room, Senator Proxmire expressed his outrage at the treacherous action of the Air Force hierarchy in disciplining a man who had told Congress the truth, then invited Secretary Charles to proceed to read his statement.

Bob Charles did, in fact, have an excellent statement, considering the material he had to work with. Very little of it was true, of course, but it sounded good. Unhappily for the Assistant Secretary, few people were listening by then. Nevertheless, Bob Charles bravely plodded through the elaborately contrived fiction, repeating the phony cost figures and the rationalization for increases I was familiar with but adding a new wrinkle. Regarding the critically ill C-5A's technical performance, he stated that: ". . . actual performance exceeds both the contractor's proposed performance and his contractual commitments by nearly 1 percent (both of which exceeded Air Force expectations by 7 percent) and in no single characteristic is there a deficiency."

I was not particularly surprised at Bob Charles' statement about the cost situation since the figures matched precisely what

* *Ibid.*, p. 290.

I had been told by my secret sympathizers, but I was astounded that he would have the audacity to proclaim the "tin balloon," as Joe Warren had labeled it, a technical success.

When my turn came to testify I did my best to set the record straight, but by then all was anticlimactic. I called attention to "suspected shortcomings in his [Lockheed's] technical conduct of the program." I also read into the record the official Air Force estimates of April 1965 and October 1968, showing a difference of $1,957,000,000 on estimated costs for the total C-5A program. In passing, I mentioned that I had experienced difficulties in determining why our internal Air Force cost reports on the C-5A had been falsified.

When I returned to the Pentagon after the January 16 fiasco before Senator Proxmire's subcommittee, I was mildly surprised to learn that Bob Charles was the new popular hero in the five-sided loony bin. In the face of overwhelming difficulties, including unexpected scandalous disclosures of Air Force treachery, Bob Charles had stuck tenaciously to the party line that all was well with the C-5A and that Lockheed, in particular, was doing a splendid job. In contrast, I had become internal enemy number one in the Pentagon.

With my ever-deepening isolation from my fellow human beings, I had leisure in which to reflect. I even recalled some of my early rudimentary philosophical training in the piney woods of Alabama. By my stubborn adherence to facts, my repeated restatement of factual indications of vast cost overruns and technical illness on the C-5, I had placed myself in opposition to the Air Force "position" that all was well with the big plane. The Air Force "position" that the C-5 was in great shape and that Lockheed was the greatest of contractors was normative or religious truth. The "position" had no basis in fact, but it did not need that. It had stronger support. It was an article of faith. Those who denied it were heretics and blasphemers. I had denied the true faith and consequently was an outcast.

Many of the cost-control advocates in the Pentagon, including most of my secret sympathizers, believed that things would change with the advent of the new Administration on January 20 and the departure of the old, sick, and frightened Democratic leadership. Things did change. They got worse. Immediately after Melvin Laird took over from Clark Clifford as Secretary of Defense, the word was passed that the military would have a stronger voice in the direction of the Pentagon's affairs. The military bureaucrats in the Air Force lost no time in asserting themselves and moving to take over hitherto civilian functions. I was particularly vulnerable both because my status as a pariah and because of my past hard-nosed dealings with the generals. Whereas my civilian bosses had previously resisted attempts by the military to usurp civilian control functions, the civilian appointees, particularly Tom Nielsen, now led the charge in giving away our controls. As a case in point, Tom Nielsen took the initiative in removing the civilian secretariat from the Management Systems Control Project. This was an effort which had been started a year or so before to cut down on the mountains of paperwork which had accompanied big procurements and to improve the quality and usefulness of information we got at the same time. We were then on the verge of killing off several of the more useless military paperwork schemes and, hopefully along with them, their attendant bureaucracies. On February 6, 1969, Tom Nielsen met with my counterpart in the Office of the Secretary of Defense, George Bergquist, and one of his assistants, David Moran, to ask them to stop dealing with me in the Management Systems Control Project. Mr. Moran could not believe his ears and afterwards wrote to his boss, George Bergquist, to confirm their understanding of Nielsen's request: "As I understand it, he said that I should deal with the Air Staff, Colonel Ayers, Colonel Shiveley, Paul Wight, and stop working with Fitzgerald. I can't quite understand this since Ernie's hang-up with the Air Staff's drafts [of instructions] is that Nielsen's office is omitted from the control loop." * George Bergquist wrote across Dave Moran's memo, "That's the way I heard it," and returned the note to Dave.

Tom Nielsen, still energetically currying favor with the newly

* "The Dismissal of A. Ernest Fitzgerald by the Department of Defense," hearings before the Subcommittee on Economy in Government of the Joint Economic Committee, Ninety-first Congress, Second Session, Nov. 17 & 18, 1969, p. 94.

confident generals, wasted no time in confirming my outcast status with the new presidential appointees. When Dr. Robert Seamans, Jr., replaced Harold Brown as Air Force Secretary on February 15, 1969, Nielsen collared Dr. Seamans immediately after the swearing-in ceremony to get permission to do something about his principal problem, A. E. Fitzgerald. A few days later Nielsen called me to his office to inform me that I "had no future with the Air Force," and that he had cleared this appraisal with Dr. Seamans. Since Dr. Seamans and I had never met (I was specifically requested not to attend the swearing-in ceremony), this seemed a little strange to me. It seemed probable to me that Dr. Seamans had acquired all his knowledge about me and my capabilities from people who would clap and cheer if I were being drawn and quartered. I expressed the hope that I might be allowed to talk with Dr. Seamans personally.

On March 4 I had a half-hour "get acquainted" meeting with Dr. Seamans. Tall, affable, with unruly white hair and black hornrimmed glasses, the new Secretary was the very picture of a successful professor of engineering, which he had been during much of his adult life, between stints in high-level posts in industry and government. Among other important jobs he had filled, Dr. Seamans had been for a time the Deputy Administrator of NASA, the National Aeronautics and Space Administration. We had a pleasant chat, but all I learned from the Secretary was that "the staff doesn't like you." I already knew that, of course, and I tried to alert the new Secretary to some of the causes of the conflict and to caution him about some of the problems he had inherited. The meeting ended pleasantly but inconclusively.

As soon as Tom Nielson got confirmation from the new Administration that Fitzgerald was also on their list of unfavored people, he went to work in earnest to strip me of my most important responsibilities. I had been excluded from direct contact with the big weapons programs since just after my November 1968 testimony, and Nielsen had told my counterparts in OSD to stop working with me, but I clung to my control of the performance measurement project until after Dr. Seamans took over. As soon as it became obvious that I was in deep trouble with the top brass in the Pentagon, the Air Staff and the Systems Command had made preparations to begin whitewashing and approving the phony systems offered by the big contractors for telling us whether they were underrun or overrun on completed portions of on-going contracts. All the systems being offered were still affected by the rubber baseline and other invalidating ailments. Nevertheless, the Systems Command and the Air Staff announced in December 1968 that they intended to approve the systems being offered by Boeing for the SRAM missile and by General Electric for the Mark 12 MIRV reentry vehicle. Neither were acceptable, and I had previously rejected them.

I found that the Systems Command spokesman, Brig. Gen. Hal Tuebner, had pronounced the Boeing and General Electric schemes successful before the reports of the inspection teams were submitted. It didn't matter, though, because the teams' criteria for acceptable performance measurement systems had been changed, especially in the case of General Electric, to match what the contractor was offering.

When I complained about this to Tom Nielsen, he called in the responsible people in the Air Staff and Systems Command to verify my accusations. Our military associates had in fact changed the rules, and on February 20, 1969, Tom Nielsen wrote to the Air Force Vice Chief of Staff concerning his meeting: "During our discussions, it became apparent that the teams which have been conducting the demonstrations [i.e., inspections] have not followed, during the conduct of the demonstrations, practices which this office believed were previously agreed to and would be followed." *

Although Nielsen agreed with me that the Systems Command was approving less than adequate performance measurement systems, his solution was astoundingly illogical. The military proposed, and Nielsen tentatively agreed, to remove me from the approval chain. I summarized the state of affairs in a letter to him on February 27, 1969:

---

* "The Dismissal of A. Ernest Fitzgerald by the Department of Defense," hearings before the Subcommittee on Economy in Government of the Joint Economic Committee, Congress of the United States, Nov. 17 & 18, 1969, p. 88.

1. Based on the evidence of demonstration reports and back-up documents, AFSC demonstrations are poorly done.

2. I detect and report the shortcomings of AFSC demonstrations.

3. You acknowledge these shortcomings.

4. AFSC and the Air Staff are unhappy.

5. As a solution, it is proposed to remove me from the approval chain.

This apparently stung Nielsen, so he made a trip to the GE plant to see for himself what we were approving; then wrote a long report once again confirming my assessment. Then, on March 27, he took away my authority to approve the performance measurement systems.

Until March 4, 1969, I was theoretically in charge of weapons systems cost analysis and control for Nielsen's office. This assignment covered the work I had previously done on the Minuteman program, the F-111, including the Mark II program, C-5A, and other big programs, mostly multibillion-dollar undertakings. On March 4 these assignments were taken from me. In place of these big jobs, I was given a number of new and smaller assignments. Among my new projects were "Cost of Food Service" (mess halls) and "Minor Construction in Thailand."

On inquiry, the Thailand project turned out to deal principally with a bowling alley then under construction. My civilian assistant found that the bowling alley project was greatly overrun (about 300 percent). When we reported this, along with our questions of why the Air Force was building a bowling alley in the first place, we lost that job too. We questioned the necessity for the project because both my assistant and I had been in the service as youngsters, and neither of us could recall ever having had the slightest inclination to go bowling when we had liberty.

Meanwhile the staff and the members of the Joint Economic Committee continued to follow up on my submissions for the record and my testimony, particularly that of January 16, in which I had mentioned my attempts to get at the bottom of apparently falsified internal reports of C-5A cost overruns. Congressman William Moorhead, a member of the Joint Economic Committee, was also a member of the House Government Operations Committee, and Mr. Moorhead pursued his inquiries through both committees. The Government Operations Committee was at that time conducting hearings on government procurement and contracting, and Mr. Moorhead had asked the General Accounting Office to follow up on my January 16th testimony to obtain results of the audit of C-5A cost reports I had requested. Since no hearings on the subject were then being conducted by the Joint Economic Committee, Congressman Moorhead planned to pursue the question in the Government Operations Committee hearings. The GAO obtained the key document in the affair directly from Dr. Seamans' office. This memorandum, written by Trenton Boyd, Deputy Auditor General of the Air Force, on October 9, 1968, stated, among other things, that "SPO personnel readily confirmed the inaccuracy of this report, as it relates to projected program overruns." * When questioned about this matter, a very nervous Col. Kenneth Beckman, who had replaced Guy Townsend as C-5A Systems Program Director, admitted that the reports had been changed because "the nature of the estimates was such that if publicly disclosed, they might put Lockheed's position in the common market in jeopardy." †

The report that the Air Force had deliberately falsified the internal C-5A cost reports to protect Lockheed's interest in the stock market made sensational news, including a front-page story in the Washington *Post* headlined "AF Data Doctored, Hill Told," and "Colonel Says Superiors Hid C-5A Cost Rise." Caught once more in a dastardly act, the Air Force hierarchy was again driven to frenzy, and I was blamed for another "leak" in spite of the fact that the incriminating document had come directly from Dr. Seamans' office.

On May 6 the C-5A controversy came up in hearings before the House Committee on Armed Services, headed by Mendel Rivers. Even though these hearings were secret and were not published for a long time afterwards, congressional friends conveyed the gist of them to me. In answer to questions posed by Chairman Rivers, who was fiercely protective of anything military and especially of Lockheed and the C-5A, Melvin Laird conceded

---

* "Government Procurement and Contracting, Part 4," hearings before a Subcommittee of the Committee on Government Operations, House of Representatives, Ninety-first Congress, First Session, p. 1217.
† *Ibid.*, p. 1179.

that the project had an overrun problem but stated that the figures had been "exaggerated." Mr. Laird told the Committee that he understood the GAO report on the subject due on May 15 would set the overrun at $500,000,000, that his own estimate was $400,000,000, and that the Air Force estimate was only $382,-000,000.*

Mr. Laird was accompanied by General McConnell, the Air Force Chief of Staff. General McConnell staked out his position in the following exchange with Chairman Rivers:

Chairman Rivers: These people over in the other body [the Senate] are talking about $2 billion.
General McConnell: They have not got the right information, Mr. Chairman.

Secretary of Defense Laird may have been misled by his advisers, but General McConnell knew for a fact that Senator Proxmire's figures were precisely accurate. I had been present at meetings in which the Chief of Staff had been given the identical C-5A cost figures I read into the record of Senator Proxmire's hearings on January 16.

Secretary of the Air Force Seamans appeared before Chairman Rivers' committee the next day, May 7. Dr. Seamans was accompanied by Lieutenant General Crow, the Comptroller of the Air Force, and between them they restated the C-5A cost growth fairy tale that had been concocted by Bob Charles and the Air Staff. Dr. Seamans was immediately set on by a number of Congressmen who wanted clarification of the conflicting cost figures then being circulated. I was identified as the dissenter in the affair and as a civilian employee of the Air Force. "On paper, he works for the Air Force," † Seamans responded viciously, thereby setting the tone for what followed. Under challenges to point out specifically where my testimony was incorrect and to confirm reports of retaliation against me after my testimony, Seamans took verbal evasive action, twisting and turning to avoid direct answers to questions put to him, and interspersing gratu-

* "Hearings on Military Posture," before the Committee on Armed Services, House of Representatives, Ninety-first Congress, First Session, Part I, pp. 2498 and 2499.
† *Ibid.,* p. 2591.

itous attacks on me. Dr. Seamans was particularly critical of the way I spent my off-duty hours and seemed outraged that I had attended an evening seminar of congressional staff aides interested in military procurement at the same time I had been invited to make a speech on the West Coast. (I had declined to make the trip to the West Coast when I learned that the affair where I was to speak was arranged for the private profit of a West Coast consultant. I had suggested that Tom Nielsen, already on the West Coast, speak to them instead.)

Otis Pike, a Congressman from New York and a bitter enemy of Chairman Rivers, wondered if this was wrong in the following exchange:

Mr. Pike: If it isn't wrong, why is it pertinent, or do you really consider that it is wrong?

Secretary Seamans: It is very interesting that in the testimony in front of a number of committees, documents keep appearing, some of which are confidential, that are obtained from Mr. Fitzgerald.

In this response, Secretary Seamans had not only evaded Congressman Pike's question but also had told a bald-faced lie. The only confidential document involved in the whole furor had been the October 9, 1968, letter from the Air Force auditors confirming that the C-5A cost reports had been falsified. Even this document had been improperly classified as confidential and was declassified by Dr. Seamans' own office prior to his releasing it to the General Accounting Office.

The Air Force's own definition of the term "confidential" illustrates how viciously the Secretary had slandered me. Air Force Regulation 205-1 (c-5) stated, quoting Executive Order 005501: "The use of the classification 'confidential' shall be authorized by appropriate authority only for defense information or material the unauthorized disclosure of which could be prejudicial to the defense interest of the nation."

The Air Force regulation went on to give examples of the kinds of information subject to the confidential classification. These included operational and battle reports which contained information of value to the enemy, intelligence reports, secret military radio frequencies, cryptographic devices, and so on.

The Secretary had leveled a grave and criminal charge against me and apparently just to make clear that the charge was not a slip of the tongue, he repeated it,* along with miscellaneous additional slander. About midway through Bob Seamans' vicious tirade, the powerful Chairman Mendel Rivers was moved to remark, "If I had a fellow like that in my office, he would have been long gone. You don't need to be afraid about firing him."

Shortly after Dr. Seamans' savage attack on me in Mendel Rivers' closed hearings, Brig. Gen. Joseph Cappucci, the Director of the Air Force Office of Special Investigations (OSI), was unleashed to probe my personal life for defamatory material which could be used to discredit me or even subject me to criminal charges. Ordinarily, the OSI gumshoes operate with the utmost secrecy, with some of their activities financed through secret accounts not subject to the customary checks on public funds. The OSI dirt-gathering project was started formally on May 17, 1969, but due to the secrecy surrounding their operations, I did not learn of the project until much later, even though some secret sympathizers were involved. My friends and I heard rumors of the investigation, but our first solid evidence that it was actually under way came on July 22 when a secret sympathizer, a former government spook himself, informed us that one of his old service buddies, working for a major Air Force contractor on the West Coast, was involved in the project. According to our secret sympathizer, the big contractor, whom I had bruised, was jubilant that at long last, in concert "with the DOD," they were finally going to "get Ernie." Our secret sympathizer said that the investigation was aimed at establishing my (1) relationship with women other than my wife, (2) overuse of alcohol, (3) use of drugs, or (4) homosexual contacts.

Since I was too busy, too old, and too poor to have serious problems with items one and two and had never been attracted by items three and four, I was not concerned that the gumshoes could dig up factual information which might damage me. On the other hand, I knew the rascals well enough to realize that they were perfectly capable of fabricating incidents, so I passed word among my friends that I would like to learn all I could about this investigation. Eventually we learned that an OSD in-

* *Ibid.*, p. 2596.

vestigation number HOD 24-12052 had been started on May 17. We also learned that the prefix "24" denoted a so-called "Special Inquiry," or fishing expedition. Even though the gumshoes were unable to find anything interesting in my sex life or drinking habits, they did manage to unearth some anonymous informants, identified only as T-1, T-2, T-3, and T-4, who were willing to pass on some juicy gossip about me.

After cautioning the gumshoes that "Fitzgerald is a very disarming person with a country-boy approach," the informers went on to reveal the amazing information that I was married, had three children, and lived in a "large home" in McLean, Virginia. Also, I apparently was considered a threat to the Republic because I was a "pinchpenny type of person" as evidenced by the fact that I drove an old Rambler automobile. I was also accused of working late. The T's also passed on a rumor that I was guilty of a conflict of interest with my former firm, PTC, and this gave the OSI spooks something they could investigate.

General Cappucci's fearless warriors immediately launched a widespread field investigation, confident that they would find that I held a secret interest in PTC and that together we had found a way to get rich by kicking big contractors in the shins. This turned out to be a tougher assignment than the gumshoes had anticipated. For one thing, as a result of their success in spotlighting fat in the big weapons boondoggles, PTC had by then expired. For another, I had sold my stock in PTC at the time I entered the Air Force and had received no money whatever from PTC subsequent to my termination pay.

When these facts were transmitted to the OSI Washington headquarters in the first RUC (Referred Upon Completion) reports from OSI's field agents, disappointment and gloom pervaded the atmosphere in the Air Force headquarters' spook shop.

However, the chief spooks had not risen to their positions of eminence by becoming easily discouraged when facts got in the way of their character assassination efforts. Rumor had it that my former boss, Ted Marks, back in civilian business on the West Coast, no longer regarded me as the outstanding Deputy for Management Systems he had described in his official personnel evaluations while in the Pentagon. Hoping to collect some more

juicy gossip and to confirm that which he already had, General
Cappucci dispatched his sleuths to interview Dr. Marks. I received conflicting reports of this interview, which took place in
Ted Marks' office at the Times-Mirror Corporation in Los Angeles
on June 24, 1969. Much later, Ted Marks told me that he sent
General Cappucci's investigators packing, saying: "You go back
to your boss and tell him that Ted Marks says you are on a wild
goose chase. If this gets out, it's only going to hurt the Air
Force." *

However, none of this appeared in the OSI's "Memorandum of
Record" of their conversation with Ted Marks. Instead, OSI
recorded a collection of faint and heavily qualified praise from
Ted Marks, some misinformation, and some gratuitous bad-
mouthing. The OSI memorandum recorded Ted Marks as saying
that he "felt Mr. Fitzgerald was sincere and dedicated *but* [em-
phasis mine] things were either 'black or white,' 'right or wrong,'
and usually his own ideas were the ones he considered right," ad
nauseam. They also quoted Ted Marks as saying that "Fitzgerald
was impatient for results" but became "increasingly belligerent"
when results were not forthcoming. OSI noted also that Ted
Marks said that Fitzgerald had violated an agreement to resign
as Deputy for Management Systems in May of 1968. This was
complete fiction, but I never learned whether the author was Ted
Marks or OSI. OSI quoted Marks as stating that he was "not
socially acquainted with Fitzgerald" despite the fact that we
had visited one another's homes, attended social functions together, and traveled extensively in one another's company.

In the end, though, OSI was disappointed in their interview
with Ted Marks. They got no confirmation of the conflict of interest slander. On the contrary, their memorandum stated: "Mr.
Marks said he knew Fitzgerald was President and part owner of
Performance Technology Corporation (PTC) prior to engaging
his services, but he knew Fitzgerald sold his stock in the company
to other principals at the time he entered the Air Force." And
that: "Mr. Marks was of the opinion Fitzgerald had never aided
his former company (PTC)."

This was naturally a bitter disappointment to General Cappucci
and his Keystone Kops. They could not have been too surprised,

* Jack Anderson's Special Report, San Francisco *Chronicle*, Dec. 26, 1969.

though, because in addition to the usual disclosures of stock holdings, then required by Pentagon conflict of interest regulations, I had voluntarily filed a complete statement of *all* my financial interests—cash, bonds, real estate, stock, and all—when I entered the Pentagon. My complete financial statement would have been easy to verify factually. The trouble was the OSI did not want facts which would have cleared me of malicious gossip. They wanted ammunition. So, after stumbling about a while longer, Cappucci's associates directed their field agents to "try again" to come up with something on the conflict of interest charge. Once more their hopes were dashed. In August of 1969, another RUC report cleared me of the absurd allegations.

While General Cappucci's secret agents were charging about the country confirming my lack of social accomplishment and attempting to build a case against me on the baseless conflict of interest gossip they had obtained from their informers, I was extremely busy on other fronts. I had lost the most important functions of my office to the military officers of the Air Staff and the Systems Command, but I was managing to keep abreast of developments in the big weapons programs through unofficial personal channels. In addition, congressional testimony kept me hopping. The sensational disclosures that the Air Force had deliberately falsified internal C-5A cost reports to protect Lockheed's position in the stock market renewed congressional interest in the disaster. The disclosures had repercussions in the Pentagon also. Colonel Kenneth Beckman had confirmed the records-doctoring episode on April 29 and 30 before the House Government Operations Committee. On April 30, an angry Melvin Laird, stung by the storm of criticism, issued a statement:

> I am very concerned by the situation which was inherited surrounding the C-5A contract and procurement actions. Rapid corrective action is essential and is being taken.
> I am determined to insure that full and accurate information on C-5A procurement and on all other procurement matters is given to the Congress and to the public promptly.*

That same day, Secretary Laird announced the resignations of Assistant Secretaries Robert H. Charles and Thomas H. Nielsen. News media reporters immediately connected the resigna-

* Washington *Post*, May 1, 1969.

tions of the two Assistant Secretaries with disclosures of the C-5A fiasco. However, Laird later issued a statement saying that Tom Nielsen's resignation "has no connection with yesterday's C-5A statement by Secretary Laird." The Pentagon statement was silent on the subject of Robert H. Charles' departure.

An outside observer might have assumed that my position in the C-5A tragedy would have been vindicated, but as the then secret Seamans' attacks on me and the subsequent Cappucci caper indicated, I was still in the soup. The Pentagon may have rejected Bob Charles, but it had gathered unto its breast his favorite project and adopted his weird story that all was well with the project. Just so there would be no mistake about where the new Administration stood, Melvin Laird, Robert Seamans, and Robert Charles held a press conference in the Pentagon on May 2. Secretary Laird praised Mr. Charles' performance but fled the scene before substantive information was presented. However, Mr. Laird's Air Force Secretary, Robert Seamans, "sat by Charles' side and supported his arithmetic." *

I was invited to testify before Mendel Rivers' House Armed Services Committee on the C-5A. This invitation meant very serious trouble for me. Even though Bob Charles had resigned, the party line that he had shared with the military side of the Air Force had been endorsed by the new Nixon appointees in the Pentagon. I would be placed in a position of contradicting my new bosses unless I recanted and changed the testimony I had given before Senator Proxmire's Committee. Mendel Rivers could be depended upon to endorse whatever position the Air Force generals took. As usual, Chairman Rivers planned to hold closed hearings on the C-5. His style was not suited to performing in public. As was the case prior to Senator Proxmire's hearings in January of 1969, the Pentagon procurement weenies gloated over my anticipated dismemberment in a forum where they could not lose. I could not hope to "win," of course, in the sense that I could convince the Armed Services Committee that I was right in my stand on the C-5A situation. On the other hand, I was confident that I could hold my own if the hearings were open to the public and the press.

* Washington *Post*, May 3, 1969.

A number of the members of Mendel Rivers' Armed Services Committee agreed that the C-5 hearings should be open, and they badgered the Chairman and his staff assistants until they finally and reluctantly agreed to hold extremely rare open hearings. Fortunately for me, there was absolutely nothing subject to military security regulations in the C-5A disaster. As it turned out, the presence of the public and the press in the hearing room did wonders for Chairman Rivers' disposition. When I appeared before his Committee on May 22, the Chairman was polite and restrained in his treatment of me throughout most of the long and rather dreary hearing, only occasionally allowing himself a snide comment.

In an effort to avoid fights I could not win, I kept my testimony as dry and technical as possible. I stuck exclusively to official Air Force figures and placed in the record a huge stack of Air Force documents supporting my testimony.* My strategy was to lay out the facts of the Air Force's own analyses, then let the gaggle of generals and colonels present to refute my testimony thrash around explaining their own figures. This strategy did little to clarify matters in the public mind, but at least it got me through the hearings alive. It might even have done a little good too. One of the documents I put in the record (one furnished me by a secret sympathizer) outlined an Air Force plan to confuse further the cost situation on the C-5.

Because of the madcap repricing formula, dubbed the "Golden Handshake" by the press, Lockheed stood to make a huge profit on the second batch of C-5As which would offset losses then estimated for the development and the first batch of airplanes. The Air Force plan to conceal this idiocy, as outlined in their own document, was to leave Lockheed's net estimated losses unchanged but to "adjust" the price of the second batch downward so that Lockheed would exactly break even on the second run, then add the amount of this downward "adjustment" on run B to the price of the first run, thereby jacking up the price of the then current first C-5A order so that Lockheed would take only

---

* "Hearings on Military Posture," before the Committee on Armed Services, House of Representatives, Ninety-first Congress, First Session, Part II, pp. 2949 to 3020.

the calculated net losses on it. The purpose of this complicated and farcical maneuver was explained in the Air Force document: "This technique is used to avoid the appearance of excess profit for Run B aircraft." *

Even though this fancy financial footwork had already been approved prior to my testimony, according to the documents I had obtained, nothing more was heard of the scheme afterward. Perhaps public disclosure headed off at least this one small bit of madness.

My next appearance as a congressional witness was on June 11, 1969, before Senator Proxmire's Joint Economic Committee subcommittee, who were holding hearings on "The Military Budget and National Economic Priorities." In contrast to my previous congressional appearances, the prelude to this testimony was quiet and uneventful. As a consequence, I had time to prepare a statement which briefly but thoroughly explored the worst effects of loose military acquisition policies and mismanagement of major weapons programs. I also proposed a number of specific actions which I believe would improve the efficiency of our acquisition of major weapons systems.

The statement was well received by the subcommittee. In the questioning that followed, Senator Proxmire, Congressman Moorhead, and the lone Republican present, Senator Len Jordan of Idaho, carefully probed and commented on the suggestions I had made. They seemed especially interested in my comments about attitude problems in the military procurement community, including the prevalent notion that excessive costs had to be allowed in buying weapons to facilitate the attainment of "social goals." The Mark II fiasco was much in the news at that time, and Senator Proxmire indicated that he wanted to look more deeply into that program. He asked that I return to testify again two days later, on June 13, and to bring with me cost information on both the Mark II and the SRAM programs. The Senator had questioned me about the technical health of the C-5A, and I had confirmed that I had heard of some relaxations in the Air Force's technical requirements. The Senator asked me to furnish documentation of this situation when I returned. Finally, he re-

* *Ibid.*, p. 2979.

quested that I give a specific example of a situation in which the "social goals" excuse had been employed to thwart cost reduction and control efforts.

I had a busy day and a half, but I finally got together most of what Senator Proxmire had requested. I had been given the "idiot treatment" by the Air Force procurement people in response to my questions about the C-5A technical performance. (The "idiot treatment" takes many forms, but the usual sort is a kind of bureaucratic mendacity in which the response, usually in enormous detail, is a correct answer to some question but not the one asked.) I expected this, of course, because Dr. Seamans and his associates were then frantically covering up the C-5A's growing technical problems. The SRAM cost information the Senator had requested was improperly classified secret, but Tom Nielsen had agreed to declassify it and to forward it to Senator Proxmire through the GAO. My big task had been assembly of a case study on the attitude problem. Fortunately, Bill George had written an excellent, scholarly summary of the Mark II program's unhappy history, and I had a file of correspondence dealing with the generals' interposition of the "social goals" argument to block the Mark II should-cost study. On June 13 I bundled up my submissions for the subcommittee and sent them to Tom Nielsen with an accompanying letter requesting declassification of the SRAM cost data and his approval for presenting the material to the subcommittee. Later, on the evening of June 12, and again early the next morning, I spoke with Tom Nielsen about my upcoming testimony. Tom, very pleasant and relaxed since his resignation, said that he saw no problem with the submission except that more time would be required to get the SRAM data declassified and submitted after my June 13 testimony.

I arrived in the big New Senate Office Building auditorium where the hearings were to be held about 9:30 on the morning of the 13th. As I sat reviewing my written statement and arranging the various exhibits I had prepared, my secretary from the Pentagon rushed breathlessly into the auditorium and handed me a letter, telling me very excitedly that Mr. Nielsen had told her the letter must reach me before the hearings started.

Tom Nielsen's letter explained that Senator Proxmire had also submitted a long list of questions to be answered by Assistant Secretary of Defense Shillito who had also testified on June 11, and that Pentagon staff people were then working to prepare the answers. He went on to instruct me:

. . . your response to questions concerning these matters should acknowledge the efforts now under way to assemble complete information on these subjects for the Committee.

In view of the efforts under way by OSD to respond to Senator Proxmire's request, I believe it would be inappropriate for anyone from this office to release additional information concerning the programs mentioned in Senator Proxmire's letter of May 14, 1969, especially in open hearings.

It was then a quarter of ten, fifteen minutes before hearing time, and the big room was nearly full, as were the press tables and TV camera alcoves. I was the only witness scheduled that day. I could not believe my leaders in the Pentagon would be so stupid as to attempt to muzzle me again after all that had gone before, especially so blatantly and in front of so many witnesses. Hurriedly, I telephoned Tom Nielsen's office. He was not available. However, I did talk with one of Assistant Secretary Nielsen's military assistants, who assured me that the letter meant exactly what it said. I was not to talk about the weapons programs, especially the SRAM and the Mark II. Sure enough, I was muzzled.

All I could do was go forward and explain the affair to Senator Proxmire. I reached the bench just as the Senator was preparing to gavel the hearing to order. The Senator listened to my explanation, then asked me to take my seat at the witness table.

After the hearing was opened, I explained all I knew of the affair, which wasn't much, to the subcommittee and the incredulous assembly of newsmen and spectators. Then Senator Proxmire took over. The Senator was at the top of his form in expressing shock, outrage, and disbelief. He announced that he was going to convey all these sentiments and more in a letter to Secretary of Defense Melvin Laird that very day. The press and television people had a field day at the expense of the Pentagon's anonymous bureaucrats. What would have been otherwise a quiet and somewhat esoteric discussion of big weapons systems management problems was transformed instead into a display of Pentagon stupidity and arrogance on the front pages of newspapers, on the radio, and on television during the evening news.

Senator Proxmire was as good as his word, and within an hour or so after the brief hearings he dispatched his blast to Melvin Laird. The Secretary of Defense immediately relayed the scorching protest to the office of the Secretary of the Air Force where, with unheard-of speed, the normally torpid bureaucrats drafted a reply the same day.

The Air Force's response was a forerunner of things to come. Their letter, signed by John L. McLucas, the new Under Secretary of the Air Force, told Senator Proxmire that a big effort was under way in the Pentagon to provide him with "detailed, correct information" which would be developed "in a complete and orderly fashion."

"However," Dr. McLucas wrote, "if you feel that a partial presentation of the information would be of assistance to the subcommittee, we would be pleased, as we have before, to make Mr. Fitzgerald available." In other words, if the Senator wanted "detailed," "correct," "complete," and "orderly" information, he couldn't get it from Fitzgerald. At that time I had not met Dr. McLucas at all, but clearly he was not one of my fans.

The Pentagon's retreat on muzzling me gave the news media another opportunity to expose the oxlike but arrogant mentality of the military bureaucrats. Senator Proxmire got in his licks as well.

My reappearance to testify unmuzzled on June 17 was anticlimactic. The prospect of my presenting the well documented case example of the Mark II fiasco had triggered another unreasoning frenzy among the generals, but when I finally presented it there was remarkably little stir. The military bureaucracy's lack of enthusiasm for cost reduction and control just wasn't news to the jaded old hands of the Washington press corps. (Incidentally, even though Senator Proxmire once again requested facts on the technical status of the C-5A and held the record open for that purpose, he never did receive the "detailed," "correct," "complete," and "orderly" information promised by the Pentagon.)

My testimony in June of 1969 was apparently the last straw

for the Air Force bureaucracy, which was already furious with me. On the afternoon of my testimony on June 11, I was summoned to meet with Secretary of Defense Melvin Laird and his deputy, David Packard. Secretary Laird was friendly and seemed somewhat sympathetic but made it clear that I would have to be moved out of the Air Force. We discussed possibilities of my working elsewhere in the Pentagon. I met with Mr. Laird and one of his assistants several times thereafter, but nothing ever came of it.

On June 24, 1969, Tom Nielson was replaced by Spencer Schedler as Assistant Secretary of the Air Force for Financial Management. Mr. Schedler had earned his appointment by good work in the 1968 election campaign of Vice President Spiro T. Agnew. He had extremely close relations, both business and personal, with the auditing firm of Arthur Young & Company, whose most lucrative client was the Lockheed Aircraft Corporation, producer of the C-5A.

From then on I was subjected to an intensive and apparently well organized campaign of personal bad-mouthing by Air Force spokesmen. The gist of the criticism, direct and implied, was that my congressional testimony had not been "balanced." By then, rising C-5A costs had forced the Air Force to concede that my testimony on the big plane's cost increases was more or less accurate, but they complained that I had not balanced the testimony by pointing out that the project was a magnificent technical success. Perhaps unknowingly, the White House also adopted this line. For example, many letters addressed to President Nixon complaining about the Pentagon's treatment of me following my testimony were bucked to the Air Force for answering. The form letters prepared for these responses "on behalf of President Nixon" always avoided specific questions raised by angry taxpayers or else lied about them. Then they cautioned the complainer: ". . . when assessing the personal views of any one individual as related to such issues, it should be emphasized that they represent a single opinion rather than a balanced picture of the situation."

Simultaneously, the Air Force military dreamed up a "conspiracy theory" to account for my apparent excess of zeal. For example, the Philadelphia *Bulletin* on July 22, 1969, carried a syndicated column which charged:

> Senator Proxmire's agent within is A. Ernest Fitzgerald. He is a civilian employee inside the finance section of the Air Force. Fitzgerald came in under Secretary McNamara and became one of the civilian operatives who scooted around and wrote out-of-channel reports on various projects.
>
> In recent weeks he has been giving damaging testimony against associates and superiors alike at the Defense Department, and it's widely supposed that he is in cahoots with the Pentagon-baiting press.

The *Bulletin*'s syndicated columnist, one Holmes Alexander, gave as his source a "military guy, an Air Force officer." According to Mr. Alexander's bold but anonymous sky warrior, "the military guys" bitterly resented criticism of the military-industrial complex. In fact, they even objected to the word "complex." "The military guys," wrote Mr. Alexander, "prefer the word 'partnership' to the word 'complex' in discussing their arrangement with industry."

The team of anonymous "Air Force guys" and Mr. Alexander made the big time in their ad hominem attacks on me when Senator Barry Goldwater picked up their themes. On September 3, 1969, during his successful fight to defeat Senator Proxmire's attempt to get the facts on the C-5A, Senator Goldwater placed another of Mr. Alexander's columns in the Congressional Record. This masterpiece, employing the vague literary techniques beloved of various lunatic fringe groups, pictured me as a member of "an interlocking directorate of intellectuals who oppose law and order, national defense, the two-party system, and the majority rule of our American palefaces." (I had not met most of my alleged co-conspirators and had never even heard of some of them.) The demonic conspiracy was not against everything, however. It favored pornography, race riots, U.S. disarmament, and Eldridge Cleaver.*

The irony of this bit of bureaucratic paranoia which imagined me a member of a left-wing conspiracy is that the washroom gossip in the Pentagon during my 1968 arguments with the "social goals" faction pictured me as the only known member of a

* *Congressional Record*, September 3, 1969, p. S10109.

gigantic *right-wing* conspiracy. Apparently the change of presidential administrations had reversed the orientation of bureaucratic dementia.

All during the summer and early fall of 1969 I received calls every few days from the Joint Economic Committee staff inquiring about my submissions of C-5A technical status for the hearing records. Congressman William Moorhead was also clamoring for information on the big plane's technical problems. I knew that the Air Force "position" was that the C-5 was a technical marvel despite factual indications to the contrary. However, by then it was clear that I would be fired as soon as the military procurement bills passed the Congress, so I was progressively less concerned with the Air Force "position." Since I was to be canned anyway, I thought I might as well get the facts as I had been requested by the Joint Economic Committee. I rarely saw my superiors, but I could still write letters, and I did. I compiled a thick file of memoranda requesting C-5A technical information and "idiot treatment" responses from a variety of bureaucrats in the Air Force Headquarters.*

On July 13, the Air Force acknowledged that the C-5A had suffered a cracked wing at less-than-specified strength in ground tests. A couple of weeks later, a report on the C-5A by Assistant Secretary Phillip Whittaker, Bob Charles' successor, acknowledged that the airplane would have to be restricted to about 80 percent of its anticipated load-carrying capabilities for landing on rough airfields.

The Air Force hierarchy reminded me of flat-earth cultists in their ability to ignore the rising tide of facts rebutting their official "position" of C-5A technical excellence. This was partly explainable by the fact that Dr. Seamans, with his reputation as one of the country's top engineers, was playing Charley McCarthy to the generals' Edgar Bergen. Another explanation was that Seamans and the top military people were telling a majority of the Congress what the people's representatives wished to hear and pass on to their constituents in order to justify continued support of the catastrophic boondoogle.

* "The Dismissal of A. Ernest Fitzgerald by the Defense Department," hearings before the Subcommittee on Economy in Government of the Joint Economic Committee, Ninety-first Congress, First Session, pp. 183–187.

On September 9, 1969, the Senate defeated Senator Proxmire's amendment to get full disclosure of the C-5A situation before continuing with the program by the resounding score of 64–21. A similar amendment in the House of Representatives was defeated on September 26 by 136–60. After that, reactions to my requests for C-5A technical data degenerated from evasive to ugly. Spencer Schedler, who was given to rather salty language even when he was on his good behavior, was particularly abusive in telling me on October 14 to go to hell. He said that if Senator Proxmire still wanted the information, he could take the matter up with the Secretary of the Air Force. The next day, October 15, I closed out my official attempts to get the facts on the C-5A's carefully concealed technical problems by writing a personal note to Senator Proxmire apologizing for my failure to comply with his request.*

When the previously secret transcripts of Chairman Rivers' hearings of May 7, 1969, were released in late September, my earlier information about Secretary Seamans' slanderous attacks on me were confirmed in the publicly distributed documents. I had to do something about the charges. On September 26, I clipped the pertinent section of the transcript and sent it to Spencer Schedler with the following note:

"I learned of the exchange recorded in the attachment for the first time today. I am concerned that the statements accusing me of releasing confidential documents were not corrected prior to printing of the transcript. They are false. Dr. Seamans never spoke to me about this matter and I do not know where he received the information. With your permission, I would like to talk with Dr. Seamans to attempt to clarify this serious matter."

The note was never answered, nor did I get an audience with Seamans. After listening to Seamans' false charges being repeated for nearly another month, on October 22 I again wrote to Schedler:

"On September 26, I wrote you concerning Dr. Seamans' accusations before the House Armed Service Committee. According to the Committee transcript of the hearings, Dr. Seamans

---

* "The Military Budget and National Economic Priorities," hearings before the Subcommittee on Economy in Government of the Joint Economic Committee, Ninety-first Congress, First Session, Part II, Appendix II, p. (A3).

stated that I had given confidential documents to congressional committees without permission of the Air Force. I would be most grateful if you could obtain for me copies of the confidential documents which I am supposed to have transmitted to the congressional committees."

This note was not answered either.

I was fired on November 4, 1969. Late in the afternoon, around five o'clock, Spencer Schedler called me to his office, where he was sitting with his military assistant, Colonel Dudley Pewitt. After a few minutes of nervous, rambling chitchat from Spencer and Dudley, Schedler said, "We're reorganizing the office," and handed me a document to read. It was headed:

Subject: Notice of Proposed Separation Due to Reduction in Force
To: Mr. A. Ernest Fitzgerald, ASFFM

The document went on to notify me that I would be "separated" in sixty days, and described at great length and in bureaucratic language my rights as a civil servant, which appeared minimal from the document. It was signed by Mrs. A. Y. Kent, the Chief of the Civilian Personnel Division in the Air Staff, the military part of the Air Force headquarters. I had never met Mrs. Kent, and the only time I had heard from her previously was when she had notified me of my conversion to career tenure status in September of 1968. Mrs. Kent's previous action had been described as a "computer error," but not this time. She had been promoted from computer to real, live bureaucrat, and I was really canned. Incidentally, the method finally used to fire me was the second of the three alternatives suggested in the Lang Memorandum of January 6, 1969.

Simultaneously, the Air Force's public relations experts (called flacks) issued a "Memorandum for Correspondents" announcing that the Office of Deputy for Management Systems was being eliminated as part of an economy move. For once the flacks had written a press release in hopes that the news media would *not* pick it up. My name was not mentioned. Moreover, my firing and the simultaneous press release were carefully timed. November 4 was election day in my adopted home state of Virginia and in many other states. The two Air Force officers who planned the caper later told mutual friends that they expected the announcement of my firing to be buried in the welter of election returns. My firing had been announced late in the afternoon so that it would miss the afternoon papers entirely and leave little or no time for reporters to prepare a comprehensive story before the early evening deadline for most morning papers.

Once again the Pentagon bureaucrats were so devious that they outsmarted themselves. They had overlooked the fact that most television and radio stations devote only limited time in the evening for news on an ordinary day but that news departments are often on the air continually on an evening after election day. On election evenings, especially in the early hours before heavy returns start pouring in, there are long, blank periods with little to report. Oftentimes the announcers will fill in these blank spaces with general news announcements. As luck would have it, November 4, 1969, was a rather dull day for news, and the report of my firing was announced every few minutes on many stations rather than only once or twice during an evening, as would have been the case on a normal day.

The next day's papers revealed that the Pentagon flacks' amateurish maneuver had not worked. News of my firing was widespread, and even though the Air Force claimed the action was "absolutely not" related to what it called my "previous notoriety in relation to congressional testimony," nobody believed them. Senator Proxmire issued a blast stating that my firing was "a clear message from the Pentagon to its employees. That message is, do not reduce costs, do not aim toward efficiency, do not attempt to achieve economy in government. If you do, you will be isolated and fired." * Senator Proxmire also announced that his subcommittee would hold hearings to inquire into my firing.

On November 7, the Washington *Post* carried a story describing an incident which probably marked the all-time high in bureaucratic stupidity, arrogance, and plain old-fashioned crookedness. On the same day that he had fired me, Spencer Schedler had hired as a consultant his old college roommate, John Diment,

---

* Newark, New Jersey, *Evening News*, November 5, 1969.

a partner in the accounting firm of Arthur Young & Company, to assume part of the duties previous assigned to my office in the Pentagon. Arthur Young & Company, as Lockheed's auditors and management advisors, were then being sued for their role in helping Lockheed conceal the monumental C-5A cost overruns. Although Joe Warren and his underpaid tiger team had managed to identify the C-5A overruns in 1966, Arthur Young & Company's experts, highly paid by Lockheed, had somehow managed not to notice.

After attending Harvard Business School with John Diment, Spencer Schedler had gone to work for an Arthur Young & Company client in Houston, Texas, a company run by an alumnus of Arthur Young & Company. Not long afterward, he had gone to work for another and larger Arthur Young & Company client, a major oil company, where he eventually became Deputy Director of Budgets.

To make matters worse, Spencer Schedler's wife, Judy, was then working for the Arthur Young & Company office in Washington. Previously she had worked in the Arthur Young & Company office in New York but had been promoted and transferred to the Washington office when Schedler completed his work for Agnew and moved into the Air Force job. Judy's boss in New York, the Arthur Young & Company partner in charge of the office, also moved to Washington to look after the interests of Arthur Young & Company and its clients. Representative William Moorhead, commenting on the employment of an Arthur Young & Company partner to help oversee the costs of major Air Force contractors, including their big client, Lockheed, accurately described the situation as "sending a bulldog to guard the hamburger."

On November 8, only one day after the Washington *Post* disclosure of the Schedler-Diment scandal, the Pentagon, unable to stand the heat of publicity, dismissed John Diment as their management systems consultant.

On November 7, sixty members of the House of Representatives signed and sent to President Nixon a letter strongly protesting my firing. They were particularly critical of the ridiculous "economy" excuse for the action, calling it "an incredible irony." To me, this was a very gratifying and faith-restoring gesture. Most of the sixty signers of the letter, including both Democrats and Republicans, had no direct constituent interest in my case. It was almost purely an endorsement of fairness and good stewardship. I was sobered, though, by the thought that 375 House members did *not* sign the letter. This score (sixty for Fitzgerald, 375 against or indifferent) must have impressed the White House too, because Congressman Moorhead, the originator of the letter, got the following brush-off from one of the President's aides, William E. Timmons:

"Thank you for your letter to the President in which you were joined by 60 other Members of the House of Representatives. Your concern over the separation of Mr. A. Ernest Fitzgerald from the Department of Defense will be called to the President's attention at the earliest opportunity, as I know he will be interested in having your views on this matter."

November 1969 was a bad month for me, but it was probably an equally bad time for the Air Force and their pet dinosaur, Lockheed. On November 14, the Pentagon announced that it had abandoned its plans to buy 120 C-5As and had cut the planned program to the eighty-one airplanes already authorized by Congress. The Pentagon announcement stated that "budget restraints" were responsible. The Air Force explained that they had made a review in July of 1969 which put the cost at $5,300,000,000, which just happened to be the figure I had testified to the previous November. Actually, I had made my own estimates in July and August of 1969, which indicated that the program would probably cost at least $5,800,000,000, with the expectation of even higher future costs under the Air Force's grotesque "Golden Handshake" repricing scheme. By fall, the combined effect of continuing cost increases on the first batch and the Golden Handshake had pushed the estimated cost for the full 120-airplane program past $6,000,000,000, which the Office of the Secretary of Defense probably concluded was a politically intolerable figure, especially in view of all the vilification directed my way for testifying that 120 of the big planes might cost $5,300,000,000 in the absence of corrective actions by the Air Force.

On November 17 and 18, Senator Proxmire held his hearings to inquire into the circumstances of my firing. The Senator opened the hearings by reading a section of the law, Title 18, Section 1505 of the U.S. Code, which stated that persons endeavoring to influence, intimidate, or impede congressional witnesses or to retaliate against them afterwards should be fined not more than $5,000 or imprisoned not more than five years or both. I then testified before a generally sympathetic subcommittee of both Democrats and Republicans for about three hours.

The next day I returned to the subcommittee hearings to hear the testimony of Secretary Seamans and Assistant Secretaries Schedler and Whittaker. After Dr. Seamans had read his prepared statement, reasserting the party line that my job had been eliminated in order to save money, both Senator Proxmire and Congressman Moorhead questioned the distinguished looking Secretary about his secret but outrageous lies before Mendel Rivers' committee in which he had accused me of leaking confidential documents. Dr. Seamans squirmed, evaded, and dissembled but was finally forced to acknowledge that his earlier statements were not true. Dr. Seamans said that he was sorry for the way his statements had been "interpreted," but, significantly, he did not offer to undo the damage to me.

With his lack of veracity thus established, Secretary Seamans had a difficult time thereafter in the hearings. Each time one of the subcommittee members referred to my firing, Dr. Seamans would object that I had not been fired at all, but instead my job had been eliminated. When the large audience laughed loudly and disrespectfully at Seamans' stubborn, bureaucratic semantics, the Secretary would turn deep red from his collar to the roots of his white hair.

Like a good military mouthpiece, Dr. Seamans again turned mendacious when questioned about General Cappucci's OSI investigation of my private life. He stated categorically at one point, "I know from my knowledge that an investigation was never called for, nor was an investigation ever carried out." * Seamans was not unprepared on this point either. The gentlemanly Congressman Moorhead had called him the night before

---

* "The Dismissal of A. Ernest Fitzgerald by the Defense Department," hearings before the Subcommittee on Economy in Government of the Joint Economic Committee, Ninety-first Congress, First Session, p. 117.

to alert him to the fact that we knew about OSI File HQD-24-12052. In the interim, Seamans had concocted a bit of bureaucratic obfuscation based on definition of terms. The prefix "24" in the file number designated a "Special Inquiry" and according to Seamans was not an investigation at all, but rather a simple, passive collection of "clippings from newspapers, summaries of meetings with individuals, and so forth."

We, of course, knew that this was not true. The OSI gumshoes had in fact made strenuous efforts all over the country to dig up dirt which could be used to discredit me personally and thereby cast doubt on my testimony. Actually the prefix "24" differentiated the "Special Inquiry" from the other types of investigations. For example, the prefix "36" referred to a background investigation; "58" to an investigation of alleged conflict of interest; and "34" to security violation investigations.

With the publication on November 7 of the letter to President Nixon signed by sixty Congressmen protesting my firing, Spencer Schedler had gone into action to head off political trouble. Having performed well in Vice President Agnew's successful campaign, Spencer was confident of his political ability and exercised it by calling on Republican Congressmen who had signed the letter to the President. His purpose was to explain to them the "real reason" he had fired me. He had explained to some that I had to go because I had been leaking information to Capitol Hill, and to some that my recommendations, particularly on "should cost," were no good. Assistant Secretary Schedler's dominant theme, however, was that I was not a "team player." Clearly I had not supported the Air Force "team" when they chose to lie and conceal the C-5A difficulties. He invoked a principle sounding somewhat like the Divine Right of Assistant Secretaries to hire and fire employees on the public payroll without regard for guidelines other than their supposed prerogatives to assemble their own "team." Schedler's political strategy may have been good, but his tactics were lousy. Among the Congressmen he called on were several representing my numerous family in Alabama and my own Congressman in Virginia, three of whom relayed Schedler's explanation to me.

Congressman Moorhead had also been told of Schedler's explanation to Republicans on Capitol Hill. He questioned Schedler sharply on the subject. Schedler took standard bureaucratic evasive action, but Congressman Moorhead persisted. After being asked the same question five or six times, Schedler finally admitted that he had made the trips to Capitol Hill to explain my firing. However, despite the fact that some of the visits had taken place only a few days prior to the hearings, Schedler claimed to have forgotten what he had told the Congressmen. He had lost his memory completely. He made this absurd excuse not once, but three times.

As Mr. Moorhead bored in with his line of questioning, Schedler literally hung his head, would not look at his questioner, and mumbled his evasions. The kindly Congressman finally let him off the hook.

Schedler may have lost his memory, but the Congressmen he called on had not, at least not all of them. The next day, newspaper accounts quoted Congressmen Broyhill (R–Va.) and Dickenson (R–Ala.) as confirming that Schedler had told them I was fired because I was not a "team player." *

Several members of the subcommittee questioned Seamans and Schedler on the extent to which animosity toward me by Air Force officials I had wounded in past actions had affected the new appointees. Both Seamans and Schedler admitted they had held conversations on the subject. (As a matter of fact, their only evaluation of my performance and abilities from people in the Pentagon came from hold-over bureaucrats. I had previously seen Dr. Seamans only once, in the brief meeting on March 4, 1969, and had met with Schedler only four or five times before my firing.) Seamans testified that I had hurt my "relationship with people in the Air Force," and offered in evidence the letter I had written to General O'Neill on December 15, 1967, on the Minuteman fiasco. Dr. Seamans was particularly offended by my comments to General O'Neill about the problem of habitual lying in managing the Minuteman program. He said, "I have yet to meet any responsible person in the military or in the civilian side of the Air Force that I can accuse of lying, so I feel myself that this was

* Washington *Post*, November 19, 1966.

a false accusation." * I wondered at the time if Dr. Seamans used a mirror to shave.

Assistant Secretary Phillip Whittaker's principal contribution to the hearings was to chant a couple of paeans of praise for the C-5A's technical excellence.

Quite aside from my personal stake in the proceedings, I found the hearings into my firing fascinating. We had just begun to draw aside the bureaucratic curtain behind which the Air Force had conducted its shenanigans, and I was hopeful that further inquiries might prove instructive to the public as well as helpful to me. However, Senator Proxmire had seen and heard enough. In fact, he had seen and heard so much that he was convinced that criminal proceedings should be instituted to identify positively and prosecute the Pentagon officials who had impeded the work of a congressional committee, attempted to impede my testimony, and retaliated against me afterwards. The law seemed so simple and so clear, and the actions taken against me and the Joint Economic Committee so brazen and so much against the public interest, that most objective observers at the time agreed that the Justice Department would be moved to investigate the matter, at least. As Senator Proxmire put it:

Now we know a crime has been committed. The provisions of this statute have been clearly violated.

We know the victim is Ernest Fitzgerald, and we know an attempt was made to obstruct a congressional hearing.

It is therefore the duty of the Department of Justice to identify the perpetrators of the criminal acts and to take the necessary action against them whoever they may be.

The Senator made these statements in a press release which accompanied his formal request to the Honorable John H. Mitchell, the Attorney General of the United States, to investigate my firing. Dr. Seamans had slyly implicated Secretary of Defense Laird in my firing. Consequently, the Attorney General should have included Mr. Laird's role in my firing in his investigation. From the superior vantage point of historical retrospection, even the implicit assumption that John Mitchell might put

* "The Dismissal of A. Ernest Fitzgerald," p. 159.

Melvin Laird in jail seems naïve in the extreme. However, the attitudes and assumptions current in late 1969 must be recalled to understand why turning the matter over to the Jusice Department appeared to be the best course of action at the time.

The judgment that my firing was a proper subject for the Justice Department's Criminal Division was shared by other members of the Congress. A few days before, Representative Jack Brooks of Texas, a senior member of the powerful House Government Operations Committee, had also asked Mr. Mitchell to look into these affairs.

In running for President, Mr. Nixon had presented himself as a man of principle. He had committed himself to holding the federal bureaucracy accountable for its actions. He had dedicated himself to fiscal responsibility and economy in government. Once elected, President Nixon had promised an "open administration." The President, Vice President Agnew, and Attorney General Mitchell were all staunch advocates of law and order.

The President's views on the right of government employees to testify before Congress without fear of retaliation were strongly held and of long standing. For example, on April 26, 1951, while still a United States Senator, Mr. Nixon had offered a strong bill to protect government witnesses testifying before congressional committees from discharge by superior officers. His speech was a classic:

"I have introduced in the Senate today a bill to make it a violation of law for any officer of the Federal Government to dismiss or otherwise discipline a government employee for testifying before a committee of Congress." Further on, the President-to-be said: "It is essential to the security of the nation and the very lives of the people, as we look into these vitally important issues, that every witness have complete freedom from reprisal when he is given an opportunity to tell what he knows." Addressing himself to upcoming congressional hearings, Senator Nixon continued: "Unless protection is given to witnesses who are members of the Armed Services or employees of the Government, the scheduled hearings will amount to no more than a parade of yes men for Administration policies as they exist." *

* *Congressional Record,* April 26, 1951, pp. S4393 and S4394.

The bill which Senator Nixon introduced (S. 1390, 82nd Congress, 1st Session) was most explicit on the definition of retaliation for testimony:

The demotion, dismissal or retirement (other than voluntary or for physical disability) of such witness *within one year* [emphasis mine] after attending or testifying in such inquiry or investigation, unless such testimony discloses misfeasance, malfeasance, derelictions of duty, or past reprehensible conduct on the part of such witness, shall be considered prima facie evidence that such witness was demoted, dismissed, or retired because of such attendance or such testimony.

I had been fired nine days short of one year after my fatal testimony. Using the President's own criterion, the case against my bureaucratic tormentors seemed ironclad.

While I awaited the Nixon Administration's decision on my fate, things began looking up for me, at least according to newspaper reports. On December 2, the Washington *Star* reported that Secretary of Defense Laird had acknowledged that I "was fired," contradicting Air Force Secretary Seamans' dogged instance that I had not been fired and strengthening my case for appealing my dismissal. On December 8, *Aerospace Daily*, a defense industry trade paper, stated that I had been given a "pat on the back from Defense Secretary Melvin Laird." *Aerospace Daily* reported that Mr. Laird had testified before the House Defense Appropriations Subcommittee that "Mr. Fitzgerald's position on the C-5A cost overruns had been correct."

However, there was too much at stake for the Air Force bureaucracy to remain idle, and they didn't. Dr. Seamans' old, discredited security violation charges and the gossip General Cappucci had collected from informers about conflicts of interest on my part were peddled all over Washington by Air Force officers and civilians. Reacting to persistent pressure from Congressman Moorhead and Senator Proxmire to expose OSI's dirt file on me to fresh air and sunshine, the Air Force compiled a bowdlerized version of the file on me which they showed to Senator Proxmire and Congressman Moorhead in private. The file shown to Mr. Moorhead and Senator Proxmire included only newspaper clippings and the scurrilous rumors and silly misgivings of anonymous informers T-1, T-2, T-3, and T-4. They omitted both their interview with my former boss, Ted Marks, and the field investigation reports which cleared me of the gossip. It was only after columnist Jack Anderson loosed a real blast in a special report [*] revealing this hatchet work that the Air Force acknowledged the Ted Marks interview which refuted the conflict of interest gossip. The Air Force explanation to Senator Proxmire and Congressman Moorhead was that they "forgot" to include Marks' interview. They had, of course, also "forgotten" to include the exonerating field investigation reports.

In an attempt to make sure the favorable field reports never surfaced, General Cappucci sent orders to his field commanders across the country to destroy all their notes and reports concerning me. We learned that these orders went at least to OSI Districts 1, 2, 4, and 18. The Air Force OSI file containing anonymous charges against me but omitting the proof of innocence was widely circulated. The charges were peddled on Capitol Hill, to the business community, to the FBI, and to the White House. Spencer Schedler, with good White House connections through his former boss, Spiro T. Agnew, was delegated the task of convincing the President's staff that my firing should stick because I was guilty of conflict of interests and security violations. Once again the hapless but apparently invulnerable Schedler had bad luck. He told his vicious fairy tales to Clark Mollenhoff, a Pulitzer Prize winning investigative journalist then serving as a special advisor to President Nixon. Unfortunately for the devious Schedler, Clark Mollenhoff had years of experience with the Pentagon bosses' tactic of using vague and unsubstantiated charges circulated in the dark to destroy critics. When Mr. Mollenhoff challenged Schedler to put his allegations against me in writing as a basis for action by the President, Schedler backed down.[†]

Clark Mollenhoff was disgusted with the Pentagon's handling of my case, and on December 5 he wrote President Nixon that "the Fitzgerald case is untenable." In the same memorandum he accurately described the testimony of Seamans and Schedler before Senator Proxmire's subcommittee as "ludicrous." Mr. Mol-

[*] San Francisco *Chronicle*, December 26, 1969.
[†] Des Moines *Sunday Register*, October 10, 1971.

lenhoff recommended to the President that I be kept on in the government and was under the impression that President Nixon agreed with his assessment. Clark Mollenhoff expected the President to announce my reinstatement in a televised news conference on the evening of December 8.* However, Mr. Nixon was noncommittal on the subject during his news conference. During the question-and-answer period Sarah McClendon, an especially tenacious reporter, recited the injustice of my treatment and asked:

"Can you do something about this, please, sir?"

While the other correspondents laughed nervously, the President grinned and then replied, "Miss McClendon, I better, after the way you put this question."

Two days later, on December 10, the Chicago *Tribune's* veteran reporter, Willard Edwards, who had excellent connections at the Nixon White House, wrote a story about my situation which the Tribune headlined "Nixon Acts to Reinstate Cost Expert."

Mr. Edwards reported that the White House decision to reinstate me was based on the judgment "that the Nixon Administration should avoid even the appearance of retaliation against an employee whose sole offense was truthful testimony when called upon by a congressional committee to give it." Mr. Edwards went on to state that the White House had taken note of my "unblemished record" and added: "The clinching point was that Fitzgerald's testimony was embarrassing only to the Johnson Administration and the Nixon regime would be implicated only if its actions appeared to be part of a coverup."

As the 1969 Christmas season came and went, rumors persisted that I would be given a job somewhere in the government, if not kept on in the Pentagon. However, as my departure date approached, the rumors dried up and I reconciled myself to the certain prospect that my long fight inside the Pentagon was finally over.

On January 2, 1970, Clark Mollenhoff made a final appeal to have me reinstated. He wrote to John Ehrlichman, one of Mr. Nixon's top advisers, warning him that my firing could have

* Interview with Clark Mollenhoff.

serious political repercussions if the opponents chose to use it against Mr. Nixon. "It is obvious," Mollenhoff wrote, "that Prox-mire does not intend to drop this case."

The final appeal had no effect, however, and on January 5 I packed my briefcase and had my picture taken by well-wishing newsmen—first in front of the framed copy of the government servant's Code of Ethics on my wall in my Pentagon office and then in front of my blackboard, where someone had written "Time wounds all heels." I then took the long walk down the art-hung hallway leading to the Pentagon's Mall entrance. In many ways, I came out the same door wherein I went, four and a half years older, somewhat poorer, and infinitely wiser. I got in the old Rambler which had so offended the sensibilities of General Cappucci's unidentified accusers, and drove away.

SEVEN

THE GREAT PLANE ROBBERY

As a result of my troubles with the Pentagon, I became an outlaw. The Department of Defense is far and away the world's largest customer. Every large manufacturing company, every big bank—in fact, every major commercial institution in the country—has an interest in staying on the good side of the Department of Defense. Therefore, all such organizations assiduously avoid associations with people marked as unacceptable by the Pentagon. My status as a Pentagon outcast automatically made me an outcast in the big business community as well. Before going to work for the Air Force, I usually had more consulting business than I could handle. Now I was completely cut off from similar work.

Soon I began to hear from other outcasts from the military spending coalition. For the most part, they were specialists who had been intensively but narrowly trained to function as a part of large, complex organizations. When they were excluded from employment in large organizations, their specialized skills were not salable, and most of these unfortunates were reduced to working at jobs well below their capacities or to living on welfare or the charity of friends and family. One military contracting officer, cast out after a long and successful career for refusing to approve some particularly outrageous contract changes was reduced to a life as an itinerant dishwasher.

Another case was that of two officials of a government employees' union local. These two men became concerned about acceptance by the military of faulty helicopter parts. At the time, accidents were causing more casualties among helicopter crews in Southeast Asia than enemy action, and some helicopter specialists blamed faulty parts for a significant portion of the deadly mishaps. Working-level civil servants who tried to correct the situation were overruled by their supervisors and, in frustration, brought the problem to their union local. The local passed a resolution calling for corrective action and sent the resolution to Congressmen and other highly placed officials. At once the two union officials who had led the protest found themselves in trouble with the military, and both eventually were removed from their government jobs. Before being fired, however, one of the union officials was found beaten nearly to death on a government reservation. The victim claimed he recognized his assailants and tried to press charges, but the courts ruled that the alleged assailants, government security officers, were protected from prosecution when the government invoked the doctrine of absolute immunity for its agents. The case was dismissed.

Neither of the union officials was able to get responsible employment thereafter, and both impoverished themselves in expensive, futile efforts to get justice through the courts.

Another man, a physicist and mathematician in his fifties who had worked most of his adult life as a weapons analyst, was ruined because he refused to alter a devastatingly accurate study he made of a useless and expensive new weapons systems proposed by the military. This man also chose to fight the injustice done to him through both legal and political means, and was soon reduced to abject poverty. When he was unable to pay the taxes on his home, his property was sold at public outcry. After payment of past-due taxes and deduction of the costs of seizing and disposing of his home, this poor man received fifty-seven cents for property in which he had thousands of dollars of equity. While petitioning his government for redress, he subsisted on one meager meal a day. Unable to afford any sort of transportation, he walked many miles every day between his room and the various congressional offices and the government agencies who should have been interested in helping him but who in fact acted in concert to destroy him.

I was much luckier. In addition to the fact that I had been fortunate enough to acquire a little money and other property before going to work in the Pentagon, I was rich in family and friends. Although I was effectively excluded from my former profession, I was able to get work. Shortly after I was fired, I contracted with a businessmen's group to tour the country in an effort to alert the public to the Pentagon's continuing raids on the national treasury. In addition, I was retained as a part-time consultant to the Joint Economic Committee of the Congress. Both Senator Proxmire, who was Chairman of the Committee in 1967 and 1968, and Congressman Wright Patman of Texas, who was Chairman in 1969 and 1970, were greatly concerned about the impact of the enormous military waste on our economy, on true military capability, and on public confidence in government. They were also interested in my welfare, which was comforting. In addition to enabling me to earn money, my assignments with the Joint Economic Committee also kept me in touch with the military systems procurements.

Immediately after my departure from the Pentagon in January of 1970, I began hearing from old friends in the Air Force that the C-5A program was going from bad to much worse. I learned that such people, my old secret sympathizers, were called "secret patriots" by the Joint Economic Committee staff. The secret patriots reported that Lockheed was threatening to go bankrupt and default on their military contracts, including the C-5A, if they were not granted relief from the terms of their contracts. When spiraling increases in C-5A cost estimates forced a cutback in the number of airplanes to be bought, the value to Lockheed of the "Golden Handshake" repricing formula in the C-5A contract was greatly reduced. Under the original plan, Lockheed would have reduced their losses by almost $1.70 for each additional dollar of overruns on the first order of fifty-eight airplanes. However, since the formula yielded a *percentage* price adjustment, the reduced number of airplanes in the second order reduced the dollar amount of the get-well adjustment. Reduction of the planned second order from fifty-seven to twenty-one airplanes diminished the offset to overruns from $1.70 to $.73 for each additional dollar of overrun. In other words, Lockheed would, in theory, recover only seventy-three cents for each dollar of additional overrun, losing twenty-seven cents per overrun dollar. I say "in theory" because there was little doubt that Lockheed had been deliberately inflating the costs of the first run of C-5As and probably could have reduced costs sharply once the contract prices were jacked up by the repricing formula. I and some of my secret patriot friends estimated that Lockheed could just about break even on the eighty-one-plane order with the repricing formula *if they could meet the contract specifications.*

This last mentioned qualification was the hooker. In spite of the drumfire of Pentagon propaganda proclaiming the virtues of the C-5A, it was increasingly obvious that Lockheed had no chance of meeting its contractual specifications. The facts would be exposed sooner or later, and if the Pentagon should be moved by public opinion or congressional pressure to enforce the terms of the contract even partially, Lockheed would be in deep trouble. Correcting the C-5A's technical troubles would cost many hundreds of millions of dollars, and if the Pentagon enforced the contract, Lockheed would have to pay for the work out of their own funds.

The fact that the C-5A's technical troubles could not be concealed much longer was evident from both trade gossip and a smattering of solid evidence which was beginning to surface. On December 15, 1969, Congressman William Moorhead revealed that the first C-5A, due for delivery to the Air Force for crew training on December 17, was sadly deficient. In addition to the structural weaknesses which had plagued the plane from its early designs, the C-5A had major problems with its landing gear, flight control systems, radar, and numerous other components and systems. Severe restrictions had to be placed on operating the big plane. Its speed was reduced, and the allowable load it could carry was cut from 110 tons to fifty tons. Because of its flimsy structure and other problems, it could not be operated from unimproved fields at all. The prohibition against operating the C-5A from rough fields meant that its highly advertised tactical mission of ferrying troops and heavy equipment to the FEBA (Forward Edge of the Battle Area) would have to be abandoned.

Congressman Moorhead called for suspension of C-5A production until the plane's problems could be worked out. Both he and Senator Proxmire demanded that the Air Force stop taking delivery on airplanes known to be defective. The suggestions of Congressman Moorhead and Senator Proxmire were brushed off by the Pentagon, of course. Outwardly, the joint reaction of Lockheed and the Air Force was to tell bigger lies more loudly in proclaiming the C-5A's technical excellence. Inside the club, things were different. Lockheed's agitation for a bailout increased markedly.

Lockheed's clamor for contractual relief drew a sympathetic response from the giveaway faction in the Air Force. With the already feeble, traditional restraints on contract cost increases practically junked, on the theory that the new magic contracts would solve all problems, plans were being made to remove the remaining contractual restraints on Lockheed's money consumption.

Even so, Lockheed was nervous. There was low-level but insistent opposition inside the Pentagon to the bailout, and Lockheed had everything at stake. Their potential losses on the C-5A were several times the net worth of the corporation. In addition, Lockheed faced the prospect of disastrous losses on the SRAM missile, for which they had contracted to provide rocket motors; on the Cheyenne helicopter, one of the all-time weapons system fiascos; and on contracts held by their shipyard, which had an unbroken record of huge cost overruns and performance failures. So on January 19, 1970, Lockheed management filed an appeal with the Armed Services Board of Contract Appeals (ASBCA) contending that the government had breached the C-5A contract by exercising production options for only the first twenty-one airplanes of the second run of C-5As.

Alerted by the secret patriots to the Air Force's plan to surrender in negotiations with Lockheed, Senator Proxmire wrote to Assistant Secretary Philip Whittaker on February 26, 1970, urging the Air Force not to give in to Lockheed's threats. In a reply to Senator Proxmire dated March 4, Whittaker denied any knowledge of the situation described by the secret patriots. Notwithstanding Whittaker's profession of ignorance, our information on the situation had already been confirmed. On March 2, 1970, Lockheed Board Chairman Dan Haughton wrote an unprecedented letter to David Packard, the Deputy Secretary of Defense. Mr. Haughton demanded an additional $500,000,000 for the C-5A, an "immediate increase" of $71,000,000 in advance payments for disputed shipbuilding costs, and another $25,000,000 of immediate money for SRAM overruns. Haughton also requested an increase in progress payments for the Cheyenne helicopter.

In many ways the Cheyenne situation was the strangest of all. On May 19, 1969, the Army had canceled the Cheyenne production contract for default after a series of catastrophic test failures, including one in which one of the machines disintegrated in flight, killing the test pilot. The Army had gotten a great deal of favorable publicity for their seemingly tough action in "calling the sheriff" to Lockheed for their Cheyenne failures, and much of the taxpaying public thought they had been relieved of the financial burden of the misbegotten Cheyenne. At the time of the 1969 default termination, the estimated cost of Cheyennes had grown from the high starting figure of $900,000 each to somewhere between three and four million dollars each for a greatly degraded product. With this background, many people who had not followed the project closely were surprised that the Pentagon was still pouring money into the project. The Army, after taking bows for toughness in enforcing the Cheyenne contract, had quietly agreed to bail out Lockheed by buying their inventories, production tooling, and substandard hardware, and by continuing the expensive development contract.

Packard reacted immediately and favorably to Haughton's letter by speeding up preparations to bail Lockheed out of its difficulties. On March 9, 1970, Packard testified before the House Armed Services Committee, and the next day, March 10, before the Senate Armed Services Committee. Mr. Packard's statements were effective in frightening the jumpy committees and dismissing such objectionable alternatives as the enforcement of contracts. Packard's testimony dealt almost exclusively with *how* to bail out Lockheed rather than *whether* to bail them out. It was assumed, without saying so, that enforcing Lockheed's contracts with the government would lead to reorganization of the company, merging with a healthier and better managed firm, or bankruptcy proceedings. Packard rejected all such alternatives without substantive reasons.*

Dan Haughton's letter to David Packard and Packard's congressional testimony verified most of what we had been told by the secret patriots: Lockheed was threatening to die if they did not get their way, and the powers in the Pentagon were planning to give up after a little play-acting in the upcoming "fight" with their big partner.

Lockheed's game and the Pentagon's complicity were clear enough, but the timing was curious. It was possible that Senator Proxmire's knowledgeable and well focused probing had tipped off the conspirators that the Senator and his staff knew what was going on, and that there was, therefore, no further point in concealing the facts. On the other hand, the Pentagon had ignored the Wisconsin Senator's pointed questioning before and could probably have brazened it out as they had done on other occasions.

Lockheed's threats of default and backruptcy were premature if their only problems were military contracts. It is true that Lockheed faced monumental future losses if the Pentagon failed to come through with contract nourishment or some other form of bailout. At the same time, there was little possibility that the Pentagon would actually hold Lockheed to its commitments. Big bailouts took time, and usually the game was to stall, delay, and lie as necessary to conceal the real situation until the bailout could be consummated. Indeed, these had been the tactics on the C-5A for three and a half years, and they had been successful despite periodic flaps in the news media following congressional inquiries and other disclosures. Even though the supposedly rigid ceiling on the C-5A price posed a theoretical problem for Lockheed, this limitation on payments was not a practical problem in early 1970. Lockheed had been reimbursed for essentially all of their overruns all along, so the C-5A, the biggest of their fiascos, could not be causing their immediate *cash* problems at that time. I and others had challenged the legality and propriety of the cost-plus

---

* Hearings on Military Posture, Committee on Armed Services, House of Representatives, March and April, 1970, pp. 7032–7033.

reimbursement of Lockheed's overruns on their fixed-price incentive contract, but these concerns had been brushed aside, and Lockheed was then being paid for their overruns more or less as they were incurred, à la Max Ajax.

It was true that Lockheed was being reimbursed "only" 90 percent of their costs as they were incurred, with the rest of the cost plus any profits being held back until specified segments of work were completed. However, due to the combination of early recording of "incurred" costs, rapid (daily) payment of these costs by the Air Force, and slower actual outlays of cash by Lockheed, most analysts estimated that Lockheed's requirement for operating capital on the C-5A was approximately zero. Secretary Packard confirmed this appraisal in his testimony before the House Armed Services Committee, stating:

Air Force progress payments can be continued through the current fiscal year with funds presently available at a rate which we believe will meet Lockheed's expenditures.*

Our secret patriots told us the Air Force was prepared to fund Lockheed's expenditures through most of the *following* fiscal year under the existing contract, provided Congress ponied up the money as usual. Lockheed's other military customers were no less solicitous.

What had panicked Lockheed into threatening backruptcy just then? Lockheed's performance on contracts was dismal, but they were generally considered to be the best cash managers in the aerospace business. Getting money from the government was a focus of Lockheed's managers, and they were good at it. (An illustration of their finesse in this field was their boasting before a meeting of the Defense Industry Advisory Committee—DIAC was the board of directors of the Military-Industrial Complex— concerned with contract financing. According to Arnold Bueter, Deputy Comptroller of the Air Force, Lockheed's chief financial officer, Dudley Brown, was very proud of his record. Reporting on a July 19, 1967, DIAC meeting, Mr. Bueter wrote to Ted Marks: "Mr. Dudley Brown of Lockheed later mentioned that Lockheed had earned $900,000 last year by investing its excess

* *Ibid.,* p. 7030.

cash in short-term Treasury notes for periods that averaged only three or four days.")

The notion that these superb manipulators could be in *cash* trouble on military contracts seemed inconceivable to me. Yet Packard had testified, "I have asked the company for additional data which will support, by specific periods and programs, *their short-term cash needs.*" (Emphasis mine.)

After considerable study of the scanty facts available to us, the Joint Economic staff and I concluded that Lockheed's immediate cash problems could not be due to their military contract troubles, and unless the Pentagon made a complete turnabout and became strict constructionists on contract enforcement, Lockheed faced no serious future threat from that quarter. By elimination, Lockheed's cash problem, which appeared real enough, had to have its origins in nonmilitary projects. Lockheed's only major civilian project at the time was the L-1011 trijet airbus. Therefore, the unidentified sinkhole for cash at Lockheed had to be the L-1011.

From my viewpoint, all this was in the nature of suspicions confirmed. Since my first visits to Lockheed's C-5A operations in early 1966, I had suspected that Lockheed was deliberately overrunning the C-5A project, partly in order to help finance their upcoming commercial projects through shared indirect expenses. Just as Max Ajax could have used his vastly increased government contract overhead allowances to expand and improve his coat-hanger business instead of hiring his girlfriend, so could Lockheed (or any other big contractor in a similar situation) use its increased overhead allowances to finance at least part of a new commercial venture.

I should point out that playing the allocation game in order to have the government pay for "company funded" private ventures is not only widespread but also legitimate under the Pentagon's convoluted procurement and contract financing rules. More direct methods of financing commercial work through government contract payments, such as mischarging (politely called "migration") of direct labor costs and diversion of materials were not legitimate but were also widespread, though seldom reported by the audit agencies.

As soon as he was told about the probable major cause of Lockheed's near-term cash bind, Senator Proxmire began trying to get the facts of the situation from both the Department of Defense and the General Accounting Office. All during the spring of 1970, the Senator kept firing off letters requesting cash flow analyses and projections on the Lockheed situation. The cash flow should have shown the timing of outlays and receipts of money for each major program. At any point in time, the difference between the cumulative amount of money paid out and the cumulative receipts for a program would show the cash financing required for that program. This is probably the most rudimentary of financial analyses, and one that every small-town banker requires before financing a business venture. We were certain that such an analysis of Lockheed's cash requirements would show that they were being well taken care of on their military programs (possibly illegally) but were being bled white by their big commercial project, the L-1011.

When Senator Proxmire first requested the cash flow figures for Lockheed, experienced government accountants in both the Pentagon and the General Accounting Office took refuge in a form of the idiot treatment, the bureaucrats' first line of defense. In meetings with the Joint Economic Committee staff, these protectors of the taxpayer's purse would profess not to know what cash flow analyses and projections were. After it was explained to them, they said they did not have such information but would try to get it for us. After a long period of stalling, during which the GAO once again refused duty in obtaining the information, the Pentagon finally admitted that they had some cash flow analyses for Lockheed but that the United States Senate could not see them. Why? Lockheed wouldn't allow it. As usual, Lockheed's attitude was, "Send money. Never mind what for."

By then it was clear that the Pentagon and Lockheed, aided by the inertness of the GAO, were cooperating to keep the Congress and the taxpayers in ignorance in order to obtain unearned money for Lockheed. Moreover, the treasury raid had nothing to do with "defense." The evidence was strong that the Pentagon was feigning ignorance on several counts in order to mislead the public. For example, the Pentagon's supposed initial inability to provide cash flow data ignored the fact that the Air Force not only maintained a large bureaucracy to keep track of such matters, but it also had a computerized "progress payment model" which routinely produced contractor cash requirements for big Air Force contracts. The computer model had been in use since 1967. Further, the DoD's Systems Analysis Section had performed a major study of Lockheed's problems which pinpointed the L-1011 as a developing disaster. The Systems Analysis study showed that Lockheed was experiencing huge cost overruns on the L-1011. As a result, the systems analysts estimated that Lockheed would have to sell almost 400 L-1011s in an oversold airplane market in order to recover their start-up costs. At the time, Lockheed had firm orders for only about 100 airbuses.

Lockheed faced the possibility of shocking future losses on the L-1011, but the near-term problem was the main worry. Who would finance the L-1011 overruns? Lockheed's commercial customers didn't have the money, and their bankers were not inclined to take further chances, so who else was left? The Pentagon, of course. How? By converting Lockheed's big military contracts to allow 100 percent reimbursement of "cost incurred." Lockheed was to become a gigantic, complicated, real-world version of the Ajax case. Significantly, this solution was proposed by the Air Force, not by Lockheed.

Senator Proxmire's persistent demands for the facts on the Lockheed cash crisis were just as persistently rebuffed or ignored by the Pentagon and the GAO. However, the Pentagon hierarchy became nervous when Proxmire began talking about a really serious attempt to hold up the annual C-5A appropriation unless he got the brazenly concealed facts. In theory, the appropriation appeared vulnerable. To begin with, the magnitude of the technical disaster was so great that the C-5A was kept out of the public press only by a strange, unreal reluctance of most probers in the Congress and the news media to demand unclassified facts on the situation. It appeared that there was nearly universal tacit agreement that the general interest would not be served by airing the calamity.

In addition, the fiscal year 1971 authorizations and appropriations requests for the C-5A did not add any airplanes, any "capability," to what had already been approved by Congress. The total FY 1971 request was for $544,000,000, which included $344,000,000 to cover "unfunded prior year commitments" (overruns) and $200,000,000 for "contingency funding" (more overruns). The basic reason for the distinction between the two parts of the request was that even the ever-generous Pentagon could not say that Lockheed had any legitimate claim to the $200,000,000 contingency fund. It was pure slush, and was clearly the down payment on the Lockheed bailout which would ultimately shake down the taxpayers for billions of dollars with no return.

Thus, the Congress was confronted with the indisputable fact that the huge C-5A money request in the spring of 1970 bought only overruns; no additional airplanes at all, just overruns. The absurdity of recurring annual appropriations of hundreds of millions of dollars to purchase pure overruns, unsullied by hardware, threatened to register on the congressional consciousness.

Against this background, the Pentagon attempted to answer Senator Proxmire's request for specific hard facts on the source of the Lockheed cash bind with an informal briefing. On May 18, 1970, Assistant Secretaries of Defense Robert Moot, the Comptroller, and Barry Shillito, the procurement chief, briefed Senator Proxmire on the situation. The Senator invited two of his staff and me to sit in. Moot and Shillito were very friendly, even gracious. "Yes," they conceded, "You've been right all along. The real problem is the L-1011."

Moot and Shillito went on to explain that Lockheed and its subcontractors figured to lose about $700,000,000 on the L-1011 as things then stood. They stated that such an industry disaster could not be allowed to happen. The Pentagon wanted to do their share by making sure that military contract financing problems did not contribute to Lockheed's downfall. Therefore, the Assistant Secretaries said, the entire $544,000,000, including the $200,000,000 slush fund earmarked for the C-5A in the coming year, was desperately needed. They urged Senator Proxmire to reconsider his opposition and to help get approval for Lockheed's slush money as soon as possible.

Senator Proxmire asked if Moot and Shillito were suggesting

that the C-5A appropriations might be diverted to help finance Lockheed's commercial program. "Oh no," Moot replied. "We're going to make sure that doesn't happen." However, Moot, the Pentagon's top financial expert, could not explain *how* he was going to prevent misuse of the military funds, particularly how he planned to prohibit excessive overhead absorption or diversion of the "float" of extra progress payments. Neither could Moot explain how bailing Lockheed out of their military contract difficulties would keep Lockheed afloat if the bailout funds could not be used on the L-1011. The Assistant Secretaries' arguments became weirdly illogical, and they retired in gentlemanly confusion.

The strange Moot-Shillito confession seemed to have no effect on the military spending coalition, who immediately organized to muscle the annual C-5A outrage through Congress. The Pentagon speech-writing mill ground out reams of material for the Defense Department's congressional friends, and special interest groups benefiting from the handouts were mobilized to oppose the rather mild and innocuous amendment to the C-5A authorization offered by Senators Proxmire and Schweiker of Pennsylvania. The Proxmire-Schweiker amendment required that the GAO establish that the extra $200,000,000 of unowed money was really needed *for the* C-5A before the slush fund money could be spent. This was an even milder request for facts than Senator Proxmire's ill-fated request of 1969, and given the C-5A's limitless appetite for money along with the GAO's obeisance to the C-5A supporters, the amendment appeared to offer no threat whatever to continued unfettered spending on the program.

However, advocates of infinite contributions to Lockheed reacted as though the pallid little amendment would have wrecked the national economy and esconced the Bolsheviks in the Pentagon in one fell swoop. The usual lobbying gaggles of contractors and military men were joined by community leaders, businessmen, labor union leaders, and big bankers who came out of the woodwork in Lockheed's behalf. The business press was particularly shrill.

The epitome of hysteria was probably an article in *Barron's*, a journal grandly advertising itself as the "National Business and

Financial Weekly." The piece was a frantic attack on the Prox-mire-Schweiker amendment or, more precisely, an attack on the Senators themselves. After erroneously stating that the Senators' amendment would bar use of the $200,000,000 slush fund "unless Lockheed goes broke," *Barron's* wrote that passage of the Prox-mire-Schweiker amendment "would make the Senators heroes in the eyes of all who seek to dismantle U.S. defenses and achieve 'peace in our time' through unilateral disarmament." *Barron's* repeatedly misrepresented the terms of the proposed amendment in a transparent attempt to generate panic, warning of the certain bankruptcy that would somehow ensue should the intended use of the $200,000,000 slush fund be identified. Their nameless writer intoned, "Such a disaster would ripple far and wide."

The factual errors in the *Barron's* piece typified the cavalier attitude toward facts common to the most vocal Lockheed special pleaders. *Barron's* presented a worshipful but error-filled introduction, citing such Lockheed contributions as the "U-4" [i.e., the U-2] spy plane, the F-104, "Since 1952 . . . the main-stay of NATO's air defenses." (The NATO F-104 was fielded in the early '60s and immediately began setting records for crash-ing, killing more than 100 allied pilots.) They went on to attempt to minimize Lockheed's C-5A overruns by overstating Lockheed's initial bid by $1,400,000,000 and to falsely state that Lockheed's C-5A problems were partly due to "DoD insistence on higher per-formance characteristics than called for in the original specifica-tions." The specifications were in fact degraded, and even the degraded specifications were not being met, despite *Barron's* claims to the contrary.

The "National Business and Financial Weekly" went on to de-clare that the big C-5A "carries its phenomenal cargoes at a cost of 2.5 cents per mile." Using then-current acquisition cost estimates and Air Force operating cost estimates, C-5A cargo-carrying costs would have been about 17.8 cents per *ton-mile,* assuming a full load of 100 tons of cargo. Thus the 17.8 cents per ton-mile figure (later, experienced costs were much higher) was roughly 700 times the *Barron's* fantasy.

Barron's also pushed the Moot-Shillito line that without the C-5A slush fund, "the whole L-1011 program might crack up.

With it might go creditors and customers alike." (*Barron's* compounded their inaccuracies and ineptness by arranging for their Lockheed piece to appear in the August 17, 1970, issue, a date nearly three weeks after the Senate vote on the Proxmire-Schweiker amendment.)

Other purveyors of the same line were more timely though, and worked more effectively to help Lockheed and the Pentagon avoid exposing the facts on their monumental mess. The senators representing Lockheed were especially tenacious in appealing to the greed and fears of beneficiaries of future handouts to Lockheed. After a few ritual tips of their oratorical hats to "national security," the Lockheed senators got right down to pork-barreling. Senator Herman Talmadge of Georgia declaimed in a Senate floor speech, "I make no apology for not wanting to throw 40,000 people out of work in one fell swoop." *

Not to be outdone in supporting pork-barrel jobs, California Senator Alan Cranston, another Lockheed supporter, upped the estimate of unemployed which would be created by obtaining Lockheed cash flow analyses:

And, of course, it would be a disastrous result for the 87,000 workers who hope to continue their employment with Lockheed and with the benefits of seniority, retirement plans, and so forth.†

Cranston, ignoring the fact that Senators Proxmire and Schweiker were trying to get information which would clear up confusion and uncertainty about the Lockheed fiasco, went on:

The C5A involves enormously important national interests. Too much uncertainty already surrounds the fate of both the C5A and the Lockheed Corporation. At a time like this, when the Nation is in an economic recession with high unemployment, the Government dare not risk deliberately sinking a giant corporation which could take thousands of jobs down with it."

Verbal attacks by Senators Talmadge and Cranston on the strawman they had substituted for the central issue (disclosure of facts) did little to enlighten their colleagues on the Proxmire-Schweiker amendment, but the debate was instructive neverthe-

* *Congressional Record,* July 26, 1970, p. S14268.
† *Ibid.,* p. 14275.

less. The public façade of the Great Military Boondoggle was crumbling. As the false front of "military security" fell away, the economic justification, the Boondoggle's main prop, was plain for all to see.

Some of the Senate debate was just plain ludicrous. A prime example was the speech of Senator Milton Young of North Dakota, a reliable supporter of Pentagon spending proposals. Senator Young apparently had been assigned the unenviable chore of upholding the C-5A's technical excellence. The big plane's technical failures had featured a number of structural failures of the wing in ground tests. Senator Young defended these disasters as follows:

> There has been one criticism of the wing. As I said earlier, I think Lockheed should be congratulated for having come up with this kind of trouble. The wing is really too strong, but it is too strong at a point just upward of the aileron. That is giving it some trouble in maintaining the flexibility needed in that type of wing. But that can be easily corrected. In fact, the Secretary of the Air Force has received the results of an analysis made by a study group appointed for purpose [sic], and I quote just one part of it:
>> The flight performance of the C5A meets the guarantees of the contract within the accuracy limitations of good flight test measurement.*

Senator Young's quotation certifying the C-5A's excellence was from a report prepared by Raymond L. Bisplinghoff, formerly Dean of Engineering at Massachusetts Institute of Technology. Dr. Bisplinghoff was reputed to be one of the world's best aeronautical engineers and was an old friend and associate of Air Force Secretary Robert Seamans. Just how Dr. Bisplinghoff was induced to endorse the C-5A technical fiasco remains a mystery.

On the basis of such arguments, the Proxmire-Schweiker amendment was defeated by a score of 48–30.

Having thus disposed of the last obstacle to unlimited C-5A spending, the Air Force lost no time in going ahead with its plans for making Lockheed well again. Middle-level Air Force officers concerned about the deliberate waste of appropriations furnished Senator Proxmire a copy of the Air Force's official plan to abandon all contractual protection against further C-5A cost increases.

* *Congressional Record,* August 26, 1970, p. S14267.

The plan was outlined in a set of twenty-five "Official Use Only" briefing charts (VuGraphs) dated August 31, 1970. In summary, the plan contained these provisions:

1. Lockheed would agree to accept a "fixed loss" (an indefinite amount, but a fraction of their loss otherwise), which would be lent back to them with repayment to begin in 1974 *if* the Pentagon should choose to ask for repayment, and *if* the Pentagon wouldn't choose simply to give Lockheed more money.
2. The Pentagon would remove contractual ceilings on Lockheed's expenditures, converting the contract from fixed-price incentive to cost-reimbursement.
3. Lockheed would be absolved of guaranteeing the performance of the airplanes and of managing the program.
4. Penalties for substandard performance and late delivery would be removed.
5. Lockheed and the Pentagon would agree to circumvent the normal legal procedures designed to protect the taxpayers.
6. The Air Force would get whatever Lockheed chose to produce in the way of C-5As.

Senator Proxmire expressed his shock, outrage, and disappointment in the Air Force's total abandonment of stewardship and their caving in to Lockheed's private interest. He inserted the entire disgraceful plan in the *Congressional Record* * as a sort of epitaph to the Miracle of Procurement in particular and to the contract approach to procuring big weapons systems in general. The total abandonment of the contractual safeguards on the C-5A needed only David Packard's approval, and that was certain to come.

From that point onward, several basic facts became increasingly clear as the Lockheed disaster slowly unfolded to public view:

1. The C-5A was an unmitigated and almost unprecedented disaster.
2. The L-1011 program was also in deep trouble.
3. Lockheed's military and civilian businesses were viewed as an

* *Congressional Record,* September 18, 1970, S15754.

entity by Lockheed representatives on the government payroll.
4. The Nixon Administration was willing to sacrifice anything—sound procurement precedent, honor, safety, honesty, and the taxpayers' money—to keep Lockheed fat and happy.

In short, the stage was set for the Great Plane Robbery.

Curiously, as pieces of the drama surfaced bit by bit, the foreign press covered some aspects of it better than our own. While most of our business writers were parroting Administration happy talk, readers of foreign papers frequently got the news straight. The London *Times,* perhaps because of British interest in Rolls-Royce's contract to furnish engines, followed the situation particularly well. On September 18 and 19, 1970, the *Times* ran stories, including interviews with Lockheed Chairman Dan Haughton, reporting that "development and scheduling problem exist for the Lockheed TriStar airbus propulsion system supplied by Rolls-Royce," and that the L-1011 project was in difficulty commercially "because of disappointing sales."

Incidentally, the London *Times* had also been quick to report the C-5A's technical troubles. On June 29, 1969, in an exceptionally perceptive article which linked Lockheed's C-5A and airbus troubles, the *Times* stated: "The full story of the difficulties of the C-5A has yet to be revealed and fresh disclosures on the downgrading of performance specifications are likely soon."

At that time, most U.S. papers were still reprinting the Pentagon's glowing accounts of the C-5A technical excellence. Typically, Lockheed had reacted with a vicious, slanderous attack on the *Times* reporter, Miss Victoria Brittain. In a letter to Miss Brittain's superiors, Lockheed, after reasserting the party line that C-5A performance was "at a level from over 100 percent to 108 percent of design guarantees," called Miss Brittain "an incompetent reporter" who had written an "unfair, one-sided and erroneous report," full of "boobish" oversimplifications, and characterizing her style as a "silly schoolgirl attempt at smart writing." *
Apparently, ad hominem attacks on critics of Lockheed were international in scope.

I was reminded of Miss Brittain's earlier troubles because my

* Letter to the London *Times* from Lockheed's New York office.

own difficulties with the campaign against me were intensified in September 1970. The businessmen's group I was working with was infiltrated by a man with close relationships with the same New York office which had slandered Victoria Brittain. This individual attacked my congressional testimony and other criticisms of the C-5A so steadily that I found myself spending much of my time defending my stand on these issues to other members of my client organization. My would-be censor, a man well connected in the New York financial community, seemed to have an endless supply of reprints of the idiotic *Barron's* article of August 17, 1970, and would hand them out and elaborate on their contents to anyone who would listen. The party line enunciated by *Barron's* was amazingly durable and, like a true article of religious dogma, seemed proof against facts.

Things got tougher, though, for defenders of the Lockheed faith. The first C-5A Lockheed had produced exploded on the ground at the Marietta, Georgia, plant on October 17, 1970. After this tragedy, in which one man was killed and another badly injured, presures on the GAO to tell the truth about the C-5A increased. The offices of Congressman Moorhead, Senator Proxmire, and the Joint Economic Committee pressed the reluctant auditors steadily for facts and explanations. Congressional staff gossip indicated that even the ever-protective Chairman of the Senate Armed Services Committee, John Stennis of Mississippi, was growing restive. Indeed, Senator Stennis had shown incipient impatience with his unruly ward, Lockheed, during the slush fund debate. When Senator Proxmire described the scenario for using C-5A slush fund money to benefit the L-1011 and suggested that the money would probably be diverted, Senator Stennis replied darkly, "It better not be."

Senator Stennis later wrote provisions into the $200,000,000 slush fund authorization bill (Public Law 91-441, Section 504) which prohibited use of the slush fund for certain categories of Lockheed's general and administrative expenses and for Lockheed intercompany profits (the various Lockheed companies made extra profits by subcontracting government work among themselves). The bill also required the GAO to make audits of slush fund spending and report to Congress on it each quarter.

Since Senator Stennis' restrictions did not close all the loop-holes, and the intent to bail out Lockheed was undiminished, the financial effect was to increase the total amount of money required to make Lockheed well. Nevertheless, the Stennis requirement had a mildly stimulating effect on the GAO, which stirred itself to provide a few facts.

Richard Kaufman of the Joint Economic Committee staff and Peter Stockton of Congressman Moorhead's staff made determined efforts to keep up with the Pentagon's exertions in Lockheed's behalf. I did what I could to help, but it wasn't much. Even though our efforts had no practical effect on the eventual outcome, the inquiry was educational. However, I must confess I was more content before I was enlightened.

The statutory authority cited by the GAO and the Pentagon for giving money to Lockheed was Public Law 85-804, popularly called the bail-out law, passed by Congress in 1958. It authorized the Executive to set aside contract limitations and to give payment to contractors without consideration in connection with the national defense. We wondered about its applicability to the case at hand. For one thing, the law's legislative history made clear the intention to invoke the authority only during national emergencies declared by Congress or the President. Testimony before the House Judiciary Committee on June 19 and 20, 1958, was explicit on this point. For example, Robert Dechert, then General Counsel of the Department of Defense, said: "I call attention to the fact that this is not a permanent extension [of the previously existing bill]. This is a bill which is merely effective during periods of national emergency.

We asked the GAO what emergency was in effect in the fall of 1970 which would authorize using the bail-out law for Lockheed's benefit. The GAO didn't know but promised to find out. They did. It was President Truman's Proclamation No. 2914, of December 16, 1950. President Truman's Korean War emergency was still in force. No one had thought to declare that crisis over.

The legislative history of 85-804 also highlighted the intention to use the bail-out procedures to make sure the government got what it needed when it needed it. Under the Pentagon's proposal, the government was not assured of *ever* receiving a satisfactory product.

Finally, the focus of attention of the bill's authors was assistance to relatively small businesses with limited credit and resources. This intent was confirmed by the history of use of the bill's authority. According to Library of Congress researchers, the total amount spent on 85-804 bailouts from 1958 to 1970 was $60,000,000, with the largest single prior amount being $5,500,000. The Lockheed bailout figured to be at least a billion dollars. "Wasn't this a violation of the intent of Congress?" we asked the GAO.

The GAO squirmed and avoided these and many other questions, even ignoring written congressional correspondence. Finally, however, the issue was forced into the open when on December 30, 1970, Secretary Packard announced the Pentagon's proposal to bail out Lockheed. It was the same as the plan outlined in the Air Force's August 31, 1970, documents given to us by the secret patriots. Packard stated that Lockheed had to be bailed out because their "operations are so entwined with many other companies which also contribute to our national defense effort that it was necessary for us to consider the chain reaction upon other companies as well." *

This rationale, a kind of domino theory of defense spending policy, ignored the fact that a Lockheed bankruptcy, even if it should occur, would probably result in little more than the loss of the services of Lockheed's existing management team—a small loss, it seemed to some of us. Why was the existing management so important? For that matter, why was the corporate entity so vital? The divisions of the company could be operated separately if need be. In fact, the government already owned many of Lockheed's facilities, including the C-5A assembly plant. Lockheed was only a tenant. New managers for the facilities would be easy to find.

Finally, after much badgering, the GAO gave us a ruling. On January 25, 1971, Mr. Robert Walters of the GAO General Counsel's office, interpreted the authority granted by PL 85-804 and its implementing Executive Order 10789 as follows:

1. The Department of Defense or any of ten other executive departments may designate *any* company "essential to the

* *The New York Times,* December 31, 1970.

national defense." It is important to note that the *company* receives the designation "essential," not the company's products nor a particular contract.

2. Firms designated "essential" may then be given contracts, modifications to contracts, and funds with or without consideration. This can be done, according to the GAO, without regard to other laws or restrictions except for a few minor ones such as prohibitions against cost-plus-percentage-of-cost contracts. The GAO spokesman evaded direct answers to whether the over-obligation statute applied.

3. Determinations of essentiality and subsequent contracts or grants do not require justification, and are not subject to challenge (Mr. Walters said the GAO could not "look behind" such decisions).

The proposed elevation of Lockheed to privileged, protected status was in stark contrast to the government's treatment of unanointed, smaller contractors. As luck would have it, just at that point in time a small firm in Pittsburgh, headed by a constituent of Congressman Moorhead, was in deep trouble on a government contract because it overran a fixed-price contract by $22,174. The contractor claimed they were not being paid their due for a government-directed change in the scope of their contractual effort. Mr. Moorhead asked the GAO's legal counsel to look into the matter. The GAO's prompt, stern response to the smaller contractor was a model of seemingly even-handed stewardship and endorsement of the sanctity of contracts:

You have assumed the responsibility of furnishing the required services at the agreed upon price and the government is not obligated to pay additional amounts for contract performance solely by reason of difficulties you have experienced in performing the contract. . . . It is a well settled principle of law that contracts are to be enforced and performed as written. . . .

It was too bad that the same law did not apply to the privileged giants. But it didn't, and that unhappy fact was to be demonstrated repeatedly in the course of the Great Plane Robbery.

Already in enormous difficulties with their ill-timed L-1011 airbus, Lockheed and its supporters had a stroke of luck. In early February of 1971, Rolls-Royce, the maker of the RB-211 engine for the Lockheed L-1011, went broke and repudiated its contract with Lockheed. Ironically, the British Government, which had taken over the collapsed aero engine division of Rolls-Royce, made demands on Lockheed almost identical to those presented by Lockheed to the United States Government a year earlier: tear up the contract and raise the prices, or no engines will be delivered. This presented Lockheed and the Nixon administration with an opportunity to blame the pre-existing financial illness of the L-1011 solely on the Rolls-Royce collapse. The new development also raised the possibility of using the L-1011 debacle to help divert attention from the events taking place in the Pentagon.

Congressman Moorhead and Senators Proxmire and Schweiker redoubled their efforts to prod the GAO into exercising their unquestioned legal right to examine the Pentagon's records on Lockheed. The Cleveland *Plain Dealer* summarized the result succinctly:

The Defense Department refused to allow a thorough inspection because of what Deputy Defense Secretary Packard said was the "extremely sensitive" nature of Lockheed's commercial ventures. . . . The GAO accepted this refusal.*

None of the information the Pentagon was concealing was properly subject to military security classification. Mr. Packard had invented a new classification, "Sensitive," for bad news from Lockheed.

At the time, in March 1971, after a long, sorry record of complicity in the Lockheed cover-up, the GAO partially redeemed themselves. They issued a staff study on the C-5A. For the first time, the GAO gave official confirmation of the C-5A technical disaster. Summarizing a seemingly endless list of shortcomings, the report stated:

The Air Force is accepting C-5A aircraft with major deficiencies, in the landing gear, wings, and avionics. The deficiencies have restricted the C-5A to performance of its basic cargo mission only. *The C5A*

* Cleveland *Plain Dealer*, February 21, 1971, p. 25.

cannot perform its tactical mission until certain deficiencies are corrected. [Emphasis mine.] °

Expanding further on the C-5A's inability to operate at the FEBA (Forward Edge of the Battle Area), the report added:

Although the landing gear was designed to permit landings and take-offs from forward area runways (matted or bare soil), the aircraft have been restricted to hard surface runways. Flight tests on unimproved runways caused severe damage to jet engines, matted runways, and the aircraft. The tests were subsequently discontinued.†

The report confirmed the predicted results of the 1966 decisions to "flimsy up" the airplane's structure:

. . . analysis indicate the possibility of a very serious reduction in fatigue resistance which would require modification to delivered aircraft, serious degradations of operational capability, or both.

The GAO study also contrasted the Air Force's shameful actions in knowingly accepting bad airplanes with practices of commercial airlines:

Commercial airlines, on the other hand, do not accept new aircraft having performance restrictions.

The GAO wrote that Lockheed would have been required to correct the C-5A difficulties at no additional cost to the government under the original contract, but that the so-called "restructured" contract would shift this cost to the government.

Meanwhile, advancing behind a continuing barrage of scare propaganda, the Nixon administration moved steadily toward bailing out Lockheed in their commercial as well as their military difficulties. Pentagon financial specialists told Congressman Moorhead and his staff that they had been told to pay Lockheed as much money as possible as fast as possible. In addition to the bureaucracy set up in the Pentagon to pump money to Lockheed, task forces were formed in the staffs of the Federal Reserve Board and in the Treasury Department to work on Lockheed's problems.

° U.S. General Accounting Office Staff Study on the C-5A Weapon System, March 1971, p. 43.
† *Ibid.*, p. 45.

The British Government demanded that the United States Government guarantee that Lockheed would not collapse before the L-1011 Tristar project was completed. The British Government wanted this guarantee as a condition for their own continued support of the Rolls-Royce RB-211 engine project. By early April, the business press was quoting unnamed high administration sources to the effect that President Nixon had decided to guarantee Lockheed's continued existence.*

The impending adoption of Lockheed as a ward of the United States Government became more certain with each passing day. On April 21, the London *Times* confirmed the prospect publicly in reporting on a debate in the British House of Commons:

Mr. Robert Selston asked Mr. Heath, the Prime Minister, to say whether he was prepared to continue with the contract [i.e., with Lockheed] in the absence of guarantees about the future of Lockheed. Mr. Heath replied, "No, we consider it essential to have guarantees about the future of the aircraft in order to implement the future of the engine."

On May 6, Secretary of the Treasury John Connally announced formally that the Nixon Administration would seek congressional approval for $250,000,000 in federal loan guarantees for Lockheed's commercial airplane program. Mr. Connally explained the matter very simply. Lockheed, he said, needed the money "to keep it from going broke." † Connally pictured the proposed bailout as necessary to avoid economic disaster. He failed to mention that other U.S. companies were eager to build and supply engines for the L-1011 or replacement airplanes if the L-1011 should be canceled, and that one of Lockheed's competitors, McDonnell-Douglas, was offering the airlines a nearly identical airplane, the DC-10. The DC-10 was being built in Long Beach, California, just across Los Angeles from Lockheed's L-1011 plant in Burbank, which would have minimized area unemployment problems if the L-1011s were not built.

Predictably, a great flap ensued. Senator Proxmire announced he would go all out in fighting the proposed legislation. Con-

* One of the best of such stories was in *The Wall Street Journal* on April 9, 1971.
† *The New York Times,* May 7, 1971.

gressman Moorhead denounced the plan as a scandalous propping up of Lockheed's miserable management, saying among
other things:

As a result one has to admire Daniel Haughton, Chairman of the
Board of Lockheed, who, by sheer guts and bailing wire, has kept his
group of incompetents afloat by intimidating the Federal Government
with threats of corporate suicide and then walking out with the taxpayers' money. *

Representative Wright Patman, Chairman of the House Banking and Currency Committee, turned loose his excellent committee staff to pull together the facts on the proposal. Although
the Banking and Currency Committee staff's report was never
publicly disseminated, and Mr. Patman himself eventually voted
for a heavily qualified bail-out bill, the information the staff
gathered was of great assistance to opponents of the measure.
Mr. Patman's staff obtained documentary proof that the Pentagon had been working on Lockheed's *commercial* airplane
problems at least since early 1970, that Lockheed and the British
Government signed a formal document on May 10, 1971, which
clearly showed that the British anticipated U.S. Government
guarantee of Lockheed's corporate existence, and much additional evidence of the conspiracies underlying this affair.†

Meanwhile, aided by Secretary Connally's L-1011 diversionary
action, the Pentagon's more expensive portion of the "Great
Plane Robbery" was proceeding apace. In addition to the Pentagon, the Armed Services Committees and the Appropriations
Committees of both houses of Congress were involved. A few
last-minute attempts were made to avert the catastrophe. For
example, on May 25, Mr. Jack H. Vollbrecht, President of
Aerojet-General Corporation, a medium-sized military contractor,
urged the House Administrations Committee to insist on enforcement of the C-5A contract:

I just tell you, gentlemen, you have a good opportunity to make an
example of a contractor who is a bellwether in this industry either way

* News release by the Office of Congressman William Moorhead, May 6,
1971.
† Staff study transmitted to members of House of Representatives Banking
and Currency Committee by Chairman Wright Patman on July 2, 1971.

and the industry will read it exactly the way you treat them. It is common talk among the industry and they are waiting to see, and don't think they won't read those signs. There is no way you can cover them up. So if you want to continue having troubles with an industry who will come right back and say, "Well, what are you treating me different for? What is different about me? My problems are just as real to me as Lockheed's are to them." I think that is fair. I would expect to be able to come in and say, "My God, we made a horrible mistake," and I'd want to know why you are not going to bail me out. If you say no, I want to know why.

Unfortunately, this and other pleas for sanity were made in secret. The public was kept in the dark until the deed was done. On May 31, 1971, the Lockheed C-5A contract was "restructured," that is to say, it was torn up and replaced with an agreement almost identical to the Air Force's August 31, 1970, proposal which had so outraged the secret patriots in the Pentagon.

The "restructured" contract was highly touted as a tough settlement. The facts can be summarized from the public record.

1. On May 23, 1970, the Air Force told the Joint Economic Committee that the maximum total price of the Lockheed contract under Air Force interpretation of legal disputes was $2,516,000,000.
2. At that time, the Air Force thought Lockheed's legal case was worth about $70,000,000, versus Lockheed's claim of about $600,000,000, for a difference in dispute of $530,000,-000.
3. The May 23, 1970, estimate of $2,516,000,000, plus the difference in positions of $530,000,000, equals $3,046,000,000.
4. On June 8, 1971, Assistant Secretary of Defense Shillito stated that the Air Force's estimated cost for development and production without initial spares, without Air Force adds, and after deducting the $200,000,000 fixed loss, is $3,048,000,000.
5. When initial spares, Air Force adds, and the fixed loss are added, Secretary Shillito said, "3.6 billion is the total estimated to complete the Lockheed contract. . . ."

Far from imposing a "tough" bargain, the sham battle between Lockheed and the Pentagon had culminated in giving Lockheed all they asked and more in the initial pricing of the "restructured" deal. Beyond this, Pentagon analysts estimated that keeping the decrepit C-5A patched up would cost hundreds of millions of dollars over the big plane's lifetime. Lockheed would be paid to fix their own mistakes. Estimates for this work ranged from $200,000,000 to $1,000,000,000, depending on how closely the Air Force should attempt to approach the C-5A's original specifications. To minimize future political embarrassment, plans were set to hide as much as possible of this additional cost in budget categories other than the C-5A line item. "Aircraft Procurement—Other" and "Operations and Maintenance" were favored as hiding places.

The American taxpayer probably will never know exactly how much Lockheed was given in return for vastly degraded military hardware in the "restructuring" of their military contracts, including the C-5A, the Cheyenne, the SRAM, the shipbuilding claims, and miscellaneous spurious additions to contracts during 1970 and 1971, but the immediate giveaway of at least a billion dollars represented the largest single theft in history.

Meanwhile, Congressmen Moorhead, Koch, and Reuss of the House of Representatives, and Senator Proxmire were fighting a tenacious legislative battle against the guaranteed loan. The scenario was familiar, but now there were new variations. Supporters of the loan pictured the defeat of proposals to ship money to California and to England as catastrophic for the United States economy and the national defense. Whereas the 1970 argument held that the C-5A had to be bailed out in order to save the L-1011, Lockheed, and the country, the 1971 argument was based on the proposition that the L-1011 had to be bailed out to save the C-5A, the entire aerospace industry, and the economies of *two* countries. Lockheed and their agents in government had thereby established a somewhat distasteful but eminently effective pattern for perpetuating the existence of giant corporations: arrange to surface one shocking flop each year, then demand taxpayer support in return for continuing to function as a conduit for public money to pork barrel jobs, corporate profits, and risk-free interest payments to the big banks.

This pattern became clear for all to see. Admiral Hyman Rickover repeatedly denounced the evolving political-economic set-up as one characterized by "private profits and public losses." Expanding on this theme, the crusty old Admiral said:

. . . We in this country pride ourselves on the superiority of our free enterprise capitalistic system and we proclaim hatred of the Soviet Communistic system. . . . However, when men in Communist Russia fail in government or in industry, they are summarily dismissed. We, on the other hand, protect those who fail and grasp them to the Government's bosom. We let them privatize profits and socialize losses. . . . I am reminded of Herbert Spencer's aphorism that "To protect men from the results of their folly is to fill the world with fools."

. . . You should bear in mind that there are about 10,000 business failures in the United States each year. And almost all of these involve very small businesses where a man loses all his savings and faces the situation on his own. If, as is being claimed, the Government has an obligation to rescue a giant defense firm, then the Government has the obligation to see that the firm is properly managed. This will inevitably lead to state socialism.[*]

The nature of the upcoming arrangement was illuminated when hearings on the new Lockheed bail-out bill opened on June 7, 1971, before the Senate Banking Committee. The reality of the privileged status of giant corporations was established on the first day of hearings. Senator Proxmire was concerned about the precedent the bail-out legislation would set in rewarding incompetence, and he questioned Secretary of the Treasury John Connally on the subject:

Senator Proxmire: If the Congress approves the Lockheed loan guarantee, why wouldn't firms run to the Administration, to the Congress, whenever they got into financial trouble? Why wouldn't this be a precedent for all of them to do it?

Secretary Connally: I say this not too facetiously, I think it will set a precedent for all of the companies that employ in excess of 75,000 people, that have 35,000 subcontractors, 71 percent of which have less than 500 employees, that are the largest defense contractors in America, that are—

Senator Proxmire: It is only for the big boys.[†]

[*] Quoted by Congressman Moorhead in his press release of May 6, 1971.
[†] Hearings before the Committee on Banking, Housing, and Urban Affairs, U.S. Senate, Ninety-second Congress, Part I, June 7–16, 1971, p. 17.

The next day the issue of subsidy of failing giant firms was wrung out. Some opponents of the bailout termed the measure a subsidy, and proponents of the bill, especially Secretary Connally and Senator Tower of Texas, disagreed vehemently. Senator Proxmire agreed with Connally and Tower, but for reasons polar to their thinking, as illustrated in the following exchange.

Senator Proxmire: . . . I think you are absolutely right in saying this might be something that can have profound effects on our economy. What bothers me so much about this, Mr. Secretary, is that Lockheed's bailout, I would agree with Senator Tower, is not a subsidy, it is different from a subsidy, it is the beginning of a welfare program for large corporations.

I would remind you in a subsidy program it is different, there is a quid pro quo. You make a payment to a railroad and in return they build trackage; you make a payment to an airline, and they provide a certain amount of service for it.

In welfare, of course, you make a payment and there is no return. In this case, the Government gives a guarantee and there is no requirement on the part of Lockheed to perform under the guarantee. A guarantee of $250 million and no benefit, no quid for the quo.

Secretary Connally: What do you mean no benefit?

Senator Proxmire: Well, they don't have to perform.

Secretary Connally: *What do we care whether they perform?* [Emphasis added.] We are guaranteeing them basically a $250 million loan. Why for? Basically so they can hopefully minimize their losses, so they can provide employment for 31,000 people throughout the country at a time when we desperately need that type of employment. That is basically the rationale and justification.

In summary, the Connally position was that we should not concern ourselves over the productiveness of huge corporations. They had to be supported, period. The taxpayers would just have to accustom themselves to providing money to the big companies in accordance with their needs and getting products from them in accordance with the big firms' abilities.

Hearings on the Lockheed bill before the House Banking and Currency Committee were equally educational. Chairman Wright Patman had representatives of all the twenty-four big banks backing Lockheed appear before his Committee at one time. These witnesses represented banks having deposits of more than 103 billion dollars. Together, the big banks had already set aside more than a billion dollars as a bad-debt reserve for Lockheed's L-1011 loans. Concerning the banks' ability to absorb losses arising from possible Lockheed default, Mr. Patman quoted one of the leading bankers:

My own bank could absorb this loss without financial strain and without raising a question of public confidence in the safety of the institution. While I should not presume to speak for the other banks, I dare say they are in the same position.*

"If this is true," Mr. Patman asked, "why is anyone suggesting that the taxpayer take the risk and become the fall guy?"

As the bankers testified in turgid concert, imparting practically no new information but sticking doggedly to the party line demanding the Lockheed loan, the answer to Mr. Patman's question emerged: The Lockheed coalition was shifting the risk to the taxpayer simply because they could get away with it.

Deputy Secretary of Defense David Packard also testified. Having persuaded the public to believe that Lockheed's military contracts had to be torn up in order to "maintain capability," Secretary Packard blandly conceded that the disgraceful abandonment of the Government's contractual protection had not really been necessary. Speaking of theretofore undisclosed testimony rooted out by the Banking Committee staff, Mr. Packard stated:

Mr. Packard: It is very important that we have a strong defense industry. I said in my first testimony before one of the Armed Services Committees that the Defense Department has a very great interest in maintaining the capability of the Lockheed Company. I put it in those terms because that capability could be preserved in a number of ways other than by preserving the company itself.

Actually, Mr. Packard's testimony before the Armed Services Committee was even more specific on the alleged interdependence of the L-1011 and Lockheed's military projects and the supposed need to keep the corporation alive. "I am convinced," he said, "that we can keep all of the essential defense programs

---

* Hearings before the Committee on Banking and Currency, House of Representatives, Ninety-second Congress, First Session, July 13, 14, 15, 19, and 20, 1971, p. 132.

going in an acceptable way whether the L-1011 program goes forward or not." *

Regarding alternatives for keeping the C-5A program going in the event of a Lockheed collapse, Mr. Packard had testified, "I frankly would have no trouble in having somebody go down and run that plant [in Marietta, Georgia] independently of the rest of the company."

So, having done the deed, Mr. Packard admitted that the most notorious bailout in military procurement history had been unnecessary. In effect, he had given Lockheed a grant of money at least four times the net worth of the corporation.

Packard supported the loan guarantee in spite of an obvious lack of enthusiasm on his part. His friends and apologists claimed he did so only because of White House pressure. However, just what kind of "pressure" the White House could put on a man reputed to have a personal fortune of $300,000,000 is hard to perceive. Had Mr. Packard possessed any real dedication to serving the taxpayers' interests, the issue would have been an excellent point of principle on which to take a stand. Presumably Mr. Packard would have not suffered greatly from being fired for his views.

After an unusually spirited fight in the normally docile House of Representatives, the Lockheed loan bill was approved on July 30. The close vote of 192 to 189 followed some of the most extraordinary arm-twisting ever seen in the House. Amused but disgusted spectators in the House visitors' gallery were treated to the spectacle of one hapless member being physically pulled into the Chamber to vote for the bill over his audible protests.

The floor fight in the Senate was equally rousing. At the time, the United States was in the midst of the most serious international money crisis in its modern history (due, some feel, in large part to just the sort of idiocy epitomized by the Lockheed debacles). Lockheed supporters deluged listeners with a flood of rhetoric claiming (without supporting facts) that saving the L-1011 would help reverse the deteriorating U.S. trade balance

---

* Staff study transmitted to members of House of Representatives Banking and Currency Committee by Chairman Wright Patman on July 2, 1971, p. 4 of "Congressional Testimony Summaries."

situation. Senator Proxmire refuted this claim by inserting in the record a study showing that continuing the L-1011 program would most likely result in a *negative* international trade balance of $1,376,000,000. The enormous flow of U.S. dollars to the United Kingdom for Rolls-Royce engines and spares more than offset predicted foreign sales of the airplanes. *

Unhappily, logic and facts were not quite enough to offset the intensive lobbying of the well heeled (mostly with taxpayers' money) special interest groups and pressures from "the highest levels" in two governments. On August 2, 1971, the Senate approved the Lockheed loan by a vote of 49–48. Senator Proxmire, who usually took such defeats with good grace, commented bitterly, "Any objective observer must think we're out of our minds." †

Lockheed, newly elevated to official privileged status, entered a period of smooth financial sailing. On August 4, only two days after the Senate vote, the company announced that it had made a profit of $11,300,000 during the first 6 months of 1971.‡

Then on October 6, 1971, the Senate passed the annual authorization for C-5A overruns (again, no new airplanes, just overruns). The $472,000,000 was approved virtually without opposition.

With Lockheed's commercial venture underwritten by the taxpayers and their military programs safely tucked back into the Pentagon's cost-plus womb and hooked up to the Treasury's umbilical cord, the Great Plane Robbery was an accomplished fact.

Once they had made sure their pet dinosaur could suffer no harm, the Pentagon relaxed a little in their tenacious concealment of the C-5A technical debacle. On September 29, while a C-5A was preparing to take off at Altus Air Force Base in Oklahoma, one of the big plane's engines took off without the rest of the plane. The engine had ripped loose from the too-flimsy pylon by which it was attached to the wing. Air Force men who observed the incident said the display was "quite spectacular"

* *Congressional Record,* July 28, 1971, pp. S12347–12357.
† Washington *Post,* August 3, 1971, p. A8.
‡ Washington *Post,* August 5, 1971, p. K11.

as the huge engine rose high in the air before bouncing down the runway and finally skidding to a stop in flames. This mishap was even more bizarre than the ill-starred plane's previous failures. The previous high point had occurred when a wheel fell off—just fell off—as the C-5A was landing before a collection of dignitaries at Charleston Air Force Base in South Carolina on June 6, 1970. The only injury in the Charleston incident was to the pride of House Armed Services Committee Chairman Mendel Rivers, who was in the assemblage on hand for ceremonies marking the activation of the first "operational" C-5A.

Fortunately, no one was hurt in the Altus incident either, and this facilitated the Pentagon's ploy of "neglecting" to announce the engine episode for a week after the event—until after the Senate had passed the yearly C-5A overrun authorization. The Department of Defense apologized to Washington newsmen for the delay in the announcement, but Air Force spokesmen were defensive, claiming that they had announced the weird accident —not in Washington, but in Altus, Oklahoma. To whom the announcement was made was not clear.

On November 2, after receiving numerous reports from secret patriots about additional concealed C-5A failures, Senator Proxmire wrote a strong letter to Air Force Secretary Seamans demanding that he come clean on the C-5A problems. Senator Proxmire got the answer to his request from the newspapers. On November 29, the Air Force announced another study of C-5A technical problems (at least the third such) by yet another group of "experts." The general press didn't say who these people were, but the insider news letters confirmed the expectation that Lockheed and the Air Force would be investigating themselves. As announced in the newspapers, the C-5A Systems Program Director was assigned to head the team. The Air Force team was headed by Dr. J. W. Lincoln, technical adviser to the Air Force's Aeronautical Systems Division, and the contractor team was headed by F. A. Cleveland, Lockheed Vice President of Engineering. The rest of the technical team would include "loaners" from other aerospace firms.

At that point, the high-powered technical experts who had

been helping cover up the C-5A technical disaster decided to begin telling the truth. This seemed to be good strategy for a number of reasons. First, Lockheed's money was safe. Opposition to continuing appropriations for overruns had been beaten down decisively.

Second, sufficient time had passed to permit many of the technical troubles to be attributed to the mysteries of Extending the Frontiers of Man's Knowledge rather than to blunders. Most taxpayers and their elected representatives had forgotten that the big plane had long since been pronounced an outstanding technical success and that it had undergone the most extensive initial technical definition ever undertaken in military procurement. During that early phase, the semiofficial *Air Force/Space Digest* (published by the U.S. Air Force Association) had proclaimed that ". . . the C-5A is technically well within the state of the art. There is nothing in its design or production plan that hasn't been done before. It rides a strong backlog of experience in the development and operation of high subsonic-speed transports." *

A third factor favoring C-5A technical problem disclosures was the need to begin laying the groundwork for the next generation of military transport planes. With Lockheed taken care of, the public story of the capabilities of the C-5A could be safely downgraded in order to make a case for the next multibillion-dollar Miracle.

Fourth, there were genuine safety-of-flight concerns at the working levels in the Air Force. As usual, the welfare of the forgotten men in flight crews had been subordinated to Lockheed's interests.

Finally, the top cover-up artists needed to salvage their technical and scientific reputations.

This last-listed reason for the long delayed disclosure apparently motivated Air Force Secretary Seamans and Dr. Raymond Bisplinghoff in extensive interviews they granted to Patrick Sloyan, the Hearst newspapers' sharp, hustling Washington reporter. In articles published on December 19 and 20, 1971, Pat

* *Air Force/Space Digest*, March 1966, p. 31.

Sloyan wrote that Secretary Seamans had stated that "You're going to have to give this plane [the C-5A] a mother's love." *
He wrote that there was universal agreement among the experts that the C-5A would "never measure up to its original conception." Seamans blamed Lockheed and was on record as saying, "I'd call it engineering negligence."

Seamans' old sidekick, Dr. Raymond L. Bisplinghoff, agreed but spread the blame, reportedly saying, "Lockheed did a lousy job, but so did the Air Force." Bisplinghoff accused Lockheed of deliberately designing the C-5A under-strength, then neglecting to provide for sufficient and timely testing to detect and correct failures before producing airplanes. "They did it the insane way at Lockheed. Insane," Bisplinghoff was quoted as saying.

In his earlier whitewash, Bisplinghoff had cast doubt on the C-5A's fatigue life estimates before finally pronouncing the project successful. Originally the C-5A wing was supposed to have a lifetime flying expectancy of 120,000 hours, and the entire airframe was supposed to last 30,000 flying hours. Pat Sloyan reported that fatigue cracks began showing up in the wings at 2,000 hours and that failures showed up throughout the wing at 8,000 hours of simulated flying. With continual patching, the Systems Program Director predicted an overall airframe life of 15,000 hours, half the former guarantee.

Seamans also reported numerous other failures in the landing gear, the avionics systems, and many other areas. Pat Sloyan summarized the situation by writing: "Fat Albert [i.e., the C-5A] is sick, fragile, and will require a mother's love for what promises to be an all too short lifetime."

According to Pat Sloyan, only Lockheed was optimistic. They were looking forward to building the Air Force's next big transport plane, a monster envisioned to be one-third larger than the C-5A.

With the taxpayers already thoroughly violated, the C-5A news kept getting worse. In secret congressional testimony on January 25, 1972, Secretary Seamans said that the C-5A life expectancy was then only 7,000 flying hours instead of the

* Seattle *Post-Intelligencer*, December 20, 1971.

specified 30,000 hours.* Seamans went on to outline the government-financed patching program and plans to fly the C-5A both gently and seldom in order to make it last.

The bad news went on and on. In March, the GAO issued its annual staff study on the C-5A which indicated that Fat Albert was sicker than ever. Among the long list of horror stories in the GAO report was the news that the plane's miraculous twenty-eight-wheel landing gear had a mean time between failure of four hours and had suffered 3,327 failures in the six-month period ending August 31, 1971. Other reliability indicators were almost equally dismal.

By March of 1972, unit cost estimates, excluding the hundreds of millions of dollars of hidden costs, had risen to more than $61,000,000 for the degraded C-5As, and promised to go higher.

A final footnote to the Great Plane Robbery was the story of Henry Durham. I first heard of Henry Durham in July 1971, at the height of the congressional debate on the Lockheed loan bill. He was a former middle-level manager at Lockheed's Marietta, Georgia, plant. After nearly twenty years of successful service at Lockheed, Mr. Durham had come to a parting of the ways with the company because of his inability to persuade his management to correct what he called "disastrously rotten management" on the C-5A.

After leaving Lockheed in May 1971, Henry Durham began writing letters to politicians, from President Nixon on down, seeking support for reducing waste of public money at Lockheed. His letter to Senator Proxmire was referred to the Joint Economic Committee staff, who asked that I evaluate the information in the letter. Mr. Durham charged that the material and parts situation on the C-5A project was "completely out of control," with millions of dollars being wasted because of double and triple ordering of material, needless scrapping of parts, vast pilferage, and blatant overpricing of common hardware items ordered from favored, sole-source suppliers. He reported that airplanes were being moved from one assembly station to another with thousands of parts missing but with production and inspection records falsified to show the missing parts

* *The New York Times,* April 7, 1972.

installed so that Lockheed could get credit for accomplishing the work. Mr. Durham's most serious charge was that Lockheed's records were deliberately falsified in order to facilitate an unchecked flow of money for progress payments and partial completions of contract work.

This was strong stuff, but it had the ring of authenticity. For one thing, the case was well documented and Henry Durham's description of the situation was authoritative, obviously drawn from long experience in aircraft manufacturing. In addition, I had long been convinced that Lockheed was manipulating their records and warping procedures to collect money as fast as possible. As far back as 1968, I had attempted to get facts to test my assumption, but without success. After my fateful testimony in November 1968, I was interviewed by GAO representatives supposedly looking into the C-5A mess. I told the GAO of my conviction about the overpayment problem and suggested that they test the thesis by comparing the performance measurement reports for which I was responsible to the progress payment records, which were the direct responsibility of Deputy Comptroller of the Air Force Arnold Bueter. Because of the importance and sensitivity of progress payments, they were monitored closely by my boss, the Assistant Secretary for Financial Management. Since I was in disgrace at the time because of my testimony on the C-5A overrun, I was denied access to meaningful Air Force records and could only suggest investigations to others.

On December 13, 1968, Mr. George Gearino of the GAO's Atlanta Office met with R. W. Andrews and G. L. Allen, both civilian officials in the Air Force Plant Representative's Office at Marietta, to review the performance measurement reports (called Cost Status Analysis Reports) in preparation for an upcoming meeting with me. According to Mr. Andrews' memorandum of the meeting, Gearino "indicated that Mr. Fitzgerald desired that he discuss this report with him as well as the possibility that Lockheed was kiting funds in their use of progress payment procedures. We talked at length on both subjects and suggested that he (Gearino) contact Lockheed relative to progress payments."

It will be remembered that Mr. Gearino was the leader of the

GAO team who specialized in Finding No Evidence in examinations of the C-5A, so nothing more was heard from Gearino's investigation of alleged overpayments.

My discussions with Arnold Bueter and my boss, Tom Nielsen, on the overpayment problem had degenerated into Bueter and Nielsen castigating me for accusing Lockheed of "kiting," which was not even my description of Lockheed's manuevers. Predictably, I heard nothing more on the subject before leaving the Pentagon, and I was not then able to substantiate my convictions on Lockheed's overpayment.

With this background, my attention was captured by Durham's charges, and I immediately telephoned him to discuss his material. Our conversation convinced me that Henry Durham was on to something, and I reported this to Senator Proxmire's office. Senator Proxmire decided to ask Mr. Durham to testify before his Subcommittee for Economy in Government, but he could not schedule early hearings because of the on-going L-1011 bailout fight.

Meanwhile, Morton Mintz, the Washington *Post's* fine investigative reporter, visited Durham in his home in Marietta, examined his evidence, and wrote a long story on Durham's charges, which was published on Sunday, July 18. The story was carried in an Atlanta paper. The reaction was immediate and shockingly vicious. The Durhams' home came under virtual siege. The family was subjected to almost constant profane and threatening telephone calls and other threats. Angry callers threatened to kill Durham and his family and to burn their home. One particularly depraved caller told Durham, "You have a pretty daughter now, but she won't be pretty long."

Henry Durham had to take his telephone off the hook so his wife, daughter, and son could sleep at night. Durham himself did not sleep at night, but kept armed watch while his family slept.

Signs appeared in the Lockheed plant which read "Kill Durham," and "Kill Proxmire." However, it was reliably reported that Lockheed Chairman Dan Haughton wrote a letter stating that such measures were against company policy.

Senator Proxmire asked the FBI to investigate the threats

against the Durham family. The threats were genuine and dangerous. As a prospective congressional witness, Henry Durham was entitled to government protection, and at the request of Senator Proxmire, federal marshals were assigned to protect the Durhams around the clock.

The presence of rotating shifts of armed federal marshals guarding the Durhams relieved Henry of guard duty and provided reasonable assurance of the family's physical safety, but the Durhams' troubles in the community had just begun. The family became social outcasts; former friends turned away from them on the street, and neighborhood children were forbidden to associate with the Durham youngsters. The local newspaper labeled Henry Durham "Public Enemy Number Two." (Senator William Proxmire already held down the Public Enemy Number One spot in the eyes of these Georgians.)

Henry Durham's wife, Nan, was an energetic and devout worker in her church, where she had taught Sunday school for many years. When Henry's charges against Lockheed were publicized, Nan Durham's coreligionists told her they "understood" that she no longer wanted to teach Sunday school. The Durhams' preacher remained silent and aloof. Nan Durham was crushed by the behavior and amorality of her "Christian" neighbors. She wrote an anguished letter to Billy Graham, whose gospel ministry she had long admired and supported, telling the great revivalist of her family's troubles and imploring Dr. Graham to help. Time passed with no word of comfort or support from Billy Graham. Finally, after a follow-up letter, one of Reverend Graham's assistants mailed Mrs. Durham some Bible tracts.

Henry Durham testified before the Joint Economic Committee's Subcommittee on Economy in Government on September 29, 1971. He repeated his charges of gross mismanagement and falsification of records to facilitate progress payments on the C-5A. He supported his case with a huge collection of documentation and examples of vastly overpriced items of common hardware and materials. He also told of the personal and family trials he had undergone.

Lockheed was invited to tell their side of the story at the same hearing. They were represented by H. Lee Poore, Executive

Vice President of the Lockheed-Georgia Company. Mr. Poore declined to respond in detail to Durham's specific charges. Instead, he attempted to belittle Durham's former role at Lockheed and stated that Durham had seen only a small part of a huge picture. He also pontificated at length about the mysteries of managing high technology. His most profound statement was that ". . . without disciplined disciplines and a willingness to relinquish individual aims for the good of the whole, the process would falter and finally fail."

Senator Proxmire was unimpressed by Mr. Poore's response, and asked the General Accounting Office to investigate. After the GAO had made a cursory examination of Durham's documentation, the GAO's Washington headquarters' people tried to worm out of taking a stand on his charges. They told the Joint Economic Committee staff that there was no doubt that Henry Durham's charges were substantially accurate, and they questioned the necessity for a written GAO report. The Committee staff insisted on a written GAO report, however, and the reluctant congressional watchdogs finally went to work.

Once the GAO field office in Atlanta was unleashed, they did a thorough, workmanlike job of investigating the Durham charges. The Atlanta office's work was completed in late February 1972, and their report was delivered to GAO's Washington headquarters on March 8, 1972.

GAO headquarters sat on the report and would not release it to the Joint Economic Committee. After a test of wills, Comptroller General Elmer Staats finally released the report to the Joint Economic Committee on March 24 but qualified it with numerous disclaimers, including Staats' attempt to downgrade the report's findings by calling the highly detailed sixty-seven-page report "an unevaluated staff study."

It was easy to see why Mr. Staats was nervous. The GAO audit was devastating. It corroborated nearly every aspect of Henry Durham's charges. The report on the overpayment charges was especially damaging. In a way, Lee Poore's contention that Henry Durham had not seen the whole picture was right, but what Henry had not seen was even worse than what he had reported.

The Pentagon's Defense Contract Audit Agency (DCAA) had confirmed the overpayment situation in 1969 and had written a series of reports on the subject. By early 1970, the DCAA reported that Lockheed had been paid at least $400,000,000 more than its due on the C-5A. Programs payment policy applicable to the C-5A contract was intended to pay the contractor the target price for completed work and to finance 90 percent of his cost incurred on work in process. In theory, the Pentagon's policies and procedures were supposed to bar on-going payments for overruns on fixed-price incentive contracts. Lockheed, with the aid of manipulated records and a conspiring customer, was getting paid for overruns.

The Air Force's response to the DCAA's report on the $400,-000,000 overpayments was to authorize additional paments of $705,000,000. Finally, the whole arrangement was sanctified when Lockheed's C-5A contract was "restructured" on May 31, 1971. At that time, the conversion of the contract from fixed-price incentive to cost-reimbursement was made retroactive to cover the overpayments.

From the standpoint of the operators in the Pentagon and at Lockheed, the violent reaction to Henry Durham's charges was understandable. He had caught them in the act of stealing more than a billion dollars.

As a troublemaker, Durham had to be put down, and he was. Despite his excellent work history, he had great difficulty finding employment. He finally got a part-time job at a small chemical company whose owner was personally sympathetic to Durham's cause, but it appeared that Henry Durham was permanently excluded from the world of big business.

Durham had been warned that this would be his fate before he left Lockheed. He reported that his boss at Lockheed had cautioned him not to talk publicly about conditions at the company after he left its employ. According to Durham, this executive, Paul Frech, the Director of Manufacturing at Lockheed-Georgia, asked him if he had ever heard of Fitzgerald. Durham replied that he had, and said that Frech then told him that Fitzgerald had made the mistake of criticizing Lockheed in public. Of Frech's warning, Durham reported, "He said Fitzgerald would never be able to get a good job as long as he lives. He gave me to understand that anybody who bucks Lockheed or the Air Force is in for a rough time for the rest of his life." *

Strangely enough, the most cogent explanation of how such arrogance prospers came from the Comptroller General, Elmer Staats. During his reluctant testimony on the Durham charges before the Subcommittee on Economy in Government on March 27, 1972, Staats was asked by Senator Proxmire to explain the universal reluctance of responsible public officials to do their duty in the Lockheed affair. The squirming Staats could only mutter, "There's such a thing as bigness."

* See *The Progressive,* January 1972, p. 19–24.

WHAT TO DO TILL THE
DOCTOR COMES

The Lockheed affair was an un-
mitigated disaster from the standpoints of sincere advocates of
military effectiveness and the taxpayers. At the same time, it contained the seeds of a political bonanza for proponents of good
stewardship. Realization of this potential benefit depends on what
we learn from the experience. To anyone who followed the
disaster closely, it was obvious that the highest officials of the
Government's civilian and military bureaucracies had lied and
cheated systematically for the benefit of special interest groups
at the expense of the taxpayers. Toward the end of the operation,
it became equally apparent that military necessity arguments, the
original justifications, were at best secondary considerations.

It was not so obvious that the Lockheed caper was unique
mostly in that it was generally known to the public. It is true
that this Treasury raid was one of the largest in history, as well
as one of the most brazen. However, setting aside these pecu-
liarities, the Great Plane Robbery was not essentially different in
either technique or result from the other horror stories I was involved in, such as the Minuteman missile program, the Mark II
avionics project, the TF-30 engine for the F-111, the SRAM
missile, and the Mark 48 torpedo. Practically all of the flood of
books on the Military Industrial Complex published in the late
1960s and early 1970s contained detailed accounts of technical
and financial disasters in procuring big weapons systems. They
followed the same general pattern: glowing early promises suc-

ceeded by concealed troubles, deception, continued excuses, bail-
out of failing contractors at public expense, rewards for the
blunderers and liars, and punishment of economy advocates.

Learned writers, analysts, and academicians delve deeply into
the mysteries of managing giant projects on the Fringes of Man's
Knowledge. In most cases the big spending programs are pictured
as subject to only marginal improvement through complex schemes.
As a result, the military budget is viewed as virtually uncuttable
unless we forego buying weapons supposedly needed to deter the
Bolshevik. The managers of the Pentagon are viewed as high-
minded, dedicated people applying their great talents to the
Herculean task of getting maximum yield for the huge amounts
of public monies spent for weapons. Even though the giants of
management labor mightily, the big military weapons programs
are depicted as resistant to their best efforts.

This is Public Myth Number One in the Pentagon's religion
of waste. My own experience convinced me, and I believe would
convince any reasonable person, that the first cause of high costs
is that they are planned that way, and the programs are managed
in ways which ensure ever increasing costs with little if any
incentive to excel in quality of product. I believe that most of
the managerial giants in the Pentagon understood this perfectly.
Those who did not were for the most part victims of programmed
ignorance. High-level military managers were especially prone to
self-inflicted ignorance. "If you're ignorant, you're innocent," was
the watchword, and woe be unto him who disturbed their tran-
quillity with bad news or alarming concepts.

In short, the military weapons budget is fat because the people
who really matter in the process either like it that way or are
unwilling to take the hard actions needed to squeeze the fat out.
Fat means high, risk-free sales for the giant corporations, an easy,
comfortable, prosperous life for all the feeders at the procurement trough, and immense economic and political power for dis-
pensers of this largesse. From the standpoint of the beneficiaries
and manipulators of this greatest of all patronage pools, the compelling question is "*Why not* continue to let nature take its
course?" Given the feeble nature of countervailing forces for
economy and good stewardship, and the rich rewards for ration-

alizing and perpetuating waste, it would be surprising indeed if the Pentagon's Treasury raiders did not behave greedily and cynically.

At the same time, acceptance of the distasteful fact that Pentagon spenders have bad intentions greatly simplifies the job of squeezing the fat out of the military budget. Citizens can easily understand this and can undertake the task of changing the situation once they recognize that most of the high-flown gobbledygook about the dark esoteric mysteries of defense management is largely propaganda to excuse the military contract thefts.

Unfortunately the problem of bad, or at least misdirected, intentions is not restricted to the political, military, and corporate élite who mastermind the Great Military Boondoggle. Millions of ordinary citizens are converts to the Pentagon's religion of waste. In this religion, the Pentagon serves as a combination of the temples of Mars and Ceres, the War God and the Corn Goddess, and citizens are asked to believe that unquestioning donations to the Temple will keep them both safe and rich. Although the unpopular Asian wars and the disclosures of procurement horror stories in the late 1960s and early 1970s combined to erode public faith in the infallibility of the Pentagon's high priests, belief in the old religion remained widespread. Instead of reacting to the Pentagon's failures and misdeeds by demanding reform, many supporters of the old faith simply demanded an end to heretical criticism, harassed and persecuted the heretics, and fought for intensification of the old, unthinking childlike remedy of attempting to make the Pentagon's troubles go away by pouring money on them. Sincere supporters of the Pentagon should pause and consider the results of Pentagon procurement policies and practices.

The first major casualty of the Great Military Boondoggle was true military readiness. Almost invariably, the ever increasing prices for big weapons systems overrun even the generous slush fund provisions, and quantities of airplanes, missiles, ships, and other hardware are reduced to maintain some semblance of fiscal order and to minimize political embarrassment. In addition, quality and performance of the equipment are frequently compromised as a result of the government's failure to require the giant companies to make good on their contract commitments. In many cases, specifications are modified to match whatever the big contractors are able to produce. In some instances, notably the C-5A, there are no operative or effective contractual specifications at all.

In my travels around the country, I encountered many people with antimilitary bias who thought the Pentagon's incredible inefficiency was a good thing and who hoped the military would become so inefficient as to be completely ineffectual, thereby bringing peace to the world. Although these people failed to realize that the awesome power of modern weaponry makes even the most bumbling military establishment catastrophically destructive, their attitudes were understandable, given their bias. What I found continually appalling, though, was the steadfast defense of the most odious boondoggles by the vast majority of high-level military men and their noisy claque of supporters. During the years I worked in and around the military spending complex, the only high-ranking military officer to speak out consistently against the unconscionable waste in Pentagon procurement and its effect on military readiness was Vice Admiral Hyman Rickover. The Admiral summarized his dogged efforts in congressional testimony in the spring of 1971:

I have testified many times in past years about deficiencies in defense contracting and the waste of billions of dollars which have resulted from it. In testifying on defense procurement I express my own views, which as you know, rarely coincide with those of my superiors in the Department of Defense.*

Unhappily, Admiral Rickover's superiors not only disagreed with his views but also stubbornly resisted his suggested reforms, despite the fact that the Admiral was motivated primarily by the desire to buy more and better weapons for less cost. In the same testimony, he made this motivation plain:

First, let me make it perfectly clear that I am deeply concerned about the rapid decline in the military posture of the United States relative to that of our potential adversaries. The weapons systems we must

* Statement of Vice Admiral H. G. Rickover, U. S. Navy, before the Joint Economic Committee Subcommittee on Priorities and Economy in Government, "The Acquisition of Weapons Systems," Part 3, April 28 and 29, 1971.

have in order to maintain the strength to defend ourselves are inherently expensive. Therefore, it is essential that we conduct our military procurement in a manner which insures the maximum amount of defense for our defense efforts, since such waste undermines our national security.

As the only long-surviving military maverick in the procurement business, the venerable Admiral was unique, but his pleas for economy were ignored, especially by his fellow officers who were constantly clamoring for more boondoggle money.

After my ejection from the Pentagon, I got a broader look at weapons buying through my work with the Joint Economic Committee. This experience confirmed my earlier conviction that the Army and Navy were not significantly different or better than the deliberately wasteful Air Force. Nevertheless, it seemed to me that the Navy had a larger number of people who were willing to speak out about their service's failure to buy workable hardware at reasonable prices. In addition to the pointed, well documented testimony given to the Joint Economic Committee by Admiral Rickover, the Committee invariably heard excellent and enlightening testimony from Gordon Rule, who had made such a good effort to save money in the should-cost study for the Pratt & Whitney TF-30 engine.

This concern within the Navy for the degradation of military readiness traceable to poor procurement practices and attitudes was also voiced by lower ranking individuals. The best example was an extraordinarily candid essay written by Captain Robert H. Smith of the Navy, highlighting the shortcomings of the DE-1052 class of destroyer escorts. Prior to publication of Captain Smith's essay, the Joint Economic Committee had revealed that the DE-1052 ships had suffered enormous cost overruns and that the Navy had connived with the shipbuilding contractors not only to pay for the overruns but also to accept substandard ships and equipment. In his essay, Captain Smith called the DE-1052 program "the greatest mistake in ship procurement that the Navy has ever known." * Among other criticisms of these expensive ships, which cost about $35,000,000 each, Captain Smith wrote that the DE-1052 ships were "lacking a single solid capability

---

* See U.S. Naval Institute Proceedings, March 1971, pp. 18–25.

across the entire spectrum of naval warfare," and that "the 1052s cannot compete in the threatening environment of today; they cannot defend *themselves,* let alone provide protection for others."

It was widely suspected that the Navy allowed publication of Captain Smith's essay partly to justify buying a new generation of escort ships (just as the Air Force later did with the long-delayed confession of the C-5A technical disaster), but Captain Smith's candor and concern were refreshing nonetheless.

Even the Senate Armed Services Committee acknowledged that runaway military procurement costs were threatening our very ability to acquire meaningful quantities of weapons. Senator Stennis' Committee raised the alarm in the report on the fiscal year 1972 military procurement authorizations:

If the geometric cost increase for weapons systems is not sharply reversed, then even significant increases in the defense budget may not insure the force levels required for our national security.*

The Senate Armed Services Committee followed up their alarm by holding hearings into probable causes of the geometric increases in weapons costs. In the course of these hearings, Senator Stennis' Committee discovered for themselves some of the facts which had been disclosed in Joint Economic Committee hearings years before. On December 7, 1971, Senator Stennis and his associates heard testimony from RAND Corporation representatives charging vast overstaffing in United States weapons programs as compared to foreign programs producing excellent weapons at relatively low costs. The RAND experts testified that government project offices in the United States normally employed five times as many engineers, technicians, and other specialists as counterpart foreign programs, and that United States companies actually doing the work employed two to ten times as many specialists as their foreign competitors.†

According to newspaper reports, both Senator Stuart Symington of Missouri and Senator Barry Goldwater of Arizona said they were "ashamed" of comparative United States performances.

* Report No. 92–359 (to accompany H. R. 8687) authorizing Fiscal Year 1972 military procurement and other appropriations, Senate Committee on Armed Services, September 7, 1971, p. 17.
† Washington *Post,* December 8, 1971.

The reaction of Senator Goldwater was particularly ironic. He had been an unwavering supporter of the grossest Pentagon boondoggles and had led the charge in the vicious personal attacks aimed at discrediting and destroying the reputations of advocates of economy in military spending.

Senator Stennis' warning was pointed, but since the Committee made only token cuts in the Pentagon's money requests, the big spenders in the Nixon administration interpreted the Committee's alarm as no more than a rhetorical opiate for public consumption. Their reaction was to increase the military money requests, then issue literal and specific instructions to waste the money.

The Pentagon's fiscal year 1973 budget request was $83,378,-000,000, an increase of $6,234,000,000 over the previous year. This election year request was the largest Department of Defense budget request in history. Hard on the heels of this staggering request, instructions were passed to the military procurement and finance offices to loosen the already flaccid restraints on price levels and spending. These instructions to get rid of money did not represent a basic change of policy but did state the policy in brazenly explicit terms.

Secret patriots in the Navy gave the Joint Economic Committee staff copies of the Navy's orders to blow money. These were outlined in a telegram from Admiral Elmo Zumwalt, the Chief of Naval Operations, to his major subordinate commanders.* This telegram (called a "Z-Gram") admonished all hands to recognize the "importance of avoiding shortfall [i.e., underspending] in meeting newly established FY 72 targets *to avoid resultant adverse effects on anticipated FY 1973 outlay ceilings.*" (Emphasis added.) Not a word was included about tooling up to smite the Bolshevik, and just to make sure that no one misunderstood the intent of the order, Admiral Zumwalt listed a number of specific suggestions for squandering the excess money. The first two suggestions were "settlement of claims in FY 72 vice FY 73," and to "expedite provisional payments on claims and unadjudicated change orders."

At the time, the Navy was faced with almost a billon dollars in shipbuilding contract claims, with the shipbuilders contending

* The complete text of Admiral Zumwalt's order is included as Appendix C.

that their cost overruns were due mostly to "constructive change notices," or informal instructions, from the Navy. Admiral Zumwalt's suggestion that the Navy make "provisional payments" on these claims was a suggestion to weaken the Government's bargaining position by paying the contractors' claims before they were settled.

The Chief of Naval Operations, the Navy's top officer, also requested his commanders to "increase used of unpriced purchase orders and fast pay procedures." Unpriced purchased orders are, in effect, blank checks for the contractors.

Admiral Zumwalt's instruction to "increase in amount, timeliness and coverage of progress payments to contractors" had the effect of giving the contractors interest-free loans—or grants, in cases of nonperformance—which further reduced the contractors' incentive to perform. The Navy's top admiral went on to suggest other schemes to unload the excess cash. He listed payments before receiving billings and reduction of funds withheld for performance surety as useful devices for increasing expenditures without getting anything in return. Then he wound up his money-wasting suggestions by requesting his commanders' "evaluation of the use of unlimited overtime during remainder of FY 1972."

Many students of the military contend that the United States overkill capacity is so huge that the degradation of readiness through waste is immaterial. This contention is probably accurate, and it is also true that unlimited money can be used to offset some of the predictably calamitous results of the Pentagon's cynical policies. Given unlimited money, flimsy C-5As can be continually patched up to fulfill at least some of their missions. With enough of the taxpayers' hard-earned cash, some of it can be used to adapt substandard F-111s to some kind of service. Extra equipment can be bought to replace junky Minuteman missile hardware designed to incinerate Russians and Chinamen. All this is undoubtedly good for the businesses of the giant contractors who make money correcting their own errors.

On the other hand, it is extremely difficult to rationalize, even on the basis of greed, the second major adverse effect of the Pentagon's deliberately wasteful practices. The impact of the United

States fiscal health in general and on the nation's competitive position in world markets has been disastrous. Spurred on by the missile gap fraud of the late 1950s and early 1960s, when the Pentagon removed practically all restrains on cost levels, wages, and salaries, the costs of services and some material prices shot up sharply in the plants of the big missile contractors. Other contractors and commercial companies had to follow suit to remain competitive for personnel, services, and supplies. Then the increase in volume of military procurement, which occurred with the expansion of the Asian War in 1965, compounded the price level problem, and we were off and running to general inflation.

By 1968, the federal government faced a $25,000,000,000 annual deficit, punishing inflation, and an international monetary crisis. Still we continued our wild and deliberate waste.

My former associates and I had been concerned as far back as the early 1960s that the poor work habits and bad management in military contracting would infect other industries and damage our competitive position in world markets. In 1971, this concern materialized. The combination of waste-engendered inflation and deteriorating efficiency finally rendered our domestic industries noncompetitive with foreign producers in most markets. For the first time since 1888, the United States bought more from foreigners than it sold to them, and the deficit in our trade balance accounts reached $1,961,000,000. As the problem began surfacing during the year, apologists for the mismanaged United States economy belittled the resulting concern, claiming it was merely a hangover from an outmoded mercantilist outlook. But foreign money managers didn't buy the excuses, and on August 15, 1971, the United States went bankrupt. The catastrophe was clouded by a flurry of Presidental actions including higher import duties, dictatorial economic controls, *de facto* devaluation of the dollar in relationships with other major currencies, and reneging on our national promises to redeem foreign-held dollars in gold.

The fact that the actions surrounding our national bankruptcy were pictured as a great stroke of genius on the part of President Nixon was a tribute to the efficacy of skillful propaganda but did nothing to change the grim reality of the situation. We could no longer compete as an industrial trading nation as we had before.

We could not pay our bills and were requiring our creditors to accept something less than 100 cents on the dollar. As a result of devaluation, we were to pay more for things we bought from abroad and get less for things we sold.

Most nations facing similar situations react with fiscal belt-tightening and a call to go back to work. Not us. As we have seen, we increased parasitic, economically nonproductive military outlays and instructed our spenders to blow more money faster.

The United States' loss of its competitive edge in selling manufactured goods in world markets would be difficult to reverse even if our leaders were trying. The low efficiency and bad habits of the big contractors that infected our other industries involve people's behavior patterns which, once set, often take a generation to change completely. If only factory workers and other people whose jobs are subject to easy definition, routinization, and perhaps mechanization were concerned, the cure would not be too formidable. Unfortunately, those who must eventually straighten things out, the managers of the big companies, have been infected too. Although the Typhoid Marys of military and aerospace contracting cannot be blamed completely for this predicament, their financial success with nonmanagement set the pattern. Again, the perceptive and articulate Admiral Rickover put his finger on the problem:

Today the businessman who demonstrates acuity in business acquisitions, cash flow, and financial manipulation gets more recognition in the business world than his counterpart who spends his time trying to manufacture high quality products efficiently. Consequently, many large companies today are virtually unmanaged while their officers are busy acquiring new businesses, lobbying for more favorable laws and regulations, or devising new ways to make their actual profits look higher or lower depending on whether they are talking to stockholders, to the customer, or to the Internal Revenue Service. Many corporate officials, particularly in conglomerates, couldn't care less whether they sell manure or missiles, so long as they can show a profit.

There are many ways to make profits. A contractor can undertake to improve the management and efficiency of his day-to-day operations and so produce a product for less cost. To sell a common product, like bread or bolts, in highly competitive markets, a company must constantly strive for greater efficiency in order to stay in business and turn a profit.

Defense business is different, however. Only about 11 percent of the defense procurement budget is awarded under truly competitive conditions. Fifty-seven percent of the defense procurement budget is spent under sole source contracts. Because of the complexity and high cost of today's military weapons, the Department of Defense is dependent on these contractors. Knowing this, large defense contractors can let costs come out where they will, and count on getting relief from the Department of Defense through changes and claims, relaxations of procurement regulations and laws, government loans, follow-on sole source contracts, or other escape mechanisms. Wasteful subcontracting practices, inadequate cost controls, shop loafing, and production errors mean little to these contractors since they will make their money whether their product is good or bad, whether the price is fair or higher than it should be; whether delivery is on time or late. Such matters are inconsequential to the management of most large defense contractors since, as with other regulated industries, they are able to conceal the real facts concerning their management ineptitude from the public and from their stockholders, until they stumble finally into the arms of Government for their salvation.*

In brief, the Admiral was describing an unnatural selection process in which the least fit not only survive but prosper more than their competitors, and in which the Max Ajaxes inherit the earth.

A third bad effect of the Great Military Boondoggle, perhaps the most serious of all, is the erosion of morality, of respect for law and of confidence in our national leadership. Following the hearings into my firing by the Joint Economic Committee, Bernard Nossiter commented on this effect:

Organized society depends in the end on trust and belief. If the Government's highest servants draw raucous laughter when they testify—and such was Seamans' unhappy fate on Tuesday—serious damage has been done. The former Marine commandant, General David Shoup, tells us that "the military is indoctrinated to be secretive, devious, and misleading." This may be sound tactics for war, but it is not the way a country can be run. In the end, the Seamans, the Schedlers, and the disingenuous generals may be doing more to tear down the fabric of society than the wild-eyed guerrilla bands that smashed windows in Dupont Circle and the Department of Justice.†

* Statement before the Joint Economic Committee, April 28, 1971.
† Washington *Post*, November 21, 1969, p. A26.

Captain Robert Smith, in his essay cited earlier, also deplored the military's loss of public confidence. "The lack of faith was deep," he wrote. "It has been truly earned and it is justified." Captain Smith went on to quote what he called the "familiar, disgusted lament" so often heard in the Pentagon: "We've lied to 'em so often that now they don't believe a word we say." The enormity of this problem was such that Captain Smith had difficulty accepting it: "In an unreal world, the bending of facts, the adoption of questionable hypotheses, and the suppression of adverse evidence do not seem quite real, either."

Unhappily, though, it is all too real, as I and others learned the hard way. So is the disregard for law as it applies to the Pentagonal thieves. Falsifying government records to protect big contractors' stock market interests and to facilitate paying them hundreds of millions of dollars of unearned money is against the law. So are retaliating against congressional witnesses and obstructing the work of congressional committees. Mendacity, called lying or perjury when done by the lesser orders, is often punished outside the privileged classes.

Lying, cheating, and stealing to assist the military spending coalition is not only tolerated but is rewarded with continuation in high posts and promotions for government officials and with additional and softer contracts for the inept industrial giants. Conversely, objectors to the thefts get the back of the government hand.

In such a climate, it is difficult to condemn a deprived person for minor thefts or to convince the young that a little light shoplifting is terribly wrong. When big, rich industrialists are lionized for successful billion-dollar deceptions, how can we honestly contend that a delinquent ripping off of a six-pack of beer should be punished?

The late Supreme Court Justice Louis Brandeis wrote that government "is the potent, the omnipresent teacher. For good or ill, it teaches the whole people by its example." Emulation of our government's example may be seen all around us.

With all these bad effects and more, it would seem that mobilization of diverse forces to bring about reform in the Pentagon's stewardship would be easy. It is not easy, of course, mostly because of the disparity in the strengths of mobilized political forces. Beneficiaries of military boondoggling are a small minority of our total population—no more than 10 to 15 percent, including indirect beneficiaries—but they are so highly mobilized to protect and advance their interests that they usually overwhelm the vast majority who pay or are deprived by the Pentagon's excesses. The military spending coalition is rich, smart, ruthless, and deeply entrenched. Composed as it is of the country's military establishment, top industrialists, key politicians, big banks and other financial institutions, labor chieftains, and community leaders, the spending coalition controls practically all the levers of power in the country, including the largest and most all-pervading propaganda machine the world has ever seen.

Conversely, the payers have no effectively organized lobby or other means of concentrating and bringing to bear their latent political force. Lacking vehicles for systematic, continuing application of their potential political power, the victims of the spending coalition are reduced to isolated and limited expressions of indignation and anger at periodic disclosures of Pentagon outrages. Secure in the knowledge that the taxpayers are largely impotent, the perpetuators of the system follow the advice to bureaucrats attributed to former President Lyndon Johnson. Collectively, they just hunker down like a jackass in a hailstorm and wait for it to blow over. The bureaucratic turtle act works too. As Ralph Nader has said, "Persistent private greed always overcomes sporadic public virtue."

In order to begin correcting the situation, citizens must prepare themselves individually and collectively to counter the highly effective special interest lobbies. Short of armed revolution, which is undesirable and probably wouldn't work anyway, concerted political action is the only practical cure for the military waste disease which has been so costly to our society.

Ultimately, the permanent cure must include changes in our political economy to remove the sources of the problem. This is a long-range solution and beyond the scope of this book. Meanwhile, citizens can begin preparing for the ultimate cure by educating themselves in the interrelated political and economic underpinnings of military boondoggling and by taking a few simple actions to stabilize the situation in the short run.

First on the list of what to do till the doctor comes is to understand the nature of the beast we must control. The military spending juggernaut runs on money. If the fuel supply can be controlled, the juggernaut will respond; in my experience, it can be controlled *only* by controlling the flow of money to the Pentagon. Public indignation, demonstrations, and even congressional restrictions on the way money should be spent have little effect on the Pentagonists. When I was in the Pentagon, the military and civilian chiefs drew sharp distinctions between what Congressmen said and what they did. For example, the Pentagon chieftains were completely unworried about the congressional rhetoric opposing the Asian war. One day at lunch, the Air Force Comptroller told me, "They'll let us know when they're serious. They'll cut off the money."

Admittedly, cutting the Pentagon's money supply is a simplistic solution and a crude one to boot. Objectors will first scream "unilateral disarmament" and the like. Pay no attention to them. The Pentagon is drunk on money. Like an alcoholic with the shakes on a fifth a day, they demand another pint of their poison. As Captain Smith wrote in his notable essay, "One main root of the Navy's problem has derived from the very abundance of its resources, the immense sums of public money, and the choices involved, that are inextricable from considerations of political power." In fact, the Pentagon's preoccupation has been with how to dispose of its superabundance of funds for maximum political effect. This problem can be solved by removing the superabundance of money and with it the vast patronage power that goes with the huge sums that can be spread about to buy support. Once the financial squeeze is truly felt at the Pentagon, sincere advocates of military preparedness inside the spending complex will become increasingly influential in the Pentagon's internal politics.

Adherents to Admiral Rickover's school of thought, who are numerous but silent and without power, will grow more influential relative to the "inefficiency is national policy" crowd. In the short run, the hawkish elements in the Pentagon may be the taxpayers' best friends. In the event of a genuine money shortage at the Pentagon, I believe these warlike folk would be sufficiently alarmed at what they perceive as real threats to readiness to kick over the traces and demand an end to buddy-buddy arrangements with big contractors and to boondoggling in general.

The general public can easily detect this healthy fight if it can be fomented. Being basically political, both factions will try to enlist public and congressional support, and citizens can read about the struggle in the newspapers and watch adversary congressional testimony on the television evenings news.

Citizens can also tell who is winning. As the economy advocates gain strength, they will begin publicizing big contractor failures instead of covering them up. Some Pentagon officials will be fired for allowing overruns and other failures, and some big contractors will go broke.

Another signal of an effective financial squeeze on the Pentagon will be a deterioration of the sweetheart relationships of big contractors and their labor unions. Strikes over work standards and other management demands are practically unheard of in the big military contractors' plants, whereas they are fairly common in commercial, competitive industries. An outbreak of such disputes in major military contractor operations will indicate that financial pressures at the Pentagon are being passed on to other segments of the spending complex.

Another sign of a healthy financial outlook in the Pentagon would be an increase in spontaneous cancellations of marginal programs. Money-eating dinosaurs such as the C-5A and the F-111 would be allowed to become mercifully extinct if the Pentagon's managers were truly concerned about stretching scarce resources.

I believe that successive annual 10 percent across-the-board cuts in the military budget could bring about the badly needed purging of the Pentagon's bad habits in three or four years. Starting with the fiscal year 1973 budget request of $83,400,000,000, successive 10 percent cuts would bring the budget down to about $61,000,000,000 in three years and roughly $55,000,000,000 in four years. Militarily, this would be a safe level of spending, assuming no major war and inflation no worse than in other periods of declining military outlays. Such a reduction should provide sufficient incentive for management reform in the military, both in procurement and operations, and also reduce the Pentagon's patronage power to manageable proportions.

The modest and progressive nature of the cuts would provide ample time for the Pentagon to adjust to the new situation if they choose to adjust and would permit citizens to play the situation by ear. If the signals of good stewardship appear sooner than expected, the cuts might be curtailed or slowed down. If favorable signs do not appear, the remedy can be extended.

The reaction of the military spending complex to deep budget cuts is completely predictable. They will appeal to the people's most primitive instincts: fear and greed. Such appeals are time-tested and will not be abandoned until they fail. General Douglas MacArthur, certainly not a unilateral disarmer, commented on the government's appeals to fear:

Our swollen budgets constantly have been misrepresented to the public. Our Government has kept us in a perpetual state of fear—kept us in a continuous stampede of patriotic fervor—with the cry of grave national energency. Always there has been some terrible evil at home or some monstrous foreign power that was going to gobble us up if we did not blindly rally behind it by furnishing the exorbitant funds demanded. Yet, in restrospect, these disasters seem never to have happened, seem never to have been quite real.*

One of the principal fears which has served to justify the Great Military Boondoggle has receded in our society. That is the stark, unreasoning panic generated by allusions to an amorphous ill-defined something called "Communism," which can be fended off only by unlimited sacrifices of money and blood. The most devastating antidote has been simple quantification of the Soviet military threat. Whereas the public responded without question to the government's demand for diversion of resources to close the mythical missile gap of the late 1950s and early 1960s, questions were raised and opposition was mounted when the same phony alarm was raised again ten years later. In 1970, the American Security Council (ASC), a military spending lobby led by retired generals and admirals, industrialists and Pentagon-contracting university professors, tried the old "gap" dodge again. The ASC ran full-page ads in newspapers all over the country claiming that the United States was in imminent danger of being

---

* From an address to the annual stockholders' meeting of the Sperry-Rand Corporation, New York City, July 30, 1957.

overwhelmed by a burgeoning Soviet strategic nuclear weapons arsenal.*

The ASC's deceptive panic pieces had tables comparing alleged strength of the U.S. and Soviet nuclear arsenals. The "Soviet" tabulation included practically every delivery vehicle—airplanes and missiles—they had built since World War II. Ancient, subsonic short-range bombers, obsolete air-breathing cruise missiles, and long outmoded strategic missile were all counted. Conversely, only the modern missiles and airplanes then in the U.S. first-line inventory were shown for comparison.

The comparative picture was further distorted by the ASC's choice of measures of relative destructive power. ASC used "megatonage" (an equivalent of one million pounds of TNT) as their measure and avoided showing numbers of nuclear warheads deliverable by the opposing forces. This made the Soviets look stronger because the Soviets are believed to use larger warheads (often five megatons) than the United States. Most knowledgeable weapons analysts believe the Soviets are forced to use bigger warheads because of relatively poor delivery accuracy. We formerly used the giant warheads too, but as our relatively inaccurate first-generation strategic missiles were superseded by more accurate missiles, smaller warheads were chosen. It should be noted that "smaller" is a strictly relative term and that a typical single U.S. warhead of one megaton is fifty times as powerful as the bomb that destroyed Hiroshima.

Although the ASC's continuing campaign of hysterical, misleading propaganda was partially successful, the response of the opposition was encouraging. The defects already noted in the ASC panic piece were widely disseminated in Congress and to segments of the public. Public-spirited citizens gathered additional facts to counter the spending. For example, Henry Niles, a Baltimore insurance company executive, picked information from documents in the public record to compile the following table showing trends of deliverable nuclear warheads ("Offensive Force Loading") for the Soviet Union and the United States:

* A typical example was the ad run in the Washington *Evening Star*, October 13, 1970, p. A24.

	USSR	U.S.	Gap (in favor of U.S.)
12-30-70	1,800	4,000	2,200
11-1-71	2,100	4,700	2,600
Mid-1972	2,500	5,700	3,200 *

At the time of my Pentagon service, our strategic planners believed that 200 to 400 of these warheads could destroy the Soviet Union as a functioning industrial society. On this basis, our estimated mid-1972 overkill capacity would be more than 1,400 percent. Clearly, such overwhelming might would impress and deter any sane leader of the Soviet Union. If the Soviet leaders were irrational, no amount of overkill would be likely to deter them.

Such logical quantification of assumed Communist military threats does not seem to have much effect on Pentagon dogma. Admiral Thomas Moorer, the Chairman of the Joint Chiefs of Staff, argued that we should keep expanding our overkill "even if that superiority would have no practical effect on the outcome of an all-out nuclear exchange." †

However, try as they will to keep alive their religion of rendering tribute to exorcise the Communist demons, the Pentagon chiefs will have increasing difficulty putting down the heretics who keep bringing up facts about the true size and nature of the Soviet threat and insisting on logical responses to it. The futility and illogic of ever-increasing overkill is slowly seeping into the national consciousness, and the old-fashioned hysterical attitudes toward the Communist threat are simply dying out.

Nowhere was this more evident than in the age distribution of prowar and antiwar demonstrations in Washington. The most vocal and unreconstructed advocate of immediate all-out war on all Communists everywhere was the Reverend Dr. Carl McIntire. Reverend McIntire, a fundamentalist radio preacher, had a loosely organized but large following which the irreverent called

---

* Testimony of Henry E. Niles submitted to the Subcommittee on the Department of Defense of the Appropriations Committee of the House of Representatives, April 26, 1972.
† Quoted in "Overkill Is Not Enough," *The Progressive*, April 1972.

the "Kill a Commie for Christ Crowd." They were indeed a most forthright group. Exhorting his followers to all-out war against the Communist heathen, the Reverend Dr. McIntire said, "The fear we have against full war is a fear that has been instigated by Communist propaganda." *

On May 24, 1972, Reverend McIntire led a large prowar anti-communist demonstration in Washington. Just two weeks before, there had been a big antiwar rally in Washington, and *Washington Post* reporters surveyed participants in both rallies to determine age distributions. Results of the survey † were as follows:

Age Group (Years)	Prowar Rally	Antiwar Rally
Under 20	15%	30%
20—30	18	54
31—45	23	7
Over 45	43	8

Thus, using the magic age of thirty years as the line of demarcation between young and no longer young, the antiwar group could count 84 percent of their number as young, while the prowar folks drew only 33 percent of their strength from the under-thirty age group. (The disparity between the numbers of young people in the two groups was probably even wider in terms of meaningful participants. Observers reported that many of the "under 20" group at the prowar rally appeared to be children accompanying their elders.)

Moreover, the depth of commitment of the prowar group was suspect. The National Taxpayers' Union, a Washington-based citizens' lobby, detected this in a solicitation of Reverend McIntire's followers. Most members of the Taxpayers' Union didn't particularly care if Reverend McIntire's adherents marched off to a religious war, but they did not want to go themselves, and they did not want to pay for it. Members of the National Taxpayers' Union circulated among Reverend McIntire's crowds and tried to get signatures on pledges to join the Army infantry or

* Washington *Post*, April 11, 1970, p. B9.
† Washington *Post*, May 9, 1971, p. A17.

the Marine Corps to help with the fighting. They did not get a single volunteer. This was not too surprising in light of the age and sex distribution of the prowar crowds (there were uncommonly large numbers of nice but bloodthirsty elderly ladies). Even so, considerable numbers of Young Americans for Freedom (YAF) were present, and according to their rhetoric, some of these young men should have volunteered. Apparently the YAF types felt they could contribute more in executive positions.

The Taxpayers' Union also asked for signatures on pledge cards which read, "I pledge to pay to the U.S. Treasury $_____ in addition to my present taxes to cover the added cost of the Indo-China War." The Union had hoped to collected sufficient pledges to justify a proposal to shift financial support of the Asian War from an involuntary to a voluntary basis. Once again they struck out. They didn't collect a dime.

The gradual passing of the people's willingness to make unthinking and nearly unending sacrifices whenever the Red Menace is invoked is not an unmixed blessing. As cold war panic-mongering declines in effectiveness, it is increasingly necessary to have real shooting wars to insure the ascendancy of emotion over common sense. The temptation will grow to keep alive whatever active wars are at hand and to grasp new opportunities for military action.

All in all, prospects for the Pentagon's chiefs' countering an economy drive on the basis of knee-jerk anticommunism will probably continue to grow dimmer. However, they can expect more success when they appeal to the next primitive fear in their bag of tricks. Even though the Mars division of the Pentagonal temple may have increasing difficulty selling their line, the Ceres division's pitch will continue to have great appeal.

Actually, jobs, corporate sales, easy profits, and free working capital have been the principal and most compelling justification for the crushing military budget for some time. As the veneer of the Communist threat argument has grown progressively thinner, an even greater share of the Pentagon's budget justification task has shifted to their half-baked economic arguments.

The notion that boondoggling makes us rich has been sold very effectively, both on the folklore level and in academic economic circles. The pervasiveness of the idea in our folklore is particularly evident in industrial workers' support of war spending. One of my close friends was employed in a helicopter plant at the time of the invasion of Cambodia in 1970. He reported that some workers in the plant openly cheered the news of helicopter losses in the action. Their work was running low, and the anticipated replenishment orders assured continued employment at familiar tasks for them.

The same sentiment was expressed by Joseph Beirne, President of the Communications Workers of America, AFL-CIO. According to newspaper reports, Mr. Beirne was also cheered by the job-making aspects of the Cambodian invasion, saying in part:

Suppose last night instead of escalating into Cambodia, President Nixon said we are pulling every man out in the quickest manner with airplanes and ships. If he had said that last night, this morning the Pentagon would have notified thousands of companies and said, "Your contract is cancelled." By tomorrow millions would be laid off.

The effect of our war, while it is going on, is to keep the economic pipeline loaded with a turnover of dollars because people are employed manufacturing the things of war. If you ended that, tomorrow those same people wouldn't start making houses.*

The American Security Council also depended heavily on this approach in rationalizing ever larger military budgets. In 1968 the ASC distributed a comic book extolling the job-making virtues of big aerospace boondoggles. (The medium of communication tells us a lot about their sales pitch.) The comic book's story line was a kind of catechism, with clean-cut, wholesome looking citizens asking questions which were answered, more or less, by a good, gray father image, General Thomas S. Powers, USAF (Retired). In one sequence, the General dealt with waste. One worried looking citizen protested, "But we keep pouring money into MILITARY things, General," and another added, "And there's so much duplication and WASTE!"

The General, casting his eyes heavenward, responded, "Well, if a BUSINESSMAN were faced with someone entering HIS plant—KILLING some of his employees—destroying his ma-

* Washington *Post,* May 15, 1970.

chines—his property—his attitude toward efficiency would change! There MUST always be another man and another machine ready to do every job—the military is YOUR insurance against losing your country—its requirements must be met!" Then in the next panel, as the assembled citizenry gazed up in awe and adoration at their protector, the General added, "REGARDLESS OF THE COST!"

Well, THAT settled those nitpickers who kept carping about giveaway contracts for junk hardware, 10 percent efficiency levels, runaway overhead expenses, and Taj Mahal office buildings.

After too many pages of this fare, General Powers, glowing with an aureole like the Angel Gabriel in a Sunday School tract, hammered home the blessings brought about by limitless offerings to the Pentagon for DETERRENCE. Against a backdrop of crowds of happy workers streaming forth from smoking factories, ecstatic family groups, a policeman, church spires, and other wholesome symbols, the General explained that the blessings included "a soundly stimulated economy and prosperous industry," "law and order," "better schools," "the practice of religion," "high moral standards and wholesome family life" (the latter illustrated by Daddy cooking hot dogs on the patio grill for Mother and the kiddies), and assorted lesser goodies.*

On a somewhat more sophisticated level, most academic economists have done their share in selling the Great Military Boondoggle. When the bungled Asian War and procurement scandals brought the military under fire in the late 1960s, many leading economists threw bones to the opposition by conceding in speeches and learned papers that military spending spurred inflation by sending more money chasing after fewer goods and deprived us of opportunities to buy more desirable things. Some even began referring to military spending as "parasitic."

However, once the academic economists stopped speaking and writing and got back to their computations, most of these new thoughts went away. The spending for blowing holes in the ground in Asia, for overruns on flimsy C-5As, and for cutting off legs in Army hospitals all adds to the gross national product

* *Design for Survival* (comic book edition) by General Thomas S. Powers, USAF (Ret.), American Security Council Press, 1968.

(GNP) as conceived by the economists. Such spending increases something called "gross aggregate demand," which, in turn, is said to "make jobs."

The very phrase "makes jobs" convicts the concepts and shows the shockingly shallow nature of modern economic mechanics. Obviously the nation is poorer, not richer, by the cost of waste in nonproductive activities, not to mention the human loss in the warfare so highly esteemed as an economic spur. The employment generated by wasteful spending is nothing more than a restatement of the costs in different terms. Many, if not most, of our economists seem to have lost sight of the importance of end products. It is only in terms of the useful products of labor, capital equipment, land, and natural processes that true economic output can be measured.

A prime reason some economists miss the whole point of economics is the preoccupation of these experts, especially those in the universities and in the government, with "making jobs" as a means of redistributing income. This preoccupation stems from the fact that redistribution of income through government taxation and spending has become the primary function of government. Taxation for military spending just happens to be the easiest way to squeeze money out of people for redistribution. As the "social goals" spending faction of my Pentagon days observed, the taxpayers probably wouldn't put up with it without the military security rationalization.

From a cold-blooded point of view the process is an exceptionally effective way to control the masses of people. The Henry Durham episode was a chilling example of how people can be manipulated by this system. Henry Durham's neighbors, having settled into daily attendance at the Lockheed boondoggle as their primary, if not sole, means of support, were driven to murderous frenzy by Durham's truthful testimony. It was not that Durham was a hateful person or that he had violated traditional standards of behavior. I found Durham quite likable, and he had in fact behaved ideally as a citizen. What he did to incur his neighbors' enmity was to threaten the patron from whom all blessings flowed. It didn't matter whether or not Lockheed was guilty of his charges. What did matter was that Durham, in blowing the whistle on Lockheed, made his neighbors fearful that their fountain of blessings might be dried up, and some of the good Georgia Christians were ready to kill Durham, burn his house, and disfigure his daughter.

This is the kind of primitive emotion that the Pentagon spending coalition has called forth and will continue to use to fight off economy moves. And it is to this point that the main forces of any Pentagon economy efforts must be directed.

It would be pleasant if we could depend entirely on positive measures to remove the economic fear obstacles to cutting out military fat. If Henry Durham's homicidally inclined neighbors could have been assured that their jobs would be safe even if Henry's disclosures shut down the C-5A line, that Lockheed would employ them building nice things like sewage treatment equipment or clean-air devices, the would-be killers, maimers, and arsonists would probably have been less rabid. The process of directing the likes of Lockheed away from military boondoggling into economically useful or desirable activities is called "conversion," a modern variation of beating swords into plowshares.

It would also be heartening to see some real evidence of humanitarian concern on the part of the politicians who shed crocodile tears over the plight of Durham's neighbors in the event of slush-fund cutoffs. Their rhetorical tears would have been much more convincing if they showed equal vigor in addressing the economic problems of *all* these people (including Durham) directly instead of feeding money to the Lockheed dinosaur in the expectation that the giant's servants would benefit indirectly.

It would be delightful if the learned economists who justify military spending on the grounds of income redistribution would turn their attention to other means of support for those now solely dependent on money they receive for attendance at boondoggles. If leading economists were to shift their focus from symbols to the condition of man, they might even find means of helping and encouraging people to acquire a variety of sources of income other than wages and salaries. Federal and state income tax forms list half a dozen such major income sources, and income from nonwage sources would greatly facilitate individuals' kicking the boondoggle habit.

Unhappily, our political system responds more readily to problems than to opportunities, so positive means of reducing the fuel supply of the military spending juggernaut probably won't work initially. The vast majority who pay for or are deprived by the Pentagon's bad stewardship must create a climate conducive to constructive solutions by cutting off the money, and doing it in a way which makes it clear that the cuts are permanent and will not be restored by panic-mongering or intimidation. Citizens who pay must demonstrate that they are unwilling to support unnecessary spending any longer. Once this message gets across to beneficiaries of the boondoggles, they will join in supporting positive solutions. Until this message is received and believed, appeals to fear, tantrums, and other immature behavior will continue to be used to maintain the status quo.

Veterans of attempts to cut the military budget will object that this simplistic approach to Pentagon reform has been tried and won't work. This is only partly true.

In the first place, the congressional military spending debate which got underway in earnest in 1969 was not a total flop, despite the fact that economy advocates lost practically every floor fight and the Pentagon budget rose to record levels. Toward the end of my tenure in the Pentagon in 1969, internal projections envisioned a total DoD budget of $96,000,000,000 for FY 1973. This compares to an actual total request for FY 1973 of $83,400,-000,000. Although it is impossible to assess its effect, I am convinced that the congressional questioning and debate has had a restraining effect, though not nearly enough to stimulate management reforms.

In the second place, the congressional debate was not an all-out attempt to save money for the taxpayers and hence did not attract broad support. Much of the public support for trimming the Pentagon's budget stemmed from disenchantment with the Asian War, and most of the military economy advocates spoke in terms of federal spending "priorities," not in real savings. The priorities argument was widely interpreted as favoring a shift in federal spending from the Pentagon to other agencies such as the Department of Health, Education, and Welfare (HEW) and the Department of Housing and Urban Development (HUD). The difficulty with this proposition was that the stewardship of HUD and HEW was as suspect as that of the Pentagon in the public mind, and very few overburdened taxpayers could grow enthusiastic at what they perceived as a shift of boondoggles from the Pentagon to HEW.

As a matter of fact, the HEW budget ranked ahead of the Pentagon in spending reduction desires of the members of the National Taxpayers' Union. In a nationwide poll of 5,000 irate taxpayers in 1971, the least popular federal spending was for foreign aid, and the activities of HEW (excluding Social Security) were a close second. Pentagon spending cuts ranked third.

The flabby stand of some of the best known "new priorities" groups on Pentagon spending cuts was a major factor in the indifferent results of military economy efforts. During the congressional fight to cut the military budget in 1970, it became apparent to me that the new priorities movement did not have enough political muscle to bring about meaningful shifts of military spending. At the same time, the would-be taxcutters were equally frustrated and had little chance of pushing through legislation which would significantly reduce their members' financial burden. Clearly, neither group had much chance of achieving their respective goals until Pentagon spending could be brought under control. So, even though the ultimate goals of the new priorities people and the taxcutters were inconsistent, they had a community of interest in reducing military spending. I arranged a meeting between the head of the National Taxpayers' Union and the Action Council, the lobbying arm of the National Urban Coalition, the leading Washington advocates of new spending priorities. I explained my analysis of the situation to both factions, and I suggested that they form a temporary alliance to take the first step in both their programs, cutting the Pentagon's budget. After the savings were realized, they could then fall to fighting over the spoils if they wished.

The Taxpayers accepted my suggestion immediately. The Action Council, whose principals later helped form the huge citizens lobby, Common Cause, rejected the idea out of hand. The Action Council representatives said they would support deep cuts in military spending only if there were simultaneous and at least equally large increases in federal spending for domestic agencies.

Both the Taxpayers representative and I pointed out that the Congress considered and voted on one bill at a time and that it would be impossible under rules as they existed to get simultaneous votes on cuts for the Pentagon and increases for HUD. We also pointed out that insistence on allies' acceptance and support of the entire Urban Coalition program would leave the political base for opposition to Pentagon excesses right where it was, with little chance of pushing through the tough cuts.

The new priorities advocates would not be swayed, however, and the whole idea of a temporary alliance collapsed. Later appeals to similar groups suffered the same fate. The lesson learned was that the most powerful of the new priorities factions may have wanted to cut the Pentagon's budget, but their proposals for cuts were so embedded in conditions and so heavily qualified as to amount to no real commitment at all.

A third reason for the relative ineffectiveness of Pentagon budget-cutting attempts in the late 1960s and early 1970s was excessive dependence on Congress. Many bruised veterans of these attempts rail bitterly at the lack of congressional leadership in this field. Most of these veterans realized early on that the Executive Branch, which presides over the distribution of the Pentagon's largesse, was not about to cut patronage money, but they expected better from Congress. Such people are bitter because their expectations were unrealistic. Where they expected leadership, they should have been fortunate indeed to get representation. Given the power of the Executive to grant or withhold favors, the number and influence of well-heeled special interest groups, and the weakness or misdirection of citizens' lobbies, consistent action by the Congress in behalf of the great masses of ill-informed, brainwashed, and passive citizens is too much to expect to occur spontaneously. Congressional action will be necessary in the corrective process, but pressure for reform will have to come from citizens themselves.

Citizens are most effective in influencing their government when they are in a position to withhold support for unpopular programs. Recognizing this, and despairing of redress through conventional politics, many individuals began practicing tax resistance in order to withhold support of the Asian War. Many of these brave souls withheld taxes by deliberately reducing their incomes to subsistence levels and by supplying many of their needs directly outside the market economy. Others simply refused to pay taxes and dared the government to prosecute them.

The courage and dedication of war tax resisters are admirable and serve as inspiration for other people wishing to influence their government. However, the effectiveness of the approach is severely limited. For one thing, there are too few people willing to make the considerable personal sacrifices necessary to the success of this type of action. Others, even though sympathetic to the objectives, are turned off by violations of law involved in tax refusal. Finally, any tax resistance movement not involving a major proportion of the population is limited in effectiveness if the movement avoids conventional politics. This is true because of the ability of our government to finance reckless spending levels by borrowing even when the tax take is limited.

This is not say that tax resistance cannot be effective. As a matter of fact, a largely unorganized, almost subliminal resistance to *all* federal taxes, not just war taxes, grew apace after imposition of the personal income tax surcharge in 1968. Politicians favoring tax increases approached the subject obliquely if at all. Proposed increases were described as "tax reform" (increased taxes for somebody else) or "hidden" like the so-called "value added" tax, a form of national sales tax which originated in the Soviet Union.

It is true that resistance to higher taxes was most evident at the local level, but this was mostly attributable to the handiness of objects of taxpayer dissatisfaction and outlets for expression. For example, new school bond issues were rejected with great frequency. From my observations, this was not due to antipathy toward education, and was based on dissatisfaction with school boards' management efficiency only to a small extent. For the most part, taxpayers voted against school bond issues because these were among the very few tax issues, sometimes the only ones, that they could express themselves on directly.

More and more, politicians choose to finance income redistribution by increased government borrowing, which is an indirect current tax (through inflation of the money supply) and a lien against citizens' future earnings. Between 1965 and mid-1972, the national debt increased by $122,000,000,000, with $85,000,000,000 of the increase occurring during the administration of President Richard Nixon, who was elected to office on a platform emphasizing the old-fashioned fiscal virtue of the balanced budget.

Because of the debt-financing loophole, tax resistance to force Pentagon reforms probably won't work unless conventional political action to stop congressional approvals of increases in the national debt ceiling are part of the resistance program. A further disadvantage is that successful tax resistance coupled with a stop on debt expansion would probably cause cuts in nonmilitary budgets before affecting the Pentagon.

Furthermore, even when the squeeze is felt at the Pentagon, the big procurement boondoggles will be protected fiercely. The big industrial faction will want to cut bases and operating budgets first. Eventually, the true hawks will rise up against operating budget cuts, but until they do, the military risks will be small. Military operating budgets are almost as fat as procurement.

Notwithstanding all the difficulties and drawbacks, I believe a dignified, legal tax resistance effort should be part of the program to cut the Pentagon's excess money. The principal difficulty, other than lack of organization and resources, has been the orientation of taxpayer groups. Most taxpayer indignation has been directed toward visible and easily understandable examples of poor stewardship such as welfare abuses, bureaucrats' expense accounts, nepotism, and the like. Taxpayers grow livid when they read of welfare families being lodged in the Waldorf at an extra cost of a few hundred dollars, but often they don't react at all to billion-dollar corporate military boondoggles. The causes of such inconsistency are easily understandable. The bureaucratic ineptness and insensitivity behind the welfare family in the Waldorf are splashed all over the newspapers, the news magazines, and the television screen, while billion-dollar welfare grants for Pentagon contractors often go by almost unnoticed by the news media and the public. Furthermore, the Pentagon grants, besides being mostly secret, are easy to camouflage as something else since they are both complicated and represented as "defense."

Several Congressmen I know who represent fiscally conservative constituencies take advantage of this situation by quietly and regularly voting for the most odious military and aerospace boondoggles ("supporting the President"), then burnishing their "conservative" image by filling their newsletters with tales of welfare agencies paying for belly-dancing lessons and HEW bureaucrats covering their office building roof with Astro-turf to make a play area.

Once the great majority of exploited taxpayers understand that the Pentagon is far and away the biggest protector of welfare chiselers and law and order violators, some of the same hot indignation that has settled upon the hapless welfare mothers will be directed against military waste. Moreover, this kind of indignation has been woefully short in congressional and "new priorities" groups' opposition to military waste. For the most part, established opposition has been too gentlemanly, too timid, and too fearful of offending to be completely effective. On the other hand, the typical irate taxpayer suffers none of these shortcomings in a fight. When it becomes clear to him that fiascos like the Great Plane Robbery are paid for out of his pocket, he won't be put off by fuzzy economic arguments. He will not grieve that the creep who threatened to disfigure Durham's daughter might lose his seat on the gravy train. When sufficient numbers of taxpayers are so aroused, they will simply outvote the beneficiaries of the boondoggles. Politicians intimidated by economic fear-mongering tactics will become more attentive to the interests of the taxpayers.

Mobilization of the ill-informed, misled, and often inert majority will not be easy, of course, and will be fought every step of the way by the Pentagon's gigantic propaganda machine. The educational requirements are formidable. Practically speaking, every citizen who wishes to keep informed in order to oppose military boondoggling needs to affiliate with some properly oriented organization to take advantage of shared knowledge. Unless one is rich or influential, it is also a practical necessity to be a member of a well organized political group in order to have appreciable political clout.

Thus the first down-to-earth step in containment of the military boondoggle is to join something, then recruit your friends, neighbors, and anyone else you can sign up. But be careful about what you join. Even though enough new members can set any organization on the right track, there is no point in starting with initial handicaps of misdirection or heavily qualified dedication. Make sure the organization you join is willing to cut the Pentagon budget with no qualifications save unavoidable war. Be careful not to get involved in organizations dedicated to supporting their own bureaucracies. Avoid outfits with expensive, fancy offices and huge paid staffs. Most such organizations spend most of their time and energies raising money to finance the next fundraising venture. Also make sure the group you join is willing to join temporarily with other groups having differing overall objectives.

I believe this latter point is the key to near-term success. Too many political action groups insist that their potential allies pass tests of ideological purity before joining forces. Consequently, they often end up talking to themselves, failing to broaden their base of support, and getting nothing done.

My optimism for the effectiveness of narrowly focused, single-minded one-time coalitions is based on the fact that they have worked. The government subsidy of the supersonic transport (SST) program was defeated by one such coalition. The environmentalists, who paid most of the bills for education and lobbying, were against the SST because of ecological fears. The new priorities groups were against it because they wanted to spend the money elsewhere. Antiwar groups saw their opposition as striking a blow at the war-profiteering aerospace contractors. Some traditional conservatives opposed the program because it appeared to be a step toward socialization of industry. Many economists were against the SST because they believed the incredibly expensive machines would not be efficient people transporters and would crush the already overequipped airlines. Tax-payer organizations fought the program because they opposed public subsidy of what they viewed as a frivolous toy of the jet set.

About the only thing these groups had in common politically was opposition to the SST. Senator Proxmire, who had been fighting the project doggedly for eight years prior to its defeat in 1971, skillfully kept the heterogeneous opposition glued together and narrowly focused on the objective long enough to defeat the subsidy. For the first time, the aerospace lobby was soundly defeated in a congressional floor fight over a major program.

Admittedly the SST was not a military program, but the project was so draped in the American flag by its supporters as to give it most of the patriotic appeal of expenditures to keep the Viet Cong out of Denver. All the stops were pulled in the "make jobs" argument too. SST supporters circulated tables showing that some of the loot would flow to almost every state in the union in the form of contracts to work on the plane.

The counter to the SST "make jobs" argument was a perfect example of how to defeat similar arguments for big military programs. SST opponents compiled a list of each state's share of the bill for the program and made a state-by-state comparison of costs and dollar volume of projected contracts. On this basis, only five of the fifty states would have received more than they paid.

The pork-barrel argument for any big military program would suffer from a similar comparison. If such facts were highly publicized in an understandable way, it would be difficult to convince taxpayers in Kentucky that shipping money to California or Georgia was good for Kentucky. It would require considerable bravery on the part of a Kentucky Senator to try to justify support of sending Kentucky money to California on grounds of theoretical redistributionist economics.

The fact that such appeals to self-interest are not employed more often by opponents of military programs illustrates the need for tough citizens lobbies. Congressional log-rolling, or mutual back-scratching, inhibits such ungentlemanly arguments but need not affect hardnosed outsiders.

This is not basically a political book, but a few more hints may be helpful for sharpening the effectiveness of citizens' work for military cuts.

First, don't be misled by ideological political labels such as "liberal" and "conservative." Years ago, "conservatives" could reasonably be expected to oppose big spending plans, especially those frankly aimed at income redistribution. As a child in the late 1930s, I remember my conservative relatives' complaints about President Franklin Roosevelt's tax-spend redistribution schemes. One of my relatives practically memorized Colonel McCormick's editorials on the front page of the Chicago *Tribune* complaining of President Roosevelt's spending. Sometime between the presidential tenure of Franklin Roosevelt and that of Richard Nixon, "conservatives" lost their distaste for tax-spend redistribution schemes. In all probability the government's adoption of military spending, with its high industrial contract content, as the prime vehicle for income redistribution was the most important factor in making redistribution more popular with business-oriented conservatives. A good indicator of overall attitudes toward tax-spend redistribution is the rating of the U.S. Senators in the ninety-first Congress by the National Taxpayers' Union (NTU). This rating was based on voting records on seventeen key spending and tax issues. The issues were not intended to reflect any particularly ideological cast or indirect economic effect, but only whether the votes saved or cost the taxpayers money. The issues ranged from the food stamp bill to the military procurement authorizations, with weighting factors assigned according to NTU's assessment of impact on taxpayers' pocketbooks. (A complete list of the issues is included in Appendix D.) As usual in voting record ratings, a score of 100 would indicate a perfect record from the NTU standpoint, and 0 would be perfectly awful. The top ten and bottom ten scores were surprising.

Top Ten

Ranking	Score	Senator	Party	State
1	70	Williams	Republican	Delaware
2	55	Proxmire	Democrat	Wisconsin
3	55	McGovern	Democrat	South Dakota
4	48	Nelson	Democrat	Wisconsin

5	48	Tydings	Democrat	Maryland
6	48	Allen	Democrat	Alabama
7	48	Mansfield	Democrat	Montana
8	45	Fulbright	Democrat	Arkansas
9	42	Burdick	Democrat	North Dakota
10	42	Church	Democrat	Idaho

Bottom Ten

Ranking	Score	Senator	Party	State
91	6	Murphy	Republican	California
92	6	Dodd	Democrat	Connecticut
93	6	Cannon	Democrat	Nevada
94	6	Long	Democrat	Louisiana
95	3	Anderson	Democrat	New Mexico
96	3	Inouye	Democrat	Hawaii
97	3	Jackson	Democrat	Washington
98	3	Young	Republican	North Dakota
99	0	Mundt *	Republican	South Dakota
100	0	Allott	Republican	Colorado

Source: *Dollars and Sense,* April 1971.
* Senator Mundt's low score could be attributed to illness which caused him to be absent. The NTU held that Senators should be present and voting, and consequently counted an absence as a bad vote.

With the exception of Delaware's Senator Williams, an old-fashioned conservative, and Alabama's Senator Allen, former lieutenant governor under George Wallace, the Senators in the top ten presented a decidedly "liberal" image. The reason for their relatively high scores was their rather consistent opposition to military and aerospace boondoggles. Most of the "liberals" consistently voted for social legislation, but the higher price tags for military and aerospace programs far outweighed the cost of social programs in the rating. Although the bottom ten were a somewhat more mixed bag, one could generalize that the low-ranking Senators had more "conservative" images on the whole.

This example of deceptive labeling should be a particularly good lesson for those who expect "conservatives" to be economical.

As the NTU ratings would lead one to suspect, party labels can also be deceiving. Fiscal integrity, balanced budgets, and a generally tightfisted outlook have long been associated with Republicans. Deficit spending has generally been considered the domain of Democrats. To test these assumptions, let's look at voting records on proposals to increase the national debt ceilings in the House of Representatives.*

Debt Limit Voting Patterns
(House of Representatives)

		REPUBLICANS		DEMOCRATS	
		For	Against	For	Against
Year	Vote	[increase]	[increase]	[increase]	[increase]
1961	231–148	40	113	191	35
1962	251–144	60	98	191	46
1962	211–192	9	153	202	39
1963	213–204	1	172	212	32
1963	221–175	2	158	219	17
1963	187–179	0	147	187	32
1964	203–182	0	154	203	28
1965	229–165	6	122	223	43
1966	199–165	1	121	198	44
1967	215–199	2	173	213	26
1967	211–197	0	176	211	21
1967	217–196	0	176	217	20
1969 *	313–93	140	41	173	52
1970	236–127	107	59	129	68
1971	228–162	105	62	123	100

* Nixon administration inaugurated.

As the tabulation indicates, much depends on *whose* deficit is being voted on. Shifts in Republicans' outlook are especially striking. Republican opposition was unanimous to the last two debt ceiling increases under President Johnson, yet "Republicans for" debt increases jumped from zero to 140 when President Nixon's first debt increase was voted on. Obviously, the Republicans' philosophical underpinnings did not undergo mass metamorphosis. The basic change was in control of patronage disbursed by the White House and Executive agencies.

Rather than relying on labels and pious promises, find out how

* *Congressional Record,* February 9, 1972, p. H 970. Note and bracketed material added.

your Congressman and Senators have voted and intend to vote on future military spending issues. Have your citizens' lobby threaten to work for his defeat if he votes wrong. If he doesn't come around, try to get him on a national citizens' coalition priority retirement list. The environmentalists have made good use of this device. Before the 1970 House of Representatives elections, a list of twelve Congressmen with bad environmental voting records was selected for concentrated attention. The environmentalists did not have enough money or other resources to take on all Congressmen with bad records, so they decided to focus on a relatively small number for maximum political and psychological effect. Of this list, called "The Dirty Dozen," seven were defeated. Most were high-seniority Congressmen who had every expectation of easy reelection. Concentration on just a few bad actors let others, many equally bad, escape unscathed, but the focusing of scarce resources yielded a few defeats rather than lots of scares, and the high percentage of defeats inflicted on the Dirty Dozen had a salutary effect on candidates for future selection to the list.

When you or your citizens' lobby puts the heat on your Congressman and Senators, some of them will probably tell you that the Pentagon is already going all-out to cut costs, so no further push from Congress is needed. How do they know this? Why, the Secretary of Defense *himself* said so, just a few nights before at a White House event. Be polite, and impressed too, if you are so moved, but then ask and insist on answers to these questions:

1. What are the cost-reduction goals (numbers, please), especially for the big weapons programs, expressed in terms of both total programs and unit costs?
2. When are these results scheduled to be achieved?
3. What is the name of the individual who will be disciplined if the goals are not achieved?
4. Will the savings be returned to the Treasury or spent someplace else?

In addition to being suspicious of political labeling and the intent of politicians, citizens pressing for military cuts should be leery of Pentagon "management image" improvements. Don't be put off by the study commission dodge. Big, drawn-out and highly publicized "studies" are devices for avoiding action. Ignore reorganizations. Admiral Rickover commented many times on Pentagon bureaucrats' propensity to fake corrective actions by reorganizations. "Every time they have trouble," he said, "they change the organization. Generally, they change the telephone numbers."

Also beware of loudly proclaimed Pentagon management systems improvements. Not that the systems don't need improving. They do. Given the proper intent and dedication to true cost reduction, lots of things could help—things such as objective evaluations of true need for the weapons in the first place; such as writing sound, well defined, binding contracts, with improved definition resulting from competitive prototypes where possible; such as enforcing the contracts, even if some of the lodge brothers lose money occasionally; such as finding ways to get more competition, both in initial awards and in continuing programs; such as negotiating tough prices, based on what the work should cost with the fat squeezed out; such as keeping track of program status and insisting that problems be fixed before they become national disasters; such as controlling spurious get-well contract changes; such as setting difficult, specifically quantified cost reduction goals for Pentagon managers; such as fixing the Pentagon's rewards and punishment system so that those who underrun are promoted and those who overrun are disciplined.

Lacking proper intent, however, "improved" management schemes serve only to lull critics into complacency while adding more sterile overhead expense. Examples abound. The Nixon-Laird Pentagon abandoned the total-package procurement concept with great fanfare. Forbidding the use of the C-5A approach was hailed as a giant step forward. The approach was faulty, of course. The "Golden Handshake" provisions plus the Air Force's unwillingness to enforce contract provisions made the whole process a bad joke. However, there were potentially beneficial aspects also. Getting commitments on production prices during initial competition is a good idea. Airlines routinely buy airplanes as complex as C-5As this way, with good results.

The "giant step" forward in contracting was a return to cost-plus contracting. To get rid of the embarassing Golden Handshake, the Pentagon got rid of practically all contractual restraints on overruns. They threw out the baby with the bathwater.

Other examples of image building can be found in the Pentagon's use of my old pet schemes: performance measurement and "should cost" pricing. Looking for something good to say about Department of Defense management, the baleful report by the Senate Armed Services Committee on the FY 1972 procurement bill praised the Pentagon's use of performance measurement and should-cost.* There had, in fact, been a revival of performance measurement, but for the most part the applications were complete reversions to the old PERT/Cost scheme, mad formula and all.

As for should-cost, the name had been given to a completely different approach which emphasized long, drawn-out, subjective, qualitative reviews of contractor operations rather than incisive, objective, quantitative identification of fat and waste. The new approach made lots of jobs for analysts and consultants, but it saved very little money. The original money-saving version of should-cost was employed only on relatively small programs by an isolated group at the working level of one of the services. This small, embattled group did some good, even though their approach was opposed by other parts of their own service, the other two services, the Office of the Secretary of Defense, and the GAO. Even the isolated good should-cost applications had limited effect, though, because identified savings potential often was not negotiated or was given back to the contractor in subsequent contract nourishment changes. Furthermore, even the relatively well intentioned analysts were so intimidated by the enormity of the waste they encountered that they sometimes settled for cost levels up to twenty times expected levels for competitive private industry.

In short, don't get delayed or diverted from the prime goal of cutting the Pentagon's budget. Look and listen for the signals that the squeeze is being felt, and don't let up until then.

Getting the military spending complex off our backs will be an enormously long and difficult job. At best, many thousands of citizens will have to devote lots of their free time and some of

* Senate Armed Services Committee Report, September 7, 1971, pp. 20–21.

their money to just the first step of metering the spending jugger-naut's fuel supply. There will be hardships, too, before the giant is caged. Beneficiaries and overseers of the military spending will make the initial cuts as painful and disagreeable as possible. Just as local political potentates respond to pressures for economy by curtailing garbage collection, our national leaders may threaten to cut off aid to widows and orphans instead of trimming Penta-gon fat in the face of shortages of funds from the taxpayers. We may even be a little poorer for a while (some of us already are). Long-standing Marxist dogma holds that Western capitalism, es-pecially in the United States, would collapse without the spur of military spending. Modern supporters of Pentagon boondog-gling make the same claim. Even though it doesn't seem reason-able, it may be that Lenin, General Powers, and John Connally were right, but the prospect of more freedom and integrity in government make the remote risk worthwhile.

Although the people cannot expect to take back control of the federal treasury from the Pentagon spenders without many bitter battles and tests of wills, a base for success was laid during the period 1968 through 1972. For one thing, the process of chal-lenging Pentagon money requests in Congress was institution-alized, albeit weakly. Some small victories were won and other issues were more or less fought to draws. Most importantly, pub-lic disclosures of the Pentagon's endemic bad stewardship, bad morals, arrogance, and overall disregard for the general welfare had a cumulative educational effect on our citizens. Many were angered and some were frightened, and these are good motiva-tions for setting things right.

From a personal standpoint, my own experience changed my outlook profoundly. My brush with ruthless, irresponsible, un-accountable authority gave me a new appreciation of liberty and an abiding fear of unchecked government power. The manifesta-tions of unaccountable power should worry us all and should serve as a goad to make the fight needed to bring our spenders to heel. The government's ability to liquidate people economically may be more genteel and neater than physical intimidation, but it is about as effective in stifling dissent. Organized high-level slander, character assassination, and blacklisting are workable substitutes for rescinding work permits.

The fate that Henry Durham's tormentors had in mind for him was not vastly different from plans made for Jews by good Germans in the early 1930s. Except for differences of degree and emphasis, the New Economic Policy instituted when we went bankrupt on August 15, 1971, did not differ too much from the policies of Dr. Hjalmar Schacht.*

Most of the bad things which have happened as a result of letting our military spenders get out of control were foreseen by wise and experienced men long before they happened. Generals MacArthur and Eisenhower both warned us against losing control of our military spending machine. However, the first Senator Robert Taft was equally perceptive and even more specific in his prophecies. In a long and remarkable speech in January 1951 on the nation's then developing militarily oriented foreign policy, Senator Taft asked the question, "Is such a military policy possible for any period of years without inflation and loss of liberty at home?" †

The Senator's answer to his own question could be summarized as "Probably not," and he predicted that the spending would be partly financed by huge deficits and that "tremendous taxes will be imposed which will reduce the income and standard of living of every American citizen." Then Senator Taft summarized the situation in a way which was important in 1951 and urgent in 1972:

The key to all the problems before this Congress lies in the size of our military budget. That determines the taxes to be levied. It determines the number of boys to be drafted. It is likely to determine whether we can maintain a reasonably free system and the value of our dollar, or whether we are to be weakened by inflation and choked by government controls which inevitably tend to become more arbitrary and unreasonable.

Sometimes outsiders, being more detached and dispassionate, see our situation more clearly than we see ourselves. Often these

---

* For a full account of Dr. Schacht's schemes for getting rich while going broke and for using dictatorial controls as both compensations and cosmetics, read *The Rise and Fall of the Third Reich* by William L. Shirer (Simon & Schuster, 1960), especially pp. 259–263. Mr. Shirer's book also gives a hint of what to expect from addiction to military spending and recounts some difficulties of kicking the habit.

† *Congressional Record*, Senate, January 5, 1951, p. 60.

observations by friends of the family jolt us into awareness and action when nothing else will. Late in 1971, I had a long interview with a foreign television team that was touring the United States recording our attitudes toward military spending in general and Asian War spending in particular. I was one of the last people they interviewed, and they had heard all sorts of "Don't knock the war that feeds you" speeches and "Boondoggling makes us rich" theories. After he finished questioning me, the interviewer sat and talked for a few minutes.

"You know," he said, "all this war economy talk is very familiar to us. Not too long ago, we had a politician who was pushing the same line. His schemes seemed to work all right for a while, but later on things sort of came apart."

The interviewer, Herr Bitthoff, was from Germany. The name of the economic system he was referring to was *Wehrwirtschaft.* The promoter of the scheme was Adolf Hitler.

APPENDIX A

Memo to Dr. Leonard Marks Jr.; from
Col. Joseph Warren, USAF, dated December 13, 1966.

OBSERVATIONS ON THE AFSC
COST MANAGEMENT IMPROVEMENT PROGRAM

The purpose of this paper is to discuss the AFSC Cost Management Improvement Program (CMIP) and suggest some things that might be considered in:

(1) Continuing the program.

(2) Planning similar efforts in the future.

The results achieved after three years of effort indicate that somewhere along the way we lost sight of the objective. The expense and effort poured into the CMIP were justified on the grounds that the Systems Command needed better control of costs and that somehow we could and should prevent the seemingly inevitable escalation of costs.

During the three-year run of the CMIP show, all facets of the problem were examined. Nothing escaped attention—organizational responsibilities, qualification of personnel, contractor overhead, contract changes, cost estimating procedures, contractor cost control methods, etc. Scores of people became involved in various projects, hundreds of milestones were achieved. Outstanding progress and significant achievements were reported through the Control Board procedure set up to direct the effort. New tools and techniques were pronounced ready for use; in fact, more new tools in the form of proposed reporting forms (CIR), generalities and principles (Change Guide), and techniques (Cost Estimating Guides) than anyone knew how to use.

In spite of these, the problem lay unchanged—lack of adequate visibility into the contractor's cost planning and control system to permit the exercise of any meaningful cost management. The term management, as used here, means working through others to achieve an objective, rather than taking direct action or control. Without adequate visibility and ability to exercise management, we had no better cost control than before and could only react to cost problems after the fact rather than participate in their solution before they became unmanageable.

When Mr. Fitzgerald became involved in the project, it was very apparent that he viewed the problem as primarily one of contract management, a problem which had its root in the relationship between contractors and the Air Force at the operating level and extended up through the Air Force procurement channels. His approach to cost control was to work on the problem at its source, to gain visibility into a contractor's operation and exert pressure for better management at that level. As he began to push hard for a meaningful cost planning and control system at contract level, a disquieting development began to take place. His view of the purpose of the CMIP and that of the Control Board began to diverge. When the project started, all key personnel involved seemed to recognize and be willing to bravely face up to the fact that improvement was needed. If improvement was needed, then it would seem to follow that these same key people were in effect admitting that the Air Force wasn't doing as good a job in procurement as we should be doing. Further, we should and could do something to improve. This, in fact, was not the case—some of the key personnel were willing to pursue the CMIP, make a great deal of noise and put on a show, yet never admit that anything was really wrong with what we were doing in the first place. Members of the CMIP Control Board reviewed the project as one of "plowing new ground." The "plowing new ground" faction was thus able to rationalize that, while we were doing the best possible job now, we might discover some magic new tool that could be painlessly applied and enable us to do an even more outstandingly effective job of cost control. Thus, the CMIP was a show piece for "management systems development," "advancing the state-of-the-art," and "providing new tools." It was not viewed as a necessary effort to correct existing deficiencies.

As the CMIP continued through the years, no new magic tool appeared. Instead, old tools were reinvented or reshaped:

OLD	NEW
WSPACS [Weapons Systems Program and Cost System]	Cost Estimating
DCPR [Defense Contractors' Planning Report]	CIR [Cost Information Reports]
CFRE [Contractors' Financial Requirements Estimate]	CFSR [Contract Funds Status Reports]
PERT Cost [performance measurement scheme]	Cost Accomplishment [performance measurement scheme]

PERT Cost—Cost Accomplishment had been ineffective in previous tests (F-111 R&D), and again fell into disfavor and was replaced by the specification approach to C/SPCS. It is noted that for over a year after embracing the specification approach, the command continued to update and maintain PERT Cost computer programs.

SAFFM maintained a position that real problems and deficiencies existed in our present system and further that an effective implementation of a system such as Earned Value was needed. This position was supported by a continuous stream of "horror stories," most of them provided by Mr. Fitzgerald. His vivid examples of problems made it abundantly clear that SAFFM felt that the present procurement system and practices left a great deal to be desired—that we were not doing the best job possible—even with present tools and talent. This position became a source of deep concern to members of the Control Board. To admit that we did not have adequate cost control was tantamount to saying that we were not doing our job properly and something would have to be done about it—possibly identify functions improperly performed, single out individuals who had failed to properly discharge their duties, or change tried and true procedures. This was not acceptable to the Control Board. Thus a gulf developed between the system and the Control Board and SAFFM as to the real objective of the CMIP.

In the meantime, the consultant contractor and project teams continued to score advances in developing new tools, break-through, achieving project milestones, producing glowing reports of progress and briefings on the project. A unique system evolved for progress evaluation. The consultant contractor pre-pared detailed reports on the status of the various projects and submitted them to the project officers, who in turn used them to make reports and briefings to the Control Board, which was dominated by the consultant contractor personnel. The net effect was to have the consultant contractor judging the effectiveness with which he was carrying out his contract. He was in a posi-tion of being able to accept his own products and approve his own recommendations. Invariably, progress was found to be outstanding, products superior and all milestones met.

Unfortunately, the CMIP show was far removed and out of touch with the System Program Offices who were to be the re-cipients and beneficiaries of the CMIP effort. This was belatedly recognized by the secretary of the Control Board, who after three years on the project reported to the Chairman of the Con-trol Board that the efforts had been misdirected toward assisting the Division staffs rather than the SPO, and should be re-oriented. This was apparently discovered as a result of the C-5A "Lessons Learned" project.

The C-5A presents an excellent opportunity to assess the effect of the CMIP. The C-5A was designated as the "model system" for management improvement. The C/SPCS specification was put on the contract in June 1965, plus all other new tools such as CIR, CFSR. The effectiveness of these tools is not yet known, but a preliminary evaluation indicates that little, if any, im-provement in cost control or visibility has been achieved. The assessment is based upon a review of the C-5A program of Lockheed-Georgia on 14–15 November 1966, and a follow-up visit on 5 December 1966.

On the first visit, the contractor stated unequivocally that in implementing the Cost Planning and Control specification he was not complying with a planned value of work concept in that sum of work package planned value does not equate to cost account budgets. This is the very heart of the C/SPCS and vital to an earned value system. The contractor was supported by the SPO in his contention that the earned value concept was superfluous and unnecessary and could lead to unwarranted meddling by the Air Force in the contractor management. On the first visit, the contractor provided the group with a briefing on the status of the program. Incipient cost problems were evident but the contractor insisted that his system was forecasting cost to complete contract within his own *budget estimate* which was significantly lower than the target price. He further insisted that his cost planning and control system, which is really PERT Cost, provided adequate visibility for the SPO, that no changes were in order.

On the return visit three weeks later, the group included senior Air Force personnel who have a vital interest and responsibility for cost management. The purpose of the second visit was to kick off the demonstration and validation of the contractor's implementation of C/SPCS. The contractor was requested to cover essentially the same subjects that had been reviewed three weeks earlier. In the second briefing, a completely different picture emerged on the status of the program. The contractor's estimate to complete had increased by $211 million and was now $38 million *over the target price.* Further, the contract provisions concerning the state of the market place were discussed. It seems that the target price is adjustable depending upon the cost of labor and material. If these exceed certain bounds, then the contract price may be adjusted upward. The bounds were reported by the contractor as being exceeded.

The contractor explained that this was the first time the new estimate to complete had been given to the SPO because it was necessary to get the Lockheed Corporate Office approval of the new budget before making it available to the Air Force. The SPO indicated he felt this was perfectly natural and proper. None of the senior Air Force personnel demurred from this concept.

The second briefing was very much like seeing the rerun of an old movie. The plot still has drama and suspense, the script was excellent, the acting superb, but the outcome will be the same as it was the first, second or tenth time it was shown. The contract costs will be exceeded.

The contractor has cut the heart of C/SPCS as described by the specification. The contractor and SPO do not use the same information for management. The contractor has interjected a massive judgment link extending through the corporate office between his management information and the data provided the SPO.

The Cost Control system operated by the contractor does not produce meaningful status and cost to complete estimates. It does not relate physical progress to planned costs. It tracks expenditures against a budget plan. The provisions of the contract will not act as a brake on cost increases. In fact, the contract almost guarantees increases. The coming cost increases will be more than justified, supported, rationalized and explained by the contractor. His position will be supported by the Air Force. The costs, whatever they are, will be duly entered into data banks to prove beyond any doubt that they are the true costs—who can argue that they should have or could have been different?

The C-5A cost control situation is not beyond redemption, but will be unless the Air Force insists on introducing the planned value of work concept and demands an effective cost planning and control system. It is quite possible that with relatively minor changes the Lockheed system can meet the criteria outlined in the specification. Thus far, the CMIP has been ineffectual as far as the C-5A is concerned.

It is important that positive and recognizable results be achieved as a result of the CMIP. The C/SPCS offers the best opportunity for this. If this effort is abandoned or modified to some sterile, ineffectual façade it may be a long time before any improvement is made in cost control. Failure of this project will be held up as proof that the concept was unsound, unworkable and unnecessary.

By way of recommendations, the following are offered:

—Objectives of the program must be clearly established. Supporting projects should be sponsored only if they contribute directly to these objectives. The purpose of the projects must be defined in terms of end results and products desired.

—Progress evaluation must be measured in terms of achieving the desired results. This will require the project to be thought through to the end and the objectives kept in sight.

—In planning and conducting the project, it is essential to keep in close touch with operating levels. Personnel assigned responsibilities for the various supporting projects must have had experience at the operating level (SPO) and be able to communicate with that level.

—Don't permit the consultant contractor to dominate and control the project. An objective assessment of his products, help and performance is necessary. This is impossible if he attends and controls all meetings and prepares all reports.

—Don't use the project as a vehicle to gain attention and notoriety for individuals. Favorable publicity which emphasizes progress is healthy, but when the purpose of the project is to create a personal image, this is quickly recognized at the lower operating levels. This discredits it, and it is thereafter ignored.

—Don't hire a contractor for his "letterhead" or to "open doors" at higher levels, or to conduct a "key acceptance" program at higher levels. The objectives of the program should not require constant selling. The value of the products must be demonstrated through results if they are to gain real acceptance.

APPENDIX B

[Letter of A. E. Fitzgerald to
Lt. Gen. J. W. O'Neill]

DEPARTMENT OF THE AIR FORCE
WASHINGTON 20330

OFFICE OF THE ASSISTANT SECRETARY

December 15, 1967

Dear General O'Neill:

As we discussed, I am sending along some of my thoughts on needed Minuteman management improvements.

Prior to reading the Minuteman Task Force Study Summary Report, I had assumed that you had reviewed the June 21, 1967, trip report which Gene Kirschbaum and I prepared. After reading the Summary Report, it appeared to me that you had not read our trip report. Consequently, I am sending along (Attachment 1) a copy of the June 21 trip report. I have gone over the document again, and I believe the recommendations it contains (Section VI) are as pertinent today as when they were written.

I want to elaborate on Section VI of our trip report, especially parts A, D, E, F, G and I (pp. 10–15). Taken together, the activities suggested in these parts would constitute a mechanically sound cost control function. However, as you might expect, there are problems.

To begin with, Minuteman cost problems are not generally recognized as such. In common with a broad segment of the weapons system management community, such problems on the Minuteman program are termed "funding problems." In general,

one of two solutions to an imbalance of money and requirements for money is recommended by the SPO: one, more money;
two, cut or "stretch" the program. With rare exceptions, this is
true even when the cost of items in the program has escalated
wildly, and avoidable inefficiencies are well documented. Some
documentation of this type is contained in the reports Gene
Kirschbaum and I had hoped to discuss with you during our September trip. I hope you have had an opportunity to review the
reports in the interim, since I intend to discuss them during our
visit next week.

In one instance, existence of a cost problem was acknowledged, and CMD made a commitment to take corrective action.
Unfortunately, nothing came of it (see Attachment 2).

As we have discussed, financial people on the Minuteman are
pre-occupied with fiscal year funding. Given this orientation,
combined with the limited recognized solutions to funding im-
balances, it is not surprising that most program financial efforts
are directed toward justifying more money. This direction is
supported and given impetus by pressures from the associate and
SETD contractors who have a community of interest with the
SPO in obtaining more money. In a commercial business situation, similar pressures are usually countered by a combination
of top management restraint and the built-in awareness that
excessive costs mean disaster to the business and those dependent on it for livelihood. There are no comparable countervailing
pressures in our situation. Indeed, the opposite is true; more
costs and, hence, more funds mean increased personal security
as long as the increases are tolerated.

In such an atmosphere, the would-be cost reducer, not high
costs, is the problem to the military manager. The cost reducer
offers a difficult, often unpleasant solution to the money/
requirements imbalance. More money is an easy solution which
makes nearly everyone happy.

If this situation could be reversed, that is, if managers could
be convinced that success in their careers depended, at least in
part, on their ability to achieve difficult cost goals without sacrifice of quality, schedule or program content, most would view
cost reduction and control practices as aids rather than an-

noyances. Some of them might even invent improved practices.

I believe that you can establish the cost goals for Minuteman and supply the motivation to assure their accomplishment.

Another major problem, or perhaps it is merely a symptom of the problem I have just discussed, is the extreme shortage of people who understand tight cost control, who are motivated to work at it and are equipped to work at it. I say this may be only a symptom because I suspect that the problem would be greatly alleviated if the current poor atmosphere for cost control were to improve. It is likely that effective cost control people, experienced and skilled in the art, would be eager to join you if more opportunity were offered for exercise of their talent.

In any event, I believe these people will continue to be in short supply for some time to come. Therefore, it would appear desirable to provide an organizational home for cost control people and their function such that they can be concentrated for maximum effect. As I mentioned earlier, I do not believe cost problems and, hence, cost control, are recognized. Certainly the function of cost control is not understood. Let me explain.

Effective cost control, like any other form of control, is a closed-loop function. Starting with the operation we are seeking to control, we identify significant variables or characteristics of the operation which we wish to measure in order to evaluate the operation. Typically, in cost control we arrange for reports of actual and anticipated costs to flow to SPOs and to various headquarters. Unhappily, some of our managers assume that such an arrangement constitutes a cost control system. Others, more astute, recognize that an effective control system must include provision for comparing actual costs to meaningful benchmarks. However, few if any appear to recognize the need for searching analyses of deviations from plan, followed by aggressive, timely corrective actions.

In short, the need for the feed-back portion of the closed-loop system is not recognized. It is not surprising, then, that there is no organizational responsibility for closing the loop.

I suggest that an organization be established to establish "should cost" levels for acquisitions, to perform variance analyses, and to assure that corrective actions are taken. Graphically, the suggested organization should be responsible for the shaded portion of the control system schematic shown below:

COST CONTROL SYSTEM SCHEMATIC

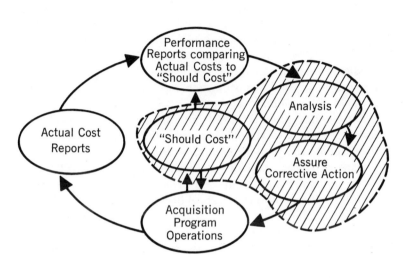

This control cycle should begin to operate in a program's concept formulation stage, and should continue, with progressive refinement, throughout the program's life cycle. In addition, certain non-program functional expense areas, such as major contractor overhead, should be continually evaluated through the cyclic process.

The suggested cost control organization could be domiciled at the level of deputy SPD, as we have discussed, or in your immediate office. The latter location might be useful for spreading the concept and its application to programs other than Minuteman.

With all the suggested improvements, your cost control efforts could go for naught if the problems of folklore are not dealt with. Principal among these are the notions that

1. economic support of the industrial base is of paramount importance, and
2. tight cost control hurts quality.

The first of these arguments has wide currency just now. I hear it from many quarters, including the Minuteman SPO. In my last visit to Minuteman, I was told that Boeing personnel could not be cut because of our fear of labor union and Congressional reaction. In the last few days, "industrial impact" arguments were used as justification for adding millions of dollars to the Minuteman budget.

The military have little difficulty selling such propositions to certain politicians. Many endorse the concept wholeheartedly. Even those who do not endorse it believe a prime purpose of our spending is to support a massive, middle-class WPA. In a recent attack on the military-industrial-academic complex, Senator Fulbright said of our industrial base,

"Together all these industries and employees, comprising 10 percent of the labor force, will earn their living from defense spending. Together all these industries and employees, drawing their income from the $75 billion defense budget form *a giant concentration of socialism* in our otherwise free enterprise economy." [Emphasis mine.]

We have convinced Senator Fulbright, among others, that we are running a latter-day WPA. The dangerous thing, politics aside, is that many of the important people in our management group are similarly persuaded, and their actions are converting their belief to reality.

Meanwhile, as you know, Minuteman cost increases are being financed, at least in part, by cutting other programs, including those for new weapons needed by our operational forces.

You can do a great deal to alleviate this situation by your actions.

The second major folklore problem is the assertion now being bruited about that reduced funding caused the Autonetics quality problems. Even the Inspector General recently cited underfunding as one of the contributing causes of our Minuteman problems.

The facts do not support this contention. If you will review the document I cited in my December 14, 1967 note to you, I believe you will agree that the basic cause of our difficulty was the gross error in technical judgement in 1963. Many of our top scientists and engineers were parties to this error. I feel free to be extremely critical of this error because I am not doing so in hindsight. I reported the dismal outlook to the Minuteman SPD in September of 1963. I do not know whether he had prior knowledge of it.

Subsequently, far from starving the program financially, massive infusions of additional money were made in attempts to buy our way out of the technical difficulty. I believe that much of this money was wasted, but nevertheless, large amounts of money were available, and, so far as I know, minimal constraints were placed on the contractors in its use.

I have even heard the 1965 Minuteman overhead review and subsequent cuts blamed for the technical problems. This is absurd on the face of it, of course. The problem had existed for at least two years, and the overhead activities under attack had nothing to do with the problem anyway.

Attachments 3 and 4 provide some significant funding and cost comparisons.

I believe that the near-automatic assumption that the cure for poor quality is more money is the most dangerous misconception now current in our business. It is true that we can absolutely ruin quality by failing to provide necessary resources. At the same time, I believe we can hurt quality with a superabundance of some resources, especially manpower.

In particular, I believe that underloading of factory personnel is a major cause of poor product quality and low yields. Underloading, that is, more people than the work requires, reduces concentration and attentiveness to a level detrimental to good workmanship, and rework soars. Some of the scrap produced invariably passes subsequent screening and shows up in field failures. Field failures too often result in the near automatic reaction I referred to earlier. More money is "turned on," more supernumeraries are hired, discipline is reduced, more failures occur, and the vicious cycle continues.

The cyclical process just described inflates the work force and reduces the apparent need for prudent, disciplined management of manpower resources. In the C/SPCS tests we have conducted to date, management discipline problems have proven to be the primary causes of failure. The contractors caught up in the fail-spend cycle, including Autonetics, have all failed our tests. The worst feature of this process and of the philosophy underlying it is that we tend to believe the theories, and therefore do not adequately examine fundamental causes of our difficulty. Let me illustrate this point with an example from my own experience.

Many years ago, when I was a young industrial engineer, fresh out of college, I was serving as quality control engineer in a manufacturing company. I was extremely interested in the business, and I studied incessantly. I took all the pertinent courses offered in the evening schools of the local universities, attended seminars and conferences and hounded all the recognized experts for scraps of knowledge. As a consequence, I learned a great deal about my specialty. Unfortunately, some of the things I learned weren't so.

One of my theories at that time was that my company's wage incentive system drove the workers so hard that quality was degraded. In order to support my theory, I compiled records of the output and quality performance of several hundred individual workers for a period of several months. I expected that this compilation would show conclusively that the faster the people worked, the poorer the quality of their product.

Exhibit 1 summarizes my findings. As you can see, the facts were just the reverse of my theory up to an extremely high level of output. *The inefficient workers were producing the scrap.*

Much sobered, I then began to study the people. It quickly became obvious that the individuals possessed of superskill, the high-output, high-quality workers, were highly disciplined people. They had learned their trades well, they knew their jobs, and they did their work with a sure hand. The best prepared, best disciplined people did good work quickly.

The lengthy example just given has direct application to Autonetics. In April, 1965, I wrote to my project officer at BSD:

EXHIBIT 1: PRODUCT QUALITY AS A FUNCTION OF WORKER OUTPUT

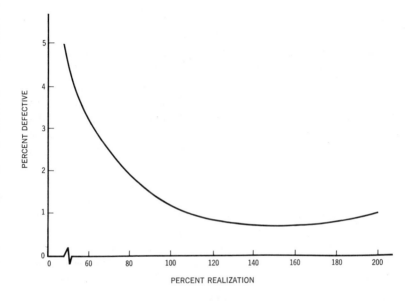

PERCENT REALIZATION

"At this point in our survey, the available analytical data for Autonetics factory labor is not as extensive or as well developed as compared to the overhead area. However, the data which is available indicates that factory labor utilization is extremely poor. Planned factors of actual to standard hours are in the range of 6–1 to 20–1, and actual recorded hours per unit are exceeding planned hours by a substantial margin. Even allowing for a high incidence of unrealistic time standards and low yields, all available data indicates that output per worker is less than one-half that being realized in manufacturing activities of other weapons of comparable complexity. Observations on the factory floor confirm the low labor utilization indicated by the control data.

"In our experience, under-loading of factory personnel is a major cause of poor product quality and low yields. We recognize that this statement flies in the face of currently popular trade-off theories, but experience supports our view. Underloading of factory workers reduces concentration and attentiveness to a level detrimental to good worksmanship, and rework soars. Every instance of dramatic improvement in factory unit hour cost we have been associated with has been accompanied by, and in part, caused by reductions in rework and improvement in product quality.

"Therefore, we are proposing a coordinated attack on the problems underlying high unit hours and high incidence of rework."

Corrective action taken as a result of this report consisted of revocation of the plant visit clearances of the BSD Project Officer, who endorsed the recommendation, me, and all of my associates.

Attributing the Autonetics quality problem to a shortage of money is, in my opinion, deceitful and hypocritical. In actuality, the experience illustrates the shallowness and lack of substance inherent in the unlimited funds theory. The real problem lies in quality of people and organization and in management discipline.

Because of the importance of the funding/quality misconception, particularly as it has affected Minuteman, I intend to give maximum publicity to my point of view and to the facts supporting my view. I solicit your assistance.

In formulating a broad management improvement plan for Minuteman, I believe you should consider the problem posed by the mass migration of Air Force officers into the management ranks of contractors with whom they have dealt. The AFPR who revoked our clearances at Autonetics is now a division manager at Autonetics. His predecessor, equally protective of the contractor's interest, is also now employed by North American Aviation. The procurement officer who blocked access by the Minuteman Program Control office to Autonetics contract negotiation records is now employed by North American Aviation. The immediate superior of the project officer who was excluded from Autonetics' plant is now employed by Autonetics. The officer cited to me as responsible for killing the cost reduction project I contracted to perform at Autonetics is now employed by North American Aviation.

It is of course impossible to assess the effect of impending employment by contractors on the actions of officers still on active duty. I am sure that many of the individuals I have cited had no idea of going to work for North American at the time they were so vigorously protecting the interests of that company vis-à-vis the Government. On the other hand, it is perfectly clear to me that these same officers studiously avoided any action which might offend their ultimate employer.

Lest you accuse me of being unfair to North American and the officers they have employed, I concede that the condition I have described is not unique. Indeed, it is common enough to be our next national scandal. However, the fact that it is so widespread makes it imperative that the practice and its corrosive effect on our stewardship be controlled.

I believe publicity is the solution to the problem just cited. However, I do not have strong convictions on this point. I should like to discuss it with you further.

Finally, I think the Minuteman program has suffered and is suffering from its own credibility gap. Some time back, lying was a way of life in the program. Financial figures were plucked from thin air, and deceptive technical information was presented as a matter of course. I believe this practice has done immeasurable harm to the program. A more serious and lasting effect is the example set for young officers and the damage done to the image of the Air Force.

The solution to this problem is ultra simple: Tell the truth, no matter how painful.

Please excuse the length and bluntness of this memorandum, I want to make sure that we share a common understanding of the background environment of the Minuteman program. As you know, many of us here have high hopes for your success. However, I believe it essential that you have a complete understanding of the genesis of the problems you now face. My reading of your Summary Report leads me to believe that you have not been fully informed on all aspects of the background problems. I intend to continue presenting my views on the situation as vigorously as I know how. In so doing, I hope I can help you in your difficult assignment.

Sincerely,

A. E. FITZGERALD
Deputy for Management Systems

Attachments
Lt. General J. W. O'Neill
Commander, SAMSO
Air Force Unit Post Office
Los Angeles, California 90045

APPENDIX C

[Wire ("Z" Gram) from Chief of Operations Admiral
Elmo Zumwalt to subordinate commands]

FM	CNO	
TO	CHNAVMAT	
	MSC	
INFO	NAVAIRSYSCOM	
	NAVELECSYSCOM	
	NAVFACENGCOM	
	NAVORDSYSCOM	
	NAVSHIPSYSCOM	
	NAVSUPSYSCOM	
	DIR SSPO	WASH DC
	NAVCOMPT	
	ONR	

UNCLAS //N07040//

FY 1972 OUTLAY TARGETS

A. SECNAVNOTE 7040 OF 4 FEB 1972

1. FY 72 OUTLAY TARGETS PROMULGATED BY REF A AS PART OF THE
PRESIDENT'S BUDGET FOR FY 1973 ARE OVER $400M ABOVE TARGETS
IN THE EARLIER FY 72 BUDGET FOR THE OPN, SCN, PAMN AND
MILCON APPROPRIATIONS. DIFFICULTY OF ACHIEVING THESE TARGETS
DURING THE REMAINING MONTHS OF FY 72 FULLY APPRECIATED BUT
IMPORTANCE OF AVOIDING SHORTFALL IN MEETING NEWLY ESTAB-

DRAFTER: 92

DIST: 00..09..090..90..01..02..03..04..05..06..093..094..095
          098..099..008..40..41..43..44..FP..BFR

CAPT C. C. BROCK, 92, 54993 2/9/72

LISHED FY 72 TARGETS TO AVOID RESULTANT ADVERSE EFFECTS ON ANTICIPATED FY 1973 OUTLAY CEILINGS DICTATE NEED FOR TOP MANAGEMENT ATTENTION. ANTICIPATE ANY SHORTFALL IN FY 72 OUTLAY TARGET COULD BE TRANSLATED INTO PROGRAM LOSS UNDER FY 73 OUTLAY CEILING.

2. IN ORDER TO PREPARE RECOMMENDATIONS INDICATED IN PARA 4D, REF A REQUEST YOUR POSITION ON THE FOLLOWING AREAS WHICH APPEAR TO OFFER THE BEST POTENTIAL FOR MEETING FY 72 AND FY 73 OUTLAY TARGETS:

A. SETTLEMENT OF CLAIMS IN FY 72 VICE FY 73.

B. EXPEDITE PROVISIONAL PAYMENTS ON CLAIMS ON UNADJUDICATED CHANGE ORDERS.

C. ACCELERATE CONTRACT CLOSE-OUTS AND SUBSEQUENT PAYMENT OF WITHHELD FUNDS.

D. ACCELERATE SHIPPING AND TRANSPORTATION BILLING PROCESS WHERE SERVICES HAVE BEEN RENDERED BUT REMAIN UNBILLED.

E. INCREASE USE OF UNPRICED PURCHASE ORDERS AND FAST PAY PROCEDURES.

F. INCREASE SOURCE INSPECTION AND ACCEPTANCE OF MATERIAL AT RECEIVING ACTIVITIES. APPLY PROMPT PROCESSING PROCEDURES FOR MATERIALS RECEIVED FOR INVENTORY.

G. INCREASE IN AMOUNT, TIMELINESS AND COVERAGE OF PROGRESS PAYMENTS TO CONTRACTORS FROM DIRECT APPROPRIATIONS AND WORKING CAPITAL FUNDS.

H. INCREASING NIF AND STOCK FUND EXPENDITURES. INVESTIGATE ADVANCE PROCUREMENT OF SHORTLEAD TIME MATERIAL WHERE FIRM NIF AND STOCK FUND ORDERS ARE ANTICIPATED IN FY 1973. ALSO SUGGEST INVESTIGATE ADVANCE PAYMENTS FOR STOCK FUND PROCUREMENTS SCHEDULED FOR FY 73 DELIVERY.

I. FORWARD PROCUREMENT OF AMMUNITION/COMPONENTS FROM SOURCES OUTSIDE THE NAVY IN ANTICIPATION OF FY 1973 INVENTORY OBJECTIVES.

J. ACCELERATION OF MILITARY CONSTRUCTION PAYMENTS TO CONTRACTORS IN FY 1972 THROUGH A SPECIAL ONE TIME EFFORT BY NAVFAC TAKING EXTRAORDINARY ACTION IN PROCESSING PAYMENT VOUCHERS IN FY 72.

K. INCREASE MILITARY CONSTRUCTION PAYMENTS TO CONTRACTORS IN FY 1972 THROUGH A ONE-TIME EFFORT BY NAVFAC REDUCING

RETENTION OF FUNDS HELD FOR PERFORMANCE SURETY UNDER PRESENT CONSTRUCTION CONTRACTS.

3. SEPARATE ACTION UNDERWAY TO REPROGRAM $33M INTO SHIP OVERHAUL AND $20M INTO AIRCRAFT REWORKS PROGRAMS. THIS ACTION PRESUMES PROGRAM ACCOMPLISHMENT DURING FY 1972 AND IS CONTINGENT UPON EASEMENT OF CURRENT OVERTIME RESTRICTIONS. AS A RELATED MATTER MAXIMUM EFFORT IS REQUIRED TO MINIMIZE NIF WORK CARRY-OVER INTO FY 1973. ACCORDINGLY, REQUEST YOUR EVALUATION OF THE USE OF UNLIMITED OVERTIME DURING REMAINDER OF FY 1972.

4. COMMENTS ON THE ABOVE AND ANY OTHER RECOMMENDATIONS TO ASSIST IN REACHING THE ASSIGNED OBJECTIVES REQUESTED.

APPENDIX D

Issues Included in Rating of U. S. Senators of 91st Congress by the National Taxpayers Union. (Published in *Dollars and Sense,* April, 1971.)

1. Sen. Williams' (R.–Del.) amendment to supplemental appropriations, reducing the number of exemptions to federal spending ceiling for fiscal 1970. Rejected 16–80, June 17, 1969, for 1, against 0.
2. Sen. Proxmire's (D.–Wis.) amendment to Military Procurement reducing funds by $533 million for the C5A. Rejected 23–64, Sept. 9, 1969, for 1, against 0.
3. Food Stamp Bill, authorizing $1.25 billion for fiscal '70, $2 billion for '71, $2.5 billion for '72. Passed 78–14, Sept. 24, 1969, for 0, against 1.
4. Sen. Byrd's (D.–Va.) Tax Reform amendment to allow surtax to lapse Dec. 31, 1969, instead of continuing for six months. Rejected 28–49, November 25, 1969, for 1, against 0.
5. Foreign Aid, Appropriating $2.2 billion for fiscal 1970. Passed 55–35, Dec. 18, 1969, for 0, against 1.
6. Mass transit bill allowing federal government $10 billion for 12-year program. Accepted 84–4, Feb. 3, 1970, for 0, against 1.
7. National Aeronautics and Space Administration authorization of over $3.3 billion for fiscal 1971. Passes 69–15, May 6, 1970, for 0, against 1.
8. Amendment to Foreign Military Sales Act authorizing $300-million ceiling instead of $350 million. Adopted 64–7, May 14, 1970, for 0, against ½.
9. Amendment to Supplemental Appropriations Bill, authorizing $587.5 million for Urban Renewal. Adopted 70–12, June 22, 1970, for 0, against ½.

10. Debt limit increase, temporarily by $18 billion and permanently by $15 billion to $395 billion and 380 billion respectively. Passed 64–19, June 29, 1970, for 0, against 1.

11. Sen. Fulbright (D.–Ark.) Independent Offices and Agencies, amendment to reduce funds for N.A.S.A. Rejected 32–37, July 7, 1970, for ½, against 0.

12. Independent Offices and Agencies-HUD Bill appropriations for, passed 84–4, July 7, 1970, for 0, against 1.

13. Office of Education Appropriations for fiscal '71 of $4.4 billion, President's veto overridden, 77–16, for 0, against 1.

14. Proxmire's (D.–Wis.) amendment to reduce ceiling on military procurement authorization by $5 billion. Rejected 31–42, for 2, against 0.

15. Military Procurement Authorization Bill, $19.2 billion, includes ABM and defense-related research. Passed 84–5, Sept. 1, 1970, for 0, against 1.

16. Agriculture Act Establishment of three-year price support program. Passed 65–7, Sept. 15, 1970, for 0, against 1.

17. Proxmire (D.–Wis.) Transportation Appropriations amendment to delete $290 million for SST. Adopted 52–41, for 1, against 0.

INDEX

391